Thirty Years of China–U.S. Relations

Challenges Facing Chinese Political Development

Series Editor: Sujian Guo, Ph.D.
San Francisco State University

In an attempt to reflect the rapidly changing political environment of the People's Republic of China, editor Sujian Guo has assembled a book series to present specialized areas of research in current Chinese political studies. Incorporating theoretical, empirical, and policy research on contemporary Chinese politics both domestically and internationally, this series contemplates the Chinese past, present, and future by utilizing interdisciplinary perspectives to approach issues related to Chinese politics, economy, culture, social development, reform, the military, legal system, and foreign relations. Aimed at bringing a greater understanding of the current Chinese political climate to Western audiences, this series is focused on the emerging voices of Chinese scholars and their perspectives on the ever-changing Chinese diaspora.

Recent titles in the series are:

The Dragon's Hidden Wings: How China Rises with Its Soft Power, by Sheng Ding

"Harmonious World" and China's New Foreign Policy, by Sujian Guo and Jean-Marc F. Blanchard

China in Search of a Harmonious Society, edited by Sujian Guo and Baogang Guo

Greater China in an Era of Globalization, edited by Sujian Guo and Baogang Guo

Toward Better Governance in China, edited by Baogang Guo and Dennis Hickey

Dynamics of Local Governance in China during the Reform Era, edited by Tse-Kang Leng and Yun-han Chu

Dancing with the Dragon: China's Emergence in the Developing World, edited by Dennis Hickey and Baogang Guo

Online Chinese Nationalism and China's Bilateral Relations, edited by Simon Shen and Shaun Breslin

Multidimensional Diplomacy of Contemporary China, edited by Simon Shen and Jean-Marc F. Blanchard

Thirty Years of China–U.S. Relations: Analytical Approaches and Contemporary Issues, edited by Sujian Guo and Baogang Guo

Environmental Protection Policy and Experience in the U.S. and China's Western Regions, edited by Sujian Guo, Joel K. Kassiola, and Jijiao Zhang

Thirty Years of China–U.S. Relations

Analytical Approaches and Contemporary Issues

Edited by
Sujian Guo and Baogang Guo

LEXINGTON BOOKS
A division of
ROWMAN & LITTLEFIELD PUBLISHERS, INC.
Lanham • Boulder • New York • Toronto • Plymouth, UK

Published by Lexington Books
A division of Rowman & Littlefield Publishers, Inc.
A wholly owned subsidiary of The Rowman & Littlefield Publishing Group, Inc.
4501 Forbes Boulevard, Suite 200, Lanham, Maryland 20706
http://www.lexingtonbooks.com

Estover Road, Plymouth PL6 7PY, United Kingdom

British Library Cataloguing in Publication Information Available

Library of Congress Cataloging-in-Publication Data

Thirty years of China–U.S. relations : analytical approaches and contemporary issues /
[edited by] Sujian Guo and Baogang Guo.
    p. cm. — (Challenges facing Chinese political development)
 Includes bibliographical references and index.
 ISBN 978-0-7391-4696-5 (cloth : alk. paper)
 1. United States—Foreign relations—China. 2. China—Foreign relations—United
States. 3. United States—Foreign economic relations—China. 4. China—Foreign
economic relations—United States. I. Guo, Sujian, 1957– II. Guo, Baogang, 1960–
    E183.8.C5T427 2010
    327.73051—dc22   2010008088

Printed in the United States of America

Contents

Part 3   Ideas, Norms, and Institutions in Chinese Foreign Policy

Part 4   Contemporary Issues in China-US Relations

List of Figures

List of Tables

Contributors

Bo Zhiyue, senior research fellow at the East Asian Institute of the National University of Singapore. He obtained his Bachelor of Law and Master of Law in international politics from Peking University and Ph.D. in political science from the University of Chicago. He is a recipient of the *Trustees' Distinguished Scholar Award* at St. John Fisher College and the inaugural holder of the *Joe and Theresa Long Endowed Chair in Social Science* at Tarleton State University. His research interests include China's elite politics, Chinese provincial leaders, central-local relations, cross-strait relations, Sino-U.S. relations, international relations theories, and global governance. He has published more than forty book chapters and articles in English and Chinese, which have appeared in *East Asia: An International Quarterly*, *Issues & Studies*, *China: An International Journal*, *Journal of Social Sciences* (in Taiwan), *Journal of Chinese Political Science*, *Asian Profile*, *Journal of Contemporary China*, *East Asian Policy: An International Quarterly*, *Russian Journal*, and *Provincial China*. He is the guest editor of *Chinese Law and Government* and *Journal of Contemporary China*. He is the guest editor of *Chinese Law and Government* and *Journal of Contemporary China*. He is the author of a trilogy on China's political elites and elite politics, including *Chinese Provincial Leaders: Economic Performance and Political Mobility since 1949* (Armonk, NY: M. E. Sharpe, 2002), *China's Elite Politics: Political Transition and Power Balancing* (Singapore: World Scientific, 2007), and *China's Elite Politics: Governance and Democratization* (Singapore: World Scientific, forthcoming).

Keith Eric Flick, a doctoral candidate in international relations at the S. Rajaratnam School of International Studies (RSIS), Nanyang Technological University, Singapore, where he also received his Master of Science degree. His doctoral dissertation focuses on the effect of domestic politics on Southeast Asian foreign policy formation in response to the rise of China. His other research interests include Sino-U.S. relations and the influence of technology on international relations.

Baogang Guo, associate professor of political science at Dalton State College, and president of the Association of Chinese Political Studies. He is a member of editorial board of the *Journal of Chinese Political Science* and research associate in China Research Center in Atlanta, GA. His research interests include comparative public policy, political culture and political legitimacy, and Chinese and Asia politics. He is an associate editor of *China Today* (Greenwood

Press, 2005), and author of nine book chapters and eleven peer reviewed journal articles. His recent publications appeared on *Asian Survey, Journal of Chinese Political Science, Modern China Studies, Journal of Comparative Asian Development, Twenty-first Century,* and *American Journal of China Studies.*

Sujian Guo, associate dean and distinguished professor of Fudan Institute for Advanced Study in Social Sciences at Fudan University, professor in the Department of Political Science and director of Center for U.S.-China Policy Studies at San Francisco State University, editor-in-chief of the *Journal of Chinese Political Science*, series editor of Rowman & Littlefield-Lexington's Chinese political studies, and former president of Association of Chinese Political Studies. He received his MA degree from Peking University and Ph.D. from the University of Tennessee. His research interests include Chinese/Asian politics, U.S.-China relations, communist and post-communist studies, democratic transitions, and the political economy of East and Southeast Asia. He has published more than thirty academic articles both in English and Chinese. His authored and edited books include *Greater China in an Era of Globalization* (2009); *Harmonious World and Chinese New Foreign Policy* (2008); *China in Search of a Harmonious Society* (2008); *Challenges Facing Chinese Political Development* (2007); *New Dimensions of Chinese Foreign Policy* (2007); *China in the Twenty-First Century: Challenges and Opportunities* (2007); *The Political Economy of Asian Transition from Communism* (2006); *China's 'Peaceful Rise' in the 21st Century: Domestic and International Conditions* (2006); and *Post-Mao China: From Totalitarianism to Authoritarianism?* (2000).

Dennis Hickey, the James F. Morris Endowed Professor of Political Science at Missouri State University. He has published over fifty scholarly articles and book chapters. Professor Hickey is also the sole-author of four books, *Foreign Policy Making in Taiwan: From Principle to Pragmatism* (2007), *The Armies of East Asia: China, Taiwan, Japan and the Koreas* (2001), *Taiwan's Security in the Changing International System* (1997) and *U.S.-Taiwan Security Ties* (1994) and the co-editor of two books, *Dancing with the Dragon: China's Emergence in the Developing World* (2009) and *Toward Better Governance in China: An Unconventional Pathway of Political Reform* (2009). For the past several years, much of Dr. Hickey's research has focused on relations between Taiwan and the Chinese mainland, and the prospects for peace in that part of the world. His article, "Beijing's Evolving Policy Toward Taipei: Engagement or Entrapment," was recently published by *Issues & Studies* (Volume 45, Number 1, March 2009), while his paper, "President Ma Ying-Jeou and Taiwan's Internal and External Challenges," was just published in an edited volume entitled, *Taiwan at a Turning Point* (Baltimore, Maryland: University of Maryland Series in Contemporary Asian Studies, 2009). In addition to these books and articles, Professor Hickey has contributed op-ed pieces to a number of newspapers including *The China Daily, The Wall Street Journal, The Los Angeles Times, The Chicago Tribune, The Kansas City Star,* and *The Taipei Times.* During the Spring semester of 2008, Dr. Hickey was a Fulbright

Exchange Scholar at the China Foreign Affairs University in Beijing, China, and that same year he was named the James F. Morris Endowed Professor of Political Science. He presently serves as a Research Associate at San Francisco State University's Center for U.S.-China Policy Studies and on the editorial board of two scholarly journals (*The Journal of Chinese Political Science* and *Taiwan Defense Affairs*). Dr. Hickey is associate editor of *Journal of Chinese Political Science*, a member of the Board of Directors of the Association of Chinese Political Studies and an associate member of the University of Chicago's Center for East Asian Studies.

Kailai Huang, professor of history at Massachusetts College of Liberal Arts. He works mainly in the area of World History, with particular interest in East Asia. His recent publication includes an article on U.S.-China commercial diplomacy after the normalization in 1979 in *Essays in Economic and Business History* (2005). His mailing address is Department of History, 375 Church Street, North Adams, MA 01247.

De-Yuan Kao, a Ph.D. candidate in the Department of Political Science at Boston University. His research focuses on U.S.-China-Taiwan relations, foreign policy analysis, East Asia security, and international regimes. He received his MA degrees from the University of Chicago in 2004, and Soochow University (Taiwan) in 2001, both in political science.

Pei-Shan Kao, assistant professor in the Centre for General Education at National Chiao-Tung University, Hsinchu, Taiwan. She has also been teaching undergraduate and graduate courses in the Institute of Public Affairs at Ming Chuan University, Taiwan. Professor Kao's research interests include International Relations Theory, U.S.-China Relations, Crisis Bargaining, Cross-Strait Relations, and Foreign Policy. She has presented her research papers in many countries such as Britain, Germany, United States, Taiwan, China, Vietnam, Mexico, and Poland, etc. She is a recipient of the 2008 Scholarship of Study of the U.S. Institute on U.S. Foreign Policy, Bureau of Educational and Cultural Affairs, U.S. Department of State. In 2009, she was a visiting professor at Maria Curie-Sklodowska University in Lublin, Poland. She is trilingual in English, Spanish and Chinese.

Yongshin Kim, Ph.D. student in the Political Science Department at the University of Hawaii at Manoa. His areas of study include international politics in East Asia, the politics of history in contemporary China and the political economy of Chinese reform. He got his BA in sociology and Chinese language and literature and his MA in political science from Yonsei University, Korea.

Ji-Yong Lee, lecturer of political science at Konkuk University, Seoul. He also is visiting professor at the Institute of Foreign Affairs and National Security (IFANS). His teaching and research interests include Chinese politics and economy, North Korean politics and economy, and Northeast Asian international relations. Recent publications include "North Korea's Internet Strategy and Its Political Implications." *Pacific Affairs*, forthcoming, 2010; "An Analysis of China's Shifting Development Paradigm: Increasing Disparity, Social Unrests, and the CPC's Survival," *International Area Reviews*, Vol.12, No.1 (Spring 2009), pp. 101-126; "The Paradox of North Korea's Ideological Radicalism: Shaky Social Basis of Strengthening Ideological Campaigns," *North Korean Review*, Vol. 5, No.1 (Spring 2009), pp. 46-61; "Making Sense of North Korea: 'National Stalinism' in Comparative-Historical Perspective," *Communist and Post-Communist Studies*, Vol. 40, No. 4 (December 2007), pp. 459-475.

LI Mingjiang, assistant professor at S. Rajaratnam School of International Studies (RSIS), Nanyang Technological University, Singapore. He is also the coordinator of the China Program and the coordinator of the MSc. in Asian Studies Program at RSIS. His main research interests include China's diplomatic history, the rise of China in the context of East Asian regional relations and Sino-U.S. relations, and domestic sources of China's international strategies. He received his Ph.D. in political science from Boston University. He is the editor of *Soft Power: China's Emerging Strategy in International Politics* (2009) and the editor of several other books on China's international relations in Asia. He has published papers in *Chinese Journal of International Politics*, *Journal of Contemporary China*, *China: An International Journal*, and *China Security*.

Yves-Heng Lim holds a Ph.D. in international security from the University Jean Moulin-Lyon III and from Peking University. He was visiting doctoral candidate at Peking University in 2005, guest researcher at NIAS in spring 2006, and exchange doctoral candidate at the Australian National University in 2007. He is currently completing an MA in Chinese Studies at the University Jean Moulin-Lyon III.

Guoli Liu, professor of political science at the College of Charleston. His main teaching and research interests are comparative politics and international relations with an emphasis on East Asia and Russia. He is the author of *States and Markets: Comparing Japan and Russia* (1994), and (with Deng Peng and Xiaobing Li) *United States Foreign Policy and Sino-American Relations* [in Chinese] (2000). His edited books include *Chinese Foreign Policy in Transition* (2004), (with Weixing Chen) *New Directions in Chinese Politics for the New Millennium* (2002), (with Lowell Dittmer) *China's Deep Reform: Domestic Politics in Transition* (2006), and (with Quansheng Zhao) *Managing the China Challenge: Global Perspectives* (2009). He received his BA and MA degrees from Peking University, and his Ph.D. in political science from the State University of New York at Buffalo.

Jing Men, the InBev-Baillet Latour Chair and professor of EU-China relations at the College of Europe. She is also assistant professor of Vesalius College and senior researcher at the Brussels Institute of Contemporary China Studies of

Vrije Universiteit Brussel. She is specialized in Chinese foreign policy and EU-China relations. Her most recent publications include: "China's Rise and Its Relations with Other Major Powers: Competitors or Partners," in Sujian Guo and Jean-Marc F. Blanchard (eds.), *Harmonious World and China's New Foreign Policy* (2008), pp. 83-103; "Crisis across the Taiwan Strait," in Stanley Crossick and Etienne Reuter (eds.) *China-EU: A Common Future* (2007), pp. 81-92; "Changing Ideology in China and Its Impact on Chinese Foreign Policy," in Sujian Guo and Shiping Hua (eds.), *New Dimensions of Chinese Foreign Policy* (2007), pp. 7-39; *European Integration: Decision-Making and External Relations of the European Union* [Ouzhou yitihua jincheng: Oumeng de juece yu duiwai guanxi], (2007), 237pp (written together with Youri Devuyst and published in Chinese); "The Construction of the China-ASEAN Free Trade Area: A Study of China's Active Involvement," *Global Society: Journal of Interdisciplinary International Relations*, Vol. 21, No. 2 (April 2007), pp. 249-268; and "Chinese Perception of the European Union: A Review of Leading Chinese Journals," *European Law Journal*, Vol. 12, No. 6 (November 2006), pp. 788–806.

Dominik Mierzejewski, assistant professor in the Department of East Asian Studies of the Faculty of International and Political Studies at the University of Łódź. He received his MA degree from the Faculty of Philosophy and History, University of Lodz (2001) and Ph.D. from University of Łódź (2006). He studied at the Shanghai International Studies University (1999–2000, 2003–2004). He is a member of: Association for Asian Studies, Association of Chinese Political Studies, European Association of Chinese Studies (board member). An author of various articles on the contemporary international relations, e.g., published by The Polish Ministry of Foreign Affairs, *China Policy Papers* at the Nottingham University and in *Journal of Contemporary Eastern Asia*. His research interests include contemporary Chinese diplomacy: ideas, concepts, strategies and rhetoric, Chinese political system: party-society nexus and party-intellectuals nexus and China's perception of the Polish transformation. He teaches comparative politics of China, international relations in Asia and international relations theory.

Albert S. Yee, professor in the Political Science Department at Colgate University and visiting professor in the Government Department at Dartmouth College in 2009-2010. His research interests are international relations theory, U.S.-China relations, international political economy, and the political-economy of development in Asia. He is completing projects on two-level negotiations of China-U.S. relations since 1989 and a constructivist analysis of China's "peaceful development."

YOU Ji, reader/professor at School of Social Science, the University of New South Wales. He is author of three books and numerous articles. The most recent ones include: "Friends in Needs or Comrades in Arms: Dilemma in Sino-Russo Weapons Business" in *Global Arms Trade* (2009); "The 17th Party

Congress and the CCP's Changing Elite Politics" in *China's Reform at 30* (2009); "The Soviet Military Model and the Breakdown of the Sino-USSR Alliance" in *The Soviet Influence on China in the 1950s* (2009); "Implications of China's Naval Deployment in Somalia," *East Asian Policy,* Vol. 1, No. 3, 2009, pp. 60-69 (with Lim Chee Kia); "China's New Diplomacy, Foreign Policy and Defense Strategy" in *China's New Diplomacy: Tactical or Fundamental Change?* (2008); "Revolution in Military Thinking" in *China Rising* (2008); "Beyond Symbiosis: Redefining Civil-Military Relations in China", in *China and the New International Order* (2008).

Quansheng Zhao, professor of International Relations and director of Center for Asian Studies at American University in Washington, D.C. A specialist in comparative politics and international relations focusing on East Asia, Dr. Zhao is the author of *Interpreting Chinese Foreign Policy* (winner of the Best Academic Book Award by the Ministry of Culture of the Republic of Korea), and *Japanese Policymaking* (selected as "Outstanding Academic Book" by *Choice*). He is editor or co-editor of *Managing the China Challenge: Global Perspectives; Future Trends in East Asian International Relations;* and *Politics of Divided Nations: China, Korea, Germany and Vietnam.* His books have been translated into Chinese, Japanese, and Korean. Dr. Zhao has been Series Editor of "Comparative Perspectives in Modern Asia" for *Palgrave* (St. Martin's Press), and a member of the editorial advisory board of the *Journal of Strategic Studies, China Review, Hong Kong Journal of Social Sciences, Journal of Contemporary China,* and *Journal of Chinese Political Science.* He received his B.A. from Beijing University, MA and Ph.D. from the University of California at Berkeley.

Yiran Zhou, a research assistant and a Ph.D. student in the Graduate Program in International Affairs and Administration at Missouri State University. His research focuses on U.S.-China relations, Chinese Politics, the Taiwan issue, and China's ethnic and religious policies. He obtained a Master's in Public Administration degree from the University of Kentucky in May, 2004. Prior to studying at Missouri State, he was a policy analyst in Beijing where he conducted research on ethnic and religious policies as well as engaging in international multicultural exchanges with more than ten countries' government agencies as well as international ethnic and religious NGOs.

Acknowledgments

This book is a collection of papers from an Association of Chinese Political Studies (ACPS) conference entitled "The 30th Anniversary of China-U.S. Relations: China's Domestic Politics and International Relations" from July 4–5, 2009 at Renmin University of China. The conference was hosted and co-sponsored by the School of International Studies at Renmin University of China. The authors would like to thank the above organizations for their generous funding for the conference.

Introduction

Thirty Years of China-U.S. Relations: Reappraisal and Reassessment

Baogang Guo and Sujian Guo[*]

The year 2009 marks the 30th anniversary of normalization of Sino-U.S. relations. Over the past 30 years, the bilateral relations have developed by twists and turns. It is not until recent years that some stability and forward-looking exchanges have returned to the central stage, albeit tension, grievances, and mistrust continue to persist. Washington has encouraged China to become a "responsible stakeholder" in the world affairs, while China has urged the U.S. to work with China to build a "harmonious world." Both sides want to work together to solve their differences through dialogs and negotiations. In the wake of the worldwide financial crisis of 2008-2009, China has contributed greatly in financing the crumbling U.S. financial market and lent a helping hand in stabilizing the world economy. Nevertheless, the foundation of the relationship remains very fragile and the long-term prospect for a constructive cooperative relationship is still full of uncertainties. For many Americans, China's increasing global reach and growing political and economic influence constitute the greatest challenge to world dominance by the United States. As a result, some perceive China's rise as a threat to Americans' core national interests.

The recent changes in the global geostrategic landscape and economic interdependence have suggested that some new ideas, factors, conditions, and elements are shaping the relations between the two countries. The task of this book is to explore these factors, issues, and challenges and their impact for the bilateral relations in the twenty-first century.

This edited book is based on an international conference titled "The 30th Anniversary of China-U.S. Relations: China's Domestic Politics and International Relations," co-sponsored by the Association of Chinese Political Studies (ACPS) and People's University of China, July 4-5, 2009. The contributors to this volume are China scholars and experts from the U.S. and from other parts of the world. Their insightful analyses will help students in this academic field understand the forces that shape U.S.-China relations.

FRIEND OR FOE: SEEKING A MIDDLE WAY

China and the U.S. seem to be an odd couple to begin with. Both sides consider each other as neither a friend nor a foe. But both sides consider the relations to be too important to put it on a frequent collision course. They are in constant search of nonconventional approaches to define and manage their uneasy, sometimes turbulent relations. Even today, there has been no clear answer to the nature of this crucial bilateral relationship. The thirty years of courtship is simply a marriage of political convenience, and is filled with ups and downs. Political leaders on both sides have tried their best to manage the relations. In the process, each side has acquired a better understanding of the other side, and has become more realistic in their expectations.

Needless to say, what drive the two largest global powers together are their shared national interests, not political ideology or friendship. Indeed, both sides can never agree on their respective ideologies, and neither side is willing to have complete trust towards the other. The U.S. side is always suspicious about China's intention and worried about the challenges China poses to it economically, politically and militarily. The Chinese side always believes that the U.S. is more interested in facilitating a "color revolution" to overturn their communist rule. Although open ideological attacks on each other have largely subsided, the U.S. never stops blaming China for its poor human rights record, and is ready to use its muscle, including economic and military sanctions, to pressure Beijing on this and many other issues. Beijing, however, is never interested in an ideological quarrel, and is forced to fight back periodically at the U.S.-led Western ideological hegemony. Suspicion and mistrust have become the unspoken words behind handshaking and smiling faces, and military capacity-building aimed at each other has never ceased for a single day.

Despite the setback in their relations in 1989 (due to the China's crackdown on the student-led democratic movement in Beijing) and 2001 (the military aircraft collision in the South China Sea), the two countries managed to break the ice and push their relations forward. Over the years, common interests have been expanded from strategic balance of power to a global war on terrorism; from bilateral trades and investment to multilateral diplomacy to restructure the world economic order. Cooperation on non-security related issues such as environmental protection, the fight against drug trafficking and the spread of AIDS, SARS and A H1N1 pandemic have also been broadened. Thanks to these shared interests, the relations today are much more mature and stable than ever before.

The relations in the past three decades can be divided into three phases. Between January 1979 and February 1989, the two sides maintained an upbeat relationship with frequent high-level official state visits. Deng Xiaoping's visit of Washington D.C. was the first official visit by a Chinese state official in history. Premier Zhao Ziyang and President Ronald Reagan exchanged state visits in 1984, followed by President Li Xiannian's state visit to the U.S. in 1985 and President George H. Bush's February visit to China in early 1989.[1]

However, the Tiananmen Incident put a big chill on the warm relations. High-level exchanges were suspended, and the relations suddenly fell to its lowest level since 1979. Between March 1989 to October 1997, there was no state visit between top leaders from either side. What made it even worse was the test-firing short-range missiles by the People's Liberation Army (PLA) near the Taiwan Strait in 1995. Though the incident was trigged by the pro-independent Taiwanese leader Lee Tenghui's visit to Yale University, the U.S. responded to PLA's provocative military exercise by sending one of its aircraft carrier battle groups to the region to deter China's further action against Taiwan. Jiang Zemin's visit on October 28, 1997 finally ended the twelve years of stalemate. President Clinton agreed to work with the Chinese to build "a constructive strategic partnership." Clinton returned a state visit to China in June 1998.

After 1999, the Sino-U.S. relations entered into the third, yet by far the most volatile phrase. On May 7, 1999 in Operation Allied Force against the former Yugoslavia, six U.S. bombs hit the Chinese Embassy in Belgrade, killing three Chinese citizens. Angry Chinese responded by holding rarely seen demonstrations in the streets of Beijing. Some attacked the U.S. Embassy building with rocks and bottles. The U.S. did issue an apology for the mistake and agreed to compensate the victims' families and pay for the repair cost of rebuilding the damaged Chinese Embassy. Things improved by November of that year when the U.S. finally agreed to China's entry into the World Trade Organization (WTO), a big breakthrough after prolonged and very difficult negotiations.

George W. Bush took a hard-line when he campaigned for presidency in 1999. He wanted to reverse the "partnership" relations Clinton agreed to and redefined U.S.-China relations as "strategic competitor." Three months after he entered into the White House, the new president was forced to deal with China in a very unpleasant way. On April 1, 2001, a U.S. Navy EP-3 military reconnaissance aircraft collided with a Chinese military J-8 fighter jet over the South China Sea. Twenty-four U.S. crewmembers made an unauthorized emergency landing on a Chinese military airfield in Hainan Island. One Chinese pilot was killed in the incident. After some intense diplomatic negotiations, the Chinese authority soon released U.S. crewmembers. But the incident was soon overshadowed by the "9/11" terrorist attack in the U.S. The two sides quickly mended their relations and vowed to cooperate on the "war against terror." Another factor that prevented further deterioration of the bilateral relations was the North Korean nuclear program. China worked with the U.S. and initiated a six-party talk between 2003 and 2007. In November 2005, Bush visited Beijing. Chinese President Hu Jintao subsequently made a state visit to the U.S. in 2006. At the end of Bush's term, he changed his definition of Sino-U.S. relations from "strategic competitor" to a more soft assessment that led to the reorganization of China being a "stakeholder," and a "strategic collaborator."[2]

Barack Obama became the 44th U.S. President in 2009. One thing that set him apart from previous presidents is that he has not taken a hard line toward China as his predecessors did in the early years of their presidencies. So far the

Obama administration has maintained a positive attitude toward relations with China. According to Obama, "The relationship between the United States and China will shape the twenty-first century, which makes it as important as any bilateral relationship in the world."[3] He calls for active cooperation and partnership with China in areas of economic recovery, environmental protection, nuclear non-proliferation, and the fight against transnational threats. This could be a sign that the bilateral relations are about to enter a new phase. The less antagonistic approach may have a lot to do with the unprecedented financial crisis Obama is facing as the new president; he has no choice but to turn his focus inward and to seek all possible helps he can to turn the U.S economy around. As a major purchaser of U.S. treasury bonds and national debts, China is now looking more like a savior rather than a foe. One thing that is clear to Obama is that China is in a much stronger position than it was in 1979.

Indeed, China's growing importance to the U.S. foreign relations has a lot to do with its rising economic and military power. From 1979 to 2006, China's real gross domestic product (GDP) grew at an average annual rate of 9.7 percent and the size of its economy increased over eleven-fold. Its real per capita GDP grew over eight-fold, and its world ranking for total trade rose from the 27th to the 3rd place.[4] It is projected that China will surpass Japan in 2010 to become the world's second largest economy, and it could be the largest within a decade. In recent years, the economy of the U.S. and China has become more and more integrated. Bilateral trade reached $387 billion in 2007. China became the second-largest U.S. trading partner in that year. With over two trillion U.S. dollar foreign currency-reserve and a 600 billion U.S. dollar economic stimulus plan, China played an important role in stopping the free fall during the 2008 global financial crisis. Today, China is the second largest holder of U.S. securities and the largest holder of U.S. treasury bonds used to finance the federal budget deficit.[5]

Militarily speaking, China has begun to modernize its army, navy and air force since the 1990s. In ten years, the PLA has been transformed into a modern, mechanized army that is capable of fighting a local, limited and high-tech warfare. Though the size of the PLA has been reduced significantly, the improvement in hardware, personnel, and logistics has made up the cutback. By 2009, China acquired key technologies in producing the third generation of fighter jets, nuclear-powered submarines, precision-guided cruise missiles, long-range ballistic missiles, and anti-satellite weapons. For decades, the U.S. was the only superpower standing after the Cold War. It was always reluctant to deal with China on an equal basis. China, after all, needed the U.S. more than the U.S. needed China. The U.S. sometime treated China more as a strategic asset to serve its own purpose; it used its leverages against China, such as the practice of annual renewal of Most Favored Nation (MFN) status for China, the admission of China into World Trade Organization (WTO), and arms sales to Taiwan, whenever it felt it wanted to. The ups and downs in the bilateral relations were in some ways singlehandedly orchestrated by the U.S.

However, with China's embracement of a market economy, free trade, and globalization since the 1990s, the U.S., which has advocated these ideas for many years, has now found itself in constant defense. Protectionist sentiments in the U.S. are running at all time high. The massive number of Chinese-made products filled U.S. stores and has caused strong resentments and China-bashing among American laborers. The fear of losing U.S. manufacturing jobs to China has provoked intensive lobbying against Chinese made products by many American trade unions and domestic producers. The accusation of China's labor rights abuses and human rights violations served as smoking guns for the underlining protectionist motives. Furthermore, China's rise is viewed by many Americans as a relative decline of the U.S., thus, it has triggered some level of insecurity and anxiety. As a result, the "China threat" claims have gained a wider audience. [6] New conservative camps proposed to contain China to minimize the economic and military threats. The U.S. has pressured China to appreciate its currency and stimulate its domestic consumption. The number of anti-dumping investigations and trade sanctions against China has grown steadily. Militarily, the U.S. has increased its military build-up in its forward bases in East Asia. It has been upgrading its naval and air forces, and intensified its space and air surveillances over China. [7]

China is keenly aware of the potential impact of its rise and the negative perception the American public have about it. To avoid unnecessary panic over China's development, Deng's Xiaoping advocated "don't stick your head out" (*bu chu tou*) and "keep a low profile and bide one's time" (*tao guang yang hui*) approach. Deng's successor Jiang Zemin invented the "keep silent while making a fortune" (*men sheng fa da cai*) approach. However, according to the realist approach, any challenge to the status quo in the existing distribution of global power will be considered a threat. [8] So in order to mitigate Western concerns, Chinese scholar Zheng Bijian proposed the "peaceful rise" theory in 1997. [9] The leaders of Chinese Communist Party (CCP) quickly adopted this new phrase, and redefined it as the doctrine of "peaceful development." CCP leader Hu Jintao further proposed the idea of "harmonious world" in order to propagate an image of nonaggression. According to a Chinese official white paper on the doctrine,

> Peaceful development is the inevitable way for China's modernization; promoting world peace and development with China's own growth; developing by relying on its own strength, reform and innovation; seeking mutual benefit and common development with other countries; and building a harmonious world of sustained peace and common prosperity. [10]

Xi Jinping, the likely successor of Hu Jintao, made a strong remark during his visit to Mexico in February 2009. He claimed that China did not constitute any threat to anyone since it did not "export revolution," "export hunger and poverty" or "cause headaches." [11]

Despite China's repeated assurance, the U.S. would rather take a wait and see attitude towards China's real intention. The extreme nationalism among the next generation of Chinese youth as demonstrated during the "Belgrade Bombing Incident" and the "military aircraft collision incident" did pose some concerns for many U.S. policy makers. How long China can keep its development "peaceful" and whether or not the government can hold the growing nationalist sentiment at bay remain to be seen.

Is China a friend or a foe? This is still a million dollar question. Two decades after the Tiananmen Incident, the American public still holds negative views about China. According to Gallup poll conducted in 2001, about a fifth of Americans consider China to be an "enemy" of the United States, while about three in ten consider it a friend, and another fifth have little idea how to characterize relations between the two countries.[12] Eight years later, a poll conducted in 2009 by Ipsos reveals almost identical results. Even though one third of respondents choose China as the most important relationship among America's bilateral partners, far exceeding that of Great Britain and Canada, only 56 percent of respondents consider China to be a "foe," and only 33 percent consider China to be a "friend."[13]

This consistent mistrust of China is also reflected in the strategic doctrines adopted by various U.S. administrations since 1979. The strategy of containment, which was the backbone in U.S. policy toward China for many years, is inherently confrontational and hostile. Its basic premise is that China is a foe. The strategy of engagement, which was a dominant theme in U.S. policy toward China since Clinton's administration, continues to show a certain level of uneasiness about China's rise and the reluctance in recognizing China as a trustworthy and equal partner.

Many policy makers or scholars have now come to the conclusion that interests of the United States and China will ease antagonism between them over time and compel them into a closer cooperation with each other. A new strategy for managing the relationships between the two superpowers in the twenty-first century is urgently needed. According to Banning Garrett, the director of Asia Program of Atlantic Council of the United States,

> The U.S. and China face many common challenges in a period of rapid globalization and growing strategic interdependence. Successful cooperation on a wide range of specific bilateral and international issues of strategic importance to both sides, such as counter terrorism and non-proliferation, could serve to reduce lingering suspicions of each other's strategic intentions and pave the way for the development of "normal" relations between the two nations.[14]

In order to do so, the new Obama administration has demanded "strategic assurance" from China,[15] and wants to exercise more "smart power" in dealing with China and the rest of the world.[16]

In the same vein, the strategy used by the Chinese to rally international support to fight against U.S. hegemony is equally hostile, and can no longer serve China's interests today. Since 1979, the relations with the U.S. has become multifaceted and multileveled. The interdependence of the two countries has greatly enhanced their common interests, making the two almost inseparable, at least in economic sense. However, it is still a wishful thinking that China will really consider the U.S. as a reliable friend with full confidence. Some Chinese believe that U.S. strategic interests will continue to be opposite to that of China's. Chinese culture and the prevailing communist ideology are inherently incompatible with American political culture and the liberal ideology. Therefore, clashes instead of cooperation will remain a reoccurring theme. What China should strive for is a normal, stable and comprehensive state-to-state relationship that can accommodate both conflict and cooperation.[17]

What will be the future directions of the Sino-U.S. relations? Former Secretary of State Henry Kissinger suggested that the U.S. and China could raise its relations to a "life community," similar to the U.S. relations with the Atlantic community. He believed that the two countries could cooperate with each other to build a "new global order."[18] Zbigniew Brzezinski, a former national security adviser under the Carter administration, also proposed to raise the bilateral relations to a special relation, equivalent to the U.S.-E.U. relations or U.S.-Japan relations. C. Fred Bergeson, the Director of Peterson Institute for International Economics in Washington D.C, suggested that the U.S. and China had already formed a *de facto* Group Two (G2), and it was poised to replace Group of Severn (G7) or Group of Twenty (G20) as a main player in global affairs.[19] Niall Ferguson, Dean of Harvard Business School, even gave a new name to the G2 concept: "Chimerica."[20] So far the Chinese side has kept cool to these ideas,[21] and some even consider these proposals to be politically motivated aimed at dragging China's feet into an unfriendly trap.[22]

The nature of US-China relations has been redefined a number of times in recent years. Clinton administration described the relations as a "strategic partnership." Bush administration in its earlier years changed it to a "strategic competitor," but later modified its position and called China as a "stakeholder" and a "strategic collaborator."

Having continued to worry about China's intention, Obama administration has demanded so-called "strategic reassurance" from China, i.e., its development and growing global role should not come "at the expense of security and well-being of others."[23] Obama has agreed to build an "active, cooperative and comprehensive" relations with China. His visit to China in November 2009 produced a range of new initiatives aimed at strengthening the existing ties, including raising the level of cooperation in science and technology, further collaboration in health and disease control, more human rights dialogs, and exchanging more students. The overall tone of Obama's China policy suggests that the U.S. has refused to treat the bilateral relations in zero-sum terms. It wants to send a clear message to China that the U.S. does not seek to contain China, and is welcoming China's rise. More importantly, the U.S. wants China to be a "board member" of the superpower club rather than just a stakeholder, and to do more in its share in maintaining world peace and security and fighting global warming.

There is no doubt that the relations between the two countries are among the most important relations in the 21st century. The papers collected in this volume will apply a number of international relation theories to the development of the bilateral relations in the past thirty years. In some ways their researches mirror some new reappraisals and reassessments, and will surely shed new light on some of the issues that have debated intensively in the academic community.

CHAPTER OUTLINE

This book is organized into four parts. Part one focuses on realist analyses; part two applies the theory of interdependency to the study of Sino-U.S. relations; part three studies the role norms, ideas and institutions played in Chinese foreign policy making process; and part four examines several contemporary issues in Sino-U.S. relations.

In chapter 1, "Manipulating the 'Balance of Power': Historical Reappraisal of the Sino-US Rapprochement," Yongshin Kim challenges some of the conventional wisdom on the motives for the rapprochement between the United States and China in the 1970s. There have been many studies of the Sino-US rapprochement as it was one of the great turning points in cold war history. Most literature, however, presumes that the Soviet Union's enormous threat had driven China to mend its relations with the United States, and this explanation has been accepted as "nearly a truism." Furthermore, this "conventional wisdom" has been regarded as hard proof of the balance of power in international politics. Nonetheless, recently declassified archives illustrate three different views. First, the Zhenbao/Damansky incidents in 1969, which were a series of armed conflicts between the People's Republic of China and the Union of Soviet Socialist Republics, were initiated by China, not by the Soviet Union. Contrary to Kissinger's widely-held perception of the Soviets as aggressors, in the initial stage, armed conflicts were perpetrated by the PRC. Secondly, during the Sino-US negotiations, China did not emphasize a Soviet threat to China. On the contrary, Kissinger and Nixon tried to persuade Zhou and Mao of the immediate possibility of a Soviet attack on China. Lastly, during secret negotiations, the United States granted major concessions regarding Taiwan without obtaining China's concession in relation to the Vietnam War. "Conventional wisdom" argues that China's negotiating position towards the United States was severely constrained by its relative insecurity vis-à-vis the Soviet threat. China, however, gained more concessions from the negotiations with the United States. This study sheds new light on how the PRC and the United States manipulated the "balance of power" secretly in order to realize their own foreign policy objectives.

In chapter 2, "The Regional Logic of the U.S.-China Rivalry," Yves-Heng Lim examines the relations between the U.S. and China using the theory of Regional System Complexes (RSC). While the post-Cold War world saw a fragmentation of the great chessboard, particularly visible in the regionalization of security questions, it also witnessed the rapid rise of a new great power—China. Drawing on recent works on regional politics by Barry Buzan and Douglas Lemke, this study examines the intersection between these major trends. Though the trend toward a "regionalization" of security dynamics has been widely noticed, debates have been beset with contradictory arguments and definitions. Among these theories, Barry Buzan and Ole Weaver's RSC theory provides us with a solid basis to analyze these trends. The author argues that one should add two qualifications to Buzan and Weaver's framework. First, as we consider regional power equilibrium, the position of any actor only depends on its relative power within the RSC; extraregional/global powers should not be given a particular status for purely geographic reasons. Second, any analysis of regional systems should pay careful attention to power dynamics, as emphasized by the Power Transition Theory. The rising rivalry between China and the U.S. should be considered through this modified RSC lens. This perspective allows the U.S. to understand the particular stakes and the asymmetry of the U.S.-China rivalry. Facing an assertive potential global hegemon, China has to limit the possible external interference within the region that it considers to be vital to its interests. China therefore has a primary interest in denying the United States the "command of the commons" —as coined by Barry Posen. China has already shaped its military modernization so as to achieve such an objective. Such choices are visible in the three major fields defined as "commons." China has focused its effort on the development of naval, air and space capabilities that will provide her with a significant denial capability but has given lower priority to the acquisition of means of projecting power.

In chapter 3, "Cooperation for Competition: China's Strategic Response to U.S. Preponderance in East Asia," Li Mingjiang and Keith Eric Flick study China's response to the strategy of preponderance of the U.S. in East Asia in the post-Cold War era. Views on China's growing influence in East Asia exhibit a wide spectrum and are usually polarized. One focal point of the debate, understandably, is the impact on the future U.S. role in East Asia. The authors believe that the sharp contrast of views is largely a result of scholars using different theoretical frameworks. Analysts who employ a realist lens tend to highlight China's efforts to increase its influence in the region at the expense of other major actors, rapaciously secure resources to continue to fuel its economic and military development, and to isolate Taiwan. In such analyses, balance of power considerations take a central role in the shaping of a Chinese strategy in East Asia and lead to a zero-sum competition with the U.S. Meanwhile, approaching the subject from a constructivist lens, others have focused on how China's strategy may be influenced and shaped through cognitive processes of socialization with regional actors and their norms. Scholars who focus on China's participation in various regional affairs and institutions describe a China that largely reflects the logics of liberal institutionalism. The various cooperative and competitive aspects of China's approach to East Asia have therefore been largely portrayed as oppositional. The authors contend that this dichotomy is arbitrary and obscures the reality and complexities in China's strategy in East Asia, particularly in response to U.S. preponderance. It could also be misleading in terms of policy implications. Flick and Li argue that instead of describing China's strategic approach through any single analytical framework, in practice, China has employed liberal institutional and constructivist means for realist purposes. In other words, China has been able to compete with the United States for influence and in securing its national interests in East Asia through cooperative means deemed benign by most countries in the region. They argue that this is the essence of China's strategic approach to its neighboring regions in response to American pursuit of preponderance in the post-Cold War era. On the basis of these analyses, the authors offer a few policy suggestions for the U.S. in meeting the China challenge in East Asia.

In chapter 4, "The Korean Peninsula as a Test Bed for the Future Direction of Sino-U.S. Relations: from Structural Realism to Neoclassical Realism and Beyond," Ji-Yong Lee investigates the role of Korean factor in Sino-U.S. relations. The Korean Peninsula is a dynamic place where the future direction of the China/U.S. relationship can be forecast. It is a venue where Cold War legacies remain, multilateralism is a daunting task, and a rising China and a transforming United States face off against each other. China has crucial interests in the Korean Peninsula, while the United States has a strategic concern about the Peninsula to deter challenges posed by a rising China. Likewise, surrounding the Korean Peninsula, new sources of conflict and cooperation are emerging in the course of a power transition in Northeast Asia. A high level of regional instability is developing because of North Korea. The current financial crisis which originated in the United States has become a global economic crisis, shaking both the United States' political and economic positions. At the same time, the new administration of the United States signals a significant change in its foreign policy, leaving the predecessor's policy to be characterized as United States unilateralism. Meanwhile, facing a rising China as well as North Korea's nuclear threat, South Korea currently leans toward strengthening the traditional alliance with the United States. In this respect, Northeast Asian international relations suggest a vision of structural realism. This chapter first examines the strengths and weaknesses of the four schools in international relations theory as an explanatory framework. It then investigates the current behavioral pattern of Northeast Asian countries centered on the Korean Peninsula, with theoretical angles of structural realism and neoclassical realism. Lastly, drawing on the realist perspective, the paper argues that the source of a peaceful power transition from the United States to China can be found in a change of the great powers' perception of each other.

Pei-Shan Kao discusses the effect of complex interdependence on the China-U.S. relations in chapter 5. In the past thirty years, the relationship between China and the United States has encountered many challenges and difficulties. Many disputes and crises on trade, human rights, and security issues had negative impact on the relationship. However, no conflict and war was fought between the two. The pessimistic predictions and viewpoints suggested by realists' power politics and the democratic peace thesis seemed to be unable to provide a satisfactory explanation for the long peace. Conversely, there have been more and more bilateral trade, economic, cultural, governmental or even military contacts and exchanges between the United States and China. If power politics and the democratic peace thesis cannot be used to explain the peaceful coexistence between the United States and China since the end of the Vietnam War, how about the theory of complex interdependence? Can we apply complex interdependence to explain the development of China-U.S. relations?

This study therefore intends to use the theory to examine the development of China-U.S. relations in the past thirty years and conclude with a discussion of the influence and effect of complex interdependence to China-U.S. relations. This chapter will also use the findings of this research to predict an optimistic future development of this relationship.

In chapter 6, "A New Era for U.S.-China Relations," Quansheng Zhao and Guoli Liu examine the new era of U.S.-China relations characterized by increasing complex interdependence. Deng Xiaoping's strategy of reform and opening requires a peaceful international environment. The normalization of relations with Washington was critical for China's move toward modernization. As China opens its door wider, Sino-American relations have matured to a much higher level. As the recent Strategic and Economic Dialogues between Beijing and Washington indicate, the bilateral relations have become truly interdependent. Complex interdependence creates both sensitivity and vulnerability. David Lampton described the U.S.-China relations in terms of "same bed, different dreams" (*tongchuang yimeng*). Considering the common challenges of global financial crisis and international terrorism, perhaps it is more appropriate to think of China and the United States as strategic partners sailing in the same boat (*tongzhou gongji*). The complex interdependence between the two countries is particularly critical in an age of global turbulence. This chapter analyzes current challenges of the new era of China-U.S. relations.

In chapter 7, "China-U.S.-Taiwan Triangular Relations since 2000: A Complex Interdependence Perspective," Dennis Hickey and Yiran Zhou employ the theory of complex interdependence to the study of cross-relations. Since 2000, ties within the so-called Chinese mainland-U.S.-Taiwan triangle have experienced dramatic fluctuations. First, Washington ramped up support for Taipei, but then declared its intention to pursue a "cooperative, constructive, and candid" relationship with Beijing after the September 11, 2001 terrorist attacks. Second, Beijing adopted the Anti-Secession Law in 2005 as a warning to Taiwan's pro-independence forces. But since that time, President Hu Jintao has made numerous conciliatory gestures and even called for a formal peace accord with Taipei. And finally, Taiwan appeared to be marching toward *de jure* independence from China under the leadership of the Democratic Progressive Party (DPP). But this changed after Ma Ying-jeou's stunning landslide victory in the island's 2008 election. Ties between the Chinese mainland and Taiwan—as illustrated by a series of goodwill gestures—provide a striking contrast to the hostile stand-off that characterized the Chen era. Examining the dynamics of trilateral relations over the past eight years, this chapter employs the theory of complex interdependence to examine the level of their mutual dependence, analyze considerations contributing to the fluctuations, and examine the possible trajectory of future relations. In conclusion, the authors suggest that long-term mutual engagement and cooperation should prevail over political containment and military rivalry, although conflicts may occur unexpectedly from time to time.

In chapter 8, "The Role of American Business in Sino-American Normalization," Kailai Huang examines the entanglement of politics and trade in the tortuous journey of the normalization of U.S.-China relations in the 1970s. The fluctuation of U.S.-China trade correlated closely with the development, or the lack of it, in Sino-American political relations. When U.S.-China reconciliation made progress, trade experienced rapid growth. Both Beijing and Washington considered growing economic ties would broaden the basis of the political relationship and generate the perception of momentum. When normalization stagnated, trade suffered sharp decline and American business felt pressured by China to lobby Washington for political concession. Caught in the crosscurrents of international and domestic politics, American business had to carefully navigate the uncharted water in the China market and to be mindful of the conservative, pro-Taiwan sentiment at home. Even more challenging was the dynamics in China's foreign trade policy that was guided more by political usefulness than by economic rationality. While generally supportive of the diplomatic recognition of China, American business refrained from playing a vigorous role in Sino-American normalization due to the political complications and the moderate assessment of the China market.

In chapter 9, "From Pragmatism to Morality: the Changing Rhetoric of Chinese Foreign Policy in the Transitional Period," Dominik Mierzejewski reviews the recent changes in China's foreign policy. During the last thirty years, along with tremendous economic achievement, China is becoming a major international player and responsible power. China's growing influence and its embracing of the globalization rivet international attention. This study will apply the constructivism approach and comparative methodology to explain the changes in political rhetoric adopted by the Chinese leadership. The major research question in this chapter is: Why has the Chinese leadership changed "pragmatic" rhetoric to "moral" rhetoric? How have the Chinese intellectuals and media approached the the new rhetoric? To what extent has the central authority responded to public opinion? The author will compare Deng Xiaoping's and Jiang Zemin's "pragmatic" rhetoric with Hu Jintao's moral-based "harmonious world" concept.

In chapter 10, "Explanations of China's Compliance with International Agreements: Configuring Three Approaches to Institutional Effects on State Behavior," Albert S. Yee analyzes China's foreign policymaking from an institutionalist perspective. Although institutionalist explanations have been pervasive and influential in the analysis of international relations, there remains much uncertainty and disagreement about how international institutions actually influence the behavior of states. Specifically, how do international institutions prompt China to comply with international agreements? This chapter seeks to address this research question by differentiating between three approaches to institutionalism and examining integrations of them. There currently exist many different explanations of the effects of international institutions on state behavior. There is some confusion, however, about the causal mechanisms that actually generate these institutional effects. To clarify these different explanations, the author delineates three approaches to institutionalism and illuminates how they offer varying explanations of Chinese foreign policies. In the first approach ("rationalist institutionalism"), international institutions provide instrumental and/or functional advantages that can render cooperative behavior more beneficial in the rational calculations of state actors. The second approach ("domestic politics institutionalism") focuses on how international institutions affect foreign policy behavior by altering the bureaucratic and domestic political actors and processes within states. The third approach ("adaptive learning/normative socialization institutionalism") emphasizes the role of "learning" and/or "socialization" in prompting states to abide by the rules and norms of international institutions. The author then examines how these three approaches have been combined in various explanations of the effects of international institutions on Chinese foreign policy. The chapter concludes by showing how the three major institutionalist explanations, and various combinations of them, explain China's compliance with international agreements across issue areas.

In chapter 11, "Searching for a New Cultural Identity: China's Soft Power and Media Culture Today," Liu Kang argues that today's Chinese culture, thoroughly saturated in ubiquitous modern electronic means of communication, embodies the fundamental tension and contradictions inherent in the globalized media culture. In addition to the new social formations that techno-media culture has produced globally, Chinese culture is further complicated by the dynamics of the political and economic developments, and new social values and identities that have emerged over the thirty-year post-Mao era reform. This paper argues that a post-revolutionary culture is taking shape in China as a result of the inseparable processes of globalization and China's reform. The paper offers a preliminary assessment of three aspects of Chinese culture today: first, discrepancy between the state ideology and China's socio-economic reality; second, fragmentation and separation of the state, the intellectual elite and the grassroots population in terms of cultural expressions, forms, and underlying values; third, prevalence of entertainment-centered consumer culture which unleashes individualistic and materialistic desires at the expense of social cohesiveness and pursuit of public good, while serving to reinforce a facile political stability. Amidst these tension and contradictions, however, a "post-80s" generation urban youth culture emerges and will inevitably become a dominant cultural formation in China in the years to come. It is media-driven, globalized, and in the meantime more inclined towards its own cultural heritage, should be understood as the core of China's soft power competing in a global new order.

Bo Zhiyue's chapter "Obama's China Policy" takes a closer look at Obama's China policy since he took over the White House. Will he follow the footsteps of George W. Bush, despite his "changed" rhetoric? Or will he introduce radical changes to the U.S.'s China policy? What Bush passed on to Obama is not only an economic recession not seen in several decades and two wars but also improved U.S.-China relations. Despite his initial adventurous, overtures along China's coast, Bush quickly learned to work with the Chinese in the aftermath of the "9/11" incident. The Obama administration has three options for its China policy. The first is simply to work with China, as Bush did in the past seven years. This will continue the trend of stability and institutionalization in the bilateral relations. The second is containment. But this will not bode well for either the bilateral relations or for the world as a whole. The third is to upgrade U.S.-China relations to a "G-2." This is likely to promote a new world order in which a declining power and a rising power coexist peacefully.

In chapter 13, "Managing the Cross-Taiwan Strait Military Conflicts in a New Era of Political Reconciliation," You Ji evaluates Obama's new concept of healthy military balance in relations to Taiwan conflict. It argues that it is politics that causes tension across the Taiwan Strait. The core of this politics is the tripartite consensus on One-China between Washington, Beijing and Taipei which is the foundation for war avoidance. Given China's rapid rise in economic and military power, Washington has to explore a new approach to deal with the inevitable change in the balance gradually titling in favor of Beijing. Therefore, the U.S.-Taiwan military cooperation in the form of U.S. arms sales to Taiwan as a way to maintain the balance will increasingly become an obstacle in managing Taiwan conflict. Obama's word *healthy* captures the changing reality and reflects a comprehensive mechanism of stability building in the region. While military deterrence is crucial, it would no longer be employed as the dominant means to deter emergence of any crisis situations: political means would be more cost-effective. And the regime change in Taipei in May 2009 has reopened opportunities for such a development.

In chapter 14, "The New Triangle of Power: China, the United States and the European Union," Jing Men and Youri Devuyst examine the triangular relationship among China, the U.S. and the E.U. and the fact that China's ascent is recognized widely in the world. As early as the 1980s, Chinese leader Deng Xiaoping had already stated that "no matter how many poles there will be in the future, China should be one of them." China's influence grows together with its rapidly developing economy. In order to realize the strategic goal of constructing a multipolar world, China has established partnerships with all the major powers in the world. Among them, the United States and the European Union are the most important. American scholar David Shambaugh in one of his articles predicted that "the interactions of the United States, China and the E.U. will be a defining feature of the international system in the years to come."[24] Professor Shambaugh's prediction is supported by the fact that both the leaders of the U.S. and the E.U. expressed on many occasions that China is important, and they need to coordinate with China in many important international affairs. Nevertheless, the cooperation and coordination between China, the U.S., and the E.U. are always harassed by disagreements and differences. Apart from ideological differences between China and the other two, a noticeable fact is that up till now, the Americans and the Europeans still treat the Chinese as juniors in the international society. A patronizing attitude from the U.S. and the E.U. to their Chinese counterparts reveals that the relationship is not equal. It will take some time for the Americans and the Europeans to treat the Chinese as their equal partners. This study will be divided into the following parts. The first part will give a review of China-U.S. and China-E.U. relations in order to find out shared interests and existed problems between China and the other two partners.

The second part will focus on China-U.S. relations to examine in which areas and why the relationship is unequal. The third part will do the same research on China-E.U. relations. The fourth part will compare the research result of part two and part three, and draw a tentative conclusion on how the triangle relations will further evolve by studying several possible scenarios.

In the final chapter, "The Change and Continuity in the U.S. China Policy after the Cold War," De-Yuan Kao studies the changeable and unchangeable elements in the Sino-U.S. relations. China is a growing power and its importance in the global society has been increasing, especially after the Cold War when China opened its door more widely to the world. Over the past two decades, it is a fact that China and U.S. had become closer, but the relationship could not be regarded as a perfectly smooth one. When we talk about the U.S. policy toward China, it is true that some parts of the policy change over time, while others remain stable under either Republican or Democrat governments. Most discussions on the topic of foreign policy focus on what factors or theories lead to policy changes, but they neglect considering that those unstable factors might be interchangeable with other fixed factors. Although we have seen great improvement in the relationship between the U.S. and China, disputes over issues relating interests such as economics, security, and Taiwan continue to flare up from time to time. These three issues could be regarded as the most important issues that Washington has to consider when making its policy toward Beijing. This chapter focuses on the U.S.-China relationship after the Cold War with discussion of three U.S. presidents (George H. W. Bush, Bill Clinton, and George W. Bush) over the past two decades. The emphases on their attitudes regarding three major issues—economy, security, and Taiwan—will be reviewed concisely and the following questions will be discussed: first, what are the changeable and unchangeable parts in the U.S. China policy? Secondly, what are the logic behind the changes and continuity? This chapter will offer a preliminary discussion on these issues according to the following structure. The first section introduces the main idea of this chapter. The two sections following thereafter briefly explain the three presidents' China policy in terms of U.S. interests in the economic, security, and Taiwan issues. It will also highlight the changeable and unchangeable elements in the U.S. China policy. The fourth section discusses some implications of President Obama's China policy, as well as the importance of these two sets of variable and in variant China policy elements. The last section provides the conclusion.

NOTES

[*] The authors would like to thank Dr. George Jones, Professor Emeritus at Dalton State College for his proofreading of this introduction chapter.

1. Kerry Daubaugh, *China-U.S. Summit, October 1997*, CRS Report 94-971F.
2. Morton Abramowitz and Stephen Bosworth, "Adjusting to the New Asia," *Foreign Affairs* 82, no. 4 (July/August 2003): 119-31.
3. White House Office of the Press Secretary, "Remarks by the President at the U.SL./China Strategic and Economic Dialogues," July 27, 2009.
4. Craig K. Elwell and Marc Labonte, "Is China a Threat to U.SL. Economy?" CRS Report, RL33604, January 23, 2007.
5. Kerry Daubaugh, *China-U.S. Relations in the 110th Congress: Issues and Implications for U.S. Policy*, CRS Report RL33877, February 10, 2009, www.crs.gov.
6. Bill Gertz, *China Threat: How the People's Republic Targets America* (Washington D.C.: Regnery Publishing, Inc., 2000); Constaine C. Menges, *China: the Gathering Threat* (Nashville, TN: Thomas Nelson, 2005), 5th ed.
7. Al Pressiin, "U.S. Moves to Counter Chinese Military Modernization," VOA News, January 27, 2009; Ivan Eland, "Is Chinese Military Modernization a Threat to the United States?" *Policy Analysis*, no. 465, January 23, 2003, Cato Institute, www.cato.org/pubs/pas/pa465.pdf.
8. Hans J. Morgenthau, *Politics Among Nations: The Struggle for Power and Peace*, Fifth Edition, Revised, (New York: Alfred A. Knopf, 1978), pp. 4-15.
9. Zheng Bijian, "The 16th National Congress of Communist Party of China and China's Peaceful Rise—a New Path," address delivered at the Center for Strategic and International Studies of the U.S., in *China's Peaceful Rise: Speeches of Zheng Bijian 1997-2004*, Brookings Institute, www.brookings.edu/fp/events/20050616bijianlunch.pdf.
10. State Council Information Office, *China's Peaceful Development Road, People's Daily*, Dec. 22, 2005.
11. Sim Chin Yin, "Chinese V-P Blasts Meddlesome Foreigners," *The Strait Time*, February 14, 2009.
12. David W. Moore, "American Divided in Feelings about China," Gallup Poll, April 3, 2001, www.gallup.com/poll/1837/Americans-Divided-Feelings-About-China.aspx
13. Reuter, "China Seen as a Key U.S. Relations, also a Foe," www.reuters.com/article/oU.Sl.ivMolt/idU.SL.TRE5A308C20091104
14. Banning Garrett, "U.S.-China Relations in the Era of Globalization and Terror: a Framework for Analysis," *Journal of Contemporary China* vol. 15, no. 48, (August 2006): 390.
15. Center for a New American Security, "Keynote Address by Deputy Secretary James Steinburg at China's Arrival: Long March to Global Power." September 24, 2009, www.cnas.org/node/3466 (accessed on November 12, 2009).
16. U.S. Senate Foreign Relations Committee, "Statement of Senator Hillary Rodhom Clinton, Nominee for Secretary of State," January 13, 2009, http://foreign.senate.gov/testimony/2009/ClintonTestimony090113a.pdf (accessed on November 12, 2009).
17. "Zhongguo nen buneng bimian yu meiguo de douzheng (Can China avoid clashes with the U.S.)?" China.com, http://military.china.com/zh_cn/critical3/27/200910 26/15679330_5.html (accessed on November 12, 2009)
18. "Kissinger: U.S. China Can Form "New Global Order," Newsmax.com, http://archive. newsmax.com/archives/ic/2007/4/3/73126.shtml?s=ic. (accessed on November 12, 2009).
19. C. Fred Bergson, "Pacific and Asia Pacific: the Choices for APEC," *Policy Brief*, July 2009, Peterson Institute of International Economics, Number PB09-16.
20. Niall Ferguson, "Team Chimerica," *Washington Post*, November 17, 2008.
21. CCTV, "Wen Rules out 'G2' Proposal," english.cctv.com/20090525/101054shtml (accessed on November 12, 2009).

22. Guo Wang, "G2: Untold Truth about Sino-U.SL. Relations," *Lianhe Zaobao* (Singapore), July 14, 2009.

23. Center for a New American Security, "Keynote Address by Deputy Secretary James Steinburg at China's Arrival: Long March to Global Power," September 24, 2009, www.cnas.org/node/3466 (accessed on November 12, 2009).

24. David Shambaugh, "The New Strategic Triangle: U.S. and European Reactions to China's Rise," *The Washington Quarterly*, vol. 28, no. 3, pp. 7-25..

Chapter 1

Manipulating the "Balance of Power": Historical Reappraisal of the Sino-U.S. Rapprochement

Yongshin Kim[*]

INTRODUCTION

China-U.S. rapprochement, symbolized by the February 28, 1972 *Joint Communiqué of the United States of America and the People's Republic of China* (or *Shanghai Communiqué*), was one of the great turning points of Cold War history. A tacit U.S.-China alliance "absorb[ed] no less than one-third of Soviet military assets" for the Far Eastern theater of operations.[1] Whereas Reagan's defense build-up "has received much of the credit for spending the Soviet military-industrial complex into the ground, the vast drain on Soviet resources caused by China's belligerence during the 1970s and 1980s should not be underestimated."[2]

Most of the literature on Sino-U.S. rapprochement argues that China reconciled with the United States in order to enhance its security against the threat from the Soviet Union; this explanation has been accepted as "nearly a truism."[3] Moreover, such conventional wisdom is regarded as evidence of the balance of power in international politics. For example, Doak Barnett, a renowned China specialist, argues that the *demarche* represents the workings of a realistic balance of power.[4] Scholars from the realist school, including experts on China like Henry Kissinger,[5] Thomas Robinson,[6] Melvin Gurtov and Byong-Moo Hwang,[7] Harry Harding,[8] Robert Ross,[9] and even Chinese scholar Wang Zhongchun,[10] assume that the enormous Soviet threat drove China to rapprochement with the United States. These ideas, however, were not supported by archival evidence. These archives have only recently been declassified and published in the *Papers Relating to the Foreign Relations of the United States Vol. XVII, China 1969-1972* (henceforth: *FRUS*) and Electronic Briefing Books in the National Security Archives (henceforth: *NSA*). Access to these archives provides a new opportunity to revisit and re-evaluate a subject that was considered one that we "already knew and understood."[11] The declassification of these archives enables us to in part overcome "old interpretive shackles" imposed by a lack of freedom, a lack of access, or a lack of interest.[12]

In this chapter, I do not claim to refute balance of power theory as an analytical tool in international relations, but my aims have been more restricted. I limited myself to illustrating how China and the United States, but especially the United States, manipulated the concept of balance of power to bring about the 1972 rapprochement. The conventional balance-of-power-centered explanations focusing on China's weakness have been overplayed by established historical accounts. This chapter, which takes an historical approach, sheds new light on the Sino-U.S. rapprochement by analyzing recently declassified archives. The historical approach would be different with a wide-spread methodology in the field of social science, which tries to separate independent variables and dependent variables; however, it would be more helpful to close on historical reality. [13] In most of the studies regarding the Sino-U.S. Rapprochement, the Rapprochement (dependent variable) is considered to be an outcome of the Soviet military threat (independent variable). The author, bearing in mind problems of oversimplification, has factored in many variables in the study of historical structures.

"BALANCE OF POWER" AS A UNIVERSAL LAW OF HISTORY?

The balance of power is an elusive and polysemous concept, "which can evoke a wide range of different and incompatible meanings."[14] In this vein, the concept has been under attack. For Richard Cobden, the balance of power is a "chimera . . . a mere conjunction of syllables, forming words which convey sound without meaning," and for A.F. Pollard, it is a "speculation on what 'permutation and combination' could be extracted by mathematicians from the Oxford English Dictionary's 20 meanings for 'balance,' 63 for 'of' and 18 for 'power.'" [15] Despite its elusiveness, in the realist tradition of international politics, "balance of power" has been treated as a universal law of history, wherein the whole universe is pictured "as [a] gigantic mechanism, a machine or clockwork, created and kept in motion by the divine watchmaker." [16] The founding father of neo-realism, Kenneth Waltz, also argues: "As nature abhors a vacuum, so international politics abhors unbalanced power." [17] Like Jean-Jacques Rousseau's explanation, "the balancing . . . is more the work of nature than of art."[18]

In the realist tradition, Stephen Walt tried to refine balance of power theory with balance of threat theory. In the former, imbalance of power causes alliances against the *strongest* state; in the latter, imbalance of threat causes alliances against the *most threatening* state. Walt succinctly points out the differences between them: "Whereas balance of power theory predicts that states will react to imbalances of power, balance of threat theory predicts that when there is an imbalance of threat (i.e., when one state or coalition appears especially dangerous), states will form alliances or increase their internal efforts in order to reduce their vulnerability."[19] While there are huge differences between balance of power and balance of threat theory, the former tends to absorb the latter with its historical richness in real politics. Furthermore, emphasizing the act of "balancing" makes both indistinguishable. Even Walt himself argues that balance of threat theory "should be viewed as a refinement of traditional balance of power theory."[20] The assumptions upon which balance of threat theory is grounded are also components of balance of power theory; hence, the former is usually interchangeable with the latter, but not vice versa. Consequently, when we are talking about balance of power, balance of threat theory is also part of it.

When it comes to the Sino-U.S. Rapprochement, the concept of balance of power has been employed without archival evidence. Historian Jerald A. Combs, in his book *The History of American Foreign Policy*, summarized the reason for the rapprochement in this way:

> Nixon and the Chinese arranged for Kissinger to be spirited into Beijing from Pakistan on a secret trip to improve Chinese-American relations and pave the way for a summit meeting between Nixon and Mao in China. Kissinger and Chinese Premier Zhou Enlai found they had much in common in their strategic thought. *Zhou*, obviously reflecting Mao's thought throughout his conversations with Kissinger, *was terribly worried by China's 4,000-mile border with the Soviet Union.* China had never recognized its border with the Soviets, which actually divided Mongolians from Mongolians and Manchurians from Manchurians, rather than Russians from Chinese. *The Soviets, steadily building their forces along the border,* had stationed twenty-one divisions there in 1969, increasing that number to thirty-three by 1971 and to forty-five by 1973. *China feared that as Soviet power grew,* the USSR would be tempted to use force to prevent the rise of another great enemy. Mao and Zhou wanted to enlist the United States in Beijing's confrontation with Moscow. *Zhou urged the United States to organize an anti-Soviet coalition* stretching from Japan through China, Pakistan, Iran, and Turkey to Western Europe. China, the most revolutionary of Communist States, was willing to cooperate with capitalists and reactionaries to deter a Soviet attack.[21] [*Emphasis* added.]

His argument is not an exceptional one, but rather a typical explanation of the Sino-U.S. Rapprochement, which already had become "nearly a truism." It contains two common assumptions: first, the USSR steadily increased its military capability along the Sino-Soviet border, and second, China feared increasing power from the Soviets, hence urged the United States to form an anti-Soviet coalition to balance the USSR. As a corollary, these assumptions bear three subsidiary assumptions: (1) The Soviet Union was the initiator of a series of Sino-USSR conflicts dating back to 1969;[22] (2) during the Sino-U.S. negotiations, the Chinese strongly emphasized the threat from the Soviets and urged the United States to form a military coalition;[23] and, (3) China's negotiating position toward the United States was severely constrained by its relative insecurity vis-à-vis the Soviet threat.[24] Like Lord Palmerston's old maxim, "The enemy of my enemy is my friend," the Sino-Soviet conflicts and the Sino-U.S. rapprochement came together from the very beginning. Kissinger recollected it in this way: "Nixon decided to concentrate on the broader issue of

China's attitude toward a dialogue with the United States. Priority was given to determining the scope of the looming Sino-Soviet-American triangle. If we could determine what we suspect—that the Soviet Union and China were more afraid of each other than they were of the United States—an unprecedented opportunity for American diplomacy would come into being."[25]

Recently, neo-classical realists have questioned the balance of power as "nature" or "universal law" and ask how the "art" of balance of power works. For example, Schweller[26] examines the domestic politics of balance of power; Christensen[27] asks "why leaders inflate external threats to sell costly internal mobilization campaigns"; and, Wohlforth[28] scrutinizes "how perceptions of the balance of power affect state behavior." These collective attempts "have incorporated the insights of classical realist theorists that domestic politics and statesmen's perceptions matter, and often critically, in explaining state behavior."[29] Rather than accepting balance of power as a "universal law," this chapter tries to understand how Chinese and American statesmen work together to bring about the "balance." In the following section, I will examine three subsidiary assumptions mentioned above in the light of the material uncovered from the recently declassified archives.

THE DEMISE OF THE SINO-SOVIET ALLIANCE AND THE ZHEN BAO/DAMANSKI INCIDENTS OF 1969

Conventional wisdom regarding the series of Sino-Soviet clashes on the Ussuri (*Wusuli*) River in 1969, known as the Zhenbao/Damanski Incidents, holds that the USSR was the aggressor toward China. Thus, the United States responded by forming a tacit alliance with China. In 1973, after visiting China and the Zhenbao Island (Damanski Island in Russian), Neville Maxwell published his "Report from China: The Chinese Account of the 1969 Fighting at Chenpao" in *The China Quarterly*. In this article, he complained that "[in] the west, as usual, the weight of credence quickly swung against China," and claimed that the Chinese commander gave the order to fire "only after taking sustained fire from the Russians."[30] Henry Kissinger, who was the executor of the Sino-U.S. negotiations and an adherent to the "balance of power" theory, agreed with Maxwell: "the skirmishes invariably took place near major Soviet supply bases and far from Chinese communications centers—a pattern one would expect only if the Soviet forces were in fact the aggressors."[31] Aligning with the logic of the "balance of power," Kissinger believed that "China needed us precisely because it did not have the strength to balance the Soviet Union by itself."[32]

Recently conducted researches from China, however, question whether the Soviets had initiated armed conflict in 1969. Although they have no incentive to reject the conventional wisdom regarding the Zhenbao/Damanski incidents (doing so could place them in political danger), many respected Chinese historians like Yang Kuisong now describe the event of 2 March 1969 as an ambush (*maifu*), not simply a clash (*chongtu*), and clearly indicating that certain revisions to historical texts are now in order.[33] Other eminent Chinese historians like Xu Yan[34] and Li Danhui[35] also suggest that the Chinese action was planned beforehand and strictly supervised by Mao Zedong and the Central Chinese Communist Party Committee. Even Maxwell, while discounting the historical significance of "who fired first," has changed his former conclusion, writing that: "It [Zhenbao Island Incident] is most likely that it happened through Chinese planning and maneuver."[36]

According to Chinese archives, Chinese leaders did not consider the possibility of the Soviets provoking all-out war against China as likely. On March 15, 1969, after finishing the second battle at Zhenbao, Mao Zedong mentioned in a rather contradictory way: "Let them invade. Then we will mobilize. In front of big enemy, preparation of mobilizing will have an advantage." At the same time, he ordered: "Stop in here, we don't need to fight."[37] On March 22, at a meeting with Chen Yi, Li Fuchun, Li Xiannian, Xu Xiangqian, Nie Rongzhen, Ye Jianying and members of the working group for Cultural Revolution, Mao again concluded that: "I'm pretty positive. About the clash on March 2 [Zhenbao/Damanski Incident], their leaders do not know and the Politburo has not discussed it like us." Furthermore, Mao informed Lin Biao that during the 9th National Congress of the Chinese Communist Party (*jiuda*) it did not need to deal seriously with clashes on the border.[38] After the 9th Congress, Mao asked four marshals, Chen Yi, Ye Jianying, Xu Xiangqian, and Nie Rongzhen, to analyze the international situation. Xiong Xianghui, who attended the four seniors' meeting as a secretary, stated that the first written report, "Preliminary Estimate on the War Situation," submitted to Mao on July 11, contained three parts: (1) struggles between the Sino-Soviet-U.S. three powers; (2) opinions on an anti-China war; and (3) analysis of Soviet-U.S. contradiction. On the second part, the four seniors argued:

> Soviet Imperialism considers China to be the archenemy and poses a greater threat to Chinese security than does the United States, but it is too early to initiate an anti-Chinese war. . . . If the Soviet Union waged a war against China, it would be a protracted war and would entrap the Soviet Union itself. The Soviet Union has exploited the terror of war on the domestic front for a long time. In the process, the Soviet government has lost the support of the people. The strategic location of Soviet industry closer to Europe would dangerously extend supply lines in a war with China. . . . Soviet military relocation to the east would not alter the primary Soviet strategic focus: Europe (the same focus held by the United States). Then, can the Soviet Union and the United States conduct a nuclear surprise attack? China, of course, has to prepare for that, but use of nuclear weapons is a military option not taken lightly.[39]

The Zhenbao/Damanski Incidents reflect deteriorating Sino-Soviet alliance and increased Chinese power relative to the USSR. Many scholars have pointed out different factors in the rupture of Sino-Soviet relations: ideological confrontation, inequality between Soviet and Chinese Communist parties owing to Soviet "great-power" chauvinism, and enmity between their leaders.[40] Chinese renowned cold war historian, Shen Zhihua, however, claims that structural contradictions inherent in the communist bloc are the fundamental reason for the demise of the Sino-Soviet alliance. One of these structural contradictions was that Communist bloc countries could not avoid conflicts between internationalism and nationalism. The USSR concealed its national interest in the name of internationalism and compelled other communist countries to accept the USSR-managed internationalism. When China was weak, it had no choice but to remain loyal to the Soviet-managed internationalism. In proportion to its rising status in the Communist bloc (although negligible on the world stage), China did not want to sacrifice its own national interest for internationalism. Relations between parties and countries were intermingled in the communist bloc then; thus, there was a contradiction between the organized principle of the parties, which is hierarchical, and the principle of Westphalian sovereignty, which is equal.[41] In other words, the Zhenbao/Damanski Incidents occurred when China decided not to sacrifice its own interest for Soviet-led internationalism.

"Conventional wisdom" also cites the Soviet crushing of Czechoslovakia in 1968 as evidence of an increasing Soviet threat toward China. Gurtov and Hwang specified threats that China confronted, and they included the 1968 Soviet invasion of Czechoslovakia as one of them.[42] New evidence from the archives in Moscow, however, indicates that the "Soviet crushing of Czechoslovakia in 1968 was not so much the behavior of a ruthless superpower as the reaction of a nervous power fearing a loss of control in eastern and central Europe and pressurized into action."[43] Arkady N. Shevchenko, former member of the Soviet Politburo, described the Soviet threat from China vividly in his memoir: "the events on Damansky had the effect of an electric shock in Moscow. The Politburo was terrified that the Chinese might make a large-scale intrusion into Soviet territory. . . . A nightmare vision of invasion by millions of Chinese made the Soviet leaders almost frantic. Despite our overwhelming superiority in weaponry, it would not be easy for the USSR to cope with an assault of such magnitude."[44] Unlike the "Realists'" assumption, the Soviet Union was not the "aggressor" in the Sino-Soviet armed conflicts in 1969. Table 1.1 shows the dispositions of the two countries' forces toward each other.

Table 1.1 indirectly indicates China and the USSR's mutual threat perception. Military dispositions might reflect decision makers' threat perception; following the Zhenbao/Damanski Incidents, the number of divisions in the Soviet Far East increased dramatically. The number of Chinese divisions on the Sino-Soviet border, on the contrary, remained relatively stable until the Sino-U.S. rapprochement in 1972. For Robinson, Chinese tardiness "was to be found in Chinese domestic politics and Peking's relations with Washington: Only in late 1971 was the Lin Piao affair resolved, allowing Mao and his group to move units and change commanders, and only after the Nixon visit in early 1972 did China feel secure enough to withdraw significant forces from the Fukien [Fujian] front opposite Taiwan."[45] Before declassification of Chinese archives, we cannot be certain of the real reason for China's delay in military relocation. As mentioned earlier, Chinese leaders did not foresee the possibility of a Soviet military attack. In addition, recent testimony from the Soviet Union depicts how Soviet leaders were frightened by a possible Chinese military attack.

Table 1.1 Soviet and Chinese Forces Dispositions, 1969-1976 (Divisions)

Year	Eastern Europe	Europe and USSR	Central USSR	South USSR	Soviet Far East
1968-69	-	-	-	-	22
1969-70	32	60	8	19	28
1970-71	31	60	8	21	37
1971-72	31	60	8	21	40
1972-73	31	60	8	21	44
1973-74	31	60	5	23	45
1974-75	31	63	5	23	45
1975-76	31	63	6	23	43

Year	Fujian	Wuhan	Hainan	Southwest	Tibet	Northeast	Lanzhou	Xinjiang	Sino-Soviet Border Total
1969-70	28	25	3	12	3	32	11	4	47
1970-71	28	25	3	12	3	32	11	4	47
1971-72	28	25	3	12	3	33	11	5	49
1972-73	25	17	3	12	8	40	15	10	65
1973-74	20	17	3	12	8	45	15	10	70
1974-75	25	17	3	12	6	50	15	8	73
1975-76	25	18	3	12	6	55	15	8	78

Notes: The "Sino-Soviet Border Total" column is simply the total of the Northeast, Lanzhou and Xinjinag.
Sources: Thomas Robinson, "China Confronts the Soviet Union: Warfare and Diplomacy on China's Inner Asian Frontiers" in *The Cambridge History of China. Vol. 15, Part 2, The People's Republic. Revolutions within the Chinese Revolution, 1966-1982*, edited by Roderick MacFarquhar and John King Fairbank (Cambridge: Cambridge University Press, 1991), p. 299.

Viktor Gobarev, a former colonel in Soviet military intelligence and specialist on the Sino-Soviet conflicts, argues: "According to all estimates . . . the Chinese possessed colossal manpower superiority . . . [Soviet] troop levels reached the capacity needed to repulse the Chinese on a conventional level only in the mid-1970s . . . in 1969, the Soviets were not ready."[46] This argument is confirmed by a Russian ex-military intelligence officer, Vitaly Shlykov, who presided over the Soviet military's Office of Foreign Estimates during the 1970s. Shlykov comments: "Soviet military leaders felt very insecure in the 1960s, because of the manpower disparities, which were only rectified by the build-up in the 1970s."[47] In addition, the following excerpt from a Soviet Communist Party Central Committee document illustrates how local Soviet leaders felt insecure facing millions of hostile Chinese just across the border:

> There is a strong need for economic consolidation, the construction of reliable communications, and, above all, [more intensive] settling of this distant territory [the Soviet Far East]. Although there has been some migration to the Far East, the density of the population, for example in the Khabarovsk territory, is almost seven times lower than the average in the country. People do not stay long here. There has been great fluctuation in the level of trained personnel. There are several reasons for this, [including] the harsh climate, and the high cost of living, which is greater than in the Western regions [of the Soviet Union]. There is no remuneration for length of service nor regional time zone increases in wages for many categories of civil servants and workers . . . there has been a catastrophic fluctuation [in the number] of teachers and doctors in the Khabarovsk territory. . . . People leave, abandoning even well appointed apartments. . . . Apparently, only when we finally resolve the problem of human resources consolidation will serious development and transformation of our Far East begin.[48]

In sum, we can infer from Table 1.1 and former Soviet officials' testimonies that Chinese threat perception of the Soviet Union around 1969 was relatively slight. However, in 1972, with the declaration of the Sino-U.S. rapprochement, which symbolized the end of the Sino-Soviet alliance, China started to increase the number of its divisions in Sino-Soviet border areas.

CHINA'S THREAT PERCEPTION OF THE SOVIET UNION DURING THE U.S.-CHINA NEGOTIATIONS

Chinese emphasis on defying Soviet expansionism is a corollary of the conventional realist explanation of Sino-U.S. rapprochement. Ross, for example, contends that Chinese Premier Zhou Enlai emphasized the importance of resisting Soviet expansionism during Kissinger's first visit to China in July 1971.[49] Newly declassified archives on Sino-U.S. secret negotiations, however, refute this argument. In this section, I will examine how China perceived and represented the Soviet threat during Kissinger's and Nixon's visits to China.

During Kissinger's first visit, Zhou and Kissinger had five meetings, but Zhou explicitly mentioned the Soviet threat just once: "For example, now, Soviet troops are in the Mongolian People's Republic. We are opposed. They pose a threat to us. We are opposed to that, but we do not adopt the practice of also sending troops to fight. But if these troops pass through the territory of the MPR [Mongolian People's Republic] to invade even one inch of our territory, then we would immediately resist and fight back."[50] This explicit mention of the Soviet threat, however, was not to call attention to resisting Soviet expansionism but to emphasize the importance of non-interference. By directly referring to the

Soviet threat to China, Zhou attempted to persuade Kissinger that the U.S. should "back off" from Indochinese affairs.

In contrast with Zhou, Kissinger ardently mentioned Soviet military pressure to China: "With respect to Soviet intentions, contrary to some of my American friends, I do not exclude the possibility of Soviet military adventurism. In fact, speaking personally and frankly, this is one of the new lessons I have learned in my present position. I had not believed it previously."[51] He also confirmed that the United States had no intention to form an anti-Chinese circle: "But this is a problem essentially between you and USSR. As far as the United States is concerned, I can tell you flatly that there is no possibility, certainly in this Administration, nor probably in any other, of any cooperation such as you have described between the United States, the Soviet Union and Japan to divide up China."[52] Furthermore, he suggested providing information regarding the U.S.-Soviet bilateral negotiations such as SALT (Strategic Arms Limitation Talks), "to alleviate any concerns" China might have. In this way, he argued, the Soviet Union did not "increase the opportunity for military pressures against you [China]."[53]

During Kissinger's second visit to China in October 1971, Kissinger again attempted to convince Zhou of the Soviet threat to China by mentioning the Four Power Agreement on Berlin. By concluding the agreement, Kissinger said "the Soviet Union has a great desire to free itself in Europe so it can concentrate on other areas."[54] Zhou, however, replied to Kissinger that the Berlin question was not related to China.[55] When Kissinger reported his second visit to President Nixon, Kissinger also wrote that the Chinese tried to downplay the Russian factor, but he still maintained that China's dislike for and concern about the Soviet Union were obvious.[56]

When Nixon finally visited China, it was not Zhou or Mao but Nixon and Kissinger who emphasized the Soviet threat to China. Before arriving in China, Nixon did not receive confirmation about the possibility of meeting with Mao Zedong. Right after Nixon's arrival in Beijing, Mao ordered Zhou to bring Nixon around at once. Winston Lord, staff member of the National Security Council who assisted Kissinger at numerous security meetings, described the meeting as "a typical example of the Chinese style, where the Emperor used to keep visitors on edge, and the schedule was never fixed until the last minute." The purpose, he thought, was "partly to make us feel grateful when the actual meeting took place and that it did take place."[57] Interestingly, Nixon met with Mao without an American translator because he was afraid of leaks. On the meeting between Nixon and Mao, Mao suggested their agenda would be better if they limited it to philosophical questions.[58] Nixon, however, continued to attempt to persuade him to acknowledge the Soviet threat: "For example, Mr. Chairman, it is interesting to note that most nations would approve of this meeting, but the Soviets disapprove, the Japanese have doubts which they express, and the Indians disapprove. So we must examine why, and determine how our policies should develop to deal with the whole world, as well as the immediate problems such as Korea, Vietnam, and of course, Taiwan."[59]

During the series of negotiations between Zhou and Kissinger, Zhou and Nixon, and Mao and Nixon, the Americans emphasized the Soviet threat toward China to motivate Chinese interest for rapprochement with the United States. Under these circumstances, if China kept an ambiguous attitude toward the Soviet threat, it could receive voluntary and unilateral top-secret military intelligence regarding the Soviet Union as a reward for cooperation with the United States.

ILL-BALANCED CONCESSIONS BETWEEN CHINA AND THE U.S. DURING THE NEGOTIATIONS

If China reconciled with the United States because of the Soviet threat, the Chinese bargaining position would be seriously limited. Kissinger wrote in his memoirs: "Taiwan was mentioned only briefly during the first session."[60] Kissinger's comment demonstrates that Taiwan was not a problem in the negotiations. Taiwan, however, has always been bottom line to China, so any yielding on Taiwan corresponds to selling out their nation. If Taiwan was really mentioned in passing that indicates that the Chinese bargaining position was severely restricted. Yet Kissinger assured Zhou in their first meeting that: "[as] for the political future of Taiwan we are not advocating a 'two Chinas' solution or a 'one China, one Taiwan' solution. As a student of history, one's prediction would have to be that the political evolution is likely to be in the direction which Prime Minister Chou [Zhou] Enlai indicated to me."[61] From the beginning of the session, Kissinger assuaged Zhou with clear concessions about Taiwan. What Kissinger told Zhou even contradicted the official position of the U.S. government, announced by the State Department less than three months earlier, that sovereignty over Taiwan was "an unsettled question subject to future international resolution." In other words, if Taiwan was barely mentioned, this was only because Kissinger gave China the private assurances it sought at the beginning of the first meeting.[62]

On Vietnam, however, concessions from China to the United States were problematic. To improve the situation in Indochina, Kissinger tried to link Indochina to other issues. Zhou, however, declined Kissinger's offer and said that "[it] would be ludicrous to want us to guarantee something you had already torn up. So we can only guarantee formally that all foreign forces should withdraw from Indochina and the three Indochinese people should solve their own questions by themselves."[63] By saying this, Zhou alluded to China's non-intervention in Indochina. Although Smyser, NSC Vietnam specialist, recalled "nothing was resolved [on Vietnam]," but the U.S. could be relieved from the legacy of the Korean War two decades before. Throughout the Vietnam War, fear in Washington of Chinese intervention in Vietnam had inhibited American military escalation. By talking directly with China, the U.S. was able to mine the harbors of Haiphong and launch massive bombing raids over Hanoi with impunity for the next 18 months.[64]

Besides Taiwan and Vietnam, they haggled over relations with the Soviet Union and Japan, the South Asian subcontinent, and the establishment of a secure channel of communication and arms control.[65] Regarding relations with other major countries, Zhou asked for the withdrawal of the U.S. troops from Korea, Japan, the Philippines, Indochina and Thailand. Kissinger, in response, urged the Chinese to help end the Vietnam War by linkage of troop reduction and the progress of the Vietnam War.[66] Furthermore, Kissinger linked the progress of the Vietnam War with the improvement of Sino-U.S. relations,[67] withdrawal of the United States forces from Taiwan,[68] and diplomatic normalization.[69]

On February 1972, just before leaving for China, Nixon wrote a personal memo about what they would exchange.

What they want:
1. Build up their world credentials
2. Taiwan
3. Get U.S. out of Asia

What we want:
1. Indochina (?)
2. Communication: To restrain Chinese expansion in Asia
3. In Future: Reduce threat of confrontation by China Super Power

What we both want:
1. Reduce danger of confrontation & conflict
2. A more stable Asia
3. A restraint on U.S.S.R.[70]

This memo clearly indicates what the United States side was willing to grant to and accept from China. Like Kissinger, Nixon also started bargaining with China by confirming the U.S. Taiwan policy. At the meeting with Mao, Nixon, more succinctly than Kissinger, put forward five principles regarding Taiwan:

(1) "There is one China, and Taiwan is a part of China;"
(2) "We have not and will not support any Taiwan independence movement;"
(3) "We will, to the extent we are able, use our influence to discourage Japan from supporting a Taiwan independence movement;"
(4) "We will support any peaceful resolution of the Taiwan issue that can be worked out;" and
(5) "We will seek the normalization with the People's Republic."[71]

In preparation for his second meeting with Zhou, Nixon wrote the following memorandum:

Taiwan-Vietnam = tradeoff
1. Your people expect action on Taiwan

2. Our people expect action on V. Nam
Neither can act immediately—But both are inevitable.
Let us not embarrass each other.[72]

To create a tradeoff between Taiwan and Vietnam, Nixon needed to establish a shared antagonism toward the Soviet Union; hence, he used a carrot and stick strategy. As a stick, Nixon exaggerated the Soviet threat to China. For example, Nixon claimed to Zhou that: the Soviet Union had been shifting the nuclear power balance at a very alarming rate; the Soviet Union had deployed more forces on the Sino-Soviet borders than it had arrayed against the Western Alliance; moreover, by supporting India the Soviets posed a very present threat to China.[73] As a carrot, Kissinger handed over top-secret information on Soviet military forces, e.g., a run-down of Soviet forces deployed along the Sino-Soviet border, including ground forces, tactical aircraft and missiles, strategic air defenses, and strategic attack forces. Additionally, the U.S. guaranteed military support if China was under pressure or attack from the Soviet Union. Vice Minister of Foreign Affairs Qiao Guanhua asked for clarification of the status of United States military support. Kissinger assured him that the United States military would support China if it was subject to pressure or attack from the Soviet Union. Kissinger, added, on an extremely confidential basis, that the United States would provide additional information, if China requested it, without reciprocity.[74] Concessions between the United States and China during the negotiations were far from what conventional realists supposed. In general terms, China gained much more than the United States did. This imbalance of concessions signals that the Sino-U.S. rapprochement in 1972 cannot be explained by the conventional balance of power approach.

CONCLUSION

This chapter identified the problems with realist explanations about Sino-U.S. rapprochement in 1972. In summary, newly declassified American and former Communist-bloc countries' primary and secondary archives negate a basic balance-of-power based assumption in three ways. First, the Zhenbao/Damansky Incidents in 1969 were initiated by China, not by the Soviet Union. This contrasts with Kissinger's perception of the Soviet Union as an "aggressor" during the initial stage of armed conflict with the PRC. Secondly, during the Sino-U.S. negotiations for rapprochement, China did not emphasize the Soviet threat. In fact, on the contrary, Kissinger and Nixon tried to persuade Zhou Enlai and Mao Zedong of the immediate possibility of a Soviet attack on China. Thirdly, during the secret negotiations between the PRC and the United States, the Americans granted major concessions regarding Taiwan, without obtaining China's concession regarding the Vietnam War. Unlike "Realist" interpretations presupposing that China's negotiating position toward the United States was severely constrained by its insecurity vis-à-vis the Soviet threat, China gained more concessions from the negotiations with the United States.

The argument stated in this chapter is not that the concept of a balance of power did not work in the process of the Sino-U.S. Rapprochement. Rather, my argument is this concept did not work in accord with conventional wisdom. The 1972 Sino-U.S. Rapprochement was not the consequence of balance of power as a universal law; rather, it was the outcome of balance-of-power oriented policies from both China and the United States. By manipulating the balance of power as more "the work of nature than of art," China and the United States could produce a "language which will meet the Prime Minister's need, but language which will not give this strong coalition of opponents to the initiative we have made." [75] When Nixon mentioned "the strong coalition of opponents," it included not only international forces like the USSR, Japan, and India, but also each country's domestic forces. For the United States, balance-of-power logic which emphasized the threat from the Soviet Union to China made Americans feel they had finally rescued China from an "evil empire" and demonstrated the idealist tradition in American foreign policy. This logic, moreover, saved the American leaders from criticism such as, "the American President went to Peking and sold Taiwan down the river."[76] For China, it enabled a breakup with its "Socialist brother" and holding hands with the "beautiful imperialist" (*meidiguozhuyi*) without abandoning a socialist system. In addition, by maintaining an ambiguous position toward the Soviet threat, China was able to gain top-secret military intelligence from the United States. In this vein, even the communiqué, which proclaimed the two countries' rapprochement, was written in an unconventional way. It emphasized differences as well as common ground between Beijing and Washington in order to make "running room," something that Nixon argued the communiqué language needed to provide.[77]

Secret diplomacy, which was unprecedented in contemporary international affairs at this level, allowed both parties to create this "running room." American-led secret diplomacy finally drove a wedge between China and the USSR under the banner of balance of power, but the 1972 rapprochement was not the result of balance of power doctrine, which presumes an alliance against the strongest power. The rapprochement was not a result of the balance of power dynamic; rather, it was the result of manipulation of the balance of power. Without question, until the opening of the Chinese archives, any conclusions on the subject must remain tentative. However, the examination of newly declassified archives allow for alternative explanations.

NOTES

* This research was supported by the Brain Korea 21 project, "Rediscovering Asia for Political Science," Yonsei University and an award from the Center for Chinese Studies, University of Hawaii at Manoa. The author is grateful to Myongsob Kim, Ki-Jung Kim, Sukhee Han, Jungmin Seo, Jing Men, Dominik Mierzejewski, and anonymous reviewers for their helpful comments and insights.

1. Craig Nation, *Black Earth, Red Star: A History of Soviet Security Policy, 1917-1991*, (Ithaca Cornell University Press, 1992), p. 267, quoted from Lyle Goldstein. "Return to Zhenbao Island: Who Started Shooting and Why It Matters." *The China Quarterly*, vol. 168, (2001), p. 985.

2. Goldstein, "Return to Zhenbao Island," p. 985.

3. Robert Ross, *Negotiating Cooperation: The United States and China, 1969-1989* (Stanford: Stanford University Press, 1995), p. 1.

4. Doak Barnett, *China and the Major Powers in East Asia* (Washington, D.C.: Brookings Institution, 1977), pp. 227-228.

5. Henry Kissinger, *White House Years*. 1st ed. (Boston: Little, Brown and Company, 1979) and Kissinger, *Diplomacy* (New York: Simon & Schuster, 1994).

6. Thomas Robinson, "China Confronts the Soviet Union: Warfare and Diplomacy on China's Inner Asian Frontiers" in *The Cambridge History of China. Vol. 15, Part 2, The People's Republic. Revolutions within the Chinese Revolution, 1966-1982*, edited by Roderick MacFarquhar and John King Fairbank (Cambridge: Cambridge University Press, 1991).

7. Melvin Gurtov and Byong-Moo Hwang, *China under Threat: The Politics of Strategy and Diplomacy* (Baltimore: Johns Hopkins University Press, 1980).

8. Harry Harding, *A Fragile Relationship: The United States and China since 1972* (Washington, D.C.: Brookings Institution, 1992).

9. Ross, *Negotiating Cooperation* (Stanford: Stanford University Press, 1995).

10. Zhongchun Wang, "The Soviet Factors during the Sino-US Normalization, 1969-1979" (in Chinese), *Dangde wenxian*, vol. 4, (2002) and Wang, "The Soviet Factor in Sino-American Normalization, 1969-1979" in *Normalization of U.S.-China Relations: An International History*, edited by Robert Ross William Kirby and Gong Li (Cambridge: Harvard University Press, 2005). One of the most typical illustrations of a realistic understanding about the 1972 rapprochement may be found in Zhongchun Wang, "The Soviet Factor in Sino-American Normalization, 1969-1979," p. 172., which is worth quoting at length:

> the Soviet military threat was the direct and basic impetus for China to talk to and seek reconciliation with the United States. It is unimaginable that China would have abandoned the 'leaning to one side' strategy completely and engaged in high-level-talks with the United States—once deemed China's 'fierce enemy'—without the deterioration of the Sino-Soviet relationship and the massing of Soviet troops on the Sino-Soviet-Mongolia border. The rapprochement between the United States and China alleviated to some degree China's perilous external security environment, especially the military pressure from the north.

11. John Lewis Gaddis, *We Now Know: Rethinking Cold War History* (Oxford, New York: Clarendon Press; Oxford University Press, 1997).

12. Odd Arne Westad, *Brothers in Arms: The Rise and Fall of the Sino-Soviet Alliance, 1945-1963* (Washington, D.C., Stanford: Woodrow Wilson Center Press; Stanford University Press, 1998), p. xii.

13. John Lewis Gaddis, *The Landscape of History: How Historians Map the Past*, (Oxford, New York: Oxford University Press, 2002), pp. 53-70.

14. Richard Little, "Deconstructing the Balance of Power: Two Traditions of Thought," *Review of International Studies*, vol. 15, no. 2, (1989), p. 87. For numerous realist understandings of balance of power, see Ernst Hass, "The Balance of Power: Prescription, Concept, or Propaganda?" *World Politics* vol. 5, no. 4 (1953), pp. 442-77; Martin Wight, "The Balance of Power and International Order" in *The Bases of International Order: Essays in Honour of C. A. W. Manning*, edited by C. A. W. Manning and Alan James (London, New York: Oxford University Press, 1973); and Paul

Schroeder, "The Nineteenth Century Balance of Power: Balance of Power or Political Equilibrium?," *Review of International Studies*, vol. 15 (1989), pp. 135-153.

15. Wight, "The Balance of Power and International Order," p. 211.

16. Hans Morgenthau, *Politics among Nations: The Struggle for Power and Peace*. 4th ed. (New York: Alfred Knopf, 1996), p. 197.

17. Kenneth Waltz, "Structural Realism after the Cold War," *International Security*, vol. 25 (2000), p. 28.

18. Jean-Jacques Rousseau, *Extrait Du Projet De Paix Perpetuelle De Monsieur L'abbé Saint Pierre*, as quoted in Hass, "The Balance of Power: Prescription, Concept, or Propaganda?," p. 453.

19. Stephen Walt, *The Origins of Alliances* (Ithaca: Cornell University Press, 1987), pp. 263-266.

20. Walt, *The Origins of Alliances*, p. 263.

21. Jerald Combs, *The History of American Foreign Policy*. 3rd ed. Volume 2 (Armonk: M.E. Sharpe, 2008), p. 235.

22. "Originally, I had accepted the fashionable view that the Chinese were the more militant country. However, I looked at a detailed map and saw that the Sinkiang [Xinjiang] incidents took place only a few miles from a Soviet railhead and several hundred miles from any Chinese railhead, it occurred to me that a Chinese military leader would not have picked such an unpropitious spot to attack. After that, I looked at the problem differently." Kissinger, *White House Years*, p. 177. This argument persists in the more recently published Kissinger's *Diplomacy*, pp. 721-722.

23. "Zhou emphasized the importance of resisting Soviet expansionism." Ross, *Negotiating Cooperation*, p. 38.

24. "Taiwan was mentioned only briefly during the first session." Kissinger, *White House Years*, p. 749.

25. Kissinger, *Diplomacy*, pp. 722-723.

26. Randall Schweller, *Unanswered Threats: Political Constraints on the Balance of Power* (Princeton: Princeton University, 2006).

27. Thomas Christensen, *Useful Adversaries: Grand Strategy, Domestic Mobilization, and Sino-American Conflict, 1947-1958* (Princeton: Princeton University Press, 1997).

28. William Wohlforth, *The Elusive Balance: Power and Perceptions During the Cold War* (Ithaca, N.Y.: Cornell University Press, 1993).

29. Nicholas Khoo, "Realism Redux: Investigating the Causes and Effects of Sino-US Rapprochement," *Cold War History*, vol. 5, no. 4 (2005), p. 537.

30. Neville Maxwell, "The Chinese Account of the 1969 Fighting at Chenpao," *The China Quarterly*, vol. 56 (1973), pp. 734-735.

31. Kissinger, *Diplomacy*, p. 722; see also Kissinger, *White House Years*, p. 177.

32. Kissinger, *White House Years*, p. 749.

33. Kuisong Yang, "From the Zhenbao Battles to the Sino-US Rapprochement" (in Chinese), *Dangshi yanjiu zhiliao*, 12, 1997 and Yang, "The Sino-Soviet Border Clash of 1969: From Zhenbao Island to Sino-American Rapprochement." *Cold War History*, vol. 1, no. 1 (2000), pp. 26-27; Goldstein, "Return to Zhenbao Island," pp. 985-986.

34. Yan Xu, "Sino-Soviet Armed Conflicts in 1969" (in Chinese), *Dangshi yanjiu zhiliao*, 5, 1994.

35. Danhui Li, "Sino-Soviet Border Conflicts in 1969: Causes and Effects" (in Chinese), *Dangdai zhongguoshi yanjiu*, vol. 3 (1999).

36. Neville Maxwell, "How the Sino-Russian Boundary Conflict Was Finally Settled: From Nerchinsk 1689 to Vladivostok 2005 via Zhenbao Island 1969," *Slavic Eurasian Studies*, vol. 16, no. 2 (2006), pp. 63-64.

37. "Mao's Speech at Preliminary Conference of the Working Group for the Cultural Revolution," quoted from Yang, "From the Zhenbao Battles to the Sino-US Rapprochement," p. 10. All translations are mine unless otherwise noted.

38. Yang, "From the Zhenbao Battles to the Sino-US Rapprochement," p. 10.

39. Xianghui Xiong, *Wode qiangbao yu waijiao shengya* [My Careers in Intelligence and Diplomacy] (in Chinese) (Beijing: Chinese Communist Party History Press, 2006), pp. 186-191.

40. Yingmei Shi, "Analysis on the Reasons of Sino-Soviet Deteriorating Relations" (in Chinese), *Journal of Heilongjiang College of Education*, vol. 23, no. 2 (2004), pp. 63-65; Guoliang Pu, "Character Conflicts between Khrushchev and Mao Zedong and Sino-Soviet Conflicts" (in Chinese), *Dangdai shijie yu shehuizhuyi*, vol. 5 (2003), pp. 101-105; Deok-kyoo Choi, "Sino-Soviet Relations and Border Disputes: Focusing on Zhenbao Island Incidents in 1969" (in Korean) in *Joonggookei byungang insikgwa galdeung* [Chinese Border Perceptions and Conflicts] (Osan: Hanshin University Press, 2007), pp. 267-276.

41. Zhihua Shen (ed.), *Zhongsu guanxi shigang* [History of Sino-Soviet Relations] (Beijing: Xinhua Press, 2007), pp. 469-475.

42. Gurtov and Hwang, *China under Threat*, pp. 187-191.

43. Caroline Kennedy-Pipe, "International History and International Relations Theory: A Dialogue Beyond the Cold War," *International Affairs*, vol. 76, no. 4 (2000), p. 743; Mark Kramer, "New Sources on the 1968 Soviet Invasion of Czechoslovakia," *Cold War International History Bulletin*, 2, 1992.

44. Arkady N. Shevchenko, *Breaking With Moscow* (New York: Knopf, 1985), pp. 164-165

45. Robinson, "China Confronts the Soviet Union," pp. 298-300.

46. Goldstein, "Return to Zhenbao Island," p. 994.

47. Ibid.

48. *Archives of President of the Russian Federation (APRF)*, Fond 53, Opis 1, Delo 448, p. 32, quoted from Viktor Gobarev, "Soviet Policy toward China: Developing Nuclear Weapons 1949-1969," *The Journal of Slavic Military Studies*. vol. 12, no. 4 (1999), p. 34.

49. Ross, *Negotiating Cooperation*, p. 38.

50. *FRUS*, pp. 418-419.

51. Nixon drew a line beside this paragraph.

52. Nixon drew parallel lines besides this paragraph.

53. *FRUS*, pp. 422-423.

54. Memorandum of Conversation, Kissinger and Zhou, "Korean, Japan, South Asia, Soviet Union, Arms Control," from *NSA* Electronic Briefing Book No. 70, "Negotiating U.S.-Chinese Rapprochement: New American and Chinese Documentation Leading up to Nixon's 1972 Trip," Document No. 13, p. 33.

55. Ibid., p. 37.

56. *FRUS*, p. 527.

57. Quoted from Margaret MacMillan, *Nixon and Mao: The Week That Changed the World* (New York: Random House, 2007), pp. 65-66.

58. *FRUS*, p. 681.

59. *FRUS*, p. 681.

60. Kissinger, *White House Years*, p. 749.

61. *FRUS*, p. 369.

62. James Mann, *About Face: A History of America's Curious Relationship with China from Nixon to Clinton* (New York: Alfred Knopf: Distributed by Random House, 1999), p. 33.

63. *FRUS*, p. 420.

64. Mann, *About Face*, p. 33-34.

65. *FRUS*, pp. 359-397.

66. *FRUS*, pp. 390-391.

67. "We believe that the end of the war in Indochina will accelerate the improvement in our relations." *FRUS*, p. 376.

68. "Let me say that, Mr. Prime Minister, that regardless of what you do, we are prepared to withdraw that part of our forces on Taiwan, which is related to this conflict [the Vietnam War] within a specified time after the conflict is over." *FRUS*, p. 376.

69. "We can settle the major part of the military question [withdrawal of the U.S. forces] within this term of the President if the war in Southeast Asia is ended. We can certainly settle the political question [establishment of diplomatic relations in consort with One-China policy] within the earlier part of the President's second term. Certainly we can begin evolution in that direction before." *FRUS*, p. 371.

70. Nixon Presidential Materials Project, White House Special Files, President's Personal Files, Box 7, Folder "China Notes," quoted from MacMillan, *Nixon and Mao*, p. 234 and Mann, *About Face*, pp. 13-14.

71. *FRUS*, pp. 698-699.

72. Nixon Presidential Materials Project, White House Special Files, President's Personal Files, Box. 7, Folder "China Notes." quoted from MacMillan, *Nixon and Mao*, p. 245.

73. *FRUS*, pp. 693-704.

74. Memorandum of Conversation, Nixon and Yeh Chien-ying, Chiao Kuan-hua, 23 February 1972, 9:35 a.m. - 12:34 p.m., from *NSA*, "Nixon's Trip to China: Records now Completely Declassified, Including Kissinger Intelligence Briefing and Assurances on Taiwan," Document 4.

75. *FRUS*, pp. 698-699.

76. *FRUS*, p. 699.

77. *FRUS*, p. 768.

Chapter 2

The Regional Logic of China-U.S. Rivalry

Yves-Heng Lim[*]

INTRODUCTION

Defining the structure of the post-Cold War international system can be a tricky task. In the classical terms of realism and power transition theory, possible trends and qualifications have been ranging from Niall Ferguson's fear of "apolarity"[1] to Christopher Layne's assertion that new powers will soon rise—putting a premature end to the unipolar moment.[2] Description of the contemporary international system also included Bradley Thayer's defense of an American empire[3] as well as an original critic by Ye Zicheng who pointed out that different polarities might be observed in the different layers of the current international system.[4] This already puzzling description of the international system gets even more complex if we choose to go beyond the traditionally static realist framework and bring power dynamics back in. Prophecies about the coming fall of American dominance over the global system might have gained new relevance in the current period, but for the time being Washington is still towering over the international system and the identity of future contenders is still uncertain. If, as stated by Kenneth Waltz, great power status "depends on how [states] score on *all* of the following items: size of population and territory, resource endowment, economic capability, military strength, political stability and competence",[5] the actual number of candidates qualifying for such status at the global level appears, at best, limited. Quite clearly, on the military chessboard, the United States remains unrivalled: no other state could realistically set up an operation of the scale of Iraqi Freedom, or seriously consider catching up with American military spending—which reached $607 billion in 2008, 41.5 percent of the whole world military expenditures—in the foreseeable future.[6]

The enduring American primacy on the global stage does not mean that the world stood still over the two decades covered by the post-Cold War era. "Dynamic differentials"[7] have benefited to some actors more than others, but the depth of changes caused by them seems to be less than a global upheaval. While, at the global level, theoreticians seem to sail partly uncharted and somewhat tumultuous waters, some scholars focused on the (re)emergence of regions. Over the last two decades, regional approaches of international affairs have been proliferating in multiple and often contradictory ways—there is little common ground between Douglas Lemke's "multiple hierarchy model"[8] and "new regionalism".[9] They nonetheless all share the view that the relevant level for analyzing contemporary international politics is located somewhere below the global level. While the Cold War was characterized by the salience of the global bipolar rivalry, which was to a large extent, overriding regional dynamics, post-Cold War trends toward regionalization have replaced a somewhat unified global order with multiple regional games, which are linked in a complex manner with the global level. As few powers—arguably only one—have a global reach, any analysis of great power relations—including relations between the lonely global superpower and regional powers—has to be replaced in the particular regional context in which they evolve.

At one of the multiple crossroads between the trend toward regionalization and the rise of new great powers, we can find the particular case of China's ascent in East Asia. China's exceptional growth since the beginning of the reforms and opening is particularly visible in the economic field where the magnitude of changes is reflected in the evolution of statistical data. Using exchange rates measurements, China's GDP reached $2,668 billion in 2006—a sevenfold increase over fifteen years; and, measured in purchasing power parity, China reached $7,903 billion in 2008 thus making China the second economic power after the United States.[10] China's impressive economic takeoff was made possible by its successful opening to the global economy. The degree of China's openness to the world economy is reflected in the steady increase of its relative share in international trade, which grew from less than one percent in 1980 to 7.8 percent in 2007.[11] In the same way, Foreign Direct Investment (FDI) in China spectacularly jumped from a very modest $57 million in 1980 to more than $79 billion in 2005.[12] Following this economic ascent, China has also devoted considerable efforts to the acquisition of military capabilities that could be commensurate with its latent power and new status. Though significant disagreements exist about the real level of Chinese military expenditures, white papers published on *China's National Defense* show that yearly increases of China's defense budget never fell below ten percent over the last twelve years.[13] In real terms, SIPRI estimates show that China's defense budget has been multiplied by three between 1996 and 2006.[14] From 2005 on, Chinese military expenditures have been the largest in Asia growing by 41 percent in real term (60 percent in nominal terms) between 2005 and 2008, while the Japanese defense budget has been slightly decreasing over the last decade.[15]

While China's ascent in the economic and military fields has been nothing less than stunning, Beijing still remains far from being a full-fledged global power able to compete on a par with Washington. Using exchange rates, American GDP was still more than five time larger than the Chinese one in 2006, and per capita figures show that the average American was still more than twenty times richer than a Chinese counterpart. On the military side, Washington has spent on its defense roughly ten times more than what Beijing was able to afford for the same purpose in 2008. By most—if not all—standards, China cannot be considered as a great power playing in the same league as the United States. Assessing the impact of China's rise through a comparison of American and Chinese performances on such crude indicators might however be misleading. China's ascent surely has serious consequences at the global level— from Africa to South America—but its strongest impact is felt within the East Asian region. This does not mean that China's rise does not, in some ways, constitute a direct challenge to United States dominance. While the post-Cold War order was characterized by an American domination over most—if not all—regional systems, China's ascent put the U.S.-centered regional order at risk in East Asia. Grasping the importance of China's challenge to the United States thus requires us to focus on the regional specificity of this rivalry.

ELEMENTS FOR A REGIONAL FRAMEWORK FOR ANALYSIS

Following Raymond Aron's classic definition, international systems are composed of political units which keep up regular relations and are likely to be all embroiled in a global, system-wide, war.[16] Considering the first condition, "globalization" is arguably turning the interstate system into a closely knit global village—though the roots of the trend toward a "unified world" can be traced much farther in the past.[17] Considering the second condition, however, the world seems much less unified, because powers with a global military reach can be considered as the exception rather than the rule. While one might be tempted to treat each of the aforementioned conditions as sufficient, disregarding the fact that both of them are necessary in any definition of regional systems leads to the somewhat awkward position Michael Haas criticized four decades ago. In his own words,

> Our attention [must be] directed toward systems containing military-strategic confrontations between poles of actors. To regard Ecuador-Ethiopia as a relevant subsystem would be as much potpourri choice as to select all national actors for the year 453, whether they knew each other's existence or not; we need precise criteria for determining membership in an international subsystem which are phrased in terms of how member states relate to one another militarily.[18]

From this perspective, the world can hardly be seen as a complete international system because most actors do not have the wherewithal to (inter)act military at the global level. Area studies aside, numerous attempts have been made to define relevant subglobal systems. Douglas Lemke provide us with an edifying list of such attempts which include: "'regions' [. . .], 'subordinate state systems'[. . .], 'subordinate international systems'[. . .], 'international subsystems' [. . .], 'hierarchical regional systems' [. . .], 'regimes' [. . .], 'regional subsystems' [. . .], 'politically relevant neighborhood' [. . .], and 'clusters of nations' [. . .]," [19] The range of frameworks compatible with realist hypothesis about the structure of international systems—which most prominently does not take into account cultural proximity and is agnostic about the war or peace proneness of regions—is however more limited. Among these multiple approaches, Barry Buzan's initial proposal for considering regions as regional security complexes—"regions as seen through the lens of security"[20]—still offers the most relevant framework to introduce "regions" in realism.

The basic logic of regional security complexes draws on the intuitive idea that a close relation exists between security concerns and distance. To borrow Buzan and Waever's words,

> If one hypothetically listed all the security concerns of the world, drew a map connecting each referent object for security with whatever is said to threaten it and with the main actors positively and negatively involved in handling the threat, the resulting picture would show varying degrees of intensity. Some clusters of nodes would be intensely connected, while other zones would be crossed by only few lines. Of the clusters that form, RSCT [Regional Security Complexes Theory] predicts that *most would be territorially based.*[21]

The existence of regional security complexes stems from the interaction of power—threat and security—and geography. To paraphrase Raymond Aron's remark about the formation of patterns of enmity and amity, security concerns are not determined by geography but by the projection "on a map" of a particular distribution of power.[22] States belong to a security complex when they can threaten one another militarily or at least when the architecture of their primary security concerns is based on the same basic features. For reasons I mention below, proximity to a given regional security system has a great impact on possible membership, but it cannot in itself be considered as a sufficient condition. Regional membership should thus be assessed by taking into account the capacity of actual military interaction between members. This capacity might remain a virtual one: states do not have actually to fight or take part in any alliance or defense agreement to belong to a given security complex. Regional security complexes might thus exist in the absence of observable institutions or even direct interaction. Using the concept of "security externalities"—the fact that actions taken by an actor affect the security level of other members of the system whatever the first actor's intents—David Lake points out that regions might exist while "there is no manifest or measurable 'interaction' between states, such as the exchange of goods and services".[23] In other words, the necessary and sufficient condition for states to belong to a same security complex is that their respective levels of security are highly interdependent, which means that they have a reasonable capacity to militarily interact and threaten one another.

Regional security systems are formed because power cannot be transported over long distances without suffering from corrosion. In Kenneth Boulding's words, all states who wish to project power have to pay "the LSG [loss-of-strength gradient, which] is a cost of transport of strength, whatever strength is."[24] Everything else being equal, the farther a state projects its power, the higher toll the loss-of-strength gradient will take of its forces. As a consequence, the ability of a state to interact with other actors will thus sharply diminish with the distance its projected forces have to cover. Beyond a certain point, the actual military power a state might be able to mobilize to wage a war or intervene in a conflict simply drops to nil—or at least to a negligible level. Global great powers aside, any state thus has a geographically limited "relevant neighbourhood", which is defined as the area within which its military might allows it to weight in the game and to be included in other states' security calculus.[25] Some states can therefore form a regional cluster—a regional security complex—because they possess overlapping relevant neighbourhood, which are characterized by a high level of inward-looking security dynamics while being comparatively insulated from interference by non-RSC member actors—because the loss-of-strength gradient is corroding too strongly power projected by the latter.[26]

In this perspective, regional subsystems differ from the global international system only in their respective sizes, and not in their "ordering principle". This difference of size implies that regions are not considered as particularly prone to peace or cooperation, as the same rules that apply at the global level are valid at the regional one. Barry Buzan thus points out: "it is [. . .] valid to see security complexes as subsystems—miniature anarchy—in their own right. From that perspective, by analogy with full system, they do have structures of their own".[27] There is thus no ambiguity in the delineation of the defining features of a regional security complex; "like the global system [. . .], regional structures can be defined by two dimensions: the ordering principle—anarchy—and the distribution of capabilities—multipolar, bipolar, and, in the regional case, unipolar."[28] The proneness to war or peace, cooperation or competition in regional systems depends directly from the same variables valid at the global level.

What makes regional subsystems quite different from the global international system is their inherent openness. Superpowers and adjacent great powers, which are powerful enough and/or close enough to a given subsystem to have their respective military might not too severely eroded by distance, will play a significant role in this regional security complex. Defining polarity in regional security complexes thus requires including not only "local" powers but any "external" actors which have the wherewithal to take part in the regional game.[29] As actual military power remains the core feature for defining the position of each actor, it appears that there is no reason to *a priori* exclude "non-local" great powers from full regional membership for only geographical reasons.[30] Extra-regional powers with sufficient capabilities should be counted in also because there is no reason to suppose that they will refrain from using their military might in the region. At least, extra-regional powers will try to prevent the rise of a local hegemon that could dominate the region—if only because such hegemon could then significantly threaten states beyond its region.[31] Endowed with sufficient power, it is even likely that these extra-regional powers will struggle for increasing their influence in the region.[32]

Whether they aim at preserving or modifying the "regional status quo," "great powers will normally be capable of projecting their power into adjacent regions and, other things being equal, can be expected to do so."[33]

Global superpower(s) and adjacent great power(s) with enough actual power in a given regional security complex should therefore be considered as "normal" actors. However, their "external" position implies that their intervention is subjected to specific constraints, especially when forces have to cross oceans. While transoceanic distances imply specific and severe requirements on the projection of military might, the "stopping power of water" [34] might be less absolute than anticipated by John Mearsheimer. Transoceanic interventions require what Barry Posen termed the command of the commons— defined as the "command of the sea, space and air."[35] In other words, obstacles created by the "stopping power of water" against transoceanic power projection might be overcome by the development of strong naval, aerial and spatial forces—the former appearing as the backbone of any transoceanic projection.[36] These particular requirements for global—or extra-regional—interventions do not imply that sea power has no role to play within regional security complexes. However, it appears clearly that in the absence of the command of the commons, global intervention is an elusive objective.[37] Sea power, in itself, cannot be considered as a sufficient condition that would automatically lead to victory and/or supremacy. However, as pointed out by George Modelski and William Thompson, "seapower (or, more precisely, ocean power) is the *sine qua non* of action in global politics because it is the necessary (though not the sufficient) condition of operations of global—that is, intercontinental—scope."[38] For states wishing to have global—or extra-regional—influence, sea power is the "multifaceted enabling capacity" [39] that allows them to make full use of Mahan's "wide common."

Replaced in our regional security complex framework, the precedent remarks simply means that, in building up their respective influences over the regional game, extra-regional powers are much more dependent on their naval forces than are the local powers. This difference between the requirements imposed upon different actors makes clear that any contest between local and regional actors is necessarily dissymmetric.[40] As mentioned above, to weigh in any given regional security complex, extra-regional powers have to secure an access to the region by commanding the commons—or at least obtaining a high degree of control over these commons.[41] In sharp contrast, when confronted with an intervention by an extra-regional power, local powers can—and usually will prefer to—play a dissymmetric game by trying to deny the command of the commons to their adversaries. The game is here dissymmetric because the sea and the commons obey to Corbettian principles rather than to Mahanian ones. In theorizing the control of the sea, Corbett points out that "[one of the commonest errors] is the very general assumption that if one belligerent loses the command of the sea it passes at once to the other belligerent."[42] Within our theoretical framework, in a struggle between local and extra-regional powers, an "uncommanded sea", or more broadly "uncommanded commons." are highly satisfying for local players but a serious problem for extra-regional ones. The situation where "commons" are "uncommanded" allows local powers to prevent extra-regional intervention while not bearing the full price of a frontal struggle against the extra-regional power.

Dissymmetry in structural constraints thus leads to different strategic priorities, which in turn lead to divergent choices in force structure. Regarding the build up of naval forces, Admiral Sergei Gorshkov pointed out:

> It is false to try to build a fleet to the model and likeness of even the strongest sea power and to determine the requirements for the building of ships for one's fleet merely by going on quantitative criteria and ratios of ship composition. Each country has specific requirements for sea forces which influence their development.[43]

In other words, it is not possible to measure the relative force of different navies only by comparing their size and firepower; one has to evaluate if and how they measure up to the specific missions they are supposed to fulfill.[44] For example, carriers might be formidable platforms for power projection, but they are not really needed if a navy's main task is to defend territorial waters. In a similar way, a strategy that aims at preventing the enemy from gaining the command of the air—so as to prevent strategic bombing—or of the space—so as to prevent the enemy from making the battlefield transparent—does not require the same capabilities than a strategy that aims at gaining control over air and space for one's own use. Under ideal circumstances, states will, of course, prefer more rather than less "command." But in a situation in which resources are limited, the allocation will usually go to the most efficient—cost-effective—method that allows the fulfillment of the objective—which means here weakening or eliminating extra-regional influence.

Though dissymmetry exists as soon as the struggle opposes a local power to an extra-regional one, its consequences are particularly pronounced in configurations where the latter is much more powerful than the former—or when a potential global hegemon is confronting a potential regional hegemon.[45] While hubris might push a local power to seek rivalry with an extra-regional or global power for the control of the commons, his relative weakness and the slim chances of success of such pretenses will usually give him sufficient incentive to look for alternative—and cheaper—ways to deceive and defeat his opponent's forces. In other words, there are some good chances that local powers will turn to strategies and force structures that will favour denial over control or command. Seen from this angle, denial is the strategy of the weak and has greater chances of success because it uses the inherent advantage of defense over offense.[46] Examining defensive fleet operations, Julian Corbett points out:

> Theory and History are at one on the point. Together they affirm that a Power too weak to win command by offensive operations may yet succeed in holding the command in dispute by assuming a general defensive attitude. That such an attitude in itself cannot lead to any positive result at sea goes without saying, but nevertheless even over prolonged periods it can prevent an enemy from securing positive results.[47]

The fact that a local power, when confronted with an extra-regional threat, will probably prefer a denial/negative strategy should not be mistaken for a general defensive trend in its posture. To the contrary, denying control to this extra-regional opponent might lead to a much more positive/assertive strategy within the regional security complex. Indeed, there are good chances that once relieved of the risk that local players could look from help "abroad", a large local power will actually look for establishing regional hegemony.

THE CHINA-U.S. RIVALRY IN EAST ASIA

The U.S.-China Political Settings

While one might debate whether the United States role in East Asia should be defined as an offshore balancer or as a dominant/hegemonic power, there is little doubt that Chinese and American interests collide in a quite frontal manner. A cursory look at how Washington defines its primary interests since the end of the Cold War provides us with a good idea of this opposition. As early as 1992, the Department of Defense stated that the United States' primary aims in the region were "to shape the security environment in ways favorable to the United States and to our allies and friends" and to oppose "the emergence of a regional hegemony".[48] Fourteen years later, the Quadrennial Defense Review Report was stating that the United States "will attempt to dissuade any military competitor from developing disruptive or other capabilities that could enable regional hegemony or hostile action against the United States or other friendly countries, and it will seek to deter aggression or coercion".[49] Concerning Asia, the 2006 Report was also pointing out:

> Of the major and emerging powers, China has the greatest potential to compete militarily with the United States and field disruptive military technologies that could over time off set traditional U.S. military advantages absent U.S. counter strategies. [...] The pace and scope of China's military build-up already puts regional military balances at risk.[50]

Below the great power game level, important frictions exist between American and Chinese interests. By any standard, the brightest flashpoint is the unsolved Taiwan question which could promptly flare up. Nancy Bernkopf Tucker considers that "at the beginning of this new century, nowhere is the danger for Americans as great as in the Taiwan Strait where the potential for a war with China, a nuclear armed great power, could erupt out of miscalculation, misunderstanding, or accident." [51] Washington's interests in Taiwan are multifaceted and include economic, political and strategic dimensions.[52] Though the United States has been officially committed to a "one China policy", it has appeared clearly that Washington has also supported—and occasionally defended—Taiwan's *de facto* independence. Though George W. Bush's open declaration that he will do "Whatever it took [*sic*] to help Taiwan defend herself"[53] appears today as little more than a false note, Washington is still keen to play the "strategic ambiguity" card. In other words, Washington will continue to strike independently the equilibrium it will prefer between its contradicting commitment toward the Three Communiqués and the Taiwan Relations Act. Relations between Taiwan and the mainland have become far better since Ma Ying-jeou replaced Chen Shui-bian. In many ways, however, though independence is not generally seen as likely or desirable, Taiwan seems to have already drifted away from unification—a trend that looks somewhat irreversible. Taiwan has also reconfirmed its special ties with the United States. In its inaugural address, Ma Ying-jeou made once again clear, that Washington was Taiwan's "foremost security ally and trading partner,"[54] and he subsequently welcomed one of the latest decisions from George W. Bush to allow Taiwan to buy a $6.5 billion arms package.[55]

On a less prominent question, the status of South China Sea, the United States posture shifted "from active neutrality to active concern."[56] While the Chinese position toward the status of the waters encompassed within the famous doted line has yet to be clarified,[57] the law on territorial sea passed in 1992[58] tends to show that China considers this zone as historic waters over which it has extensive rights. More specifically, the provision contained in article 6, which states that "To enter the territorial sea of the People's Republic of China, foreign military ships must obtain permission from the Government of the People's Republic of China,"[59] if applied to the South China Sea, would directly collide with Washington's interest for the freedom of navigation—which obviously includes the free movement of U.S. Navy warships—in the area.

As the United States intends to protect its interests in Asia—which are mainly defined as preventing the domination of "Northeast Asia, [and] the East Asian littoral"[60] by unfriendly powers—and seems to be increasingly concerned about Chinese capabilities and intentions in the region, it needs to preserve its capacity to interfere in the regional game. In other words, while the United States might have a choice in defining its role in East Asia,[61] it will need to protect its access to the region, whatever its ultimate objectives. While U.S. alliances and defense agreements with local partners provide it with a solid anchor in the area,[62] access is mainly guaranteed by U.S. dominance at sea. The post-Cold War requirements certainly pushed U.S. Navy to refocus on force projection ashore,[63] but the fact that U.S. naval power has been unrivaled over the last two decades should not lead us to mistakenly conclude that sea control has become obsolete. On the contrary, J. Paul Reason and David Freymann emphasize:

> There is no forward presence on the sea without control of the sea. There is no power projection on the sea without control of the sea. There is no initiation or support of littoral warfare from the sea without control of the seas between the United States and the engaged littoral. *Sea Control is absolutely necessary*, the thing without which all other naval missions, and most national missions, precariously risk catastrophic failure.[64]

American freedom of action and influence in East Asia, which depend on U.S. ability to project power within the region, are thus intimately linked to U.S. ability to preserve the command of the sea.

Wars in the Gulf, Afghanistan and Kosovo have demonstrated an impressive American supremacy in space and in the air. Though the exact political impact of NATO bombings during the War in Kosovo is hard to measure, air forces have seemed to be able to win a war by themselves. In the post-Cold War conflicts, "[a]n electronic flying circus of specialized attack, jamming, and electronic intelligence aircraft allows the U.S military to achieve the 'suppression of enemy air defenses' (SEAD); limit the effectiveness of enemy radars, surface-to-air missiles (SAMs) and fighters; and achieve the relatively safe exploitation of enemy skies above 15,000 feet".[65] American dominance also extended to upper layers. While great powers devoted considerable interests and efforts to space during the Cold War, "the use of space to enhance military operations on Earth has, without question, accelerated since the demise of the Soviet Union".[66] In its 2009 Joint Publication on Space Operations, the Joint Chiefs Staff considers that "space capabilities have proven to be a significant force multiplier".[67] The role of satellites is no more limited to early warning and nuclear strategic stability. Satellites are today crucial for navigation, positioning, communication, environmental monitoring and surveillance.[68] They have also acquired a more direct role in combat operations; "more than 5,000 [GPS-guided joint direct attack munitions] were employed in the Afghanistan war of 2001-02, striking as close as five meters from their aim point, and a comparable number were used in Operation Iraqi Freedom in 2003."[69]

The Chinese Challenge

While multiple constraints—including those concerning available technologies and funds—impose strict limitations to what is within the realm of possibility for the modernization of Chinese armed forces, one of the important motives of Chinese choices and priorities in modernizing the People's Liberation Army (PLA) can be found in the specific position of China within the East Asian security complex. As a potential regional hegemon, China's first priority is to secure the achievement of such a position, while not triggering a full-fledge global rivalry with the global superpower. In an analysis of Beijing's grand strategy, June Teufel Dreyer points out:

> While it has been fashionable to conclude such analyses by pointing out that, for all its increased capabilities, the PLA is no match for the United States military, this is to argue the question in the wrong way. The Chinese government has no intention of challenging the United States in a global confrontation.[70]

With primary ambitions concentrated in (East) Asia, China's most urgent need is to deal with possible extra-regional interference as its rapid ascent makes it the largest power—and a potential regional hegemon.

Though an encounter between American and Chinese forces would be characterized by the technological superiority of the former, the latter would be advantaged by the dissymmetric nature of the fight. Whereas the United States would need to preserve full access to the East Asia so as to preserve its influence in the region and its capacity to weight on regional affairs, China would have every incentive to avoid a symmetric confrontation with the United States and to prevent U.S. forces from reaching the locus where they could deploy their full superior capacities. In a war against a superior opponent, Chinese armed forces would have to "attack the enemy's key points [*da di yaohai*]."[71] As modern warfare is a "networked and systemized" warfare, Chinese armed forces will have to "thoroughly understand and analyze the internal structure of the enemy warfare systems" and strike key points that can "swiftly paralyze and dismember the enemy warfare systems, cripple and reduce the enemy's superiority."[72] Instead of trying to defeat projected forces, China could reap much greater benefit from attacking what makes power projection efficient. Cutting the sea lines of communication could prove an excellent strategy as it would "not only weaken the enemy's war potential, but also put forward-deployed enemy forces in a situation where they would be isolated and deprived of support."[73] In many ways, this explains why the modernization of Chinese armed forces can be seen as an attempt to maximize PLA's capacity to deny the free use of the commons—mainly sea, but also air and space—to its probably superior adversary in a potential local conflict. Denying access to extra-regional adversaries has been made easier by the vertical integration of the naval battlefield. In 1967, Martin Lawrence was pointing out that:

> The surface ship already faces a pincer movement between air power and the submarine, so that command of the surface increasingly becomes a prize that must be sought elsewhere. Control of both the air and the subsurface is necessary to ensure secure use of the surface: control of either can deny the surface to others.[74]

Last decades have added an upper layer to this vertical integration as the control of space has become crucial for command, control and communication. While powers wishing to preserve access have to establish their multi-dimensional control over the commons, those aiming at denying access only have to successfully contest this control in one of the commons so as to make opponent's operations costly and hazardous—if not impossible.

As PLA's priority moved "from luring deep to fighting forward" and "from a defensive campaign to an 'offensive defense' campaign,"[75] naval forces have mechanically gained a larger strategic role and a better share of the defense budget.[76] China's naval modernization has been multifaceted and has included some features that would confirm the claim that it is ultimately aiming at building a "blue-water" navy. In this sense, the purchase and refitting of the

58,500-ton aircraft carrier *Varyag* has attracted significant attention. However, Andrew Erickson and Andrew Wilson consider that the future role of this aircraft carrier will be seriously limited; the "*Varyag* [. . .] may ultimately also be used for pilot and deck crew training, as well as a 'test platform' for general research and the development of catapults, arresting gears and other ship-board systems."[77] China is still far from being able to project significant power over oceanic distances, and even large-scale operations against Taiwan are considered as beyond PLA's reach.[78]

The greatest efforts have been devoted to the acquisition of strong sea denial capabilities. While China's submarine fleet was mainly composed of obsolete *Romeo* at the end of the Cold War,[79] roughly two thirds of Chinese submarines are today considered as reasonably advanced platforms. Among these modern submarines, indigenously developed submarines—*Song* and *Yuan*—are today more numerous than imported *Kilo*.[80] These three types of submarines are considered very quiet[81] and equipped with high-performance weaponry, most notably submarine-launched anti-ship cruise missiles.[82] China has also begun to introduce *Shang* SSN which will replace the deficient *Han*, and whose performances have been compared with Russian *Victor III*.[83] China also modernized its surface forces with the purchase of *Sovremenny* destroyers and the deployment of indigenously produced *Luyang I*, *Luyang II* and *Luzhou*. While *Luzhou*-class destroyers appear to have been conceived so as to provide an area air defense capability for potential non-carrier battle groups,[84] *Sovremenny*, *Luyang* and *Luyang-II* are primarily fit for anti-surface missions.[85] However, in a confrontation against the United States, China's weapon of choice would be its large submarine fleet. In 2005, Rear Admiral McVadon was stressing that "with a total of more than fifty operational submarines, and with a substantial number of them new and quiet, China, quite simply can put to sea more submarines than the U.S. Navy can locate and counter."[86] In a very obvious way, China has chosen to fully play on the fact that "the best way to blunt American power projection capabilities is at sea, and that the highest leverage sea denial capability are provided by modern, undersea warfare weapons."[87]

Beijing also gave very high priority to the modernization of its air force. In many ways, China has moved beyond the delicate stage of building "pockets of excellence."[88] Over the last two decades, China imported—or built under license—more than 180 Su-27 fighters and 108 Su-30.[89] Richard Fisher considers that, in spite of the serious difficulties PLAAF encountered in operating the aircraft, "the Su-27SK has provided the PLAAF with a robust introduction to the complexity, expense, and improved combat potential of modern fourth-generation fighters."[90] China went a step further with the purchase of "fourth generation 'plus'"[91] Su-30MKKs designed for "deep-strike and interception missions."[92] In 2003, PLAN Air Force equally acquired the navalized Su-30MKK2 which "gave China an unprecedented level of integrated long-range power projection".[93] China indigenously developed its own air superiority fighter, the J-10, which is believed "to begin its service life with a capability comparable to an F-16 Block 30"[94] and, after decades of development, deployed the reasonably advanced JH-7 fighter-bomber.[95] China might thus possess around 500 aircrafts that could carry high performance air-to-air missiles, and deliver PGMs—more particularly anti-ship missiles.[96] In spite of the well-publicized crash of one of the KJ-2000 AWACS in 2006, PLAAF seems also to have made considerable progress in the area of C4ISR, electronic warfare and surveillance.[97] Andrew Erickson points out that "if successfully developed [. . .], these platforms [KJ-2000 AWACS and Y-8 AEW/EW/ELINT] could give China an important aerial battle-management capacity."[98] While far from being able to rival with U.S. air power, China's maturing air forces could add some difficulties to U.S. power projection if planned in the vicinity of the Mainland or in a Taiwan clash scenario. Rear Admiral McVadon notes that attack coordinated by the PLANAF might take place "several hundred miles out to sea from China (in some cases possibly much farther)" and that "at a minimum, the U.S. Navy would have to be concerned about vulnerability to such an attack."[99] PLA's ground-based missile programs might also have some utility against a deployment of American forces, as the increased accuracy of ballistic missiles and the development of long-range cruise missiles[100] could put at risk U.S. Navy battle groups.[101]

With the destruction of one of its own satellites with an anti-satellite (ASAT) weapon in January 2007,[102] China showed that it could significantly—perhaps decisively—damage one of the United States crucial assets. Though "China's ASAT test of 11 January involved a fairly primitive system, limited to high-inclination LEO satellites,"[103] the destruction of the satellite constitutes a crucial step for several reasons. First, despite China's statements that the test did "not constitute a threat to any country,"[104] the destruction of the satellite sparked widespread condemnation,[105] as it generally appeared as "first real escalation in the weaponization of space that we've seen in twenty years."[106] Second, while China's capacity to destroy satellites arose as soon as it acquired nuclear warheads and IRBMs, China proved it was able to resort to high-precision attack on selected objectives—to destroy "a bullet with a bullet."[107] Third, the use of a direct ascent ASAT weapon might seem a quite crude method to disable satellites when compared with the use of high energy laser to blind sensors or the use of electronic warfare,[108] but the use of kinetic energy ASAT tends to emphasize the persistent vulnerability of satellites that could be hardened against other forms of attacks such as jamming, radiation and electromagnetic pulse.[109] China's efforts in the ASAT area tend to emphasize that space will be considered as a "normal" battlefield in a conflict with the United States—a trend that is coherent with the idea that "the contemporary battlefield is composed of the land, sea, air, space, electromagnetic multiple battlefields."[110] Punching "U.S. military's soft ribs"[111] could be a particularly attractive option for China because disabling satellites could decisively "paralyze the enemy's war apparatus, weaken the enemy's war potential and quicken the fulfillment of [PLA's] war aims."[112] Consequences could be particularly important in a Taiwan conflict scenario where attacks against satellites could significantly delay U.S. support to the island.[113]

CONCLUSION

In many ways, China's rise in the post-Cold War has transformed the U.S.-China relation into a quite perfect illustration of the classic contest between a dominant power and a rising challenger. Appraising this trend, however, requires abandoning a "Cold War mentality"—in a way that is substantially different from the one proposed by Qin Gang in its criticism of the 2008 Pentagon report.[114] While the rivalry between Washington and Moscow was at the global level and created a condition of *overlay*[115] in all regional systems, China, in spite of its rapid growth, remains unable to compete with the United States on the global stage. The main feature of Beijing's challenge to the United States is its regional saliency. As a potential regional hegemon, China has no interest in an exhausting race to catch up with the United States. Because U.S. presence and influence in East Asia is the main obstacle on China's way toward regional hegemony, Beijing's foremost aim is to insulate the East Asian regional security complex from possible extra-regional interferences. In this sense, though Chinese armed forces are still far from being on a par with the American ones, their ability to keep their extra-regional adversary at bay has been steadily increasing. Such a change could not be without serious consequences on the East Asian security complex. As China's relative weight in East Asia is rapidly increasing, weaker states without the ability to balance and deprived of an American guarantee have little choice other than accommodating China. ASEAN engagement policy toward China might thus be a prelude to a deeper acquiescence of Beijing's dominant role. Such acquiescence might lead to a more peaceful East Asia,[116] but such a peaceful order would be rooted in power calculus rather than in a specific East Asian identity.

NOTES

[*] Yves-Heng Lim holds a Ph.D. from the University Jean Moulin-Lyon III and Peking University. The author would like to thanks members of the CLESID (Lyon) and Professor Yang Baoyun for their support.

1. Niall Ferguson, *Colossus, The Price of America's Empire* (New York: The Penguin Press, 2004), pp. 296-298.
2. Christopher Layne, "The Unipolar Illusion: Why New Great Powers Will Rise", *International Security*, vol. 17, no. 4, 1993, pp. 5-51.
3. Bradley Thayer, "The Case for the American Empire" in Christopher Layne and Bradley Thayer, *American Empire, a Debate* (London: Routledge, 2007), pp. 1-51.
4. Ye Zicheng, "Chaoyue duojihua siwei, cujin daguo hezuo" (Beyond the Multipolarity Thinking, Favouring Great Powers Cooperation) in Qin Yaqing, *Zhongguo Xuezhe kan Shijie 1: Guoji Zhixu Juan* (World Politics, Views from China 1: International Order), (Beijing: New World Press, 2007), pp. 63-86.
5. Kenneth Waltz, *Theory of International Politics* (New York: McGraw-Hill, 1979), p. 131.

6. "Arming Up", *The Economist*, 8 June 2009.

7. Dale Copeland, *The Origins of Major War* (Ithaca, N.Y.: Cornell University Press, 2000), pp. 2-3.

8. Douglas Lemke, *Regions of War and Peace* (Cambridge: Cambridge University Press, 2002).

9. See Frederik Söderbaum and Timothy Shaw, eds., *Theories of New Regionalism* (New York, Palgrave, 2003); Mary Farrell, Björn Hettne and Luk Van Langenhove, eds., *Global Politics of Regionalism, Theory and Practice* (London: Pluto Press, 2005).

10. World Bank, "Gross domestic product 2008, PPP", 1 July 2009, http://siteresources. worldbank.org/, accessed 29 August 2009.

11. WTO Statistics Database, "China (Trade Profiles)", http://stat.wto.org/; WTO, *International Trade Statistics 2008*, pp. 10-11, http://www.wto.org/, accessed 13 September 2009. China's international trade was roughly $30 billion in 1980 and reached more than $2.173 billion in 2007.

12. UNData, "Investment, foreign direct long-term net in US$ (World Bank estimates)," http://data.un.org/, accessed 4 September 2009.

13. Information Office of the State Council, *China's National Defense in 1998*; Information Office of the State Council, *China's National Defense in 2008*, both on http://www.gov.cn/, accessed 4 April 2009.

14. SIPRI, "SIPRI Military Expenditure Database," http://milexdata.sipri.org/, accessed 27 March 2008

15. SIPRI-FIRST, "China"; SIPRI-FIRST, "Japan," both on http://first.sipri.org/, both accessed 13 September 2009.

16. Raymond Aron, *Paix et Guerre entre les Nations* (Paris: Calmann-Lévy, 1984), p. 103.

17. See Eric Hobsbawn, *L'ère du Capital 1848-1875* (Paris: Hachette, 1978), pp. 75-101.

18. Michael Haas, "International Subsystems: Stability and Polarity," *The American Political Science Review*, vol. 64, no. 1, 1970, p. 100.

19. Douglas Lemke, *Regions of War and Peace*, p. 59.

20. Barry Buzan and Ole Waever, *Regions and Powers*, pp. 43-44.

21. Barry Buzan and Ole Waever, *Regions and Powers*, p. 44.

22. Raymond Aron, *Paix et Guerre entre les Nations*, p. 106.

23. David Lake, "Regional Security Complexes: A System Approach" in David Lake and Patrick Morgan, eds., *Regional Orders: Building Security in a New World* (Pennsylvania: The Pennsylvania State University Press, 1997), p. 51.

24. Kenneth Boulding, *Conflict and Defense, A General Theory* (New York: Harper Torchbooks), 1962, p. 231.

25. This definition is more flexible than the one proposed by Ronald Tammen et al., which states: "[adjusted power] defines a state's politically relevant neighborhood as comprising all those states which can move 50 percent or more of its power into the other's national capital" (Ronald Tammen et al., *Power Transitions*, p. 67).

26. Barry Buzan argues: "The boundaries between such sets [security complex] will thus be defined by the *relative indifference* attending the security perceptions and interactions across them" (Barry Buzan, *People, States & Fear*, p. 193).

27. Barry Buzan, *People, States & Fear*, p. 209.

28. David Lake, "Regional Security Complexes: A System Approach", p. 60.

29. I will use "local" as a shortcut for designating actors geographically located in the regional security complex, and use indifferently "external" or "extra-regional powers" referring to actors that do not geographically belong to the regional security complex under consideration but that have the wherewithal to intervene in it.

30. This goes against Buzan and Waever's position that the polarity of a given regional security complex is defined by the number of regional/local powers (Barry Buzan and

Ole Waever, *Regions and Powers*, p. 37); but is consistent with David Lake's idea that membership depends only on the capacity to interfere and on the existence of security externalities (David Lake, "Regional Security Complexes: A System Approach", p. 50).

31. See John Mearsheimer, *The Tragedy of Great Power Politics*, pp. 40-42. This contradicts hypotheses offered by the multiple hierarchy model which suggest that "[t]he overall dominant power is little concerned with who specifically controls these various parts of the globe, so long as the mineral riches are exported and the global status quo is undisturbed" (Tammen Ronald et al., *Power Transitions*, p. 68).

32. Christopher Layne, "The 'Poster Child for Offensive Realism': America as a Global Hegemon," *Security Studies*, vol. 12, no. 2, 2002/03, p. 129.

33. Barry Buzan and Ole Waever, *Regions and Powers*, p. 60.

34. John Mearsheimer, *The Tragedy of Great Power Politics* (New York: W.W. Norton & Company, 2001), pp. 114-128.

35. Barry Posen, "Command of the Commons: The Military Foundation of U.S. Hegemony", *International Security*, vol. 28, no. 1, 2003, p. 7.

36. It is possible to draw a parallel between Colin Gray's emphasis on sea power "multifaceted enabling capacity" and the role usually played by air and space power (Colin Gray, *The Leverage of Sea Power* (New York: The Free Press, 1992), p. 289).

37. George Modelski and William Thompson, *Seapower in Global Politics, 1494-1993* (Basingstoke: MacMillan, 1988), p. 12; Karen Rasler and William Thompson, *The Great Powers and the Global Struggle, 1490-1990* (Lexington: The University Press of Kentucky, 1994), p. 17-18.

38. George Modelski and William Thompson, *Seapower in Global Politics*, p. 13. A similar logic is present in Colin Gray's works (Colin Gray, *The Leverage of Sea Power*; Colin Gray and Roger Barnett, eds., *Seapower and Strategy* (Annapolis: Naval Institute Press, 1989).

39. Colin Gray, *The Leverage of Sea Power*, p. 289

40. "Dissymmetric conflict" is here understood as a qualitative difference in the position occupied by the actors—which determine the objective they pursue—as opposed to "asymmetric conflict [. . .] defined as a conflict involving two states with unequal overall military and economic power resources" (T.V. Paul, *Asymmetric Conflicts: War Initiation by Weaker Powers* (Cambridge: Cambridge University Press, 1994), p. 20.

41. For a differentiation between command of the sea and sea control, see Stansfield Turner, "Missions of the U.S. Navy", *Naval War College Review*, vol. LI, no. 1, 1998, p. 92 [first published in 1974 in the same journal].

42. Julian Corbett, *Principles of Maritime Strategy* (New York: Dover Publications, 2004), p. 87.

43. Sergei Gorshkov, *The Sea Power of the State* (Annapolis: Naval Institute Press, 1979), p. 254.

44. In a classical way, John Hattendorf distinguishes between "three broad objectives: (1) to secure the command of the sea, thereby obtaining control of maritime communications for oneself and denying it to the enemy; (2) to dispute command of the sea, thereby denying control of maritime communications to the enemy; and (3) to exercise one's own use of the sea whether or not one has command of the maritime communications" (John Hattendorf, "Recent thinking on the Theory of Naval Strategy" in John Hattendorf and Robert Jordan, eds., *Maritime Strategy and the Balance of Power* (New York: St. Martin's Press, 1989), p. 153. Stansfield Turner defines the four missions of the U.S. Navy as: 1. Strategic deterrence; 2. Sea control; 3. Power projection ashore; 4. Naval presence (Stansfield Turner, "Missions of the U.S. Navy").

45. John Mearsheimer, *The Tragedy of Great Power Politics*, pp. 40-42.

46. Julian Corbett, *Principles of Maritime Strategy*, p. 211.

47. Julian Corbett, *Principles of Maritime Strategy*, p. 211.

48. Department of Defense, *A Strategic Framework for the Asian Pacific Rim, Report to the Congress 1992* (1992), http://www.shaps.hawaii.edu/, accessed 16 April 2009.

49. Department of Defense, *Quadrennial Defense Review Report 2006*, p. 30, http://www. comw.org/, accessed 15 August 2008.

50. Department of Defense, *Quadrennial Defense Review Report 2006*, p. 29.

51. Nancy Bernkopf Tucker, ed., "An Introduction" in Nancy Bernkopf Tucker, ed., *Dangerous Strait: The U.S.-Taiwan-China Crisis* (New York: Columbia University Press, 2005), p. 1.

52. Ronald Montaperto and Ming Zhang, "The Taiwan Issue: A Test of Sino-U.S. Relations", *Journal of Contemporary China*, vol. 4, no. 9, 1995, pp. 8-10.

53. Full text available on "Text: Bush on ABC's 'Good Morning America'", *The Washington Post*, 25 April 2001, http://www.washingtonpost.com/, accessed 26 September 2009.

54. Ma Ying-jeou, "Taiwan's Renaissance", http://www.president.gov.tw/, accessed 8 June 2008.

55. Bonnie Glaser, "Ties Solid for Transition, but Challenges Lurk", *Comparative Connections*, vol. 10, no. 4, 2008, p. 31; AFP, "Taiwan hails multi-billion dollar US arms package", 4 October 2008, http://www.france24.com/, accessed 2 June 2009.

56. Yann-huei Song, "The Overall Situation in the South China Sea in the New Millennium", *Ocean Development & International Law*, vol. 34, no. 3/4, 2003, p. 236.

57. Eric Denécé, *Géostratégie de la Mer de Chine Méridionale* (Paris: L'Harmattan, 2000), p. 255; R. Haller-Trost, *The Contested Maritime and Territorial Boundaries of Malaysia* (London: Kluwer Law International, 1998), p. 330.

58. *China Territorial Sea and the Contiguous Sea*, http://www.un.org/, accessed 10 June 2008.

59. *Ibid.*

60. Department of Defense, *Quadrennial Defense Review Report 2001*, p. 2, http://www. dod.mil/, accessed 15 August 2008. The QDR defines the East Asian littoral as "The east Asian littoral is defined as the region stretching from south of Japan through Australia and into the Bay of Bengal".

61. For a discussion of these choices, see Robert Art, *A Grand Strategy for America* (Ithaca: Cornell University Press, 2003).

62. Most significantly, the United States stations 47,000 troops in Japan (soon to be reduced by 8,000), approximately 28,000 troops in South Korea, the Philippines ratified the Visiting Forces Agreement in May 1999, and the United States and Singapore signed the Strategic Framework Agreement in July 2005 ("No new US-Japan troop deal", *Strait Times*, 1 September 2009, http://www.straitstimes.com/; "US Forces Korea Order of Battle [as of 01 May 2009]", http://www.globalsecurity.org/, US-ASEAN Business Council, "Strategic Framework Agreement Between the United States of America and the Republic of Singapore for a Closer Cooperation Partnership in Defense and Security", http://www.us-asean.org/, all accessed 17 September 2009; Sheldon Simon, "Good News and Bad News", *Comparative Connections*, vol. 1, no. 1, 1999, pp. 33-34.

63. Edward Rhodes, "'. . . From the Sea' and Back Again" in Peter Dombrowski, ed.., *Naval Power in the Twenty-first Century* (Newport: Naval War College Press, 2005), p. 140.

64. J. Paul Reason and David Freymann, *Sailing New Seas* (Newport: Naval War College Press, 1998), p. 18.

65. Barry Posen, "Command of the Commons: The Military Foundation of U.S. Hegemony," p. 15.

66. Michael Krepon and Christopher Clary, *Space Assurance or Space Dominance?* (Washington: The Henry L. Stimson Center, 2003), p. 40.

67. Joint Chiefs of Staff, *Space Operations*, 2009, www.fas.org/, p. ix, accessed 26 September 2009.

68. Joint Chiefs of Staff, *Space Operations*, 2009, pp. II 1-3. Michael O'Hanlon reports that "[during the Afghan campaign], a U.S. military operation of some 50,000 troops in 2001-02 used five times as much communications bandwidth as did a war with 500,000 troops a decade earlier—fifty times as much bandwidth per person, on average" (Michael O'Hanlon, *Neither Star Wars nor Sanctuary* (Washington: Brookings Institution Press, 2004), p. 4).

69. Michael O'Hanlon, *Neither Star Wars nor Sanctuary*, p. 3. Michael Krepon and Christopher Clary report that the share of air-delivered satellite-guided munitions jumped from zero in the Gulf War to 3 percent during the war in Kosovo, and 32 percent during the war in Afghanistan (Michael Krepon and Christopher Clary, *Space Assurance or Space Dominance?*, p. 40).

70. June Teufel Dreyer, "China's Power and Will: The PRC's Military Strength and Grand Strategy," *Orbis*, vol. 51, no. 4, 2007, p. 654.

71. Xue Xinglin, *Zhanyi Lilun Xuexi Zhinan* [Guidebook on the Study of Campaign Theory] (Beijing: Guofang Daxue Chubanshe, 2002), p. 105.

72. Xue Xinglin, *Zhanyi Lilun Xuexi Zhinan*, p. 106.

73. Xue Xinglin, *Zhanyi Lilun Xuexi Zhinan*, p. 339.

74. Lawrence Martin, *The Sea in Morden Strategy* (New York: Praeger, 1967), p. 94. See also Wayne Hughes, *Fleet Tactics and Coastal Combat* (Annapolis: Naval Institute Press, 2000), p. 196.

75. David Finkelstein, "China's National Military Strategy" in James Mulvenon and Richard Yang, *The People's Liberation Army in the Information Age* (Santa Monica: RAND, 1999), p. 129.

76. Bernard Cole, *The Great Wall at Sea* (Annapolis: Naval Institute Press, 2001), p. 180.

77. Andrew Erickson and Andrew Wilson, "China's Aircraft Carrier Dilemma" in Andrew Erickson, Lyle Goldstein, William Murray and Andrew Wilson, eds., *China's Future Nuclear Submarine Force* (Annapolis: Naval Institute Press, 2007), p. 239.

78. Michael O'Hanlon, "Why China Cannot Conquer Taiwan," *International Security*, vol. 25, no. 2, 2000, pp. 51-86.

79. International Institute for Strategic Studies, *The Military Balance 1991-1992* (London: IISS-Oxford, 1991), p. 152.

80. China purchased twelve *Kilo* from Russia and is reported to have deployed at least thirteen *Song* and two *Yuan* (International Institute for Strategic Studies, *The Military Balance 2009* (London: IISS-Oxford, 2009), p. 384).

81. Peter Howarth, *China's Rising Seapower* (New York: Frank Cass, 2006), p. 17. Jane's Defence Weekly reports that "in October 2006, a Song-class diesel submarine was able to get within weapon range of the aircraft carrier USS *Kitty Hawk* before it was detected in international waters off Okinawa" ("Marching Forward", *Jane's Defence Weekly*, vol. 44, no. 17, 25 April 2007).

82. *Kilo*—and possibly *Yuan*—are equipped with the SS-N-27 *Klub* while *Song*—and possibly *Yuan*—are equipped with the shorter range YJ-1 and are designed to carry the more advanced YJ-2 (Jane's Information Group, *Jane's Fighting Ships 2007-2008*, pp. 118-120; Peter Howarth, *China's Rising Seapower*, p. 17).

83. "Russia helps China take new SSNs into silent era", *Jane's Defence Weekly*, vol. 28, no. 6, 13 August 1997; Peter Howarth, *China's Rising Seapower*, p. 17.

84. Jane's Information Group, *Jane's Fighting Ships 2007-2008*, p. 122.

85. *Sovremenny* are equiped with the formidable SS-N-22 *Sunburn* which was designed to defeat Aegis systems (Jane's Information Group, *Strategic Weapon Systems Issue 44 – 2006* (Coulsdon: Jane's Information Group, 2006), p. 151) while *Luyang I* and *Luyang II*

carry indigenously developed and very capable C-802 and C-803 (Jane's Information Group, *Jane's Fighting Ships 2007-2008*, p. 124-5).

86. Rear Admiral McVadon quoted in Ronald O'Rourke, *The Impact of Chinese Naval Modernization on the Future of the United States Navy* (New York: Nova Science Publisher, 2006), p. 10.

87. Owen Coté, *The Third Battle: Innovation in the U.S. Navy's Silent Cold War Struggle with Soviet Submarines* (Newport: Naval War College, 2003), pp. 85-86.

88. Avery Goldstein, "Great Expectations, Interpreting China's Arrival", *International Security*, vol. 22, no. 3, 1997/98.

89. Jane's Information Group, *All the World's Aircraft 2007-2008* (Coulsdon: Jane's Information Group, 2007), p. 511 and 514. China purchased 78 SU-27 from Russia and obtained a licence for the production of 200 Su-27/J-11. To date, only 105 units have been produced.

90. Richard Fisher, "PLA Air Force Equipment Trends" in Stephen Flanagan and Micahel Marti, *The People's Liberation Army and China in Transition* (Washington: National Defense University, 2003), p. 152. Jane's Defence Weekly reports that Su-27s benefited from an upgrade program that made them rough equivalent of the -SM version known for its better performances in air strike missions ("Chinese Su-27 upgrade funds Russian project," *Jane's Defence Weekly*, vol. 44, no. 14, 8 October 2003; Jane's Information Group, *All the World's Aircraft 2007-2008*, pp. 509-510).

91. David Shambaugh, *Modernizing China's Military* (Berkeley: University of California Press, 2002), p. 263.

92. "Air Force aims to spread its wings," *Jane's Defence Weekly*, vol. 36, no. 2, 11 July 2001.

93. "More details disclosed on China's Su-30MKK2," *Jane's Defence Weekly*, vol. 40, no. 10, 10 September 2009.

94. Jane's Information Group, *World Air Forces, Issue 26, 2007* (Coulsdon: Jane's Information Group, 2007), p. 109. One hundred J-10s have been deployed by the end of 2008, but figures about probable requirements by the PLAAF and the PLANAF vary between 300 and 1200 ("China officially unveils widely known fighter," *Jane's Defence Weekly*, vol. 44, no. 3, 17 January 2007).

95. Richard Fisher, "PLA Air Force Equipment Trends," pp. 149-150. The Military Balance 2009 suggests that the PLANAF and the PLAAF might respectively operate 84 and 72 JH-7/JH-7A (International Institute for Strategic Studies, *The Military Balance 2009*, p. 385 & 387).

96. China purchased from Russia anti-ship TV-guided AS-18 Kedge and AS-13 Kazoo, as well as anti-radiation AS-17(Kh-31P) Krypton –a copy has been reportedly produced in China (YJ-91)– and anti-ship AS-17(Kh-31A) (SIPRI, "Arms Trade Database"; "YingJi-91 (Kh-31P) Anti-Radiation Missile," http://www.sinodefence.com/). J-10s and JH-7 can also carry indigenously developed C-801/802 anti-ship cruise missiles and JH-7 might also carry the new KD-88 LACM, C-803ASCM and C-701 TV guided ASCM (Jane's Information Group, *All the World's Aircraft 2007-2008*, p. 104 & 129; "KongDi-88 (C-802KD) Air-Launched Land-Attack Cruise Missile," http://www.sinodefence.com/, accessed 19 September 2009).

97. Jane's Information Group, *World Air Forces, Issue 26, 2007*, p. 111.

98. Andrew Erickson, "Can China Become a Maritime Power?" in James Holmes and Toshi Yoshihara, *Asia Looks, Seaward* (Westport: Praeger, 2007), p. 84.

99. Eric McVadon, "China's Maturing Navy", *Naval War College Review*, vol. 59, no. 2, 2006, p. 100.

100. DF-15 A are reported to be quite accurate with a CEP around 30 to 45 meters (Jane's Information Group, *Strategic Weapons Systems Issue 44–2006*, p. 16), China has

also developed its own cruise missiles whose CEP is reduced to five meters for a range of 1800 to 3000 km (p. 36).

101. Office of the Secretary of Defense, *Annual Report on the Military Power of the People's Republic of China 2008*, http://www.defenselink.mil/, p. I, accessed 21 June 2009.

102. The target was a weather satellite in low earth orbit and the interception was made at an altitude of 865 kilometres ("Chinese ASAT test rekindles weapons debate," *Jane's Defence Weekly*, vol. 44, no. 4, 24 January 2007).

103. Desmond Ball, "Assessing China's ASAT program", *Austral Sepcial Report*, no. 07-14s, http://nautilus.rmit.edu.au/, accessed 23 September 2009.

104. Liu Jianchao quoted in Joseph Kahn, "China confirms Test of Anti-Satellite Weapon," *New York Times*, 23 January 2007, http://www.nytimes.com/, accessed 22 September 2009.

105. United States concerns about the test were shared by Japan, India, and the European Union (Joseph Lin, "Regional Reactions to ASAT Missile Test & China's Renewed Activities in the East China Sea," *China Brief*, vol. 7, no. 3, 2007, http://www.jamestown.org/,; Ministère des Affaires Etrangères (France),"Déclaration de la présidence au nom de l'Union européenne Bruxelles, 23 janvier 2007)," http://www.diplomatie.gouv.fr/, both accessed 19 September 2009.

106. Jonathan McDowell quoted in William Broad and David Sanger, "Flexing Muscle, China Destroys Satellite in Test," *New York Times*, 19 January 2007, http://www.nytimes.com/, accessed 19 September 2009.

107. Ashley Tellis, "China's Military Space Strategy," *Survival*, vol. 49, no. 3, 2007, pp. 41-42.

108. The 2002 Department of Defense Report mentioned that "Beijing may have acquired high-energy laser equipment that could be used in the development of ground-based anti-satellite (ASAT) weapons" (Department of Defense (U.S.), *Annual Report on the Military Power of the People's Republic of China*, p. 5, http://www.defenselink.mil/, accessed 16 July 2008). For a short description of electronic warfare methods see Michael Krepon and Christopher Clary, *Space Assurance or Space Dominance?* pp. 23-24.

109. Michael Krepon and Christopher Clary, *Space Assurance or Space Dominance?* p. 70.

110. Zhang Yuliang et al., *Zhanyixue [On Campaigns]*, (Beijing: Guofang Daxue Chubanshe, 2006), p. 31.

111. Wang Hucheng quoted in Ashley Tellis, "Punching the U.S. Military's 'Soft Ribs': China's Antisatellite Weapon Test in Strategic Perspective," *CEIP Policy Brief*, 51, 2007, p. 2.

112. Xue Xinglin, *Zhanyi Lilun Xuexi Zhinan*, p. 372.

113. Philip Saunders and Charles Lutes, "China's ASAT Test: Motivations and Implications," *INSS Special Report*, June 2007, p. 2.

114. Li Xiaokun, "Pentagon report smacks of Cold War mentality", *China Daily*, 3 May 2008, http://www.chinadaily.com.cn/, accessed 30 September 2009.

115. Barry Buzan defines overlay as "the direct presence of outside powers in a region [which] is strong enough to suppress the normal operation of security dynamics among the local states" (Barry Buzan, *People, States &Fear*, p. 198).

116. David Kang, "Getting Asia Wrong," *International Security*, vol. 27, no. 4, 2003, pp. 57-85; David Kang, *China Rising* (New York: Columbia University Press, 2007).

Chapter 3

Cooperation for Competition: China's Strategic Response to U.S. Supremacy in East Asia

Li Mingjiang and Keith Eric Flick

INTRODUCTION

The continuing growth of China's economic and military power, as well as its cultural influence, is having unmistakable impacts on the rest of the world, in particular East Asia where many countries share borders with China either on the land or in the sea and experience China's rise firsthand. Views on China's growing influence in East Asia exhibit a wide spectrum and are usually polarized. One focal point of the debate, understandably, is the impact on the future U.S. role in East Asia.

One school of thought believes that China's increasing influence in Asia will have dire consequences for the international order in Asia.[1] These scholars depict China's regional policy as an intentional attempt to challenge U.S. supremacy in Asia[2] or are simply suspicious of China's long-term regional ambitions.[3] Another group of analysts tends to view China as an actor for stability in the region and partner for other states.[4] David C. Kang, for instance, provides a provocative view on Asia's future by saying that East Asia's future will resemble its past: Sino-centric, hierarchical, and reasonably stable.[5]

Obviously, what has driven the debate in recent years over China's strategy in East Asia is that Beijing's approach has defied simple categorization and the sharp contrast of views is largely a result of scholars using different theoretical frameworks. Analysts who employ a realist lens tend to highlight China's efforts to increase its influence in the region at the expense of other major actors, to rapaciously secure resources to continue to fuel its economic and military development, and to isolate Taiwan.[6] In such analyses, balance of power considerations take a central role in the shaping of a Chinese strategy in East Asia and lead to a zero-sum competition with the U.S. Meanwhile, approaching the subject from a constructivist lens, others have focused on how China's strategy may be influenced and shaped through cognitive processes of socialization with regional actors and their norms.[7] Scholars who focus on China's participation in various regional affairs and institutions describe a China that largely reflects the logics of liberal institutionalism.[8]

The various cooperative and competitive aspects of China's approach to East Asia have therefore been largely portrayed as oppositional. This dichotomy is arbitrary and obscures the reality and complexities in China's strategy in East Asia, particularly in response to U.S. preponderance. It could also be misleading in terms of policy implications. Heeding Katzenstein's advice on employing "analytical eclecticism,"[9] we emphasize the merits of integrating the major theoretical perspectives to better understand China's foreign policy and international strategy. We argue that instead of describing China's strategic approach through any single analytical framework, in practice, China has employed liberal institutional and constructivist means for realist purposes. In other words, China has been able to compete with the United States for influence and in securing its national interests in East Asia through cooperative means deemed benign by most countries in the region. We believe this is the essence of China's strategic approach to its neighboring regions in response to American pursuit of preponderance in the post-Cold War era.

In making our case, we organize this chapter into three main parts. Part one looks at U.S. post-Cold War strategic policy in East Asia and Chinese perceptions of this policy. This section provides the historical backdrop for the evolution of China's foreign policy towards a strategy of cooperation for competition. In part two, we examine China's various cooperative efforts in East Asia and how these efforts have allowed Beijing to cope with U.S. supremacy in the region. The third and final part offers an assessment of the efficacy of China's strategy of cooperating to compete. The concluding section summarizes our arguments and briefly discusses some of the policy implications that are derived from the discussions in this chapter.

THE UNITED STATES STRATEGIC POLICY IN EAST ASIA AND CHINESE PERCEPTIONS

The end of the Cold War brought about a reassessment on the part of the U.S. regarding its strategic priorities in East Asia. Without a rival superpower to contain, some analysts called for a realignment of U.S. military deployments in the region. In 1992 the Subic Bay naval base was closed. Although some Asian leaders grew concerned of a U.S. strategic withdrawal from the region, a 1995 Defense Department report reaffirmed America's "commitment to maintain a stable forward presence in the region," at the level "of about 100,000 troops, for the foreseeable future."[10] Even without a rival superpower, some core strategic interests remained for the U.S. in East Asia.

First, there was the need to ensure freedom of navigation through key economic and strategic sea-lanes cutting through the region. For almost two centuries these waterways had been of importance to U.S. trade. Second, although the Soviet Union was no more, the U.S. would need to prevent the rise of a regional hegemon. Not only would this be important for maintaining U.S. influence, but Washington also viewed it as necessary for the maintenance of peace and stability among East Asian countries. Related to this, a third strategic interest was the fulfillment of commitments to U.S. friends and allies in the region.[11] East Asia also has always been regarded by Washington as a vital region of economic opportunities.

Given these interests, it is not surprising that some in the U.S. would react to the changes happening within China in the early to mid-1990s with some trepidation. China was experiencing on average almost double-digit economic growth and had embarked on its military modernization effort. In the wake of the Cold War, a "third wave" of democratization had begun to take shape.[12] However, the events at Tiananmen Square just a few years earlier offered a clear signal that China would undergo no such political transformation. These factors, along with China's assertive actions on territorial claims in the South China Sea in the mid-1990s, contributed to the "China threat" debate, which reached its apex around 1996,[13] but continued afterward, albeit with less vigor and rhetoric. Consequently, in the post-Cold war era, Washington has consistently adopted a strategy of maintaining U.S. supremacy in East Asia. This is particularly the case in the security arena.

For its part, Beijing's reaction to the "China threat" discourse, and a continued large U.S. military presence in Asia, was to accuse Washington of following antiquated Cold War thinking. Chinese scholars perceived the goal of U.S. strategy in East Asia as one of maintaining the status quo—U.S. hegemony, a term that was understood entirely negatively. From the Chinese perspective, the international system and its attendant institutions and laws were largely designed to benefit the U.S. This conflicted with China's own goal of promoting a more multipolar system.[14] Chinese officials were also critical of the alliances that some Asian countries continued to uphold with the U.S.

If the end of the Cold War brought about a strategic reassessment for the U.S., the same can be said about China. With the Soviet Union no longer a consideration, Beijing grew more concerned with what it perceived as U.S. efforts at containing China. U.S. allies in South Korea, Japan, the Philippines, and Taiwan populated China's periphery. Multilateral institutions such as ASEAN were also initially viewed as tools of American hegemony aimed at constraining China's growth.

China's criticism of American hegemony and some of its Asian neighbors' complicity in it, however, was not helping to address China's strategic interests in the region. These interests were—and continue to be—to forestall any strategic encirclement of China, gain regional influence, ensure a stable environment in which China's economy could continue to prosper, and isolate Taiwan.

By the mid-1990s, however, Chinese leaders and scholars appeared to have concluded that the world was not becoming as multipolar as they had hoped. In a survey of Chinese scholarly writing from the time, Jin Canrong notes, "they realized that the leading position of the United States would be unshakable, and its comprehensive national power would be unparalleled by any single country in the foreseeable future."[15] Therefore Chinese leaders had little choice but to seek any advantage working from within the current international system. While they would continue to strongly oppose any perceived U.S. pressure and meddling on key national security and sovereignty issues (Taiwan, Tibet and human rights), there were some areas of common ground with the U.S. Cooperation on these issues, and increased interaction with multilateral institutions, could serve as a buffer against any downturn in Sino-U.S. relations. Greater cooperation with China's neighbors, the major powers, and multilateral institutions was also important to China's leaders as they sought the recognition and status on the world stage they felt China deserved.[16]

PEOPLE'S REPUBLIC OF CHINA ENGAGES EAST ASIA: COOPERATION FOR COMPETITION

In light of the strategic pressure from the U.S., Beijing has consistently pursued a regional strategy that emphasizes cooperation with neighboring states. These major cooperative initiatives include improving bilateral relations with individual states; maintaining largely stable relations with other major powers, active participation in various multilateral institutions, downplaying sovereignty and territorial disputes, actively participating in various cooperative projects, i.e. non-traditional security matters, and providing preferable loans and assistance programs to neighboring states.

Improving Bilateral Relations with Small Neighbors

Bolstered by its dynamic economic growth, and a favorable Southeast Asian response to its actions during the 1997 Asian Financial Crisis, China's once insecure and defensive foreign policy stance gave way to a new confidence. This confidence has manifested in Beijing reaching out to improve bilateral relations with its Asian neighbors. From countries with which it has enjoyed closer relations, such as Myanmar, to former adversaries, such as Japan and Vietnam, China has feverishly worked to build closer ties.

China's approach to bilateral relations has worked in large part because it has offered its Asian neighbors much, and asked little in return. Unlike Washington's practice of linking aid to democratic or human rights reforms, China only asks that its friends adhere to its One-China policy and avoid interfering in its domestic matters, such as concern Tibet and Xinjiang.

In Southeast Asia we find, perhaps, the best example of the success of Beijing's "charm offensive."[17] For much of the latter half of the twentieth century, China's relations with most Southeast Asian countries were strained, if not hostile, due to Cold War politics, China's support for communist insurgency in the region and domestic politics. Within the span of ten years, the situation had changed dramatically and all ten members of ASEAN were now on positive terms with China. Much of the improvement in bilateral relations between

China and the ASEAN states can be chalked up to economics. But it is easy to overstate the importance of trade in Sino-ASEAN relations and economics alone cannot resolve troubled histories.

As Southeast Asian countries reached out to China in the hopes of socializing it to regional norms of peaceful settlement of disputes and noninterference, China sought to reassure states in the region that it was willing to be a responsible major power. Beijing employed a flurry of high-level diplomatic visits to all ten ASEAN states and also worked to build formal party-to-party relations between the CCP and leading parties in Thailand, Singapore, Malaysia and Indonesia. Military-to-military relations also featured prominently in China's push for improved bilateral ties, as did aid and preferential terms on loans to Southeast Asian states.

In Myanmar, Laos and Cambodia, China has assisted in major construction projects with technical expertise as well as funding. In Myanmar in particular, China's support to the largely politically isolated military junta has bolstered ties, and China has reportedly supported efforts to modernize Myanmar's navy.[18] In late 2008, China and Vietnam resolved their long-standing border demarcation. While some have noted China's willingness to settle the Vietnam border was the product of domestic politics, it no doubt also served to show China could be a responsible player in Asia.[19]

Whereas China had in the past reacted strongly to incidents of violence against ethnic Chinese in Indonesia, Beijing's reaction to the 1998 anti-Chinese riots was considerably more muted.[20] A number of high-level visits between leaders on both sides, including President Megawati's 2002 visit to Beijing appeared to further improve diplomatic ties.

In Northeast Asia, China's bilateral accomplishments are no less impressive. While it has continued to act as North Korea's closest ally and key financial supporter, China's relations with South Korea have also come a long way. China's relations with South Korea under president Roh Moo-Hyun saw significant economic as well as security exchanges and confidence building measures. Progress in the relationship faltered temporarily in 2004-2005 with a controversy over Kogoryo history, but has since recovered.[21] Beijing has continued to seek development of stronger bilateral ties under Lee Myung-bak's government, elevating a "comprehensive cooperative partnership" to a "strategic cooperative partnership," in 2008.[22] Despite signs that the Lee government has been less enthusiastic about addressing security cooperation with China than its predecessor, economic ties have continued to grow.

Maintaining Normal Working Relations with Major Powers

Another component of China's strategy in East Asia involves the maintenance of largely positive relations with other major powers. In doing so, China ensures a stable international environment, free from major conflict, in which it can continue its economic development. This has not always been an easy task.

Externally, a number of issues, such as a perceived lack of transparency on Chinese military development, concerns about China's human rights, and trade-related disputes have challenged stable relations with the major powers. Within China, the increasing accessibility of the internet has allowed Chinese citizens (or netizens) to voice their opinion on international affairs. Chinese netizens have tended to be nationalistic and vigilant against any major concession that Beijing attempts to make in its relations with other major powers, in particular Japan and the U.S. Even before the massive growth of the internet in China, incidents like the 1995-96 Taiwan Straits crisis, the bombing of the Chinese embassy in Belgrade in 1999, and the 2001 EP-3 surveillance plane incident resulted in strong negative public reaction toward the United States. While at times such nationalistic reaction can be useful to Beijing's leaders, it is a double-edged sword, which challenges China's pursuit of maintaining positive relations with major powers.

While problems of history still plague the Sino-Japanese relationship, stable relations have endured. This has occurred despite strong domestic opposition in China to any stance viewed as too accommodating toward Japan. China's interaction with Japan under the ASEAN+3 framework, the Six Party Talks, and recent discussions regarding a possible China-Japan-South Korea free trade agreement display Beijing's willingness to positively engage Tokyo.

After years of strained relations with the Koizumi administration, China's relationship with Japan began to improve in 2006,[23] and in 2008 the two countries agreed to a "Mutually Beneficial Relationship on Common Strategic Interests," which aimed to promote peaceful coexistence and cooperation.[24] Hu Jintao declared it "the first time that the two sides made positioning and planning of bilateral relations on a strategic level."[25] Ties are expected to improve further under a newly-elected DPJ government in Tokyo.

The relations between Beijing and Moscow have been on the rise ever since the mid-1990s. The 2001 Treaty of Good-Neighborliness and Friendly Cooperation outlined a twenty-year strategic and economic accord. Shortly thereafter, the "Shanghai Five" group, led by China and Russia, evolved into the Shanghai Cooperation Organization, further institutionalizing their security and economic cooperation. And the 4,300 kilometer border—long a source of acrimony between the two—was finally resolved in October of 2004. It is perhaps not an overstatement to say that current relations between Beijing and Moscow are better than at any other point in history.[26]

There is little doubt that China's ability to maintain stable relations with other powerful countries relies to a large degree on China's existing and increasing economic strength. This, however, should not obscure the fact that Beijing has carefully worked at its major power relations. As we have noted above, this does not mean Beijing will accommodate actions on the part of major powers that run counter to China's key national interests, such as sensitive issues of sovereignty. But China has moved beyond its previous ideologically driven foreign policy to a more pragmatic approach that sees the importance of cooperation with major powers on issues of mutual concern and not allowing occasional conflicting interests to derail generally stable ties.

Active Participation in Multilateral Institutions

The organizer of a 1993 track-two forum on cooperation in Northeast Asia put the level of China's apprehension about multilateral institutions in perspective. She noted, "it was easier to persuade the North Koreans to come than it was the Chinese." [27] Since the mid-1990s, China has shunned this skeptical and suspicious view of multilateral institutions and embraced its ability to address major national interests in the region.

Beijing's introduction to participation in multilateral institutions came in its dealing with ASEAN. The Association was originally formed, at least in large part, in order to constrain China. Suspicious of becoming entangled in such multilateral activity, Beijing was initially a careful observer. China eventually realized the benefits of becoming more fully engaged and the limited costs involved. It became the first non-Southeast Asian state to sign ASEAN's Treaty of Amity and Cooperation in 2003, while the U.S. refused to sign until 2009. The ASEAN+3 mechanism eventually evolved into more direct and regular dialogue between China and its Northeast Asian neighbors, Japan and South Korea. Again this allowed China to be an active participant in an organization that apparently marginalizes the U.S. Outside of the ASEAN+3 framework, China has sought a "tripartite" dialogue with both Japan and South Korea, in an attempt to counter historically strong U.S. relations with both. Early indications from the Hatoyama administration signal an interest to reassess Japan's relationship with the U.S., which presents China with a welcome opportunity. Through its involvement in multilateral institutions, China has found a means of indirectly balancing against U.S. influence in the region.

Downplaying Territorial Disputes

In the resolution of its land border disputes, Fravel sees considerable flexibility and a willingness to make concessions on the part of Chinese leaders.[28] In fact, China has resolved all but two of its contested land borders,[29] and none remain with its East Asian neighbors. While this willingness to make concessions has not led to final resolution of disputed claims in the East and South China Seas, Beijing has generally sought to downplay these remaining disputes. Its strategy seemed to be to freeze the status quo and seek opportunities to cooperate on joint development of the resources in the disputed areas. In the past decade, Beijing has attempted to balance its sovereignty, developmental, and security interests in the South China Sea disputes. China signed the Declaration on the Conduct of Parties in the South China Sea in 2002. In 2005 China, Vietnam and the Philippines agreed to the Joint Marine Seismic Undertaking (JMSU) to research potential underwater oil reserves. In 2008, however, the joint development deal was derailed when it was linked to a corruption scandal involving another Chinese corporation in the Philippines. Despite the ongoing dispute, China moved forward signing two agreements with the Philippines in late 2009 to improve bilateral ties in the areas of trade, investment and defense.[30]

On the Diaoyu/Senkaku Island dispute with Japan, China appears to be less willing to put the issue aside. According to Krista Weigand, this is because China has been able to link the dispute to other issues to gain an advantage.[31] But, while the issue may be used as a means of coercive diplomacy, China has not ostensibly escalated the dispute. In 2008 the two countries reached an in-principle agreement regarding joint development of undersea resources in the East China Sea, but such work has yet to come to fruition.

Participation in Regional Cooperative Projects

China further seeks to display its responsible role in the region through involvement in numerous regional and sub-regional cooperative projects. Here China can employ its relative technical advantage and expertise as well as its financial resources, not only for the benefit of regional states, but also for the development of its own southwestern provinces.

The Greater Mekong Sub-region development project, known as GMS, was the first Southeast Asian regional cooperative mechanism in which China participated. Joining with Cambodia, Laos, Myanmar, Thailand and Vietnam, China actively takes part in the development of dams, hydroelectric plants and infrastructure to facilitate trade among regional states. Among other cooperative development projects in the region involving China is the emerging Pan-Beibu Gulf economic zone. The Pan-Beibu project aims to expand cross border trade, develop the banking and investment sector in the region, and increase communication and tourism between the project participants.

China's cooperative efforts have recently also extended into areas of non-traditional security. Surpassing the U.S. as the world's biggest carbon emitter in 2008, Beijing was feeling pressure from the international community to join in action against climate change. Its position on the subject had been that it was unfair to expect developing nations to cut their emissions, when they were the manufacturers for the rest of the world. However, in 2009 China undertook aggressive diplomatic efforts in the lead-up to the Copenhagen summit on climate change. In remarks addressing the United Nations, President Hu Jintao committed to significantly decreasing carbon emissions and improving energy efficiency. While not declaring specific reduction targets, Hu's comments were welcomed by Western governments and raised some hopes for securing an agreement in Copenhagen.[32]

Preferable Loans and Assistance Programs

China has also become one of the largest sources of official development assistance for some Southeast Asian countries. In addition to other measures deemed favorable by ASEAN states during the 1997 Asian Financial Crisis, China provided billions of dollars in supplemental aid to states like Thailand and Indonesia. China's initiative to forge a free trade agreement with ASEAN countries, particularly the "Early Harvest" scheme, was widely perceived as Beijing's action to mitigate Southeast Asian countries' concerns of China's economic competitiveness.

Similarly, in response to the 'global financial crisis China pledged considerable aid packages and preferable loans to regional states. In April 2009 Chinese foreign minister Yang Jiechi unveiled $10 billion China-ASEAN investment cooperation fund to spur development of transportation, energy and communications infrastructure in the region. China also planned to offer preferential terms on loans of $1.7 billion to the region, along with nearly $40 billion in special aid to Cambodia, Laos and Myanmar.[33]

CHINA'S COMPETITIVE STRATEGIC GOALS

In international relations, no nation is altruistic. China is no exception. All the above-mentioned cooperative means were aimed to achieve various strategic goals. Over the past two decades, Beijing has consistently attempted to compete against the possibility of containment or constrainment led by the U.S., compete for a better China image in the region, compete to create a more propitious regional environment for its domestic economic development, compete with other major powers, especially the U.S. and Japan for regional influence, and compete to consolidate a long term solid strategic position in the region.

All the above strategic goals center on the question of how to cope with American dominance in the region and hedge against possible future U.S. efforts at containment using China's neighbors. Through active participation in regional institutions, China competes to show it is more supportive of Asian interests and initiatives than the U.S. Beijing's decision against devaluing its currency during the Asian Financial Crisis has already been mentioned. In another example, while the U.S. opposed Malaysia's proposal for an East Asian Economic Caucus (which would have excluded the U.S.) China voiced its strong support for the proposal.

In some ways China appears more of a supporter of the status-quo in Asia than the United States. Washington's aid to regional states is often accompanied by demands for liberal democratic reforms, whereas China makes no such demands. Indeed, China's strict concept of sovereignty and non-interference is more compatible with regional values, particularly in Southeast Asia.

China's regional economic cooperation has placed it in perhaps the best position to compete for a long-term strategic position in the region. The ASEAN-China Free Trade Agreement is likely to further link the economies of Southeast Asian states to China, giving the latter more influence in the region. Chinese officials have talked about reorienting their economy and increasing domestic consumption, which would provide a vast market for Southeast Asian-produced goods. And through the various regional cooperative projects noted above, China is putting in place the infrastructure to facilitate trade with regional states, as well as increase regional tourism and communication, further tying the region together.

China's active participation in regional cooperative projects also serves not only to build closer ties with its neighbors, but also as an indirect means of keeping the U.S. out. Beijing cautions its partners in such cooperative projects that the involvement of outside powers, such as the U.S., will only complicate matters and slow down progress. In this way, it encourages states to deal first and foremost with Beijing. As one author noted, "Chinese specialists . . . readily admit that China's initiatives in Asia, while designed to promote cooperation with the United States, also strengthen Chinese ability to offset possible U.S. efforts to pressure or contain China."[34]

Pursuing the above cooperative course has, in turn, allowed China to address issues of national interest in a less confrontational or threatening manner. As noted above, a review of Chinese scholarly writing in the mid- to late 1990s reveals a general consensus that direct competition with the U.S. would be impossible if China wished to continue its path of development. On the other hand, Chinese leaders had not abandoned their aspiration for a more multipolar world—one in which the U.S. was no longer a hegemonic power and in which China attained its rightful place among the world's great powers.

Here it is important to pause and further consider China's aspirations. To be sure, China aspires to more military power, as has been evident with its increasing defense expenditures. However, it also strives for international status. As Yong Deng points out:

China's struggle for status is about creating an international environment that allows the Chinese Communist Party (CCP)-state to continue self-paced reforms at home; increase power and recognition abroad to secure China's core interests; reassure other states of China's nonthreatening intent; and projects its influence in Asia and beyond.[35]

In other words, status is important for China not purely for the sake of being respected by others, but for what status will enable China to accomplish. China experienced being an outsider in the wake of the Tiananmen Square incident and does not wish to be ostracized again. Beijing understands that in order to avoid reigniting the "China threat" discourse it must convince its neighbors that it has no ill intentions toward them. This is evident given the amount of energy expended by Beijing in communicating its aim for a "peaceful rise" and "peaceful development." Through both words and action, Beijing has sought to exhibit its willingness to work within the existing system.

In doing so, Beijing has behaved recently in a manner that is very familiar to liberal institutionalist and constructivist analysts. Although tepidly at first, China has increasingly joined and become an active participant in regional and international institutions, and now appears largely "enmeshed" in the international system. Meanwhile the change from Beijing's previous revolutionary and confrontational rhetoric to its current cooperative and status-seeking overtures is easily viewed by some as an evolution in identity and acceptance of regional and international norms. However, it is clear that these changes in Beijing's approach to foreign policy are strategic adaptations to the extant system in order to achieve their national interests as outlined above.

ASSESSING THE EFFICACY OF CHINA'S STRATEGY

How then do we measure the effectiveness of China's strategy of cooperating to compete against the U.S. in East Asia? One way is to examine China's image among its neighbors. Various surveys from the Pew Global Attitudes Project over the past decade offer a glimpse at China's image in the region. The reaction appears to be mixed, and not surprisingly, opinions appear to differ between Northeast and Southeast Asia.

The 2005 Pew survey in Indonesia showed significant majorities favored China's rise, both economically and militarily.[36] Likewise, a majority of Malaysians surveyed in 2007 felt China's growing economic and military power was a positive development. Interestingly, the 2007 poll saw a significant decrease in Indonesians who felt China's military growth was a good thing.[37] And a 2006 poll indicated that more Indonesians expressed confidence in Japanese Prime Minister Koizumi's leadership than were confident with Chinese President Hu Jintao.[38]

In Northeast Asia, a 2007 poll found large majorities in South Korea (89 percent) and Japan (80 percent) viewed China's growing military power as a bad thing for their countries.[39] A review of Pew surveys conducted from 2002 to 2009 showed public favorability of China in both South Korea and Japan has dropped. In 2002 majorities in both countries saw China favorably. By 2009, only 46 percent of South Koreans and 26 percent of Japanese held a favorable view of China.[40]

Even in those states where China's image has high favorability, has this translated into influence in the region? Certainly China's positions are taken into account by regional states in the formation of policy. But it is yet to be shown whether China has the ability to shape regional policy. At the present it seems more likely that East Asian states take advantage of China's cooperation and competition with the United States when it is in their best interest to do so. In one example, Malaysia and China supported each other in plans to confine the membership of the East Asia Summit to only the Asian states of the ASEAN+3 framework, excluding the United States.

At the policy level, many observers agree that most East Asian nations now adopt a hedging policy towards China. Chinese decision-makers may be disappointed by the fact that many of China's neighbors still harbor significant suspicion of China, in particular China's future role in regional affairs. But viewed in a different angle, the hedging stance of neighboring states attests to the success of China's cooperation for competition strategy. The success lies in the fact that regional states have at least partially accepted China's rise and do not regard China's continuing rise as an immediate threat to their crucial national interests, thus forestalling any possibility of a containment or constrainment policy led by Washington. Under this hedging policy framework, regional states have no problem in cooperating with China and to some extent allowing China to play some leadership role in regional affairs. This is perhaps the best outcome that Beijing could have achieved in the post-Cold War era.

CONCLUSION

In the post-Cold War years, China faced quite daunting challenges in East Asia. None of the challenges was without the shadow of the United States. In response to these challenges, Beijing adopted a regional strategy that could be best characterized as "cooperation for competition." Beijing understood that to retain a solid strategic position in its neighboring regions in the long run China would have to focus on domestic economic growth. This understanding necessitated a regional approach of using international policy to serve the imperatives of its domestic economic agenda. Chinese efforts in solving land border disputes, participating in various multilateral forums and institutions, pushing for regional integration, and improving bilateral relations all aimed to create a stable environment in China's neighborhood and build an image of a rising but benign power. Gradually, Beijing realized that employing cooperative instruments was most effective to compete with other major actors in achieving its strategic goals and expanding its strategic influence in Asia in response to U.S. attempts to maintain its supremacy in the region.

It is important to distinguish the cooperation for competition strategy with the often-mentioned cooperation and competition approach. Beijing's strategy has been promoting cooperation in almost all policy arenas for the competition of attaining a better strategic position in the long run. Even on sensitive territorial issues, i.e., the South China Sea disputes, China has attempted to reduce competition by quietly accepting the status quo and instead pushed for cooperation. Admittedly, China would also engage with other East Asian states in many of the policy areas that are discussed in this chapter even if there had been no American strategic pressure. But the intensity and breadth of China's cooperative engagement have been so salient that we need to go beyond the usual liberal institutionalist interpretation that cooperation serves mutual interests. Cooperation for competition has been the essence of China's strategic approach in East Asia. And many signs indicate that China intends to continue to carry out this strategy in the foreseeable future.

The growth of China's strategic influence in East Asia, largely as a result of its cooperation for competition strategy, has been quite impressive. In fact, observers in the strategic circles in the U.S. are now alarmed by the increase of China's influence in the region. They worry that China is making all the strategic gains at the expense of the U.S. Indeed, China's approach of using the "charming offensive" to compete at the strategic level is a very difficult challenge to the U.S. Washington would have a much easier time to cope with East Asian international affairs if China had adopted either an aloof stance towards many of its neighbors or an assertive and heavy-handed strategic approach.

How should the U.S. respond to China's cooperation for competition strategy? Policy-makers in Washington need to understand three things. First, China's relentless efforts in managing its international relations in East Asia in the past two decades has entailed a regional situation in which containment or constrainment of China has become an unfeasible option. Second, with the increase of Chinese power and interactions with neighboring countries, Beijing will naturally become more important to other states in East Asia. Willingly or unwillingly, Washington will have to recognize the fact. Third, China's cooperation for competition strategy has also created or expanded areas of international interactions, for instance non-traditional security in the region. Officially Beijing does not seek to exclude the U.S. in any of the policy areas in the region for fear that doing so would aggravate the strategic suspicions in Washington and many capitals in East Asian, while at the strategic level China would be happy to see the gradual decline of U.S. strategic weight in the region. This essentially means that a good strategy for the U.S. is to step up its involvement in various policy areas in East Asia and to stage a similar "charming offensive" strategy.

NOTES

1. Steven W. Mosher, *Hegemon: China's Plan to Dominate Asia and the World* (San Francisco: Encounter Books, 2001).
2. Wayne Bert, *The United States, China and Southeast Asian Security: A Changing of the Guard?* (Vancouver, B.C.: University of British Columbia, 2005); Randall Doyle, *America and China: Asia-Pacific Rim Hegemony in the 21st Century* (Lanham: Lexington Books, 2007).
3. Robert G. Sutter, *China's Rise in Asia: Promises and Perils* (Lanham: Rowman & Littlefield Publishers, 2005).
4. William W. Keller and Thomas G. Rawski, eds., *China's Rise and the Balance of Influence in Asia*, (Pittsburgh: University of Pittsburgh Press, 2007).
5. David C. Kang, *China Rising: Peace, Power, and Order in East Asia* (New York: Columbia University Press, 2007).
6. For examples of realist approaches to China's strategy in Asia and beyond, see Robert Sutter, "Dealing with a Rising China: US Strategy and Policy," in Zhang Yunling (ed.), *Making New Partnership: A Rising China and its Neighbors* (Beijing: Social Sciences Academic Press, China, 2007); Robert G. Sutter, *China's Rise in Asia: Promises and Perils* (Rowman & Littlefield, 2005); Gerald Segal, "East Asia and the 'Constrainment' of China", *International Security*, Vol. 20, No. 4 (Spring 1996), pp. 107-135; Aaron Friedberg, "Ripe for Rivalry: Prospects for Peace in a Multipolar Asia," *International Security*, Vol. 18, No.3 (Winter 1993/94), pp. 5-33.
7. Alastair Iain Johnston and Paul Evans, "China's Engagement with Multilateral Security Institutions," in Alastair Iain Johnstong and Robert Ross (eds.), *Engaging China: the Management of an Emerging Power* (London: Routledge, 1999), pp. 235-72; G. John Ikenberry, "The Rise of China: Power, Institutions, and the Western Order," in Robert S. Ross and Zhu Feng (eds.), *China's Ascent: Power, Security, and the Future of International Politics* (Ithaca: Cornell University Press, 2008); Amitav Acharya, "Will Asia's Past Be Its Future?" *International Security*, Vol. 28, No. 3 (Winter 2003-04), pp.

149-64; Alice D. Ba, "Who's Socializing Whom? Complex Engagement in Sino-ASEAN Relations," *The Pacific Review*, Vol. 19, No. 2, June 2006.

8 . David Shambaugh, "China Engages Asia: Reshaping the Regional Order," *International Security*, Vol. 29, No. 3 (Winter 2004/05); Evan Medeiros and M. Taylor Fravel, "China's New Dipomacy," *Foreign Affairs*, Vol. 82, No. 6 (Nov/Dec 2003); Morton Abramowitz and Stephen Bosworth, "Adjusting to the New Asia," *Foreign Affairs*, Vol. 82, No. 4 (July/August 2003); Rosemary Foot, "China's Regional Activism: Leadership, Leverage, and Protection;" Zhang Yunling and Tang Shiping, "China's Regional Strategy," in David Shambaugh (ed.), *Power Shift: China and Asia's New Dynamics* (California: University of California Press, 2005).

9. See Peter J. Katzenstein and Rudra Sil, "Rethinking Asian Security: A Case for Analytical Eclecticism," in J.J. Suh, Peter J. Katzenstein and Allen Carlson (eds.), *Rethinking Security in Asia*, Stanford University Press, 2004; and Peter J. Katzenstein and Nobuo Okawara, "Japan, Asia-Pacific Security, and the Case for Analytical Eclecticism," *International Security*, Vol. 26, No. 3 (Winter 2001/02), pp. 153-185.

10. "1995 Annual Report to the President and the Congress," U.S. Department of Defense, February 1995.

11. Michael McDevitt, "U.S. Strategy in the Asia Pacific Region: Southeast Asia," in W. Lee, R. Hathaway and W. Wise, *U.S. Strategy in the Asia-Pacific Region*, Woodrow Wilson International Center for Scholars, Washington, 2003; Bruce Vaughn and Wayne Morrison, "China-Southeast Asia Relations: Trends, Issues, and Implications for the United States," Congressional Research Service Report for the U.S. Congress, April 4, 2006.

12. Samuel Huntington, *The Third Wave: Democratization in the Late Twentieth Century*, University of Oklahoma Press, 1992.

13. Herbert Yee and Zhu Feng, "Chinese Perceptions of the China Threat: Myth or Reality?," in Herbert Yee and Ian Storey (eds.), *The China Threat: Perceptions, Myths and Reality*, Routledge Curzon, London, 2002.

14. Jin Canrong, "The US Global Strategy in the Post-Cold War Era and its Implications for China-United States Relations: A Chinese Perspective," *Journal of Contemporary China*, Vol. 10, No. 27, 2001.

15. Ibid.

16. For more on the importance of status in China's international relations, see Yong Deng, China's Struggle for Status: The Realignment of International Relations, Cambridge University Press, 2008.

17. In addition to Joshua Kurlantzick's *Charm Offensive*, a number of other analysts have noted Beijing's drive to increase and utilize China's soft power resources in order to improve relations with other countries, Southeast Asia in particular. See Li Mingjiang (ed), *Soft Power: China's Emerging Strategy in International Politics*, (Lanham: Lexington Books, 2009); also Thomas Lum, Wayne Morrison, and Bruce Vaughn, "China's 'Soft Power' in Southeast Asia," Congressional Research Service report for U.S. Congress, January 4, 2008.

18. Bruce Vaughn and Wayne Morrison, "China-Southeast Asia Relations: Trends, Issues, and Implications for the United States," Congressional Research Service Report for the U.S. Congress, April 4, 2006, p. 24.

19. Alexander Vuving argues that China and Vietnam's willingess to settle the dispute was the product of grand strategic fit, as the settlement served both countries greater national interests. See Vuving's "Grand Strategic Fit and Power Shift: Explaining Turning Points in China-Vietnam Relations," in Shiping Tang, Mingjiang Li and Amitav Acharya (eds.), *Living with China: Regional States and China Through Crises and Turning Points*, Palgrave MacMillan, 2009; alternatively, M. Taylor Fravel argues that Beijing's willingness to compromise and settle the dispute is the result of concern for

political legitimacy. See Fravel's "Regime Instability and International Cooperation: Explaining China's Compromises in Territorial Disputes," *International Security*, Vol. 30, No. 2, 2005, pp. 76-77.

20. Rizal Sukma, "Indonesia-China Relations: The Politics of Re-engagement," in Shiping Tang, Mingjiang Li and Amitav Acharya (eds.), *Living with China: Regional States and China Through Crises and Turning Points*, Palgrave MacMillan, 2009

21. Scott Snyder, "Lee Myung-bak and the Future of Sino-South Korean Relations," The Jamestown Foundation's *China Brief*, vol 8, issue 4, February 15, 2008.

22. Jae Ho Chung, "China's 'Soft' Clash With South Korea," *Asian Survey*, Vol. XLIX, No. 3, May/June 2009.

23. Takashi Hoshiyama, "New Japan-China Relations and the Corresponding Positioning of the United States—History, Values, Realism in a Changing World," *Asia-Pacific Review*, Vol. 15, No 2, 2008.

24. Haikuan Gao, "The China-Japan Mutually Beneficial Relationship Based on Common Strategic Interests," *Asia-Pacific Review*, Vol. 15, No. 2, 2008.

25. "China, Japan vow to promote bilateral ties" *Xinhua*, September 22, 2009.

26. For a thorough analysis of the relationship, see Bobo Lo, *Axis of Convenience: Moscow, Beijing, and the New Geopolitics*, Brookings Institution Press, 2008.

27. Susan L. Shirk, "China's Multilateral Diplomacy in the Asia-Pacific," written testimony before the U.S.-China Economic and Security Review Commission, Washington D.C., February 12-13, 2004,

28. M. Taylor Fravel, "Regime Insecurity and International Cooperation: Explaining China's Compromises in Territorial Disputes," *International Security*, Vol. 30 (2), 2005.

29. China continues to have land border disputes with India and Bhutan.

30. Jerome Aning, "RP, China Ink 2 Agreements Boosting Ties Despite Conflict," *Philippine Daily Inquirer*, October 30, 2009.

31. Krista Weigand, "China's Strategy in the Senkaku/Diaoyu Islands Dispute: Issue Linkage and Coercive Diplomacy," *Asian Security*, Vol. 5, No. 2, May 2009.

32. Julian Borger and Suzanne Goldenberg, "China announces pledge to curb carbon emissions," *The Guardian*, September 23, 2009

33. "China rolls out aid package for ASEAN," *Xinhua*, April 12, 2009.

34. Robert Sutter, *China's Rise in Asia.*

35. Yong Deng, *China's Struggle for Status* (Cambridge and New York: Cambridge University Press, 2008), p.21.

36. "U.S. Image Up Slightly, But Still Negative," *Pew Global Attitudes Project*, June 23, 2005.

37. "Global Unease With Major World Powers," *Pew Global Attitudes Project*, June 27, 2007.

38. "Publics of Asian Powers Hold Negative Views of One Another," *Pew Global Attitudes Project*, September 21, 2006.

39. "Global Unease With Major World Powers," *Pew Global Attitudes Project*, June 27, 2007.

40. "Confidence in Obama Lifts U.S. Image Around the World," *Pew Global Attitudes Project*, July 23, 2009.

Chapter 4

The Korean Peninsula as a Test Bed for the Future Direction of Sino-U.S. Relations: From Structural Realism to Neoclassical Realism and Beyond

Ji-Yong Lee

INTRODUCTION

Contemporary Northeast Asia provides a laboratory for international relations theories. It is a venue where international dynamics of the Post-Cold War and the Cold War coexist, in that Northeast Asian states have strived to build multilateral international institutions, while competition between rising China and the United States is a source of conflict and cooperation. In addition, the legacies of the Cold War ideological conflicts still account for much of the interstate politics in the region. They substantially confine Northeast Asian international relations. There are two socialist party states, China and North Korea. The conflict between North Korea and South Korea provides the major source of instability for Northeast Asian regional security. The Northeast Asian regional international system is characterized as a regional multipolarity with a rising China, a normalizing Japan, and the United States, which may increase instability and complexity in the regional international politics. At the same time, Northeast Asian states have been increasingly economically intertwined in this era of globalization. Deepening economic connections in turn furnish incentives to promote regional political stability. In the international environment of globalization and regional multipolarity, each state has been seeking to build multilateral regional institutions in order to secure regional stability.

Observing a rising China, realists in international relations theory, especially power transition theorists, continue to warn of a possible conflict between the United States and China. They base their views on the assumption that a rising power comes to challenge an existing international order. In the current regional international environment, Japan and South Korea have been carefully executing both "engagement" and "hedging" strategies against a rising China. Japan has reinforced its alliance with the United States since the mid-1990s. South Korea has swung back to the U.S.-Japan alliance arrangement since Lee Myung-bak, a conservative politician, took office in 2008. The U.S.-Japan-South Korea alliance, in turn, causes Beijing serious concern, raising the suspicion that the United States and her allies may attempt the encirclement of China. On the other hand, increasing regional tension gives rise to a need for establishing regional multilateral institutions to maintain regional political and economic stability. For example, ARF (ASEAN Regional Forum) and APT (ASEAN Plus Three) were established in an effort to build security institutions and promote regional cooperation, though with little effect to date. This lack of progress confirms the complexity of Northeast Asian international relations.

Recently, Japan and South Korea have exhibited patterns of "balancing" by which they adjust themselves to the international system of bipolarity (China-U.S.). Recent relations with the United States suggest a direct correlation with domestic factors; change of political leadership at the domestic level is translated into national foreign strategy and policy. For example, the new administration of South Korea radically discarded the foreign policy of the previous administration, changing its priority in foreign policy from identifying itself as a regional stabilizer to strengthening the U.S.-South Korea alliance. If South Korea defines its role as a regional stabilizer in Northeast Asian international relations, it should redefine the traditional U.S.-South Korea alliance. This happened during the previous administration and stirred up a controversy. The current administration of South Korea has been emphasizing the strategic importance of the alliance with the United States. It again moved the pendulum toward the U.S.-side, which reinforced the traditional U.S.-Japan-South Korea alliance. It caused Beijing concern about Northeast Asian international relations, leading the Chinese leadership to seek ways of dissolving the tripartite alliance. In other words, it tends rather to reinforce the assumed confrontation between China and the United States. Meanwhile, the new administration of the United States has a different outlook on international affairs from that of the previous Bush administration. The new international affairs approach of the Obama administration may contribute, to some degree, to easing tensions between China and the United States. This will, in turn, affect the policies of states such as Japan and South Korea. In other words, Japan and South Korea should recalculate their interests in the context of revised Sino-U.S. relations; that is, they may not feel as securely backed by the United States alliance, so they may have to seek another way of ensuring their security. There are signs of change in Japanese foreign policy as new political leadership replaced the Liberal Democratic Party (LDP) in September 2009 for the first time in half a century. The Democratic Party's "Asia-focused" [1] foreign policy reflects both the new political leadership's foreign policy strategy and the changing Sino-U.S. relations with the beginning of the Obama administration.

This calls for consideration of the domestic factor in examining Sino-U.S. relations. Along these lines, realists tend to assume that a rising China will eventually challenge the international order set by the United States. But, what if

Chinese leadership actually does not have the capacity to challenge the United States in the near future? What if Chinese leadership does not have any serious intention to alter the current "rules of the game" in world affairs dominated by the United States? What if, rather, Chinese leadership wants to maintain the current order because of its need to maintain economic growth as well as stable international politics, both of which are crucial for regime survival? What if the Chinese leadership does not intend to replace the United States as a global hegemony? Similar questions arise for the United States. What if the United States seeks peaceful coexistence with rising China? What if the United States political leadership wants to cooperatively manage political and economic issues with China? What if the United States leadership needs to build a new international structure as demonstrated by the terms "G-2" and "Chimerica,"[2] thereby allowing China to make a strategic partnership with the United States, rather than dismissing China as a challenger or revisionist?

These questions may sound naïve or idealistic. Certainly, the new foreign policy of the Obama administration may come from the United States' declining material power rather than from a different worldview. Nonetheless, it is significant that a different worldview and perception of a competitor can fundamentally alter the operation of a given international system. What if China and the United State pursue co-management of international affairs, irrespective of their origin? Competition and suspicion would remain even under that scheme. However, it may alter basic perceptions of other states such as Japan, South Korea, Taiwan, and Southeast Asian states, which may create different outcomes in the same international system; that is, outcomes in an international system may vary according to the domestic politics of each nation. This would then reduce the incentives to depend heavily on one or the other major power. They should seek cooperation with the superpowers, rather than rely on balancing or bandwagoning strategies. This would reduce the tensions between the superpowers and restrain a spiraling movement of competition and conflict.

With these research questions, this chapter examines the dynamics of Sino-U.S. relations and their effects on the Korean Peninsula. The Korean Peninsula is a flashpoint of Sino-U.S. relations. It poses the legacy of the Cold War in terms of socialism versus democracy, dynamism of the assumed power transition between a rising China and the United States as the incumbent leader, and the need for multilateral collaboration to deal with the North Korean nuclear challenge. Therefore, it provides a venue where we can extract sources of conflict and cooperation of the two poles of the Northeast Asian international system.

THEORETICAL DEBATES ON SINO-U.S. RELATIONS

One of the big issues of contemporary international relations, both for international relations theorists and policy practitioners, is Sino-U.S. relations. How do international relations theorists, commentators, and policy makers view a rising China? How do they predict the future direction of Sino-U.S. relations?

Some realists tend to warn that a rising China is a serious threat to the existing international order, while others see it in a different way. Liberalists who are based in "the China threat" perspective suggest the need to build multilateral international institutions in order to place rising China in a framework of multilateralism. On the other hand, other liberalists tend to lament the relative lack of multilateral institutions in East Asia compared to the western hemisphere. Some other liberalists suggest that rising China would not necessarily be a potential threat to the international order, if China democratized, thereby sharing values with the United States and the West. This is based on the assumption that democratic states do little to challenge one another militarily.[3] Others emphasize the importance of further integration of the Chinese economy into the world. There is a different viewpoint that East Asian international security will not necessarily be threatened by a rising China. This explanation draws on the history of the East Asian international order before the nineteenth century and points out East Asian particularism in international relations. Even though each perspective is based on a different worldview and theory, they share a common perception that China will be a peer competitor of the incumbent world leader, the United States.

First, realists regard a fast-rising China as a new source of international conflict in post-Cold War international relations. From the realist viewpoint, states must secure their survival in an anarchic international system where the principle of self-help prevails. Rising China creates security concerns among neighbor states that worry about the relative decline of their power position in an international structure. This leads to greater competition between the major powers. Offensive structural realists, stressing the states' concern about their relative power, predict that a clash between China and the United States is coming because the United States will not tolerate China's hegemonic status in East Asia while a rising China is committed to being a regional hegemony. For an offensive structural realist, such as Mearsheimer, the ultimate goal of every great power is to be a hegemon and thereby to dominate the international system by maximizing its relative power. The hegemon does not tolerate the emergence/existence of a peer competitor.[4]

Mearsheimer makes a dire prediction that "the United States and China are likely to engage in an intense security competition with considerable potential for war. Most of China's neighbors, including India, Japan, Singapore, South Korea, Russia, and Vietnam, will likely join with the United States to contain China's power."[5] In the same vein, he is critical of the United States' engagement policy toward China, because a rising China comes to challenge the United States hegemonic status in Asia. On the contrary, Waltz, who is a defensive structural realist, holds that moving from the current unipolarity to multipolarity or bipolarity is imperative because states are not as wary under unipolarity.[6] Facing the formation of a new balance of power, Waltz suggests that the United States should seek a form of coexistence, rather than create unnecessary conflicts with a rising China.[7] For Waltz, bipolarity is the most stable international system. Ross adds another variable for examining Sino-U.S. relations, the geographical factor. For Ross, the time is ripe for a Sino-U.S.

strategic competition in East Asia, shaping the regional bipolarity. However, Sino-U.S. regional bipolarity will be relatively stable unlike the conflict-ridden bipolarity between the Soviet Union and the United States during the Cold War, because of the geographical division of power between China and the United States. For Ross, the United States is a major maritime power, while China is a major continental power. Because China and the United States have interests in different strategic domains, the two great powers will manage to eschew conflict in East Asia.[8]

Meanwhile, power transition theory suggests a gloomy outlook for Sino-U.S. relation in the twenty-first century. Power transition theory posits that hegemonic war can be caused by a revisionist state that challenges the incumbent leader, while offensive structural realists tend to see a hegemonic power's reluctance to accept a peer competitor as a major source of conflict. In power transition theory, a new rising power is dissatisfied with the international order set by the incumbent hegemony. As a result, it tries to alter the rules of the game by challenging that leading power, maneuvering to a hegemonic war. The super-power then tries to forestall the rising revisionist state. This results in the break out of hegemonic war.[9] In light of these assumptions, power transition theorists argue that a rising China is likely to be a revisionist challenger that seeks to alter the current international political and economic order established by the current world leader. Because the existing order is operating for the incumbent hegemon, the revisionist China will be progressively dissatisfied with the rules of the game. However, it is questionable that a newly rising great power should be dissatisfied with the current order. The current issue in power transition theory with regard to a rising China, therefore, tends to focus on whether China is a dissatisfied revisionist or a satisfied power, content with the existing international political and economic order. If China is a satisfied latecomer, it should lead to China's peaceful rise. In contrast, if China is dissatisfied with the rules of the game set by the west, a catastrophic war could result.[10]

For theorists, the question is whether China is a dissatisfied challenger or not. Johnston examines whether China is a status quo state or a revisionist one, and specifies indicators to use in assessing a rising China's identity.[11] By analyzing China's behavior, he concludes that Chinese leadership is not likely to aggressively challenge United States power, and it is hard to say that China is a revisionist state. He argues that China is not likely to be a challenger, because China has already been deeply integrated into the existing international order, increasingly shows cooperative performance, and historically has been little involved in conflicts when its territory was not encroached upon by others.[12] In the same vein, Chan contends that historical evidence shows that a rising power tends to avoid a confrontation with an incumbent power, and this is the same case with a rising China.[13] Empirical evidence of China's behavior leads to the conclusion that China is "a risk-averse latecomer."[14] Furthermore, Samuel Kim contends that there are many differences between rising China and Germany before the two world wars, a case which power transition theory draws as an historical example. Therefore, the correlation between power transition and war causation may no longer apply in the current international situation. Especially in the post-Cold War era, over-simplification of the struggle for power has little relevance.[15]

It is an over-simplification to attempt to explain contemporary international relations with only the basic assumptions of power politics. In this regard, liberalists grapple with the idea of finding sources of cooperation between China and the United States. Nonetheless, the sources of cooperation and solutions to conflict that liberalists seek are varied. Neo-liberal institutionalists emphasize the importance of establishing international or multilateral institutions for international cooperation, because institutions provide information and the incentive for a rational state to abide by shared rules. Some neo-liberals, who seem disappointed in the lack of multilateral institutions in Northeast Asia, claim that cooperative settlement of international disputes is less feasible in Northeast Asia than in the western countries.[16] Some others, however, pay attention to China's increasing commitment to international institutions both at the regional and global levels. China not only participates in most regional multilateral institutions, such as Asia-Pacific Economic Cooperation (APEC), ASEAN Plus Three (APT), ASEAN Regional Forum (ARF), and the East Asian Summit, but also initiates regional institutions such as the Shanghai Cooperation Organization.[17] At the global level, China's accession to the World Trade Organization (WTO) in 2001 was a turning point that integrated China more deeply into the world liberal economy; Chinese leadership had long been seeking active participation in international institutions.

Johnston looks at China's increasing participation rate in international institutions and concludes that "China moves from isolationism from international organizations to membership numbers approaching about 80 percent of the comparison states. High levels of development are associated with high levels of interdependence, with high demand for institutions that can regulate these interactions."[18] Pointing out the difference between international multilateralism and multilateralism with Chinese characteristics, Moore argues that China's new approach to multilateralism may result in China's integration into the liberal political and economic order, though its commitment to multilateralism is currently highly strategic.[19]

By the same token, some liberalists pay attention to deepening economic interdependence among Northeast Asian countries as well as between China and the United States. This economic interdependence creates larger shared interests among states, which contribute to peaceful settlement of international disputes.[20] Meanwhile, democratic peace theorists stress the importance of the spread of democratic rule in China and other Northeast Asian countries, such as North Korea, in promoting the possibility of peaceful regional order. Examining the historical experience of the power shift from the Great Britain to the United States, Lemke and Reed point out that democratic dyads tend to make for a peaceful power transition.[21] This implies that the democratization of China is a crucial factor for the future direction of Sino-U.S. relations; a power transition between the two powers would not be peaceful, if China keeps its current government.[22]

It is notable that some others see the Asian international order quite differently from conventional western views. David Kang contends that Asian countries centering on China have shaped a world order that is fundamentally different from the Westphalian system that shaped Europe since the seventeenth century. While the Westphalian system maintained the basic principles of national sovereignty and sovereign equality of the nation-state, rendering the international system anarchic, East Asian states shaped a hierarchical international order in which China was regarded as an emperor and other states rendered tribute to the Chinese Emperor. However, China rarely encroached on the political independence of her subordinate states unless they challenged her authority and territory. In other words, while the European international order worked under formal equality and actual inequality, the East Asian order was characterized by formal inequality and informal equality. Lastly, East Asia could maintain a stable international order when China's political and economic power remained stable.[23] In other words, the argument implies that the basic rules of Northeast Asian international relations were fundamentally different from the western international relations characterized as an anarchical world order under the Westphalian international system. If this is so, we can realize that states may shape a different form of world order according to different worldviews, as the East Asian order had exhibited before the nineteenth century. However, it should be noted that Northeast Asian states have been deeply integrated in the Westphalian international system throughout the twentieth century. In other words, the integration into the western international order has altered the worldview of the regional states. Currently, no Northeast Asian state sees China as an emperor; no state kowtows to Chinese authority. All see themselves as equal partners with China rather than as subordinates. Thus, facing a rising China, Northeast Asian states seek liberal solutions to establish regional security, while their behavioral patterns present the typical strategy based on realism.

What about domestic factors such as the characteristics of domestic political leadership or domestic socio-economic conditions that significantly constrain a state's foreign policy? Political leaders' perceptions and worldviews can substantially affect the behavior of states, even in the same international system. Historical evidence of international relations shows that suspicion of other states creates significant rivalry between/among states. For example, mutual suspicion regarding the intentions of the United States and the former Soviet Union affected the emergence of the Cold War between the two nations.[24] Mao Zedong was suspicious of Khrushchev's intentions and, simultaneously, Khrushchev and Brezhnev saw Mao's China as an unreliable ally. This mutual misperception then resulted in the spiraling Sino-Soviet split.[25] The American political leaders regarded communist China as an evil, like the Soviet Union, in spite of the fact that the Soviet leaders initially did not have such strong hostility toward the United States as they did after the Korean War. The United States president, John F. Kennedy, decided to intervene in Vietnam for the purpose of protecting Asia from Soviet expansionism. At the time, the United States policy makers adhered to the idea that Ho Chi Minh, the leader of the Viet Cong, was an instrument of Soviet expansionism, while Ho's primary purpose was to achieve national independence from a foreign country. The American decision to intervene in Vietnam was caused by the fear of communism and the assumed domino effect posed by the Soviets and the Viet Cong, which by historical analogy was associated with "the lesson of Munich" in the 1930s. [26] These historical examples suggest that politicians' perceptions of other states or their worldview can significantly affect the outcome of international politics.

One must consider domestic factors in examining the dynamism of Sino-U.S. relations. It is unlikely that international systems such as unipolarity, bipolarity, or multipolarity would all produce the same outcome. By the same token, bipolarity does not necessarily mean competition and conflict centering on two poles—China and the United States. The power transition from a rising power to an incumbent power may create either conflict, hegemonic war, or a peaceful transition. As Lemke and Reed explain, regime type significantly affected a peaceful transition from the Great Britain to the United States. [27] Regime type is not the only factor correlated with an international outcome, however. Perception or the worldview of policy decision-makers also may substantially alter the operating principles of an international system. Next, this chapter examines how changes in domestic political leadership can shake an alliance arrangement in an international system, focusing on the dynamism of Sino-U.S. relations that revolves around the Korean Peninsula. Specifically, it analyzes the effects of changes in political leadership in the United States, South Korea, and Japan on the alliance and security arrangements against a rising China.

EVOLVING SINO-U.S. INTERESTS ON THE KOREAN PENINSULA AND THE IMPACTS OF DOMESTIC POLITICAL LEADERSHIIP

The Korean Peninsula is located on the frontline where Chinese "continental interests" and United States "maritime interests" intersect. [28] Sources of Sino-U.S. conflict tend to rise to the surface over the Korean Peninsula. These potential flashpoints include the United States military presence in South Korea, North Korea and the North Korean nuclear program, the United States missile defense (MD) system and South Korean participation in it, and regime type, if there is a reunification of Korea in the future.

As Chinese capabilities grow beyond those of a regional power, Chinese leadership has come to have more strategic concerns about the United States and its alliances in Northeast Asia. At the same time, the United States has a strategic interest in maintaining a status quo in the region, because an increase in Chinese influence would mean a relative decline in United States influence. [29] In the post-Cold War era, Northeast Asian international relations have revolved around the United States and its allies' offensive strategy of encircling China and China's defensive response of strengthening bilateral relationships with East Asian countries and committing to a multilateral approach.

The strategic importance of the Korean Peninsula has increased for the United States and for China as Sino-U.S. relations have evolved. From the Chinese perspective, China's increasing influence over North and South Korea offsets the effects of the United States and its allies' encirclement of China. At the same time, the United States retains its military presence in South Korea, which is "a key component of the American commitment to a forward military posture in East Asia."[30] Maintaining the security alliance with South Korea is crucial for the United States not only to keep regional stability, but to check China. Consequently, China and the United States are pitted against each other in an effort to secure their strategic interests in the Korean Peninsula.

Historically, China has had a vital strategic and geographic interest in the Korean Peninsula, with North Korea serving as a security buffer zone for China in Northeast Asia. With the idea of "once lips are removed, teeth then will freeze," Mao decided to intervene in the Korean War in 1951. China has maintained an alliance with North Korea since 1961, although relations have fluctuated during this period. China also has been developing a cooperative partnership with South Korea since the two normalized their relationship by establishing formal diplomatic relations in 1992. Since then, China and South Korea have extended their economic and political relationship. In 1998, China and South Korea not only established a partnership, but they also extended their cooperative efforts to include the military. South Korea especially invigorated relations with China during the Roh administration. In 2004, South Korea and China signed a comprehensive cooperative partnership. Several factors led South Korea to strengthen the relationship with China. First, China became one of South Korea's most important economic partners in the 2000s. Second, politically, the Roh administration sought a new position in Northeast Asia to establish South Korea as a balancing power in Northeast Asia and to reduce its heavy dependency on the United States politically and economically, although it would not abandon the U.S.-South Korea security alliance.

It seemed that China benefited from the South Korean foreign policy shift.[31] In contrast, the United States revealed its concerns about changing relations with South Korea, because of the high potential for a shift in the status quo in Northeast Asia. As Shambaugh points out, increasing Chinese influence in South Korea and the relative decline of United States influence may be offset by the strengthening U.S.-Japan alliance.[32] The United States has been committed to building and intensifying the U.S.-Japan alliance to counter its declining influence in South Korea. Furthermore, the United States and Japan have committed to extending the security alliance to other states, such as Australia and India. Confronted with the new U.S.-Japan-Australia-India security arrangement, China has responded by making progressive partnerships with neighbor states. The competition between China and the United States is characterized by suspicion and friction. For example, the United States, Japan, and Australia held "the Trilateral Strategic Dialogue" that was accompanied by "an Action Plan" and "a Joint Declaration" between Australia and Japan at APEC 2007.[33] Furthermore, the United States, Japan, Australia, Singapore, and India held a joint military exercise. China questioned the intent of strengthening these alliances, perceiving this as a containment strategy directed against China.[34]

The change of South Korean political leadership in 2008 further intensified the alliance arrangement of the Asia-Pacific democracies. The new South Korean administration radically changed the domestic and foreign policies that had been implemented by the Roh administration. In foreign policy, the Lee administration discarded Roh's idea of South Korea as a balancing power in Northeast Asia. The new government then moved toward support for the U.S.-Japan alliance, strengthening its own strategic alliance with the United States. Criticizing the new alliance arrangement, China said that "the U.S.-ROK military alliance is something leftover from the history. As we all know, time has changed, so have situations in all countries of this region. The Cold War mentality of "military alliance" would not be valid in viewing, measuring and handling the current global or regional security issues."[35] In other words, strengthening the United States alliance in Northeast Asia further aggravated China's security concern over the assumed containment of China by the U.S. allies. The fact that China is threatened by a strengthening U.S.-Japan-South Korea alliance caused the new administration of South Korea to give serious consideration to its participation in the United States' MD system.[36] By reinforcing the strategic alliance with the United States, the Lee administration stuck to a hard-line policy against North Korea. This has escalated tension over the Korean Peninsula and over all of Northeast Asia. Given that China has a vital interest in maintaining the North Korean status quo for regional stability and in dealing with the containment policy, it would naturally follow that China would seek to strengthen a counter alliance arrangement including Russia and North Korea. This would then create a security dilemma over the Korean Peninsula, unleashing confrontation between the China-Russia-North Korea and the U.S.-Japan-South Korea alliances.

The year 2009 saw the beginning of a new phase in Sino-U.S. relations. First of all, the new Obama administration employed a quite different approach to international relations and to China. It emphasized multilateralism rather than unilateralism, engagement rather than containment, and cooperative partnership rather than strategic competition.[37] Second, the United States leadership has come to clearly recognize that the United States can no longer cope with global affairs by itself. The 2008 financial crisis in the United States and the following domestic and global economic recession imposed a heavy burden on the new administration. The Obama administration was confronted by many problems, including the domestic economic crisis, issues in the Middle East, global terrorism, energy security and environmental protection, as well as the North Korean nuclear challenge. All of these areas require an active commitment to establishing effective international cooperation. As a result, the new administration's policy toward China took a new turn, and efforts to build a new partnership with China began.[38]

The United States' new foreign policy turn toward China could partially, but significantly, shake the existing alliance arrangement (U.S.-Japan-South Korea accompanied with Australia and India) against China. It could weaken the momentum of the U.S.-Japan alliance. Japanese politicians raised worries about "Japan-Passing" as the Obama administration has developed closer Sino-U.S. ties.[39] The new Japanese political leadership has been strengthening China-Japan relationships since the Democratic Party of Japan replaced the Liberal Democratic Party for the first time in more than 40 years. Whereas the previous LDP pursued the strengthening of the U.S.-Japan alliance that was assumed to be directed against China in strategic terms,[40] the DP tends to be committed to deepening and widening China-Japan relationships in the area of security. On 27 November 2009, China and Japan agreed to conduct their first joint military exercise,[41] which means that the bilateral relationship is going beyond an economic partnership. The South Korean government, which has moved to the U.S.-Japan security alliance, would have to rethink its foreign policy strategy in the context of changing Sino-U.S. relations. It is not clear whether changing Northeast Asian international relations create a multipolarity (U.S., China, Japan, and Russia), rather than a bipolarity (United States and China), a situation which can increase uncertainty and variability in international relations. One thing is clear, however: the United States, Japan, and South Korea are all beginning to seek a cooperative partnership with China.

We could conclude from this chain of events that domestic factors,[42] rather than international ones, significantly affect the operation of international systems. Although, as structural realism holds, international structure tends to shape the nature of international politics, an explanation of international politics based only on structuralism is likely to fail to explain the effects of transforming domestic foreign policy caused by changes in domestic political leadership. Another important factor is the effect of the political leadership's perception and political orientation. To some extent, the United States' different policy approach to a rising China may be attributed to political leadership. The Clinton administration's welcoming of China into the global economy was based on liberalism. In contrast, the Bush administration treated China as a "strategic competitor" based on its realist worldview, which led the administration to take a containment strategy toward China, rather than a policy of engagement.[43] The Obama administration seems committed to principles of engagement, which is expected to soothe tensions with China. As for the Chinese, Chinese foreign policy strategy is based on its "Grand Strategy." The purpose of the strategy is to create a favorable international environment in an effort to keep steady economic growth and social stability as well as national integration. Its ultimate goals are to secure the regime survival as well as retain its political influence as a great power. It requires maintaining friendly relations with the U.S.[44] It seems that the leadership recognizes that it does not have the capacity to challenge the United States, at least in the near future and acknowledges U.S. global leadership.[45] Consequently, China may not want to alter the current rules of the game in the international order. Rather, the Chinese leadership may have strategic interests in maintaining the current order because China in some sense is the main beneficiary of the existing international economy in light of its unprecedented economic success. Furthermore, its primary concern is securing domestic political stability. Since the Chinese leadership is faced with the grave problems of social unrest, questions regarding the legitimacy of its political authority, and the integration of with independence-minded ethnic minorities, the leadership's top priority is to manage domestic affairs and strengthen their own political authority and legitimacy, not international affairs.[46] Maintaining the status quo in contemporary international relations is crucial if the Chinese leadership is to maintain economic growth and deal with domestic political stability and national integration. Therefore, the Chinese leadership is less likely to be a "challenger" to or a "revisionist" force against the international order set by the United States.[47] We can see that political leaderships' worldview and perception are no less important than the international system, because they can alter the operation of an international system and bring about a far different outcome in world affairs.

The next section examines how domestic factors in a given international system may alter the future direction of Sino-U.S. relations by analyzing three flash points of the Korean Peninsula.

THE DYNAMIC EFFECTS OF SINO-U.S. RELATIONS OVER THE KOREAN PENINSULA

There are three major issues in the Korean Peninsula that can test Sino-U.S. relations. The first issue is North Korea and its nuclear program. China and the United States have developed a multilateral arrangement to deal with the North Korean nuclear challenge. Second, China and the United States tend to struggle against each other to hold and exert influence over South Korea. The last major issue is the future reunification of the two Koreas. Whether that process creates dire consequences for both the Koreas, the United States and China will depend on the approach the latter two nations take.

Cooperation between China and the United States Evolves into Multilateralism: the North Korea Regime and its Nuclear Program

China and the United States share a strategic interest in preventing the development of nuclear weapons in the Korean Peninsula. China has a vital interest in maintaining regional stability for its economic growth. Therefore, the North Korean nuclear bid is not acceptable, because it could trigger the proliferation of nuclear weapons to other countries, such as Japan and South Korea, aggravating regional tensions and instability. The United States also has dealt with this issue, but tends to deal with the North Korean nuclear program in the context of global non-proliferation of nuclear weapons. Despite the fact that both China and the United States must confront the North Korean nuclear program, they have distinct views of the issue. First of all, China has more vital interests in the North Korea than the United States, in geographical terms. It regards North Korea as a "strategic buffer-zone" between China and the United States.[48] Second, China has strategic interests in preventing the current North

Korean regime from radical collapse or in sustaining the North as an independent and pro-Chinese state. China regards North Korea as a strategic leverage partner in the Sino-U.S. rivalry over Northeast Asia. Clearly, China is likely to have more interest in maintaining the status quo in the Korean Peninsula, including the existing arrangement of confrontation between North Korea and U.S.-South Korea.[49] On the contrary, the United States' interests are more focused on managing the disturbed Korean Peninsula created by the collapse of the despotic regime than in ensuring the current status quo of the divided two Koreas.[50] Its primary task is to protect South Korea from the North's threat, which was the origin of the U.S.–South Korea alliance made in 1953. Therefore, the U.S. puts much more weight on South Korean security than North Korea while China is more concerned about North Korea.

China's approach to the North Korean nuclear program has shifted from bilateralism to multilateralism. Chinese leadership took a passive attitude toward the United States and its allies' multilateral solutions regarding the North Korean nuclear program in the 1990s, because they saw that the United States made use of the North Korean nuclear program to strengthen its Cold War security alliances to counter a rising China.[51] In 2002, however, China began to play a major role in the Six Party Talks to solve the problem of the North's nuclear program. Two factors encouraged China's more active role in coping with the North's nuclear issue. First was the change of political leadership in China. The new leadership of Hu Jintao took seriously the issues of the Taiwan Strait and the North Korean nuclear challenge, viewing them as major flashpoints that could create regional instability. As a result, the leadership began to play a more active role in finding solutions. The Bush administration needed China to play this role in dealing with the North's nuclear program, because the United States' primary task during that period was the creation of a new order in the Middle East, making the North's nuclear issue secondary. The Bush administration called for China's commitment to the nuclear issue within the framework of the Six Party Talks. Another factor for Chinese engagement in the multilateral approach was that Chinese leadership seriously apprehended about the Bush administration militarism. The leadership worried about "the danger of a military solution by the United States, including a military strike against DPRK" that would easily result in military escalation and war over the Korean Peninsula.[52] Especially, since the second Bush administration, China and the United States have been building a bilateral framework, the US-China Senior Dialogue (now called the Strategic and Economic Dialogue: SE&D), which promotes a coalitional approach to many issues, including the North Korean issue.

China's support for a multilateral resolution of the North Korean nuclear issue is exhibited by a number of Chinese actions. For example, China voted for the 2006 and 2009 U.N. Security Council resolutions imposing sanctions on North Korea in an attempt to force it to end its nuclear program. Since the UN toughened sanctions against the North following its nuclear test in May 2009, China and the United States together have been making an effort to reach a breakthrough settlement of the nuclear issue. The Obama administration expressed support for the Six-Party Talks' effort to settle the nuclear issue.[53] This implies that the United States recognizes China's major role in the issue. China has served as a mediator between the United States and North Korea to bring about bilateral talks on the North's nuclear issue. In September 2009, Chinese State Councilor Dai Bingguo visited the North and confirmed that Kim Jong Il would be willing to join in bilateral and multilateral talks on the North's nuclear issue. In the next month, Chinese Premier Wen Jiabao met Kim Jong Il and was reassured that Kim Jong Il was "willing to attend multilateral talks, including the six-party talks, depending on the progress in its talks with the United States."[54] This was followed by the senior United States envoy's visit to Pyongyang in December 2009.[55] It shows that China and the U.S. tend to make cooperative approach to the issue within the Six-Party Talks.

However, it is equally important to note that the Six-Party Talks have not produced a remarkable achievement for denuclearizing North Korea. Rather, during the period of the Talks, the North could have time for developing its nuclear arsenal.[56] There are various factors affecting the failure of denuclearization of North Korea, such as the United States policy muddle for the nuclear issue, the North Korean regime's strong bid for nuclear weapons, and lack of commitment of both China and the United States for denuclearization of the North. Among these factors, the lack of commitment can be attributed to lack of efforts between China and the United States to narrow different interests in the North Korean issues during the Bush administration. In this respect, it is noteworthy that China and the United States recently have been seeking policy collaboration on the North Korean issues. Furthermore, China shows its support for bilateral talks between the North and the U.S. if it does not bypass the multilateral framework. The gist is that whether China and the U.S. make progress in building a multilateral framework for settling down bilateral strategic issues in Northeast Asia as well as North Korea depends on bilateral efforts to find out and form shared interests, ironing out differences in the perceived interests. On such an occasion, the Sino-U.S. coalitional approach to North Korean issues within the multilateral framework may open a road to the cooperative settlement of bilateral issues between the two states.

Competition: South Korea, the U.S. Forces Korea (USFK), and the U.S.-South Korea Alliance

South Korea is the venue for political and economic influence confrontations between China and the United States. South Korea is in the forefront of the United States' East Asian foreign policy and is where the United States has retained its military presence. As East Asia emerges as a world economic center, the United States sees its national interests in expanding its access to East Asian markets, maintaining its military force in the region. The aim of the United States force is to deter a rising China from being an East Asian hegemony and to promote democratic development of the regional states.[57] As an ally of the United States, South Korea plays a role in checking expanding China's influence in the region. As already mentioned, China has strategic interests in the political stability of the Korean Peninsula. As China rises as a great power and has to cope with the United States and its allies' collaborative efforts to check China's growing power, the strategic importance of South Korea increases.[58] In other words, the importance of relations with South Korea has grown as much as the importance of relations with the United States has increased.

South Korea is a traditional ally of the United States, while China and South Korea were enemies during the Cold War. The international environment of the post Cold War has fundamentally changed the political equation, however. China and South Korea normalized their relationship in 1992. Since the normalization, China has tried to strengthen the relationship with South Korea in order to enlarge its influence in the Korean Peninsula. In 2009, the two states' relationships in economics and politics became closer. China became South Korea's number one trade partner in 2009. China now maintains a strategic partnership with South Korea. The development of bilateral relationship can be attributed not only to increasing economic interdependence but also to Sino-U.S. competition over South Korea.

Relations between the United States and South Korea have fluctuated since the post-Cold War, even though the bottom-line of the U.S.-South Korea alliance has been untouched. While Japan made a strategic decision to strengthen its alliance with the United States based on the perception that a rising China would be a potential threat to Japanese interests in post-Cold War Northeast international relations, South Korea maintained the U.S.-South Korea alliance mainly to deter North Korean military adventure. South Korea had little concern about a rising China as a major source of future security threats. Rather, South Koreans recognized a "China opportunity." The rise of a neighboring great power, China, did not lead South Korea to take "balancing" measures by strengthening its alliance with the friendly great power, the United States, because South Korea's political leadership and people did not perceive the rising power as a serious threat.[59] Meanwhile, South Korean especially began to rethink the United States and U.S.-South Korean relations after the 1990s. Additionally, anti-Americanism increased in South Korea. South Koreans became concerned about the United States' hostile policy toward the North, which they feared could trigger military action in the Korean Peninsula and bring about disastrous results for Korea like those seen during the Korean War.[60] In particular, the Bush administration's unilateral approach to foreign policy and the war on Iraq raised the fear of war. Consequently, the South Korean government, especially during the Roh administration, distanced itself from the United States in areas such as the United States' approach to the North and its MD project. Simultaneously, South Korea sought "national coordination (*Minjok gongjo*)" with the North to promote South-North relations.[61] China appeared to welcome anti-Americanism in South Korea and the South Korean government's foreign policy,[62] because it indicated a decrease of United States influence and provided an opportunity for China to benefit in strategic terms and in terms of in its increasing influence in Korea.

A change of political leadership in 2008 was a turning point in South Korean foreign policy, however, which shifted toward reinforcing the U.S.-South Korea alliance and South Korea's relationship with Japan. The new administration radically changed South Korea's foreign policy implemented by the previous administration, executing a hard-line policy on the North. This policy shift resulted in a new alliance arrangement between the United States, Japan, and South Korea, and came to increase the United States' influence on the Korean Peninsula. This situation may well clash with China's strategic interests in the Peninsula.

The changing alliance arrangement against China also may lead China to rethink its position on a number of sensitive issues, such as the military presence of the United States in South Korea. China has tended to accept the United States military presence in South Korea, because that presence has contributed to deterring the military challenge and threat of North Korea. Likewise, it indirectly restrains the military potential of normalizing Japan, thus playing a crucial role in maintaining the status quo in Northeast Asian security. The United States presence could raise Chinese security concerns, however, because the United States Forces in Korea (USFK) could become the spearhead of possible United States action against China. The United States and South Korea have reached consensus regarding the flexibility of the USFK, "the USFK will be mobilized in case military conflicts occur in the Taiwan Strait."[63] Although the South Korean government simultaneously tried to strengthen its relations with China, the new alliance arrangement of U.S.-Japan-South Korea that was accompanied by an emerging U.S.-India-Australia alliance led Chinese leadership to be concerned about the United States and its allies' encirclement of China. China then reacted to the tightening United States encirclement by seeking the strengthening of relations with South Korea, India, South East Asian states, and Japan. It has committed to leveling the relationship with South Korea to that of a "strategic cooperative partnership." As the Obama administration emphasizes more engagement and collaboration with China, however, the client states' foreign policy behaviors—for example, South Korea's balancing behavior—is likely to have little importance to the relations of the great powers. In other words, while the great powers may be sensitive to the client states' behaviors when they are pitted against one another, they may be little concerned with them when they are engaging in collaborative relations.

In sum, the domestic political leaderships' foreign policy significantly affects Sino-U.S. competition over South Korea. U.S.-South Korea relations have been affected by the foreign policy a political leadership adopts. This, in turn, affected China's perception of the international environment and its strategy.

Coalition or Conflict: Korean Reunification

China and the United States have different interests regarding a reunified Korea. China would try to maintain its influence over a reunified Korea to ensure its own security. China's primary goal is to maintain the status quo of the divided Korea.[64] If reunification takes place, the most desirable outcome for China would be the establishment of a pro-Chinese regime. It seems that the United States does not want to see a radical change in the Korean Peninsula, either. It has been preparing for the possibility of a sudden change in the North, however. If the current North Korean regime collapses and the North becomes integrated into the South, the United States would try to establish a pro-American regime in the reunified Korea. It also would attempt to maintain its military presence in the Korean Peninsula. Despite the different outcomes desired by both sides, peace and stability are the primary goals for the both states, so it is possible that they can collaborate to reach solutions that will settle down the crisis. Therefore, whether the process of Korean reunification creates crisis and conflict or not depends on mainly Sino-U.S. relations. If Sino-U.S. relations remain characterized by competition, suspicion, and conflict, Korean reunification would create a high level of tension, because of the two nations' differing vital interests in the features of a reunified Korea.

For example, China has considered military intervention into North Korea in the case of a sudden collapse of the current North Korean regime. The Chinese action plans "include: 1) humanitarian missions such as assisting refugees or providing help after a natural disaster; 2) peacekeeping or "order keeping" missions such as serving as civil police; and 3) "environmental control" measures to clean up nuclear contamination resulting from a strike on North Korean nuclear facilities near the Sino-DPRK border and to secure nuclear weapons and fissile materials."[65] The action plan would face strong repercussions from South Korea, because South Korea would consider it a serious encroachment upon its national sovereignty. Under the conditions of a strong U.S.-South Korea alliance, acute conflicts between China and the U.S.-South Korea could arise over the North. South Korea rebuffed even the United States proposal of a "joint concept of operation plan (CONPLAN 5029)" for fear that it would limit South Korea's "sovereign prerogative in a crisis" in 2005.[66] Nonetheless, China would not be likely to abstain from taking action in the situation, given the fact that South Korea and the United States brought their alliance up to the level of "strategic alliance" in 2008. Under the strategic alliance, the tasks of the United States force in South Korea will not be limited to protecting the Korean Peninsula, but will expand to at least East Asia,[67] meaning that the alliance could threaten Chinese vital interests in the Taiwan Strait.

On the other hand, China and the United States may seek a coalitional approach to the possible sudden collapse of the North Korean regime and the issue of Korean reunification, if they shape a strategic partnership and do not consider the Korean Peninsula a venue where they have to engage in a zero-sum game. In this respect, it is a good sign that China and the United States have been making progress in bilateral relations, especially since the Obama administration took over. It is reported that China and the United States have been dealing with those issues in the U.S.-China Senior Dialogue, and now the S&ED, since the summer of 2009.[68] With a collaborative framework, the interested powers may eliminate or moderate an escalation of misperceptions of one another's intentions.[69] Furthermore, if the two poles of Northeast Asian international relations shape a non-zero-sum game over the issue of North Korea, a client state, such as South Korea, would have more incentive to seek collaborative solutions for managing and reducing tension in North Korea than to commit to balancing against China and thereby shaping a confrontational scheme.

The possibility of political crisis in North Korea increasingly looms large. There are various possible scenarios for political change in North Korea, including "managed succession, in which the top post transitions smoothly; "contested succession," in which government officials or factions fight for power after Kim's demise; and "failed succession," in which a new government cannot cement its legitimacy, possibly leading to North Korea's collapse."[70] Even though there may be differences in the impact of the shock on the political stability of the Korean Peninsula according to which direction the North will take, it surely will trigger serious tension in Sino-U.S. relations, as well as in Northeast Asian international politics. Whether the interested powers cope with the crisis collaboratively or not depends on the future direction of Sino-U.S. relations. Clearly, "[t]he United States and South Korea must coordinate with China based on mutual understandings of China's response to U.S.-ROK planning"[71] to avoid expansion of a crisis in the Korean Peninsula to North East Asia and beyond.

FROM STRUCTURAL REALISM TO NEOCLASSICAL REALISM AND BEYOND

International relations in the twenty-first century tend to revolve around Sino-U.S. relations. While international relations since the collapse of the Cold War have been characterized as "the uneasy juxtaposition of global unipolarity and regional multipolarity,"[72] it seems that a bipolar international system with the two poles of China and the United States is looming large in Northeast Asia and a global bipolarity may be emerging in the twenty-first century. The United States seems to take a rising China as a fait accompli. As for the evolving international system, defensive structural realists advise the hegemon—the United States—to seek a way to reach coexistence with the emerging great power—China. Offensive realists, on the other hand, warn about the dangerous potential of a rising China for the United States' hegemonic status. Power transition theorists propose that the time is ripe for rivalry between the United States and a rising China. In their view, a rising China will challenge the current international order in politics and economics and finally will try to rewrite the order set by the United States. It could bring about a hegemonic war. Debates continue regarding whether China is a revisionist or a status quo state, or whether China has both hard and soft power to use in challenging the United States. Empirical evidence shows that Sino-U.S. relations actually have fluctuated during the last two decades, affected by domestic factors like changes in the perceptions and worldviews of domestic political leadership. In other words, operational features and outcomes of an international system are substantially affected by domestic factors. The perceptions and worldviews of political leadership, that is, how a political leadership perceives a rival state and the world order, are at the center of the issue. Regarding this, it is meaningful to recall Alexander Wendt's remarkable thesis: "Anarchy is what states make of it."[73]

How have both China and the United States dealt with each other in the post Cold War international environment? Minxin Pei defines the United States strategy toward China since the 1990s as "hedging engagement," or "strategic hedging," which means that a containment strategy continues to be the bottom-line, but engagement continues. Meanwhile, according to Pei, China adopts a "hedged acquiescence" strategy toward the United States, whereby China has come to terms with the United States foreign policies as far as they do not encroach on China's vital interests, such as the Taiwan issue.[74] However, the United States strategy has fluctuated according to political leadership, and the pendulum of foreign strategy has swung back and forth between "engagement" and "containment." While the Clinton administration implemented its policy toward China emphasizing the United States' relationship with China as that of "strategic partner," the Bush administration treated China as a "strategic competitor." Furthermore, the primary task of United States foreign policy during the Bush administration was to maintain its hegemonic status and consolidate the international order set by the United States.[75] This stance was based on the administration's confidence in the superiority of the United States' values, such as freedom and democracy. The problem with this position was that the United States leadership did not tend to regard different political systems acceptable. This came to confine the United States foreign policy toward non-liberal democracies, because differences in values limit "the quality of interactions," which "gives rise to a 'trust deficit."[76]

With regard to Sino-U.S. relations, this perception led to a tendency to highlight differences between China and the United States, rather than to emphasize common interests. This situation has been accompanied by the strengthening of the U.S.-Japan alliance and the expansion of the alliance to include other liberal states, such as Australia and India. In particular, it was reinforced in 2008 with the reinvigoration of the U.S.-South Korea alliance as the new administration of South Korea reemphasized the importance of the U.S.-South Korea alliance, including Japan. A competitive arrangement between China and the United States alliance was, thereby, shaped, although the states involved in the arrangement apparently tried to emphasize the importance of engagement with China and to deny the doubt about the alliance raised by China. Regardless of the real intentions of the United States alliance, it surely generated Chinese suspicion. Suspicion or a "trust deficit" does matter, because it can substantially reduce the scope and range of cooperation and, at the same time, increase tensions between China and the United States. It should be noted, however, that the United States alliance arrangement exhibits signs of cracking as the new Obama administration, which has views of the world order and China that are different from those of the previous administration, seeks coexistence with a rising China.

In this regard, it can be said that the two poles' relations substantially affect the alliance arrangements of China and the United States, because the client states tend to make their strategic decisions based on the given international system and the assumed competitive scheme between the two larger nations. Currently, Japan's new cabinet is making efforts to open a new phase in that nation's relations with China. Even though the Japanese new foreign policy can be attributed to the new leadership's perspective on international relations that emphasizes its relations with China and Asia, the Japanese political leadership was dismayed, fearing Japan would not be taken seriously by Obama administration. Similarly, the South Korean government, in light of changing Sino-U.S. relations, has to follow a more coalitional strategy with China than before to manage the North Korean issues and to ensure its own security. This is necessary, because South Korea's strategic leverage is likely to be lessened in the context of Sino-U.S. competition. All interested powers tend to seek cooperation, rather than competition, with a rising China, so that any competition which exists is reduced or moderate competitive competition. An international system of regional bipolarity between China and the United States may exhibit different operational features according to domestic political leaderships and their perceptions.

Evolving Sino-U.S. relations are clearly seen in the Korean Peninsula, where the two powers come into direct contact. Due to their shared strategic interests in the North's nuclear program, the two powers have utilized a multilateral approach to that issue. China did not play a significant role in dealing with the issue during the 1990s, partially because it did not trust the United States intentions, and therefore took a defensive position, regarding it as a bilateral matter between the United States and North Korea. During the Bush administration, China began to take part in the issue, leading the Six Party Talks. Nevertheless, it failed to settle the issue. It did nothing but allow the North to make progress in its nuclear program. On one hand, this can be attributed to the Bush administration's strategic muddle in dealing with the North, [77] and on the other hand, the Chinese strategic interest in maintaining a status quo in the North. Altogether, it resulted in a weak level of collaboration between the two powers. It is important to note that the different interests of China and the United States in the future direction of the Northern regime restrained them from making more collaborative efforts. China wants neither the North Korean regime to abruptly collapse nor the Korean Peninsula to be reunified under a pro-American regime. Without assurance that a reunified Korea will not be a potential threat, China cannot choose other than to protect the current North Korean regime from the United States and pro-American South Korea. This issue, therefore, can generate acute conflicts, even including military action, between the United States and China. Simultaneously, China may seek resolution of the North Korean issue with the United States, if the United States ensures that a reunified Korea will never be a threat to China. A collaborative approach will contribute to a moderation of tensions regarding the North Korea issues, including the nuclear program. How can the two nations build cooperative relations and get beyond the vicious cycle caused by suspicion and lack of trust? It requires trust building between the two powers to reach a strategic partnership. The two powers recent move toward "trust building" with the S&ED is a positive sign. Furthermore, the Six Party Talks have potential for evolving into a multilateral institution for Northeast Asian international relations. Consequently, the future direction of Sino-U.S. relations may depend more on the perceptions and will of both sides' political leadership, than to the changing material powers of each and the formation of a balance of power in the international system.

NOTES

1. Mieko Kawashima, "Hatoyama unveils Asia-focused foreign policy," *The Daily Yomiuri*, http://www.yomiuri.co.jp/dy/national/20091116TDY01303.htm
2. "Chimerica" refers to symbiotic economic relationships between China and the United States. For more details, see Niall Ferguson and Moritz Schularick, " 'Chimerica' and global asset markets," *International Finance* 10, no. 3 (2007): 215-239.
3. For the democratic peace theory, see Bruce Russett and John Oneal, *Triangulating Peace* (New York: Norton, 2001); John Oneal and Bruce Russett, "The Kantian Peace: The Pacific Benefits of Democracy, Interdependence, and International Organizations, 1885-1992," *World Politics* 52, no.1 (1999): 1-37.
4. John J. Mearsheimer, *The Tragedy of Great Power Politics* (New York: WW Norton, 2001).
5. Zbigniew Brzezinski and John J. Mearsheimer, "Clash of the Titans," *Foreign Policy* 146, (January/February 2005): 47.
6. Kenneth N. Waltz, *Realism and International Politics* (New York and London: Routledge, 2008).
7. Kenneth N. Waltz, *Realism and International Politics*, pp. 221-222.
8. Robert S. Ross, "The Geography of Peace: East Asia in the Twenty-First Century," in Michael E. Brown et al., eds., *The Rise of China*, (Cambridge: The MIT Press, 2000), pp. 167-204.
9. Robert Gilpin, *War and Change in World Politics* (Cambridge: Cambridge University Press, 1981); A.F.K. Organski and Jacek Kugler, *The War Ledger* (Univ. of Chicago Press 1980).
10. Brian Efird, Jacek Kugler, and Gaspare M. Genna, "From War to Integration: Generalizing Power Transition Theory," *International Interactions* 29 (2003): 293-313.
11. The indicators are consisted of participation rates in international institutions, degree of compliance with international norms, behavior toward the rules of the game, revisionist behavior, and the distribution of power. See Alastair Iain Johnston, "Is China a Status Quo Power?" *International Security* 27, no. 4 (2003): 5-56.
12. Ibid.
13. Steve Chan, *China, the U.S., and the Power-Transition Theory: A Critique* (New York and London: Routledge, 2008).
14. Steve Chan, *China, the U.S., and the Power-Transition Theory: A Critique*, p. 122.
15. Samuel S. Kim, "Northeast Asia in the Local – Regional – Global Nexus: Multiple Challenges and Contending Explanations," in Samuel S. Kim, ed., *The International Relations of Northeast Asia* (Lanham: Rowman & Littlefield Publishers, 2004), pp. 3-61.
16. Ibid.

17. The SOC in some sense is said to be China's strategic reaction to the United States' encirclement of China.

18. Alastair Iain Johnston, "Is China a Status Quo Power?" *International Security* 27:4 (2003): 5-56.

19. Thomas G. Moore, "Racing to integrate, or cooperating to compete? Liberal and realist interpretations of China's new multilateralism," in Guoguang Wu and Helen Lansdowne, eds., *China Turns to Multilateralism* (New York: Routledge, 2008), pp. 35-50.

20. Avery Goldstein, "Power Transitions, Institutions, and China's Rise in East Asia: Theoretical Expectations and Evidence," *Journal of Strategic Studies* 30, no. 4-5 (August-October. 2007): 651-52.

21. Douglas Lemke and William Reed, "Regime Types and Status Quo Evaluations." *International Interactions* 22, no. 2 (1996): 143–164.

22. John Ikenberry, "The Rise of China and the Future of the West," *Foreign Affairs* 87, no. 1 (January/February 2008): 23-37.

23. David Kang, "Hierarchy and Stability in Asian International Relations," in John Ikenberry and Michael Mastunduno, eds., *International Relations Theory and the Asia-Pacific* (New York: Columbia University Press, 2003), pp. 163-189.

24. John Lewis Gaddis, "Drawing Lines: The Defensive Perimeter Strategy in East Asia, 1947-1951," in *The Long Peace: Inquiries Into the History of the Cold War* (New York: Oxford University Press, 1989), pp. 72-104.

25. Odd A. Westad, "Introduction," in Odd A. Westad, ed., *Brothers in Arms: The Rise and Fall of the Sino-Soviet Alliance, 1945-1963* (Stanford: Stanford University Press, 1998), pp. 5-32.

26. Yuen Foong Khong, *Analogies at War: Korea, Munich, Dien Bien Phu, and the Vietnam Decisions of 1965* (Princeton: Princeton University Press, 1992), pp. 72-96; pp. 174-205.

27. Douglas Lemke and William Reed (1996).

28. Robert S. Ross, "The Geography of Peace: East Asia in the Twenty-First Century," in Michael E. Brown et al., eds., *The Rise of China* (Cambridge: The MIT Press, 2000), pp. 167-204.

29. Jason T. Shaplen and James Laney, "Washington's Eastern Sunset: The Decline of U.S. Power in Northeast Asia," *Foreign Affairs* 86, no. 6 (November/December 2007).

30. Avery Goldstein, "Power Transitions, Institutions, and China's Rise in East Asia: Theoretical Expectations and Evidence," p. 659.

31. Some Chinese scholars expect that transforming the U.S.-South Korean alliance to one allowing South Korea greater autonomy would contribute to regional stability because South Korea would oppose the use of United States forces to intervene in the regional dispute. The South Korean government would object to the U.S. hard-line policy against North Korea. See Guo Xiangang, "Hanmei tongmeng xunqiu xindingwei [the U.S.-South Korean Alliance Seeking New Relations]," Guojiwentiyanjiu [International Studies], 3(2006), pp.28-32.

32. Shambaugh, "China Engages Asia," *International Security* 29, no. 3 (Winter 2004/2005): 90.

33. William Tow et al., "Assessing the Trilateral Strategic Dialogue," NBR Special Repot #16, December 2008, http://www.nbr.org/publications/specialreport/ pdf/SR16.pdf.

34. Ministry of Foreign Affairs of Peoples' Republic of China, 6 September, 2007. http://www.fmprc.gov.cn/chn/gxh/mtb/fyrbt/t359430.htm.

35. Ministry of Foreign Affairs of Peoples' Republic of China, Foreign Ministry Spokesperson Qin Gang's Regular Press Conference on May 27, 2008, http://www.fmprc.gov.cn/eng/xwfw/s2510/2511/t459519.htm.

36. At the China-South Korea symposium on "Regional Security in Northeast Asia," Chinese scholars and commentators raised concerns about South Korean new administration's policy consideration for joining the U.S. Missile Defense system while Korean asserted that it would not be against China but for protecting South Korea from North Korean nuclear ballistic missiles. See Korea-China Think Net, "Regional Security in Northeast Asia and Korea-China Strategic Cooperation," the Eighth Conference of Korea-China Think Net (Seoul: Korea-China Think Net, 2008), pp. 53-68.

37. The strategic principles for the Obama administration's foreign policy can be read in "A Phoenix Initiative Report." The report emphasizes 'international cooperation' rather than unilateral enforcement of U.S. strategic interests in other states. For more information, see "A Phoenix Initiative Report" at http://www.brookings.edu/~/ media/ Files/rc/reports/2008/07_national_security_brainard/07_national_security_brainard.pdf.

38. For example, the United States promoted Sino-U.S. ties, convening the first annual joint Strategic and Economic Dialogue (S&ED), July 2009. It upgraded the Sino-U.S. dialogue to the level of strategic meetings. The Obama administration initiated it in order to strengthen the Sino-U.S. cooperative partnership. On November 14, Obama said that "[T]he United States is not threatened by a rising China, but will seek to strengthen its ties with Beijing even as it maintains close ties with traditional allies like Japan." http://www.nytimes.com/2009/11/14/world/asia/ 14prexy.html

39. Hiroshi Nakanishi, "Will Obama's promise of change include U.S.-Japan relations?" *The Japan Times*, January 1, 2009, http://search.japantimes.co.jp/cgi-bin/ eo20090101 a1.html

40. After the Cold War bipolarity broke down, Northeast Asian states came to be more concerned about a precarious security environment. States began to engage in an arms race and border disputes over natural resources have loomed large. On the contrary, there has been little progress in building multilateral frameworks for promoting regional cooperation. Japan has reinforced its strategic relationship with the U.S. since the mid-1990s, strengthening the strategic alliance with the U.S. see Thomas Berger, "Japan's International Relations: The Political and Security Dimensions," in Samuel S. Kim, ed., *The International Relations of Northeast Asia* (New York: Rowman & Littlefield Publishers, 2004), pp. 135-170.

41. http://www.washingtonpost.com/wp-dyn/content/article/2009/11/27/AR2009112 701 388.html?wprss=rss_world/wires.

42. More specifically, the domestic factors consist of: political orientation and the vision of political leadership toward international relations, foreign policy decision-makers' perception of a rival state and its policy intention, and economic and political conditions.

43. Joshua Kurlantzick, "Broken Promises: Bush's Shameful Record on Combating Human Rights Abuses in China", dated 12 May 2008. Available from *The New Republic*, http://www.tnr.com/article/politics/broken-promises.

44. For the "Grand Strategy," see Michael D. Swaine and Ashley J. Tellis, Interpreting China's Grand Strategy: Past, Present, and Future (Santa Monica, CA: RAND, 2000). For Chinese perception on the international environment, see Yang Chengxu, ed., *Zhongguo zhoubian anquan huanjing toushi[Assessing China's International Environment]* (Beijing: Zhongguo qingnian chubanshe, 2003), p. 36.

45. Zhu Feng, "China's Rise Will Be Peaceful: How Unipolarity Matters," in Robert S. Ross and Zhu Feng, eds., China's Ascent: Power: Power, Security, and The Future of International Politics (Ithaca, NY: Cornell University Press, 2008), pp. 34-54; Wang Jisi, China's Changing Role in Asia (Washington, D.C.: Atlantic Council of the United States, January 2004), pp. 1-17.

46. Zhu Feng, "China's Rise Will Be Peaceful: How Unipolarity Matters," pp. 45-49.

47. Alastair Iain Johnston, "Is China a Status Quo Power?"

48. Shi Yinhong, "China and the North Korean nuclear problem," in Guoguang Wu and Helen Lansdowne, eds., China Turns to Multilateralism (Abingdon, Oxon; New York: Routledge, 2008), p. 91.

49. Cui Zhiying, "Meichao guanxi gaishan dui dongbeiya jushide yingxiang," Zhongguo yu Shijie Gongtongliyide Haodong, Shanghai Shehui kexieyuan shijiejingji yu zhengzhi yanjiuyuan, ed. (Beijing: Shishichubanshe, 2008), p. 309.

50. Paul B. Stares and Joel S. Wit, "Preparing for Sudden Change in North Korea," Council Special Report No. 42, Council on Foreign Relations, pp. 6-7., www.cfr.org/content/publications/attachments/North_Korea_CSR42.pdf.

51. Avery Goldstein, "Power Transitions, Institutions, and China's Rise in East Asia: Theoretical Expectations and Evidence," Journal of Strategic Studies 30 (2007), p. 661.

52. Shi Yinhong, "China and the North Korean Nuclear Problem," in Guoguang Wu, ed., China Turns to Multilateralism (New york: Routledge, 2007), p. 93.

53. David Goullist, "Clinton Backs Six-Party Talks for Ending North Korean Nuclear Program," Voice of America, January 14, 2008, www.voanews.com/ english/ 2009-01-14-voa2.cfm

54 . "Preparing for Sudden Change in North Korea," http://news.bbc.co.uk/2/hi/8373567.stm

55 . "Senior US envoy Bosworth begins talks in North Korea," http://news.bbc.co.uk/2/hi/asia-pacific/8400739.stm.

56. The U.S. Joint Forces Command included North Korea in a list of nuclear weapons states in a report released on December 4, 2008. See U.S. Joint Forces Command, "The Joint Operating Environment 2008, http://www.jfcom.mil/newslink/storyarchive/2008/JOE2008.pdf.

57. The White House, "The National Security Strategy for the United States of America," http://www.whitehouse.gov/nsc/nss/2006/nss2006.pdf.

58. Avery Goldstein, "Power Transitions, Institutions, and China's Rise in East Asia: Theoretical Expectations and Evidence," p. 661.

59 . Dong-ryul Lee, "Hankuk jeongchi kwankye-ui jaengjum-kwa kwaje" [Issues of China-South Korea relations], in Sung-Heung Chun and Jong-Hwa Lee, eds., The Rise of China: Its Implications for East Asia and Korean-Chinese Relations (Seoul: ORUEM Publishing House, 2008), pp. 242-244.

60. Yang-Sup Shim, 2008, Hankuk ui Banmi [Anti-Americanism in South Korea], Seoul: Hanul, pp. 133-136.

61. Yang-Sup Shim, 2008, Hankuk ui Banmi [Anti-Americanism in South Korea], pp. 137-144.

62. Wang Sheng, "Hanguo shumeiqinzhong xianxiang pouxi"[Analysis on Estranged Relationship between South Korea and the U.S. and Strengthening Relationship between South Korea and China], Dongbeiya luntan, 2 (2006), pp. 87-92; Cui liru, "Chaoxian bandao anquan wenti" [Problem of Security in Korean Peninsular], Xiandai guoji guanxi, 9 (2006), pp. 44-45.

63. Chul-kee Lee, "Strategic Flexibility of U.S. Forces in Korea," Policy Forum Online, 2006, http://www.nautilus.org/fora/security/0619Lee.html.

64. For China's policy calculus toward the North Korean regime, see David Shambaugh, "China and Korean Peninsula: Playing for the Long Term," Washington Quarterly 26, no.2 (2003): 44-45.

65. Bonnie Glaser, Scott Snyder, John S. Park, "Keeping an Eye on an Unruly Neighbor: Chinese Views of Economic Reform and Stability in North Korea," United States Institute of Peace Working Paper (January 3, 2008): 19.

66. Paul B. Stares and Joel S. Wit, "Preparing for Sudden Change in North Korea," Council Special Report No. 42, Council on Foreign Relations, pp. 7-8., www.cfr.org/content/publications/attachments/North_Korea_CSR42.pdf.

67. Sung-Han Kim, "Jeonsi jakjeon tongje gwon jeonhwan kwa han-mi dongmaeng ui kwaje" [Wartime Operation Control Plan and ROK-U.S. Alliance], in Hankukhayang Yeonguso, ed., *Hanbando Jubyeonkuk Jeonse-wa Hankuk-ui Anjeonbojang* [International Environment over Korean Peninsula and South Korea Security] (Seoul: Hankukhayang Yeonguso, 2009), pp. 240-283.

68. "North Korea Contingency Planning and U.S.-ROK Cooperation," Center for U.S.-Korea Policy, The Asia Foundation, www.nautilus.org/fora/security/09089 TAF.pdf.

69. It is reported that, in October 2009, the Center for Strategic and International Studies (CSIS) that is one of American research institute and China Institutes of Contemporary International Relations (CICIR) jointly held a closed seminar of which the topic was possible action plan for sudden change in North Korea. Government officials from both states participated in the seminar. It can contribute to deepening mutual understanding over the North Korean issues and reducing possible misperception each other. Meanwhile, South Korean government reacted against it because South Korea was excluded from the joint seminar between China and the United States. See "Mi-Jung, Pukhan keupbyunsatae nonui" [U.S.-China dialogue on sudden change in North Korea], *Yonhap News*, 20 October (2009), http://www.yonhapnews.co.kr/bulletin/2009/10/20/0200000000AKR 20091020083100043.HTML?did=1179m.

70. Paul B. Stares and Joel S. Wit, "Preparing for Sudden Change in North Korea," Council Special Report No. 42 (January 2009), p. vii, http://www.cfr.org/content/ publications/attachments/North_Korea_CSR42.pdf.

71. Paul B. Stares and Joel S. Wit, "Preparing for Sudden Change in North Korea," p. 17.

72. Samuel S. Kim, "Northeast Asia in the Local—Regional— Global Nexus: Multiple Challenges and Contending Explanations."

73. Alexander Wendt, "Anarchy is what states make of it: The social construction of power politics," *International Organization* 46 (spring 1992): 391-425.

74. Minxin Pei, "China's Hedged Acquiescence: Coping with U.S. Hegemony," in Byung-Kook Kim and Anthony Jones., eds., *Power and Security in Northeast Asia: Shifting Strategies* (London: Lynne Rienner Publishers, 2007), pp. 100-101.

75. Norman Ornstein, "The Legacy of Campaign 2000," *The Washington Quarterly* 24, no. 2 (2001): 99-105.

76. Richard. Armitage & J. Nye, "The U.S.-Japan Alliance: Getting Asia Right Through 2020" (February, 2007), p. 4. The report continues to say that "In the case of China, there is a growing body of evidence suggesting that the nexus between values and foreign policy could negatively affect U.S. interests. This is manifest in China's behavior toward countries like Iran, Sudan, Venezuela, Zimbabwe, and Uzbekistan. It is evident that China is engaged in relationship building, which may enable continued irresponsible behavior on the part of other governments." http://www.csis.org/media/ csis/pubs/070216_asia2020.pdf.

77. See Hazel Smith, "Bad, Mad, Sad or Rational Actor? Why the Securitization Paradigm Makes for Poor Policy Analysis of North Korea," *International Affairs* 76, no.3 (2000): 111-132.

Chapter 5

A Complex Interdependence: China-U.S. Relations

Pei-Shan Kao

DEBATES ON CHINA-U.S. RELATIONS: WHAT KIND OF RELATIONSHIP?

The year 2009 is the 30th anniversary of normalization of China-U.S. relations. Since President Carter claimed on April 11, 1978 that establishing diplomatic relations with China accorded with U.S. national interests, China-U.S. relations entered into a new period. The United States and China then established diplomatic relations on January 1, 1979. As Robert G. Sutter indicated, the evolution of U.S.-China relations vividly demonstrated that strategic factors had occupied the most important role in bringing about Sino-American rapprochement. For China, establishing diplomatic relations with the United States not only provided a guarantee against Soviet domination and ended American efforts to contain China, but also could enhance China's international influence. Moreover, Chinese leaders believed that "diplomatic recognition by the United States would speed the flow of Western and Japanese capital, which China desperately needed to foster economic modernization."[1] For the United States, cooperation with China could maintain a balance of power in East Asia, which accorded with American interests. In addition, it provided the United States with "an important source of international leverage in its ongoing competition with the Soviet Union."[2] This kind of "strategic needs" link China and the United States and promote the development of China-U.S. relations.

However, in the past thirty years, the relationship between China and the United States has encountered with many challenges and difficulties. Many disputes and crises on trade, human rights, and security issues had negative impact on the relationship hence made it fall into a low point. Realists therefore predicted that a war would occur soon between China and the United States. Realists claimed that the United States and China could not and would not develop a good relationship based on power politics theory. Realists argued that

China's being a rising power and one of the four remaining socialist countries made it become Americans' first target. Their views particularly caused response after the occurrence of the Tiananmen Square incident when China-U.S. relations reached a low point. Among the realist arguments, the theory of a "China Threat" has caused the most attention and has had important influence in the United States.[3] The theory of China Threat appeared in the beginning of the 1990s claiming that China was a rising power and represented a source of regional and international instability due to the rapid development of the Chinese economy since 1978 (growth averaging 9.9 percent per year); the authoritarian political system; China's growing military strength accompanied by intensified territorial disputes with some neighbors (the South China Sea) and the confrontation with Taiwan. In addition, the Chinese government's fear of a political and economic collapse all prevented it from maintaining a good relationship with America hence making it become an unstable factor for the stability of world politics. However, although many disputes and arguments happened between them in the past thirty years, no conflict and war was fought between the two. Conversely, their relations have gradually progressed into a positive direction and have become more and more interdependent. There have been more and more bilateral trade, economic, cultural, governmental or even military contacts and exchanges progressed between China and the United States. That is, the realists' predictions actually did not realize.

Differing from Realists' emphasis on power politics and these pessimistic views on the future development of U.S.-China relations, liberals also rejected optimistic views based on the democratic peace thesis. According to the democratic peace thesis, democratic states are more peaceful than non-democratic states and democratic states do not fight with one another. For Michael Doyle, the major reason for democratic peace is that democratic governments have to be responsible to their citizens, and if a war becomes too costly, they will lose elections.[4] Meanwhile, in a democratic state such as the United States, since the procedure of foreign decision-making regarding war is transparent, and people are as sensitive as the decision makers to the cost of war, they can debate publicly and influence governmental policy directly. In addition, Doyle considers that there is a common desire to resolve conflicts peacefully among democratic countries; this common belief requires they coordinate their relations through respect and cooperation to expand contacts. This common desire then causes finally the production of common interests.[5] Since the actions of national decision makers are supervised and constrained by people and legislature, they have to consider the cost of using military force; that is the reason why democracies rarely fight each other, and that is why liberals advocate democracy. The United States and China pertain to different polities, political institutions and societal structures. However, although there have been a number of crises and problems happened between the United States and China since the end of the Cold War, war has never occurred in their relations. In serious crises and incidents such as the cases of the Belgrade bombing and the spy plane, the two countries did not use force to resolve the problems. Conversely, by means of bargaining and consultations, they resolved their disputes peacefully. Since the end of the Cold War, not only has peace been maintained in this relationship; the two countries have close and highly interdependent economic and trade relations. The democratic peace thesis apparently has its problems to explain the development of U.S.-China relations.

The pessimistic predictions and viewpoints suggested by realists' power politics and the democratic peace thesis seemed to be unable to provide a satisfactory explanation for the long peace. If power politics and the democratic peace thesis cannot be used to explain the peaceful coexistence between China and the United States since the end of the Vietnam War, how about the theory of complex interdependence? Can we apply complex interdependence to explain the development of China-U.S. relations? This chapter therefore intends to examine the development of China-U.S. relations in the past thirty years and conclude with a discussion of the influence and effect of complex interdependence to China-U.S. relations. We will also use the findings of this research to predict an optimistic future development of this relationship.

THEORY OF COMPLEX INTERDEPDENCE

Complex interdependence—the basic and important research framework in Robert Keohane and Joseph Nye's work—is an analytical model proposed by Keohane and Nye in *Power and Interdependence*, which is used to describe an ideal type of world politics and to challenge the realist assumptions. It describes "a world in which actors other than states participate directly in world politics, in which a clear hierarchy of issues does not exist, and in which force is an ineffective instrument of policy."[6] As a result of the deep development of interdependence in international relations, Keohane and Nye intend to construct a new hypothetic model that is completely different to that of Realism. Although they emphasize that the model of complex interdependence they suggested is merely an ideal type, they claim that it increasingly corresponds to reality in many parts of the world. Their ideal type of complex interdependence emphasizes three basic concepts: (a) the development of multiple channels connecting societies, which can be inter-state, transgovernmental, and transnational; (b) the absence of hierarchy among issues, which means that military security does not consistently dominate the agenda; and (c) the minor role of military force. These three basic concepts with regard to complex interdependence are the most important components to the theory of interdependence based on the two basic characteristics—sensitivity and vulnerability. They can also be seen as reflecting the new progress interdependence theory made in the late 1970s and early 1980s.

According to Keohane and Nye, contemporary world politics are characterized by the following features: (1) Multiple Channels Connecting Societies—these channels include informal ties between governmental elites or formal foreign office arrangements, informal ties among nongovernmental elites, and transnational organizations. These communication channels help states to talk and exchange views and opinions. (2) Absence of Hierarchy among Issues—As the agenda of interstate relationships comprises multiple issues which are not arranged in a clear or consistent hierarchy, military security no longer dominates the agenda. Any issues can be discussed on states' agenda. (3) Minor Role of Military Force—When complex interdependence prevails, governments will not use military force toward other governments within the region or on the issues although force may be important in these governments' relations with governments outside that region, or on other issues. Following with close contacts and interdependence among industrialized and pluralist states, states' fears of being attacked have declined. The role of military force has decreased and force is no longer an instrument of policy. The fact of the matter is that the application of force is both costly and uncertain in most situations although Keohane and Nye do not completely reject the role of military force. In an interdependent world, the recourse to force is less likely than employing force on one issue against an independent state with which one has a variety of relationships because it may rupture mutually profitable relations on other issues. That is to say, the use of force often has costly effects on non-security goals; therefore, even authoritarian countries may be reluctant to employ force to obtain economic objectives. This hence implies that when states' relations are complex interdependent, war is unlikely to happen. Moreover, the likelihood of states' cooperation can be increased as complex interdependence provides an environment where helps sates to negotiate and resolve their problems.

This study argues that the development of China-U.S. relations accord with the assumptions of complex interdependence. The main three characteristics can be easily found in this relationship, namely, the relations are pretty closer to the ideal world of complex interdependence. And that is the reason why peace can be maintained in the relations. This chapter therefore intends to demonstrate, firstly, that China-U.S. relations do develop and progress towards complex interdependence. That is, this study will examine the development of China-U.S. economic, social and governmental relations since 1989 and discuss the effect and influence of complex interdependence to the relationship.

CHINA-U.S. INTERDEPDENT ECONOMIC AND TRADE RELAITONS

Economic and trade relations are the most important aspects of China-U.S. relations as they are the major factors that strengthen the development of bilateral relations. When the United States and China established diplomatic relations in 1979, they signed a trade agreement granting each other the most-favoured-nation (MFN) status; subsequently, the two-way trade developed and grew rapidly. China has taken important actions to open its foreign trading system and integrate itself into the world trading system. China now is world's third-largest economy after the United States and Japan with a nominal GDP of \$3.5 trillion (2007) when measured in exchange rate terms.[7] It is also now world's third-largest trading nation with \$2.17 trillion in imports and exports, following the USA and Germany.[8] According to American statistics, the bilateral trade increased sharply from $17.8 billion in 1989 to $386.7 billion in 2007;[9] it grew nearly 22 times. China-US two-way trade accounted for 17.7 percent of China's total trade amount. The United States now is China's largest trading partner. The United States is also the largest export market for China, and its fourth-largest import supplier.

For the United States, China is America's third-largest export market and also the fastest growing export market of the United States. In 2001, U.S. exports to China were $19.2 billion, it then rose to $65.2 billion in 2007; the percentage change between 2001 and 2007 was 240 percent.[10] Moreover, China has passed Canada and has become the United States' biggest import supplier. The United States chiefly exports electrical machinery, transportation equipment, and metalliferous ores, etc., to China (See Table 5.1). China mainly exports electrical machinery, apparel, telecommunication equipment, and office machines to the United States as Table 5.2 shows. This also indicates that China has gradually shifted its export structure from labor-intensive products such as textiles, shoes, and toys to capital-intensive goods. Although the bilateral trade did serve American interests and support China's development strategy, China has become the U.S.'s largest deficit trading partner. This deficit sharply increased and exceeded $266.3 billion in 2008,[11] making it a serious political issue in China-U.S. relations. Americans therefore criticized that the huge deficit was caused by China's unfair trade practices, and that is why trade issues are considered the most important but sensitive issues in China-U.S. relations.

China-U.S. trade reached a particularly high level of growth during two periods, the years after 1979, when they established formal diplomatic relations, and during the post-Cold War era. Although American and Chinese statistical data do not match completely, both sets of trading statistics indicate that the bilateral trade developed in a positive direction. All the data indicate that China-U.S. economic and trade relations have developed substantially, and quite harmoniously, in the post-Cold War era. China is a major and important source of consumer goods and cheap products for the United States, whilst America is China's major provider of important resources and equipment. The preponderance of American high-technology plays an indispensable role in China's modernization.

In addition to trade exchange, significantly American investment in China also increased sharply. After China adopted its "Open Door" policy in 1978, it received a huge amount of foreign direct investment (FDI) during the 1980s. Following the opening of China's market and economic reforms, foreign investors were allowed to manufacture and sell a wide range of goods in China and establish wholly foreign-owned enterprises. Nowadays half of China's exports are produced by foreign-invested enterprises. Foreign direct investment has played an important role in China's domestic economy and export-led economic sectors. In 2003, China became the biggest recipient of FDI in the world.[12] In 2005, China received another $60 billion, making for a cumulative total of $623.8 billion.[13] FDI in China in 2007 was $75 billion;[14] it then increased to $92.4 billion in 2008 according to Chinese Ministry of

Commerce.[15]   According to the same source, the recent increase in foreign investment chiefly flows to the Chinese service sector which attracted $38.12 billion of FDI.

Table 5.1 Top U.S. Exports to China 2007

Electrical machinery and equipment
Power generation equipment
Air and spacecraft
Oil seeds and oleaginous fruits
Plastics and articles thereof
Optics and medical equipment
Iron and steel
Copper and articles thereof
Organic chemicals
Pulp and paperboard

Source: The US-China Business Council,
http://www.uschina.org/statistics/tradetable.html, consulted in March 2009

Table 5.2 Top U.S. Imports from China 2007

Electrical machinery and equipment
Power generation equipment
Toys and games
Apparel
Furniture
Footwear and parts thereof
Iron and steel
Plastics and articles thereof
Leather and travel goods
Vehicles other than railway

Source: The US-China Business Council,
http://www.uschina.org/statistics/tradetable.html, consulted in March 2009.

Among the major investors, the United States is China's major investor country since 1979. The cumulative realized amount of U.S. investment in China was $57.13 billion since 1979 till January 2008,[16] ranking the second biggest investor of China after Japan.

All the data indicate that China-U.S. economic and trade relations have developed substantially, and quite harmoniously, in the post-Cold War era. Not only is China's immense market attractive to U.S. enterprises, as U.S. investment in China grows steeply, but also Chinese enterprises now try to enter into the American market. Since the rise of China's economy, China initiated a "Go Global" policy in 2000; this enhanced its economic relations with the United States. According to the Chinese Chamber of Commerce in the United States, by the end of December 2002, China invested $720 million in the United States; constituting 9 percent of China's total investment abroad. 681 Chinese companies were permitted by the Chinese government to do business there.[17] Chinese-invested companies mainly have been concentrated in New York, followed by Los Angeles, San Francisco, Chicago, Houston and Seattle. The majority of Chinese enterprises focus on selling manufactured products. Since the global financial crisis, China has emerged as a major investor in the world, particularly in mineral and energy resources. In 2007, China's outward FDI was $18.6 billion; it then rose 1.8 times to $52.2 billion in 2008.[18]

To conclude, China is a major and important source of consumer goods and cheap electronic products for the United States, whilst America is China's major provider of important resources and equipment. The preponderance of American capital and high-technology has played an indispensable role in China's modernization. Following China's formal accession to the World Trade Organization (WTO) in December 2001, it has gradually opened its insurance, banking, telecommunications and services markets. This certainly will enhance and promote further the development of China-U.S. bilateral trade and investment. Although some disputes arise from close trade contact and exchange, such as protection of intellectual property rights and textile problems, economic interdependence does alleviate political tensions and strengthen the development of China-U.S. relations.

ACTIVE SOCIAL AND CULTURAL EXCHANGE

In addition to changes in economic and trade contacts, social indicators also show that China and the United States have developed and advanced an extensive relationship since the end of the Cold War. Statistics such as numbers of exchange students, tourists or levels of transportation links can tell us whether social and cultural exchange is closer and more active now than before. First of all, on bilateral tourist exchange, according to American statistics, in 1990 there were only 624,000 journeys made by Americans to China. However, this level grew nearly two times to 1,181,000 in 1995, and totaled 1,476,000 in 2000.[19] The percentage increase over ten years, namely from 1990-2000, is 136 percent, and the annual growth rate is 9.0 percent. In 2000, China ranked seventh amongst foreign countries visited by Americans. In 2006, there were 1,327,000 U.S. residents travelling to China;[20] China ranked as the tenth destination for U.S. travelers. The positive growing trend also reflects on Chinese travelling to the United States. In 1990 there were 229,000 trips made by Chinese to the United States.[21] This increased to 387,000 five years later, and totaled 453,000 in 2000. China ranked, in 2002, fifteenth amongst countries travelling to the

United States. The numbers of Chinese tourists nearly grew two times within ten years. The annual growth rate is 7.0 percent. In 2008, there were 493,000 Chinese visitors to the United States.[22] There are many factors contributing to the large increase in Chinese visitors to the United States, for instance, China's steady economic growth and its relaxation of some travel regulations. These helped spur more leisure visits to the United States.

On the matter of educational exchange, according to statistics of the Chinese Education Ministry, in total there have been 700,000 Chinese students studying abroad from 1978 until 2003[23] In 2003, the number of students studying abroad totaled 117,000. In 2004, the Chinese Ministry of Public Security permitted 107,000 students going to study abroad.[24] According to Leo A. Orleans' study,[25] the majority of officially-sponsored Chinese students were sent to Europe and Japan in the early post-normalization years, but from 1983 most were going to the United States; 60 percent of the total went to study there. After establishing diplomatic relations in 1979, official education exchange and cooperation between the United States and China increased steadily, and there were also private exchanges that expanded to many sectors. China saw the fastest growth and biggest number of students studying in the United States from the late 1980s to early 1990s.[26]

According to the U.S. Institute of International Education (IIE) report,[27] in the 1980s, numbers of Chinese students grew dramatically, and in 1988 China displaced Taiwan as the leading country of origin. However, from 1994, Japanese students displaced Chinese students to rank the highest number of students entering from other countries and regions, and the number of Indian students suddenly rose to become a significant number. From 1998 to 2000, China once more overtook Japan as the leading sender of students, again until it was overtaken by India in 2001. According to Chinese official statistics, until 2000 the cumulative number of Chinese students studying in the United States was 190,000.[28] However, from 1978 to 1991, there were no more than 80,000 Chinese students studying in the United States.[29] In 2002, there were 64,757 Chinese students studying in the USA;[30] the number in 2003 was 61,765 students,[31] ranking second, after India. Until 2005, there are 640,000 Chinese students in total studying in America.[32] On the other sides, 241,791 Americans studied abroad in 2006; among them, 11,064 Americans studied in China. However, in 1995 there were only 1,396 Americans studying there.[33] The increase of American students' numbers shows a strong growth in educational exchanges with China.

In addition to tourist and educational contact, other cultural and social exchange information also can tell us how close and interdependent China-U.S. relations are in the post-Cold War era. For instance, regarding flight information, American Airlines (AA) and Hainan Airlines (HU) announced that they would provide regular flights between the United States and China. Hainan Airlines is the fourth Chinese airline permitted by the Chinese Civil Aviation Administration (CAAC) to fly on China-U.S. routes, in addition to Air China (CA), China Eastern (MU) and China Southern (CZ) airlines. According to the U.S.-China Civil Aviation Agreement, which was signed in July 2004, the number of airlines flying U.S.-China routes, based on joint cooperation between the United States and China, is allowed to increase from the present number of four to nine.[34] Moreover, the U.S.-China routes will add 195 more flights per week to increase the total weekly number of flights to 249 within six years.[35] As at present, among American air companies, Northwest Airlines (NW), United Airlines (UA) and American Airlines (AA) all provide regular flights to China. In addition, Kungpeng Airlines, the largest Sino-regional airline based in northern China, also announced to operate passenger and cargo service as well as charger flights. It is a joint venture between China's Shenzhen Airlines and Mesa Air Group of the United States. This indicates that like other American enterprises, American air companies also actively attempt to enter Chinese markets. Following closer development of China-U.S. relations, not only official but also private contacts are more active, which we can perceive from the increasing numbers of tourists, students and flights.

CHINA-U.S. GOVERNMENTAL AND CONGRESSIONAL EXCHANGE MECHANISM

In addition to close economic and trade contacts, social and cultural exchanges, the relations between Chinese and American governments and congresses also have progressed well. The most apparent examples are the establishment of a strategic dialogue regime between American and Chinese senior level officials and the establishment of an exchange mechanism between their legislative bodies. When they met during the APEC (Asia-Pacific Economic Cooperation) Summit in Chile in November 2004,[36] a talk regime between senior officials was suggested by Chinese President Hu Jintao to U.S. President George W. Bush, from which they agreed to hold "senior level dialogue" twice a year in Beijing and Washington, alternatively, and that the dialogue content was not limited to any specific economic, political and security issues. At their first senior level meeting started on August 1, 2005 in Beijing,[37] Chinese Vice Foreign Minister Dai Bingguo exchanged views on the bilateral relations and international issues of common interest and concern with his counterpart, U.S. Deputy Secretary of State Robert Zoellick. Since that meeting, a dialogue mechanism has followed with frequent high-level exchanges and visits between these two countries. This indicates that the bilateral relations are progressing in a more comprehensive direction and that the two nations intend to resolve their differences by negotiations and consultations. This helps to decrease the occurrence of misunderstanding and conflict. The two nations then held their second strategic dialogue in Washington D.C. in December 2005, and agreed to hold the third meeting in the first half year of 2006.[38] Even on military issues, both countries agreed to cooperate with one another. For instance, China and the United States announced to establish a "military hotline" in 2007 to avoid misunderstanding during any moments of crisis in the Pacific and to enhance their military exchanges at all levels.[39]

Meanwhile the two governments interact closely with one another; the contacts between American and Chinese parliamentary bodies are progressing extensively and intensively as well. According to the Memorandum of Understanding (MOU) signed by the vice-chairman and secretary-general of the Chinese NPC (National People's Congress) Standing Committee, Sheng Huaren and the president pro tempore of the U.S. Senate, Ted Stevens, in January 2004,[40] a formal exchange mechanism would be established between the two Congresses. The NPC and the Senate would establish an inter-parliamentary group to cooperate and exchange with one another to promote the development of the relations between the two nations. Moreover, they agreed to visit the other side's country every two year. This exchange mechanism has been launched in August 2004 when Republican Senator Ted Stevens led a congressional delegation to Beijing.[41] In addition to this congressional formal exchange mechanism, the U.S. Senate and the House of Representatives both also announced the setting up of working groups for a better understanding of China and for the purpose of promoting the bilateral exchanges. The first congressional group, the "China Caucus," including fifteen members was created by Representative Randy Forbes in June 2005.[42] Forbes indicated that the Caucus intended to "raise awareness and serve as a forum of discussion for U.S.-China interests in the U.S. House of Representatives."[43] The discussion would cover all issues. In addition to the Congressional China Caucus, Republican Congressman Mark Kirk and Democratic Congressman Rick Larsen also jointly initiated a "U.S.-China Working Group" in the House of Representatives in July 2005.[44] This bipartisan congressional group included more than twenty Congressmen who would work to promote the bilateral diplomatic and economic relations. They would invite important and influential entrepreneurs and academic and political leaders to discuss issues and policies related to U.S.-China trade and economic relations. In addition, the U.S. Senate established a group in January 2006 as well, "the Senate China Working Group,"[45] According to Coleman, this Working Group would serve to better understand China and its intentions. The establishment of these congressional working groups not only signifies the Congress's interest in understanding China but also indicates its desire for involving itself in the formulation of China policy. The close contacts and exchanges between Chinese and American Congresses, particularly in the post-Cold War era, explain that the two nations highly value their relations.

Similarly, the Chinese community also has fortified its presence in the United States hoping to add strength to the China-U.S. relations. For example, the Friendship Association of Chinese Students and Scholars (FACSS), one of the biggest Chinese groups in America; Asian American Business Development Centre; The Chinese Finance Association, etc., are all very active in China-U.S. relations. And as do other political interest groups, these groups are attempting to promote the relationship between China and the United States. These all demonstrate a fact, "the already formed interdependence between the two countries in terms of economy and trade, and their irreplaceable cooperation in politics and security,"[46] as explained by a Chinese scholar. Although this kind of complex interdependence is unlike that of Canadian-American relations, it does greatly promote the development of states' relations and affect their crisis bargaining and resolution.

FROM STRATEGIC NEEDS TOWARDS COMPLEX INTERDEPENDENCE

When the People's Republic of China (PRC) was founded by the Chinese Communist Party in 1949, China aligned itself with the socialist camp which was led by the Soviet Union. The relations between the United States—the leading country of the capitalist camp—and China at that moment were therefore hostile and mutually opposed, and the two countries hardly had any contact or interchange. This kind of opposition lasted almost twenty years until late 1960s and early 1970s when both China and the United States faced the same pressure and threats from the Soviet Union. The "strategic needs" made them reconsider their relations and adjust their respective foreign policies. Therefore, they tried to normalize their relations from the end of the 1960s, and finally established formal diplomatic relations in 1979.

However, the establishment of diplomatic relations did not mean that the development of their relations ran very smooth without any problems. There are still many problems interfering in the development of their relations, some problems are longstanding while others are relatively new. Aside from these issues, there have also been many incidents happening from time to time. Although there are some dissensions existing in China-U.S. relations, the need for realizing common interests and strategic cooperation, and the reality of interdependence make them maintain a stable relationship and resolve disputes by means of negotiations. If one looks at the history of the development of China-U.S. relations, one will find that their relations in the 1950s and 1960s were pretty much close to the realist assumptions. Military force was the most usable and effective instrument during this period, and it seemed that war could happen easily between China and the United States at any time. Moreover, due to the opposition of the capitalist and socialist camps, states' agenda and world politics were headed by questions of military security. In addition, there was no official contact between China and the United States. Since their relations were hostile, the United States greatly opposed China's participation in world organizations. Therefore, at that moment, international organizations and regimes did not and could not play important roles in China-U.S. relations.

Following the Sino-Soviet split and the eventual rupture of their relations in 1969 and also, the changes of international situation in the 1970s, the relationship between the United States and China had a chance to be normalized. Under the mutual need for strategic cooperation to oppose their common enemy, the Soviet Union, and their respective considerations, China and the United States adjusted their policy toward each other and gradually restored their relations in the late 1970s. That is, this kind of rapprochement and cooperation derived from realistic political considerations. This study argues that it was a "have to" choice for the United States and China; it still belonged to a kind of power politics. The major issues and topics the two nations were concerned about were still in the security area. However, since they normalized their relations, the bilateral contacts increased and the likelihood for using military force against each other decreased. Although their relations at this moment still could not be completely characterized as "complex interdependence," at least they were better connected than in the first period of their relations and were also progressing towards a closer interdependence.

Strategic needs greatly promoted the development of China-U.S. relations in the 1980s. Following the practice of China's "Open Door" policy and the establishment of formal diplomatic relations, not only official contact but also private interchange between the United States and China increased sharply. Their interdependence was not limited to strategic cooperation any longer but started to develop and extend to economic, trade, and cultural sections. Their relations gradually progressed toward complex interdependence. As this chapter has discussed and as was mentioned in previous sections, in the phase of post-Cold War, not only the bilateral governmental and congressional interchange but also the contacts on trade, economic, social and cultural sections between the two countries are very extensive and intensive. There are multiple channels connecting the two nations, they can communicate and exchange views easily and smoothly with one another. Any issue can be discussed and talked about; military security issues do not dominate states' agenda any longer. Following the close contact and exchange, a highly interdependent relationship has formed; adopting military force to resolve disputes is not only unwise but also costly. Consequently, bargaining and consultation has become the major method for resolving problems.

That is, the three main characteristics of complex interdependence borne out in China-U.S. relations. As this study has examined and demonstrated in previous sections, in China-U.S. relations, military security no longer overrides other issues, that is, it is not the dominant goal and goals of states vary by issue area. With the existence of multiple channels in states' relations, not only transnational actors started to appear and pursue their own goals, transgovernmental politics also make states' goals difficult to define. This situation is more apparent in the United States than in China as China is still a socialist country, it can maintain coherent policies and pursue coherent goals more easily. Regarding the instruments for achieving states' goals, although force remains a potential instrument of state policy, the two governments have never used it to resolve their disputes. Conversely, one can clearly perceive and find that when a dispute happens, the United States and China both are used to manipulating their economic interdependence, international organizations and transnational actors to achieve their goals. They always resolve their problems by means of negotiation. Whether exchanging trade contracts or politicizing and linking issues, they achieved their objectives in the bargaining process.

In addition to interstate contacts, transgovernmental and nongovernmental elites and transnational organizations all participate actively in China-U.S. relations. Transnational actors and international organizations not only can be the major instruments of states' policy but also intend to intervene in states' interactions. Compared with the Cold-War era, their roles are more apparent and outstanding and thus cannot be ignored. As there are many more actors intervening in China-U.S. relations than before, and they pursue their own goals, states' agendas are hence affected by numerous factors. Security threats were not the major source of agenda change. Instead, the agenda formation has been greatly influenced by the economic process. The issues that have been submitted to states' agenda comprise of a variety of topics and not just security issues any longer. Although not all of the expectations under complex interdependence conditions are borne out in China-U.S. relations, compared with that of the realist assumptions, they are closer and are progressing to the ideal world of complex interdependence. Since their relations have progressed towards complex interdependence, this definitely will help to promote the relationship.

AN OPTIMISTIC FUTURE DEVELOPMENT

Entering into the twenty-first century, the necessity for coordinating with one another on international affairs and cooperating for opposing terrorism all bring chances for the United States and China to work together. Although there have been and there may be more disputes that will happen between the two nations, complex interdependence will help them to resolve problems peacefully and avoid the occurrence of war. That is, a more positive and optimistic future of the relationship can be expected. In sum, although the progress of China-U.S. negotiations on many issues may look like a long-term game of wrestling, it at least decreases the occurrence of war. There have been and there will be more problems and disputes in the near future for China-U.S. relations; however, complex interdependence will help the United States and China to resolve problems easily and smoothly by bargaining. That is, China's being a non-democratic country does not mean that there will not be a peace existing in China-U.S. relations as the democratic peace supporters claimed. However, this study considers that following the close contact with other countries and its rapid economic growth, a more open and democratic China can be expected. This chapter argues that neither can the realist assumptions be applied to describe and explain the development of China-U.S. relations in the post-Cold War era. Some Realists based on power politics claim that a war cannot be avoided in the end in China-U.S. relations, particularly on the sensitive Taiwan issue. Although the Taiwan issue remains a sensitive issue in US-China relations, I believe that the leaders of both sides will not make any rash decision to resolve the issue by using force and will find a solution. Complex interdependence does not necessarily lead to peace; however, it did and will continue to positively influence China-U.S. relations by making the use of force less likely and making their leaders consider their relations carefully and resolve their problems peacefully. Therefore, a short-term peace can be expected.

NOTES

1. Michael Schaller, *The United States and China-Into the Twenty-First Century*, 3rd ed. (New York: Oxford University Press, 2002), p. 189.
2. Robert G. Sutter, *China-Watch: Toward Sino-American Reconciliation* (Maryland: The Johns Hopkins University Press, 1978), p. 118.
3. Regarding the discussion of the China Threat, see Herbert Yee and Ian Storey (eds.), *The China Threat: Perceptions, Myths and Reality* (London: Routledge, 2002).
4. Regarding democratic peace thesis, see Michael Doyle, "Liberalism and World Politics," *American Political Science Review*, Vol. 80, No. 4 (December 1986); and *Ways of War and Peace: Realism, Liberalism and Socialism* (New York: Norton, 1997).
5. Regarding democratic peace thesis, see Michael Doyle, "Liberalism and World Politics," *American Political Science Review*, Vol. 80, No. 4 (December 1986); and *Ways of War and Peace: Realism, Liberalism and Socialism* (New York: Norton, 1997).
6. Robert O. Keohane and Joseph S. Nye, "Realism and Complex Interdependence," in Paul R. Viotti and Mark V. Kauppi, *International Relations Theory: Realism, Pluralism, Globalism*, 3rd ed. (Massachussetts: Allen and Bacon, 1998), p. 311.
7. "China now world's third-largest economy," *Times Online*, January 14, 2009. http://www.timesonline.co.uk/tol/news/world/asia/article5514156.ece, consulted in March 2009.
8. "Jump in exports swells China's trade surplus," *International Herald Tribune*, April 11, 2006. http://www.iht.com/articles/2006/04/11/bloomberg/sxsurplus.php, "consulted in March 2009".
9. "US-China Trade Statistics and China's World Trade Statistics" *US-China Business Council*, http://www.uschina.org/statistics/tradetable.html, consulted in March 2009.
10. David Zweig, "China and the World Economy: The Rise of a New Trading Nation," *paper presented at the World International Studies Association*, Ljubljana, July 24 2008, p.19.
11. "Trade with China: 2008," *US Census Bureau*, http://www.census.gov/foreign-trade/balance/c5700.html#2008, consulted in March 2009.
12. This situation was changed in 2004. According the latest report of the UNCTAD (United Nations Conference on Trade and Development), the United States became the biggest recipient of FDI in the world in 2004, receiving $96 billion; the United Kingdom ranked the second, receiving $78 billion. China became the third recipient of FDI in the world in 2004, receiving $61 billion, but still ranked the biggest recipient of FDI in Asia. *The Central News Agency*, September 30, 2005.
13. *US Department of State*. http://www.state.gov/r/pa/ei/bgn/18902.htm#econ, consulted in September 2006.
14. David Zweig, "China and the World Economy: The Rise of a New Trading Nation," Hong Kong University of Science & Technology's Center on China's Transnational Relations Working Paper No.25, p. 20.
15. "China's FDI up 23.6% in 1008," *China Daily*, January 15, 2009.
16. *Mainland Affairs Council*, http://www.mac.gov.tw/big5/statistic/em/182/29.pdf, consulted in May 2009.
17. *China Chamber of Commerce in the United States*. http://www.chinausbiz. com/id 566. html, consulted in November 2004.
18. *World Socialist Web Site*, "China emerges as a major exporter of capital," May 19, 2009. http://www.wsws.org/articles/2009/may2009/chin-m19.shtml, consulted in May 2009.

19. *US Department of Commerce, International Trade Administration, Office of Travel and Tourism Industries*, "US Resident Travel to Canada, Mexico and Overseas Countries: Historical Visitation Outbound," http://ntl.bts.gov/lib/19000/19800/19866/PB20031 00977.pdf, consulted in November 2004.

20. *US Department of Commerce, International Trade Administration, Office of Travel and Tourism Industries*, "Selected Destinations of U.S. Residents Traveling abroad 2005-2006," http://tinet.ita.doc.gov/view/f-2006-08-001/index.html, consulted in May 2009.

21. *US Department of Commerce, International Trade Administration, Office of Travel and Tourism Industries*, "Arrivals to the US 1990-2000," http://ntl.bts.gov/lib/19000/19800/19866/PB2003100977.pdf, consulted in November 2004.

22. *US Department of Commerce, International Trade Administration, Office of Travel and Tourism Industries*, "2008 Market Profile: China," http://tinet.ita.doc.gov/outreachpages/download_data_table/2008_China_Market_Profile.pdf, consulted in May 2009.

23. *Ministry of Education of the People's Republic of China.* http://www.moe.edu.cn/edoas/website18/info5116.htm, consulted in November 2004.

24. *The Central News Agency*, February 18, 2005.

25. Leo A. Orleans, *Chinese Students in America: Policies, Issues, and Numbers* (Washington D. C.: National Academy Press, 1988).

26. *China Internet Information Centre*, November 7, 2004. http://www.china.org.cn/english/culture/79409.htm, consulted in November 2004.

27. *Open Doors: Report on International Educational Exchange*, published annually by IIE, available at http://www.opendoors.iienetwork.org, consulted in November 2004.

28. *Ministry of Education of the People's Republic of China.* http://www.moe-daoa.edu.cn/america/index.html, consulted in November 2004.

29. Wu, Tung-Lin, *The Strategy of Powers in Drastic Transition* (Taipei: Taiwan Elite, 2002), pp. 195-196.

30. *Chinese Consulate-General in Chicago*, "Growth of Chinese Students in the US Slows Down: Report," November 6, 2003. http://www.chinaconsulatechicago.org/eng/jy/t40302.htm, consulted in May 2009.

31. *Washington File*, "Door Open for Chinese Students in United States, Officials Say," March 30, 2005. http://www.america.gov/st/washfile-english/2005/March/200503300 95731aawajuk0.4669916.html, consulted in May 2009.

32. *The Central News Agency*, October 24, 2005.

33. *New York Times*, "Study Abroad Flourishes; China Attracts More American Students," November 18, 2008.

34. *The Embassy of the People's Republic of China in the United States of America*, August 11, 2004. http://www.china-embassy.org/chn/gyzg/t147031.htm, consulted in November 2004.

35. Ibid.

36. *China Times*, August 1, 2005.

37. *People's Daily Online*, August 1, 2005. http://english.people.com.cn/200508/01/eng20050801_199503.html, consulted in February 2006.

38. *The Embassy of the People's Republic of China in the United States of America*, August 12, 2005. http://www.china-embassy.org/chn/zmgx/t225567.htm, consulted in February 2006.

39. It is the first time that China implements a direct military hotline with one country. See *The Washington Post*, "China and U.S. To Establish Military Hotline," November 6, 2007, Page A16.

40. *China Times*, January 5, 2004.

41. *China News*, August 8, 2004. http://www.chinanews.com.cn/news/2004year/2004-08-08/26/469511.shtml, consulted in February 2006.

42. *The China Press*, June 15, 2005. http://www.chinapressusa.com/yaowen/200506 150078.htm, consulted in February 2006.

43. "Legislators Form Congressional China Caucus," *Hong Kong Trade Development Council*, June 9, 2005. http://www.tdctrade.com/alert/us0511d.htm, consulted in February 2006.

44. *China News*, July 1, 2005. http://www.chinanews.cn/news/2004/2005-07-01/7032. shtml, consulted in February 2006.

45. *People's Daily*, January 10, 2006.

46. "Engagement is better than isolation," *People's Daily*, January 11, 2006. http://english.peopledaily.com.cn/200601/11/text20060111_234547.html, consulted in February 2006.

Chapter 6

A New Era for U.S.-China Relations

Quansheng Zhao and Guoli Liu

China and the United States established diplomatic relations in 1979. After three decades of growing interactions, the relationship between the two great powers has entered a new era. In this chapter, we examine the changing strategic context, the broadening economic foundations, and the critical challenges in the new era of U.S.-China relations. Offensive realist John Mearsheimer argues that China and the United States are destined to become adversaries. International strategist Henry A. Kissinger believes that there is a great opportunity for mutually beneficial cooperation between China and the United States. A balanced and cool-headed analysis of Sino-U.S. relations is essential for understanding this critical relationship. With increasingly broad and active economic interactions between the two countries, it seems that U.S.-China cooperation is growing but frictions and misperceptions are rising as well. The Taiwan issue has been a most critical issue in relations between Beijing and Washington. This issue is becoming increasingly interesting due to not only changing perceptions in the two capitals but also rapid development inside Taiwan following the 2008 power transition from the pro-independence Democratic Progressive Party to the pro-status quo Nationalist Party. It is reasonable to argue that Sino-American relations have evolved from a "fragile relationship" to a truly interdependent "complex relationship." During his first official visit to China in November 2009, President Barack Obama clearly stated that the U.S. and China should "build a positive, cooperative and comprehensive relationship."[1]

Scholars have been searching for the most appropriate models to interpret Sino-American relations. There is no consensus on what is the most effective model that can lead to the best understanding of the dynamic nature of the bilateral relationship. We believe that "complex interdependence" can help us gain a better understanding of the new era of Sino-American relations. Complex interdependence is a liberal concept developed by Robert O. Keohane and Joseph S. Nye. According to them, "complex interdependence has three main characteristics: 1) state policy goals are not arranged in stable hierarchies, but are subject to trade-offs; 2) the existence of multiple channels of contact among societies expands the range of policy instruments, thus limiting governments' control over foreign relations; and 3) military force is largely irrelevant."[2] Interdependence does not only promote cooperation but also might generate conflict. After a systematic study of cooperation among industrialized nations, Robert O. Keohane points out that interdependence in the world political economy generates conflict. People who are hurt by unexpected changes emanating from abroad, such as increases in the prices that producers charge for oil or that banks charge for the use of money, turn to their governments for aid. So do workers, unemployed because of competition from more efficient or lower-wage foreign production. Governments, in turn, seek to shift the costs of these adjustments onto others, or at least to avoid having them shifted onto themselves. This strategy leads them to pursue incompatible policies and creates discord.[3] Although Keohane's analysis was based on a study of the discord and cooperation among industrialized nations before the mid 1980s, his perspective is quite relevant for examining U.S.-China relations today. In some ways, in fact, the degree of interdependence between China and the United States today has exceeded that of the relations between the United States and its Western partners in the 1970s and 1980s. This is particularly true if one focuses on the amount of merchandise trade and foreign investment each country has with the other country.

Complex interdependence is evolving in the context of turbulent globalization.[4] At the heart of globalization is an array of multiple trans-boundary forces and processes that reduce national control over what happens within national boundaries and enable a set of new political actors to project social, economic, and political influence over a long distance. The main drivers of globalization are: technological innovation, economic interdependence, demographic transition, political diversification, environmental degradation/concerns, and ideational convergence. Globalization is a double edge weapon. It can promote cooperation but also may cause new conflict.[5] China and the United States are among the key actors of globalization. It is hard to say which country benefits more from globalization. But within each country there are winners and losers in globalization. Turbulent globalization has created daunting challenges such as radical religious terrorism and catastrophic global financial crisis. The acceleration of globalization since the end of the Cold War clearly indicates that communities and nations must cooperate closely to survive the growing challenges in this turbulent world. We attempt to demonstrate that close cooperation between Beijing and Washington is particularly essential for successful management of the regional and international challenges in this globalizing world.

The chapter is divided into three sections: (1) Growing common interests and working with differences; (2) Broadening economic foundation and increasing complex interdependence; and (3) Interpreting the new era of U.S.-China relations.

GROWING COMMON INTERESTS AND WORKING WITH DIFFERENCES

Although starting from very different historical background, China and the United States have developed broad common interests in diverse areas including regional stability, international peace, economic development, and anti-terrorism. Reformers in China for a long time have looked to the United States as a leading modern country. Chinese leaders from Sun Yat-sen to Deng Xiaoping have high regard for American efficiency. International circumstances, however, were not favorable for the United States to play an active role in Chinese modernization before the 1970s. In fact, the two countries were strategic rivalries for more than two decades before the 1972 rapprochement.

The rising Cold War confrontation between the United States and the Soviet Union and China's civil wars in the late 1940s made it impossible for China to develop a normal relationship with the United States in the beginning of the People's Republic of China (PRC). Following the founding of the PRC in 1949, Mao Zedong decided to "lean to one side" relying on the Soviet Union. The outbreak of the Korean War in 1950 and the Chinese "anti-American and assist-Korea" campaign deepened the Cold War confrontation between the two sides. In addition to fighting against Chinese forces in Korean peninsula, the United States deployed its seventh fleet in the Taiwan Strait, effectively blocking the mainland from taking over Taiwan. Mao perceived the United States as the biggest threat to China's national security in the 1950s and early 1960s.

Ideological differences and conflict of national interests between Beijing and Moscow grew more serious in the late 1950s and led to open debates in the early 1960s. In 1969, China and the Soviet Union experienced armed border clashes. Confronting with the rising Soviet challenge, Mao Zedong decided to explore improving relations with the United States. From the U.S. side, President Richard Nixon and his national security adviser Henry Kissinger also took bold initiatives to open up to China. It was a common strategic consideration against the rising Soviet threat which brought Beijing and Washington together. In February 1972, President Nixon visited China. Nixon's meeting with Mao and the Shanghai Communiqué helped to build a strategic foundation for developing Sino-American relations.

Deng Xiaoping saw the establishment of diplomatic relations between China and the United States as a critical step for China's opening and reform. Soon after he came back to power in 1977, Deng took decisive steps to establish full diplomatic relations with the United States in January 1979.[6] Deng's visit to the United States in early 1979 was not only significant for improving bilateral relations but also instrumental for promoting reform and opening in China. Since the normalization of Sino-American relations, Beijing has always paid special attention to its relations with the United States. Beijing and Washington enjoyed a strategic and diplomatic honeymoon following the normalization of relations.

By 1982, however, China's leaders realized the best approach to pursue Chinese national interest is to follow "an independent foreign policy of peace." This new policy was driven by China's internal dynamics and the changing international environment. Internally, China after 1978 became fully committed to reform and opening which required a peaceful international environment. Externally, the Soviet Union was experiencing domestic decay and getting deeper into the troubled war in Afghanistan. At the same time, the United States under President Ronald Reagan took a tough stand against the Soviet Union and dramatically increased U.S. defense spending. As a result, the need for Sino-U.S. coalition to balance the Soviet power declined. Furthermore, Chinese leaders were frustrated with continued U.S. arms sales to Taiwan. Deng Xiaoping realized that China could not pursue any alliance policy with a foreign power. Therefore, an independent foreign policy of peace was officially declared in 1982. This policy helped China to normalize its relations with the Soviet Union in 1989. After the collapse of the Soviet Union, China has developed close relations with Russia and other post-Soviet states.

In the rapidly changing international strategic environment, China continues to pay special attention to its relationship with the United States. In fact, Sino-American relations are often perceived as the key bilateral relationship among China's relations with great powers. Even when major difficulties emerged in Sino-American relations after the Tiananmen incident in 1989, Deng emphasized to U.S. national security adviser Brent Scowcroft that "ultimately, China and the United States must build a good relationship. This is essential for world peace and stability." [7] Deng cared deeply about the improvement of Sino-American relations. After a period of troubled interaction following the 1989 crisis, China-U.S. relations continued to move forward.

Chinese leaders from Deng to Hu Jintao have given a great deal of thought to great power relations with an emphasis on building and maintaining a healthy relationship with the United States. Over a relatively long period of time, the United States will continue to be the main diplomatic partner (or competitor *duishou*) of China. There are conflicts and cooperation between China and the United States. Because of the leading role of the U.S. in the world economy and military, stability in Sino-U.S. relations will significantly affect China's relations with Japan and many Western countries. The United States is China's main exporting market and a main source of capital, technology, and advanced management experience. Therefore, maintaining and developing Sino-American relations has strategic significance for China. Jiang Zemin argues that Sino-American relations affect the whole picture of China's diplomacy and the strategic interests of China's politics, economy, and national security. [8] After some ups and downs, President Jiang Zemin and President Clinton exchanged presidential summits in 1997 and 1998. They even discussed building a "constructive strategic partnership."

When he first came into power in 2001, President George W. Bush considered China as a competitor rather than a strategic partner. The September 11 terrorist attack on the United States made it clear that the top threat to U.S. national security is international terrorism. In the war against terrorism, China is a partner. According to Evan S. Medeiros, Chinese leaders' hopes for stable U.S.-China relations had a strong influence on China's foreign policy priorities. Chinese leaders began emphasizing the security interests they shared with the United States, and they put nonproliferation at the top of their lists of areas of further bilateral cooperation. Chinese officials regularly stressed the need for the major powers to work together to combat nontraditional security threats, among them terrorism, WMD proliferation, and environmental degradation. China began cooperating in different ways with the United States in the global war on terrorism. For example, it supported key UN Security Council resolutions, gave aid to Afghanistan, and helped with the forensics on terrorist financing. In response, the Bush administration began to talk about China as a partner in addressing common security challenges, and no longer referred to China as a "strategic competitor." These arguments about China were reinforced in "The National Security Strategy of the United States of America," which the Bush administration released in September 2002. This important document identified strategic cooperation among major powers—and mentioned China by name—as a top priority. U.S. officials also began characterizing the U.S.-China relationship as cooperative, constructive, and candid.[9] In this situation, China and the United States reached a new level of cooperation. At the same time, China and the United States have developed comprehensive interdependence in culture, trade, finance, investment, security, and many other aspects.

The Chinese leaders continue to emphasize developing a stable and constructive relationship with the United States. President Bush visited Beijing on August 8-11, 2008 and attended the opening ceremony of the 29th Olympic Games. In his meeting with President Hu Jintao, Bush said that U.S.-China relationship is "important, constructive, and candid." Hu said that Sino-American relations have maintained a positive trend of development. The two sides have exchange and cooperation in the areas of trade, anti-terrorism, energy, environmental protection, and law enforcement. A good and continuously improving Sino-American relationship is consistent with the fundamental interest of the people of the two countries. Such a relationship will have far-reaching impact on peace, stability and prosperity of Asia-Pacific and even the whole world. China deals with Sino-U.S. relations from a strategic and long-term perspective. The Chinese side is willing to work with the U.S. to strengthen exchange and dialogue, enhance understanding and mutual trust, respect and take care of each other's interests and concerns, manage sensitive issues, and ensure healthy development of Sino-American constructive cooperative relationship. Many policymakers in Beijing and Washington consider their bilateral relations more complex and interdependent than ever before.[10]

Strategic and security issues lie at the heart of the realist-liberal debate surrounding Sino-American relations. The United States welcomes the rise of a stable, peaceful, and prosperous China, and encourages China to participate responsibly in world affairs by taking on a greater share of the burden for the stability, resilience, and growth of the international system. However, many in

Washington are beginning to fear China's inevitable military buildup, viewing China's military modernization as an "ominous sign of instability to come."[11] The question therefore on most American's minds is whether China will undergo a "peaceful rise," as Beijing claims, or whether it will further challenge the existing global order. Therefore, it is crucial for the United States to work on security issues surrounding its relationship with China, debating both national and global defense policies regarding its new military contender.

Realism has deep roots and strong influence in studying the rise and fall of nations. Classic realism and structural realism emphasize the balance of power. According to the leading neorealist Kenneth N. Waltz, China will emerge as a great power even without trying very hard so long as it remains politically united and competent.[12] In contrast to Waltz's defensive realism, John Mearsheimer advocates offensive realism. He states, "it is sad that international politics have always been a ruthless and dangerous business, and it is likely to remain that way. Although the intensity of their competition waxes and wanes, great powers fear each other and always compete with each other for power, which means gaining power at the expense of other states." In Mearsheimer's view, "the most dangerous scenario the United States might face in the early twenty-first century is one in which China becomes a potential hegemon in Northeast Asia."[13] Mearsheimer suggests that the United States should not engage China in such a way that would promote China's further rapid development. Instead, the U.S. should try to slow down China's economic growth. It seems that he fails to appreciate the interdependent nature of the U.S. economy and the Chinese economy. The fact of the matter is that any slow down in the Chinese economy might have a negative effect on the U.S. economy.

Scholars beginning with the realist tradition can often lead to different perceptions of China. Realist strategist Zbigniew Brzezinski sees the China challenge in a very different way than Mearsheimer. In Brzezinski's view, "China is determined to sustain its economic growth. A confrontational foreign policy could disrupt that growth, harm hundreds of millions of Chinese, and threaten the Communist Party's hold on power. China's leadership appears rational, calculating, and conscious not only of China's rise but also of its continued weakness."[14] Brzezinski argues that China is assimilating into the international system. Of course, tensions over Taiwan are the most worrisome strategic danger. But any Chinese military planner has to take into account the likelihood that even if China could overrun Taiwan, the United States would enter the conflict. Therefore, both China and the Unites States have strong interests in maintaining peace and stability in the Taiwan Strait. The former Secretary of State Henry A. Kissinger questions the wisdom of basing policy toward China on the assumption that it is determined to overthrow the international system by the use of military force. "A more accurate assumption is that China will seek to play a larger role within the international system, politically and economically, because of its rapid growth. And that is a challenge—of competition—to which we should pay attention." Kissinger does not see "why it would be rational to expect that a China that is surrounded by major countries with significant military budgets would challenge the United

States militarily and exhaust itself in a military rivalry while it is doing so well economically."[15]

In order to strengthen China-U.S. relations, several major points must be stressed. First, political trust and strategic dialogue are critical for managing great power relations. Direct and regular contacts at the highest level among leaders of the great powers are essential for building political trust. Strategic dialogue can enhance mutual trust and understanding. If misperceptions can be avoided, there will be a greater chance of building peace. By combining their separate dialogues into a joint Strategic and Economic Dialogue, top officials in Washington and Beijing have publicly acknowledged the significance of regular and in depth contacts in reaching a better understanding. Although improved mutual understanding does not automatically solve existing problems, such high level dialogues will help to achieve cooperation and avoid conflicts originating from misperceptions.

Second, economic common interests and economic frictions are like a double-edged sword. On the one hand, common gains can promote win-win cooperation. On the other hand, increased economic interaction might also lead to more frictions. Overall, it is reasonable to argue that economic interdependence has become a dynamic driving force for great power cooperation. As China and the U.S. both are confronting serious economic challenges at home and abroad, it is particularly important each country should avoid putting unfair blame on the other for its own problems such as unemployment and loss of investment. History has clearly indicated that trade protectionism will not improve but will aggravate economic situations. Both China and the U.S. must vigilantly work against rising protectionism in hard times.

Third, military exchange is a critical link in great power relations. Increased economic interaction and political dialogue do not automatically lead to more military exchange. In order to build lasting peace, major military leaders of different countries should have regular exchanges so that they can strengthen mutual trust and understanding. Cooperative security will be impossible without military leaders working closely with each other.[16] Building political trust and security cooperation should go hand in hand.

Fourth, social and cultural exchanges are also important. New thinking in great power relations should emphasize social and cultural exchanges. The "clash of civilization" or the "tragedy of great power politics" took place in history partly because of the lack of cultural understanding. Increased exchange does not automatically resolve the issues of potential conflicts among different cultures. Nevertheless, more cultural and social exchanges are certainly beneficial for enhancing mutual understanding, which is a key step toward identifying possible solutions to current and future conflicts.

A rising China has caused strong reactions from around the globe. The Unites States is especially concerned about the implications of a rising China.[17] Although the initial rational of strategic cooperation between China and the U.S. almost disappeared with the disintegration of the former Soviet Union, the U.S. and China have found new and broader common ground for strategic cooperation. This is particularly true since the terrorist attack on the U.S. on September 11, 2001. The most important bilateral relationship for China is Sino-American relations. A healthy relationship with the United States is critical for creating a favorable international environment for reform and opening, for defending China's national security, and for achieving China's modernization with assistance of U.S. capital, technology, and management experience. According David Shambaugh's analysis, neither the U.S. nor China seeks a deterioration of relations. Indeed, both countries are otherwise preoccupied. The United States is committed to the war against terrorism and improving the domestic economy. China faces the tough challenges of deep reform and is in the early stages of a prolonged and wrenching process of implementing the terms of its accession to the World Trade Organization. Shambaugh concludes: If wisely managed by both sides—and if the key sensitivities of each are respected rather than provoked—the new stability in Sino-American relations may endure.[18]

In spite of China's stress on "peaceful development," the United States and many other powers continue to be suspicious about China's strategic intentions. Some American analysts are not sure about how responsible China will be in exercising its rapidly growing power.[19] Perceptions and misperception will affect China's interaction with the outside world. If interdependence of China and the U.S. was just an idealist aspiration in the 1970s, it has become a reality today. China and the U.S. have developed very close economic ties. The two countries are also strengthening their strategic and political ties. Nevertheless, serious differences and misperceptions continue to exist. Future development of U.S.-China relations might experience many twists and turns.

According to Avery Goldstein, China's emerging grand strategy links political, economic, and military means in an effort to advance the twin goals of security and great-power status. Politically, China pursues multilateral and bilateral diplomacy to mute threat perceptions and to convince others of the benefits of engagement and the counterproductive consequences of containment. Economically, China nurtures relations with diverse trading partners and sources of foreign investment, weaving a network of economic relations to limit the leverage of any single partner in setting the terms of China's international economic involvement. Militarily, China seeks to create some breathing space for modernization of its armed forces.[20] China's rise is one of the most significant events in the contemporary world.[21]

The Taiwan issue is a core national interest of China. It has been a critical issue in Sino-American relations with strategic significance. The issue of Taiwan itself is the product of a combination of factors, including domestic rivalry (the civil war of 1946-49 between the CCP and KMT), the intervention of external powers and changing international relations in the Asia-Pacific region. The dynamics of the international environment frequently and significantly affects Beijing's policy considerations toward Taiwan. Beijing regards the United States as a major obstacle to its goal of reunification with Taiwan. The issue can be traced back historically to the Chinese civil war period when the U.S. supported the Chiang Kai-shek regime, and the cessation of the Korean War in the early 1950s, when the U.S. signed a Mutual Defense Treaty with Taiwan which effectively prevented the PRC from taking over the island. In the early 1970s, both Beijing and Washington were willing to normalize their relations due primarily to their mutual concern about the threat from the Soviet Union. While Washington has recognized Beijing officially and ceased its official relations with Taipei, Beijing still views the "Taiwan Relations Act" and U.S. arms sales to Taiwan as unwarranted "intervention in internal affairs."[22] Taiwan has long been the most sensitive issue in U.S.-China relations and likely will remain so for the foreseeable future. The area of greatest danger of potential conflict between China and the United States concerns security involving the Taiwan issue.

In recent times, cross-Taiwan Strait relations have experienced a series of positive developments. January 1, 2009 was the 30th anniversary of the "Message to Taiwan Compatriots" issued by the Standing Committee of the National People's Congress of the People's Republic of China. At a meeting to commemorate the important message that announced China's shift from a strategy of armed "liberation of Taiwan" to "peaceful reunification," President Hu Jintao made an important speech on December 31, 2008 and proposed six points policy for improving cross-Taiwan Strait relations. The "six-points" outlined in Hu's speech are: (1) firm adherence to the "one China" principle; (2) strengthening commercial ties, including negotiating an economic cooperation agreement; (3) promoting personnel exchanges; (4) stressing common cultural links between the two sides; (5) allowing Taiwan's "reasonable" participation in global organizations; and (6) negotiating a peace agreement.[23] Comparing with Beijing's previous policy statements, Hu's speech is more pragmatic, flexible, and people-oriented. President Hu puts aside difficult disputes and stresses cooperation in economic and other areas. This important speech is a clear indication that Beijing's policy toward Taiwan has undergone significant shifts and is likely to continue to evolve in the positive direction of peaceful cooperation for mutual benefits. This policy will contribute to building mutual trust, enhancing cooperation, and promoting regional peace and prosperity.

Leaders in both Beijing and Taipei have publically pledged to enhance cultural and economic exchanges and financial cooperation. Interestingly, Beijing has declared that it is willing to provide financial assistance to Taiwan if necessary to overcome the financial crisis. Such cooperation is certainly mutually beneficial and will contribute to not only economic development across the Taiwan Strait but also to regional stability and prosperity. The Ma administration is simultaneously trying to build closer ties with the Mainland and to stabilize and strengthen its relations with the United States. Such policies reflect the wish of the majority people in Taiwan and are likely to contribute to stability of the cross-strait relations. How Beijing and Washington respond to such calls is very critical in deciding the future of cross-Taiwan Strait relations.

Fundamentally speaking, mainland China's modernization and reform and opening policy have contributed to Beijing's shift of policy from "liberation of Taiwan" to "peaceful development." The growth of cross-strait relations is an essential component of mainland China's grand strategy of peaceful development. China has developed friendly and cooperative relations with almost all of its neighbors. The issue of Taiwan is perhaps the single most explosive issue for China if it involves Taiwan independence. Chinese leaders have attached great significance to peaceful unification. Hu has made it clearer than ever that as long as there is any hope for peaceful development, China will not resort to the use of force on Taiwan. When dealing with the Chen Shui-bian regime, Beijing confronted the dilemma of choosing war or peace. With the transition of power in Taiwan from Chen to Ma Ying-jeou in May 2008, a precious new opportunity for cross-Taiwan Strait peace and cooperation has emerged. The danger of war in the Taiwan Strait has been significantly reduced. Accordingly, Beijing's policy has further shifted from preparing for the worst case scenario to building mutual trust and enhancing cooperation. The six point proposal announced by Hu on the eve of New Year 2009 represents the most systematic and authoritative statement of Beijing's new thinking for peaceful development in cross-strait relations. Hu's policy has produced tangible results in the CCP-KMT dialogue and cooperation, the productive talks between the Straits Exchange Foundation (SEF) and the Association for Relations Across the Taiwan Strait (ARATS) which have led to the full normalization of the three links.

The international environment has experienced significant changes. (1) September 11 transformed the global strategic environment. Terrorism has become the common enemy of the United States, China, and the world community at large. The joint struggle against terrorism requires unprecedented cooperation among great powers including China and the United States. This strategic shift resulted in a transformation of U.S. perception of China as a competitor to the new thinking of China as an essential partner and stakeholder in the existing international political and economic systems. The growth in common interests between Beijing and Washington also made it easer for the two sides to settle their differences on the Taiwan issue and defend the One China policy. (2) The U.S. led war in Iraq has exhausted the power of unilateralism and increased demand for global cooperation. This has increased the possibility for China and the United States to co-manage the North Korean nuclear crisis and for Beijing and Washington to cooperate in other areas. Their success in the formal co-management of North Korea could encourage informal co-management of the Taiwan issue. This point was made clear by President Bush's public declaration against Taiwan independence. (3) The global financial crisis has exposed the vulnerability of the United States and also made it clear that no country can escape the negative effects of the global financial crisis. With a relatively fast growing economy and the world's largest foreign currency reserve of two trillion dollars, China has emerged as an indispensible partner in the common struggle against the financial crisis. At the same time, both Taiwan and the mainland have powerful incentives to strengthen economic cooperation in a joint effort to fight against the financial crisis. Tough economic times have created an urgent demand for enhanced cooperation. Closer economic interaction between Taiwan and the mainland as well as closer economic interdependence between China and the United States are likely to create a more favorable political environment for the key parties to reach better mutual understanding of each other's needs and concerns. Cooperation in the economic arena might create more good will and political trust and ultimately lead to improved political relations. If the current positive trends continue, the Taiwan issue will no longer be a source of contention between Beijing and Washington. From strategic perspective, a "landmine" has been removed in the path of developing China-U.S. relations. This is consistent with the long standing U.S. interest of maintaining peace and stability in Asia-Pacific. It is also a vindication of the success of China's grand strategy of peaceful development.

In spite of the growing common ground, there are still serious differences between China and the United States on issues of human rights, U.S. arms sales to Taiwan, intellectual property rights, trade imbalance, currency valuation, and global issues such as climate change. During his official visit to China in November 2009, President Obama discussed many critical issues with President Hu. They agreed to build on their common interests and work on their differences. Because most of the differences between the two countries are likely to continue to exist for a long time, it is important for both sides to learn to manage their differences and prevent the differences from leading to crises. In the early years following Sino-American normalization of diplomatic relations, strategic considerations were paramount for leaders in Beijing and Washington. Since China's deep reform and comprehensive opening beginning in the early 1990s, however, economic interactions have gained more and more weight in U.S.-China relations. Next we will examine the growing economic interdependence between China and the United States.

BROADENING ECONOMIC FOUNDATIONS AND INCREASING COMPLEX INTERDEPENDENCE

As a result of reform and opening since 1978, China has achieved remarkable growth in the last three decades. Following the monumental decision of reform and opening made in December 1978, the first foreign country that Deng Xiaoping visited was the United States. Deng's visit to the U.S. with extensive media coverage had profound impact on the perception about the United States. The U.S. has been the leading industrialized country. In many ways the United States has been a model for China's modernization. Due to historical reasons, U.S.-China relations started from a very weak foundation in the 1970s. Since then however, the bilateral economic relations have made enormous progress in spite of some up and downs.

U.S.-China economic ties have expanded tremendously over the last three decades. Thus, liberal scholars point to trade and investment between the United States and China as a point of compromise and cooperation. Since normalization of U.S.-Chinese relations in the 1970s, economic ties have in fact been the driving force of strategic partnership. Important to the democratic peace theory, the commercial relationship has served as a bridge between the two countries despite fluctuations in political relations. In 2005, two-way trade between China and the United States reached $244 billion, emphasizing how both countries are benefiting from the link. In 2007, total U.S.-China trade totaled over $387 billion, becoming the third largest U.S. export market, overtaking Canada to become the largest source for U.S. imports.[24] After three decades of rapid development, China and the United States have become truly interdependent. China's economy has never been so closely linked to the outside world before. The United States is China's largest trading partner (unless the European Union is considered as one unit). China has emerged as America's second largest trading partner. China has become the largest foreign holder of U.S. treasure notes with a total $776.4 billions in June 2009.[25] China has indeed become a stakeholder of the current international economic system.[26]

Recognizing the need for and benefits of strategic engagement, President Bush and President Hu launched the U.S.-China Strategic Economic Dialogue in 2006 as a means to provide economic discussion between the two nations. Sending the country's top economic policymakers, the Bush administration clearly recognized the importance of expanding its economic relationship with China long term. The talks also emphasized understanding that great opportunities may lie in economic ties to China. In its attempts to maintain close ties with its new peer in the international economy, the U.S. sees economic cooperation as a gateway to achieving political and social ties in the future. As former Secretary of Treasure Henry Paulson states, the challenge for Washington is to understand China's perception of its self-interest, identify opportunities to persuade China that its interests and those of the United States are often the same, and narrow real differences whenever possible.[27]

China's membership in the WTO since 2001 has spurred dramatic reforms, including tariff reductions, the elimination of import licenses and quotas, and mandated market openings. These comprehensive trade commitments made upon entering the WTO have lead to a sharp expansion in U.S.-China economic ties. Another recent reform was the Chinese government's decision to allow all international companies the right to import and distribute goods directly to consumers, bypassing state-owned entities. Thanks to these modifications, international companies are now able to perform operations independently of the Chinese government, giving them greater autonomy in business matters. The United States is in fact benefiting from its relations with China and the amazing growth of the Chinese market is providing new incentives for America not to rock the relationship. In all, despite differences in the political realm, the United States should do everything in its power to maintain its strategic economic partnership with China.

Realist scholars, on the other hand, might see this relationship differently, seeing that bilateral trade relations have grown increasingly strained in recent years over a number of issues, including a large and growing U.S. trade deficit with China. Realist arguments point to the fact that the U.S.-China trade relationship is far from perfect. Given that the United States is China's largest trading partner, trade disputes, which are often inherent in any high-volume trade relationship, are inevitable. China's large trade surplus with the U.S. is also another source of friction and the issue has received more attention in recent years. The U.S. deficit with China has surged in recent years as imports from China have grown much faster than U.S. exports to China. The bilateral deficit with China is therefore one of the most complicated and multifaceted challenges the United States will deal with in the future.

Some U.S. critiques insist that China is continuing to pursue a mercantilist trading strategy, restricting access to its market while aggressively supporting exports by its national firms. When China joined the WTO, it agreed to provide a full description of all its subsidy programs, but to date has failed to do so. In addition, China agreed to make its state-owned enterprises operate according to market principles, however, state-owned firms in China continue to receive direction and subsidies. When looking at the facts, it is hard to discount the notion that the Chinese government is continuing to shelter its companies from the global market. Realists are beginning to point fingers at China's "unfair trade polices" as a point of contention in U.S.-Chinese relations.

The United States recognizes that economic ties with China hold more opportunity than setback. The annual gains to the U.S. from increasing economic interaction with China are substantial—about $70 billion or $625 per household.[28] On June 6–7, 2008, CNA China Studies and Fudan University's Center for American Studies sponsored a conference on U.S.-China economic relations. The participants identified six key themes in the bilateral economic relations: (1) The U.S.-China economic relationship is increasingly complex, increasingly buffeted by outside forces, and increasingly contentious. The two economies are becoming ever more intertwined. As the size and interdependence of both economies grow, their relationship becomes increasingly subject to forces outside the immediate control of economic policy-makers. (2) The U.S.-China economic relationship rests partly on the Chinese and American citizenries' perceptions of the relationship. The bilateral economic relationship is increasingly subject to public opinion in both the United States and China. Some citizens in both countries believe that the interconnectedness of the two economies poses unacceptable risks to national and individual interests. (3) The United States and China each contend that the other side does not fully understand its priorities and concerns. (4) Trade imbalance and renminbi (RMB) revaluation—and, to a lesser degree, China's foreign exchange reserves—remain hot button issues. (5) The Strategic Economic Dialogue (SED) provides a much-needed forum for managing the U.S.-China economic relationship, but it has not yet lived up to its full potential. (6) Both sides voiced support for increased economic openness and for greater clarity of economic goals. The United States and China have shared interests in upholding a stable regional and international environment for economic growth and dispute resolution.[29]

With the deepening troubles in the U.S. financial system, Beijing is positioned to play a crucial role in any policy that Congress and the Obama administration design to address the U.S. economic problems.[30] China has amassed a huge supply of foreign exchange reserves, totaling $2.3 trillion as of December 2009, and the Chinese central government has become an ever more important purchaser of U.S. Treasuries and other U.S. debt. The financial rescue and economic stimulus program thus far enacted—and any further program that may be needed for the U.S. economy—will require a substantial level of new U.S. government borrowing, with China positioned to be a major purchaser of this new U.S. government debt. Some U.S. policymakers have expressed concern that this poses an economic risk to the United States should China's foreign exchange purchase patterns change, and a political risk should China use this position to seek advantages on other bilateral issues.

China is implementing a $586 billion stimulus package for its economy, ostensibly designed to build major infrastructure projects, which may draw investment away from U.S. Treasuries. The plan has been criticized by some in China who say that its lack of project details or spending safeguards is an invitation for corruption, misuse, and malfeasance. Economic and trade issues remain extremely complicated and are a lingering source of contention in U.S.-China relations. The PRC remains the second-largest U.S. trading partner, with total U.S.-China trade in 2008 at $409 billion. In addition to the substantial and growing U.S. trade deficit with China (which climbed to $268 billion in 2008), bilateral issues include repeated PRC inability or unwillingness to protect U.S. intellectual property rights and the PRC's trade and currency policies. As a result of the financial crisis and reduced American consumption, the U.S. trade deficits with China have declined to $103 billion in the first six months of 2009 from $119 billion during the same period of 2008.[31]

China's persistent trade surplus with the United States hit a record $266.3 billion in 2008 and has been a source of tension between Beijing and Washington. However, the global recession has hurt both countries' exports and increased the temptation for governments around the world to raise import barriers to protect local companies. The size and importance of U.S.-China trade, which totaled $409 billion in 2008, means both countries have a stake in making sure it is "fair, sustainable and mutually beneficial," U.S. Trade Representative Ron Kirk said in a statement after meeting with Chinese Minister of Commerce Chen Deming.[32] Chinese and U.S. firms signed thirty-two trade and investment contracts on April 27, 2009 worth some $10.6 billion, which the U.S. Chamber of Commerce said will support U.S. economic growth and job creation. "With businesses in both countries struggling, these deals come at a critical time and will help create jobs and stronger commercial bonds between the United States and China," said Myron Brilliant, the chamber's senior vice president of international affairs. Chen Deming stated that China "will continue to encourage Chinese companies to import more from the U.S., and we will also welcome U.S. companies and trade-promotion agencies to be more active in China."[33]

Some American analysts believe that the financial crisis may have significant long-term effects that would make it harder for the U.S. to remain the world's financial superpower. The financial crisis contributes indirectly to the rise of mainland China, since poor U.S. management of the American financial system is widely blamed as the trigger for the crisis. Accordingly, U.S. soft power and moral authority are reduced, and U.S. influence declines with them.[34]

At the same time, it must be pointed out that the global financial crisis is not only a serious threat to the United States but also to China and other emerging powers. As a result of the global financial crisis, more jobs were lost in China in 2008 than in any other country. Over twenty million Chinese peasant workers were forced to return home from factories in coastal areas due to reduced orders from overseas in late 2008 and early 2009. The world today is dramatically different from the old system of zero-sum game. In the past, the economic loss of the U.S. might be China or other countries' gain. In today's interdependent economy, however, the crisis in the U.S. inevitably leads to crisis in China and other countries. The solution to the current global financial crisis, therefore, must be global. Cooperation between China and the United States is more essential than ever for global economic recovery and development.

INTERPRETING THE NEW ERA OF U.S.-CHINA RELATIONS

The relationship between China and the United States has become the most important bilateral relationship in the world. Any significant development in this bilateral relationship will have a big impact not only on the two countries but also the global community. Since the normalization of diplomatic relations in 1979, the relationship between China and the United States has experienced many twists and turns. The initial strategic rationale was a common interest in counter balancing Soviet expansionism. By 1982 China adopted an independent foreign policy of peace. By 1989 China normalized its relations with the Soviet Union. With the collapse of the Soviet Union and the end of the Cold War, some people thought that there was no longer a need for Sino-American strategic cooperation. Such prediction turned out to be misplaced because with China's modernization and post-Cold War international transition, the common interests between China and the United States have expanded into many new areas and reached a much deeper level.

Since 1978, China has taken economic development as the central task. The success of China's modernization has significantly enhanced China's power and influence. Interestingly, it seems that the historical growth of American power has provided some valuable lessons for China. The rapid growth of the U.S. economy and expanded materials resources provided a strong foundation for America's growing world role over time. From 1978 to 2005, China's GDP grew from 364.5 billion to 18.3 trillion yuan, with an annual growth rate of 10 percent. During the same period, per capita GDP rose from 381 yuan to 14,040 yuan.[35]

With frustration in Iraq and some other areas, President Bush's main bright spot in foreign policy was that he was able to build a solid relationship with China. President Bush and his secretary of state Condoleezza Rice both claimed that U.S.-China relations achieved unprecedented progress and stability. Under the Bush administration, U.S.-China trade grew significantly. China became a "stakeholder" of the existing international system. The United States and China conducted multiple rounds of Strategic Economic dialogues. The two sides achieved a good understanding of the one-China policy. President Bush helped to curb the Taiwan independent movement by stating unequivocally that the United States "opposes to Taiwan independence," and "opposes to any unilateral efforts to change the status quo" in the Taiwan Straits.

Since coming into the White House in January 2009, President Obama made it clear that he is determined to change American foreign policy in the Middle East by initiating an orderly withdrawal of combatant troops from Iraq. At the same time, Obama has raised the stake of U.S. war in Afghanistan. On China policy, however, it seems that there will be more continuity than change from the Bush administration to the Obama administration. In their first meeting at the G-20 economic summit in London on April 1, 2009, President Obama and President Hu agreed to work together to build a "positive, cooperative and comprehensive relationship in the twenty-first century." Hu said during the meeting that no matter how the situation across the Taiwan Strait evolves, China will steadfastly adhere to the one-China policy and resolutely oppose "Taiwan independence," "One China, one Taiwan" and "Two Chinas." Obama said the U.S. government is committed to the one-China policy and the three Chinese-U.S. joint communiques, adding that this stand will not change. The U.S. welcomes and supports efforts to improve relations across the strait and hopes for greater progress in the relations.[36]

The global financial crisis which began in 2008 is one of the most significant developments in the international community. The impact of the crisis will be felt for a long time to come. Having originated in the United States, it has created worldwide repercussions. Both Taiwan and the mainland are facing the tough challenges. It is clear that there is no escape from the crisis. All countries are in the same boat of globalization. The crisis has led to a much deeper interdependence between China and the United States.

The new challenges that require China-U.S. cooperation are related to the following issues: First, both China and the United States have strong interest in maintaining international peace and stability in an increasingly complex regional and global environment. China and the United States continue to be two of the most important powers in East Asia. No major security issues in East Asia can be solved without the input from both China and the United States. Although East Asia seems relatively stable comparing with the Middle East and Central Asia, the region also has its own serious problems. The most outstanding case is the on-going North Korean nuclear crisis. At one time, co-management of the Korean issue between China and the United States seemed quite promising under the framework of Six Party Talks.[37] However, Kim Jong-il has refused to give up his nuclear ambition and has continued to conduct multiple provocative missile tests. Both Beijing and Washington are determined to achieve non-nuclearization in Korean peninsula. An enormous amount of tough work is required to achieve this objective. The U.S. tends to overestimate Beijing's influence over Pyongyang and thus wishes China will exercise more influence in the negotiation process with North Korea. China is concerned about breaking its traditionally strong ties with North Korea without achieving the objective of denuclearization. Washington wishes to avoid spending more resources in the

Korean peninsula while fighting two wars in Iraq and Afghanistan. As a result, it has demonstrated more patience in using the diplomatic approach in Korea than in other places. Cooperation between China and the United States is essential for any viable solution of the North Korea nuclear crisis. Taking a long term approach to East Asian stability, the contending views about Japan's historical role in Asia and the current Japanese demand of becoming a "normal country" might become a serious challenge to both China and the Untied States. There are political forces in Japan that call for revising the peace constitution. As a victim of Japan's past aggression, China is naturally concerned of any militaristic orientation of Japan. If Beijing, Washington, and Tokyo can achieve mutual understanding on this issue, East Asia will have a better chance of remaining stable. From Tokyo and Washington's view, however, China's modernization has caused concerns among about what Beijing might do when China becomes even stronger in the future.

Second, Beijing and Washington have become strategic partners of anti-terrorism. After 9/11, anti-terrorism has become the central security challenge for the United States. China is an indispensible partner in the international fight against terrorism. China is also a victim of international terrorist attacks, such as the bombings of buses in Xinjiang conducted by the extremist East Turkistan Islamic Movement terrorists in recent years and the Urumqi riots of "separatists" in July 2009. Both China and the U.S. are longstanding supporters of Pakistan, which is on the frontline of the war against terrorism.[38] At strategic level, both Beijing and Washington are clearly against terrorism. At operational level, however, there is ambiguity about who is and who is not a terrorist. The U.S. Department of State has listed the East Turkistan Islamic Movement as a terrorist group. When the U.S. administration considers releasing Xinjiang Uighur suspects caught by the U.S. military in Afghanistan and held at Guantanamo Bay, the U.S. is not willing to release these suspects to China for concerns about possible tough treatment by China against terrorist suspects. It seems that the U.S. does not treat Uighur Islamic separatists as terrorists. From a Chinese perspective, the past car bomb attacks and the deadly July 5, 2009 Urumqi riots indicate that terrorism, ethnic separatism, and religious extremism are "three evil forces." "China has accused Rebiya Kadeer, the leader of the World Uighur Congress who lives in exile in Washington, of masterminding the riots."[39]

Third, the Taiwan issue has long been considered one of the biggest challenges for Beijing and Washington. There has been meaningful and concrete progress in improving cross-Taiwan Strait relations. China and the United States have adopted some informal co-management of the Taiwan issue. The United States has publicly stated its position against Taiwan independence. With power transition in Taiwan from the pro-independence Democratic Progressive Party to the pro-status quo Nationalist Party, a precious opportunity for building cross-strait peace has emerged. Washington welcomes the positive development in cross-strait relations. Although differences remain between Beijing and Washington on the U.S. arms sales to Taiwan, improved mutual understanding will help to improve cross-strait exchange. Interestingly, there has been serious new thinking on the issue of Taiwan.[40] Substantial improvement in Cross-Strait relations will enable Beijing and Washington to build a stronger strategic relationship in the future.

Fourth, China's modernization has significantly benefited from a dynamic and rapidly growing relationship with the United States. At the same time, success in China's rapid economic growth has enabled the rapid growth of Sino-American economic relations both in quality and quantity. The two countries have become truly interdependent. Over the last three decades, China has learned many valuable lessons from the experience of the United States in economic development. With the global financial crisis, many Chinese are reexamining Chinese system and the U.S. system. Perhaps Americans can also take a close look at the Chinese socioeconomic system to see if the U.S. can learn something from China's best practices. Some analysts have pointed out that the Chinese save too much and the Americans consume too much. If this is true, the Americans might learn how to save more and achieve a more balanced budget instead of relying heavily on deficit financing. Of course, if the Americans learn this lesson too quickly and too well, the global market might confront the challenge of the weak consumer demand for many categories of goods. With China's success in economic modernization, there have been growing environmental degradation. As a result, China and the United States are facing unprecedented challenge in coping with global climate change and reducing natural resource waste. This presents both risks and opportunities. The risks are if Beijing and Washington keep blaming each other and cannot achieve mutual understanding and cooperation, the global environment will continue to deteriorate at an accelerating pace. There will be no hope of sustainable growth what so ever if China and the United States do not take active and measurable steps to reduce CO_2 emissions. On the other hand, if the two countries can take significant and meaningful measures to promote green development and build a healthy environment, they can set great examples for the rest of the world.

Fifth, the global financial crisis has made it clear that China and the United States are in the same boat of globalization. The financial crisis originated in the subprime lending crisis in the United States has not only severely damaged the Wall Street but also had a very negative impact on the Chinese economy. Over 20 million Chinese workers lost their jobs in 2008. The United States federal government and the PRC central government have initiated the world's two largest economic stimulus plans. The global financial crisis demands international cooperation. Close cooperation between Beijing and Washington is especially critical for resolving the current financial crisis. In the first round of Sino-U.S. Strategic and Economic Dialogue held in Washington D.C. on July 27-28, the American side proposed to recognize China's market economy status (MES) as soon as possible via a cooperative form of the Sino-U.S. Joint Commission on Commerce and Trade.[41] This is a positive step that is most likely to enhance the level of cooperation between the two countries.

As a result of China's modernization and development of U.S.-China relations, China's role in world affairs is changing. In 1978 China was a developing country that just started reform and opening to the outside world. The gap between the GDP of China and the United States in 1978 was more than 13 times. By 2008, however, China has emerged as the world's third largest economy by exchange rate and the second largest economy measured in purchasing power parity. The U.S. GDP in 2008 was only three and a half times that of China. More significantly, in terms of contribution to global economic growth, China has become the most significant emerging economy in the world. China is becoming more and more active in all major international organizations.

Historian Niall Ferguson coined a word "Chimerica" to describe the close relationship between China and United States. He described the pattern as the "Chinese did the saving, the Americans the spending. The Chinese did the exporting, the Americans the importing. The Chinese did the lending, the Americans the borrowing." Recent trends since the global financial crisis have indicated this pattern is not sustainable.[42] *Newsweek* editor Fareed Zakaria points out that the United States needs China like never before. "China is the key to America getting through the worsening economic crisis." "There is a consensus forming that Washington needs to spend its way out of this recession, to ensure that it doesn't turn into a depression. Economists of both the left and right agree that a massive fiscal stimulus is needed and that for now, we shouldn't be worrying about deficits. But in order to run up these deficits—which could total somewhere between $1 trillion and $1.5 trillion, or between 7 and 11 percent of GDP—someone has to buy American debt. And the only country that has the cash to do so is China."[43]

The global financial crisis has highlighted the growing need for close cooperation between China and the United States. Before the global financial crisis, as Henry A. Kissinger points out, China sent scores of experts to the United States and invested in major American financial institutions to learn the secrets of the system that seemed to produce permanent global growth at little risk . . . China has a major interest in a stable—and preferably growing—U.S. economy. But China also has a growing interest in reducing its dependence on American decisions. Since American inflation as well as deflation have become for China nightmares as grave as they are for America, the two countries face the imperative of coordinating their economic policies. As America's largest creditor, China has a degree of economic leverage unprecedented in the U.S. experience. At the same time, the quest for widening the scope of independent decision exists in ambivalent combination on both sides.[44]

CONCLUSION

There is no doubt that U.S.-China relationship has entered a new era. Our study suggests that complex interdependence is perhaps the most useful theoretical concept for understanding the current relationship between China and the United States. Rethinking the three main characteristics of complex interdependence identified by Robert Keohane and Joseph Nye in *Power and Interdependence*, we can draw the following tentative conclusions. Unlike the traditional realist perspective with an obsession on balance of power, the multiple goals of United States and China are not arranged in stable hierarchies, but are subject to trade-offs. The two countries have developed broad and overlapping interests in maintaining regional and global peace and security, managing financial crisis, promoting trade and investment, and protecting the environment and dealing with climate change. This is no single issue that truly dominates the bilateral relationship. Therefore it is natural for the two sides to reach compromise and achieve cooperation in managing their complex relations.

China and the United States have developed multiple channels of interactions which have expanded the range of policy instruments, thus limiting governments' control over foreign relations. Even the authoritarian Beijing government must take various domestic and international interest groups into consideration in managing its foreign relations. In the United States, more and more people have their material and ideational interests related to America's healthy and cooperative relations with China. For many Americans, it is hard to imagine a life without using products made in China. At the same time, with U.S. exports to China growing faster than the over all U.S. economy, a growing number of Americans are working in China trade related fields. As the largest holder of U.S. Treasury notes, China naturally cares about the health of the U.S. economy because any deterioration in the U.S. economy might negatively affect the value of China's assets. With an even increasing number of Chinese students and scholars coming to the United States over time and more Americans going to China, people in the two countries are gaining a much deeper understanding of each other's culture, value, and tradition. Genuine friendship and mutual understanding from students, business people, professionals, to diplomats and top leaders can bridge much traditional gaps and help to avoid serious misunderstanding. The two countries have developed multiple channels of communication so that the bilateral ties are much more endurable.

Although no one can declare that "military force is largely irrelevant" in U.S.-China relations, as Keohane and Nye envisioned for the community of industrialized nations, it is reasonable to argue that both Washington and Beijing are considering their complex relationship in much broader terms than their military relationship. Unlike during the early Cold War era when the two nations treated each other as military adversaries, the current Chinese and American administrations officially recognize each other as partners in the war against terror. In the old days security was often perceived as a zero sum game in which one side's gain equals to the other side's loss. Today both China and United States have a common high stake in maintaining peace and security in Asia-Pacific and beyond. It is important to point out that complex interdependence between China and the U.S. should include military mutual trust and cooperation. If the two militaries cannot build mutual trust and closely work together, regional stability and world peace might be endangered if unpredictable circumstances arise.[45] The two sides must take historical lessons seriously and avoid repeating past failures of the great powers in the early and mid twentieth century.

In spite of many twists and turns, U.S.-China relations have evolved into a truly complex and interdependent stage in the last three decades.[46] A cooperative relationship with the United States has facilitated the peaceful rise of China. There is no doubt that China's modernization has transformed the country from an isolated weak economy in 1978 to a dynamo today. The key question is whether China can sustain the pattern of rapid peaceful growth under the threat of global financial crisis. As our analysis indicates, China and the United States are sailing in the same boat of globalization. Broad and overlapping common interests between China and the United States far exceed their existing differences. Therefore, for their self-interests and the interests of the global community, China and the United States have greater responsibility in closely working together to achieve sustainable development and maintain world peace. Success or failure in managing the challenges of this new era will have long lasting effect on international relations in general and U.S.-China relations in particular. Because the rapidly growing common interests between China and the United States seem to far outweigh their existing differences, there are good reasons to be cautiously optimistic about the future development of this critical bilateral relationship. Nevertheless, no positive development can be achieved without persistent hard work by people on both sides of the Pacific.

NOTES

1. See Keith B. Richburg, "Obama, Hu vow to continue to strengthen partnership," *The Washington Post* November 17, 2009. http://www.washingtonpost.com/wp-dyn/content/article/2009/11/16/AR2009111603705.html?sid=ST2009111700768, accessed November 18, 2009. President George W. Bush initially considered China as a "strategic competitor." After the 9/11 terrorist attack on the U.S, however, Bush quickly realized that China is a strategic partner in the war against terror and a strong business partner with the United States. By the end of his presidency, Bush considered U.S.-China relationship as "better than ever." See James Fallows, "What *xiao* Bush got right," http://www.washingtonmonthly.com/features/2008/0808.fallows.html, accessed August 28, 2009.

2. Regarding the third point, Robert O. Keohane and Joseph S. Nye point out, "Military force is not used by governments toward other governments within the region, or on the issues, when complex interdependence prevails. It may, however, be important in these governments' relations with governments outside that region, or on other issues. Military force could, for instance, be irrelevant to resolving disagreements on economic issues among members of an alliance, yet at the same time be very important for that alliance's political and military relations with a rival bloc." Robert Keohane and Joseph Nye, *Power and Interdependence*. Second edition (New York: HarperCollins, 1989): 25, 255.

3. Robert O. Keohane, *After Hegemony: Cooperation and Discord in the World Political Economy* (Princeton: Princeton University Press, 1984).

4. For turbulent globalization, see the following three books by James Rosenau. *Turbulence in World Politics: A Theory of Change and Continuity* (Princeton: Princeton

University Press, 1990); *Along the Domestic-Foreign Frontier: Exploring Governance in a Turbulent World* (New York: Cambridge University Press, 1997); and *Distant Proximities: Dynamics beyond Globalization* (Princeton: Princeton University Press, 2003). Rosenau considers *Turbulence in World Politics* his most important book. According to his "turbulent model," the boundaries between domestic and foreign affairs have become porous.

5. For contending views on globalization, see James H. Mittelman, *The Globalization Syndrome: Transformation and Resistance* (Princeton: Princeton University Press, 2000); and Peter Berger and Samuel P. Huntington, eds. *Many Globalizations: Cultural Diversity in the Contemporary World* (New York: Oxford University Press, 2002).

6. For a detailed and interesting account of the Sino-U.S. negotiations for normalization of relations, see Patrick Tyler, *A Great Wall: Six American Presidents and China: An Investigative History* (New York: PublicAffairs, 1999): 227-285.

7. Deng Xiaoping, *Deng Xiaoping Wenxuan* (Selected works of Deng Xiaoping), vol. 3. (Beijing: Renmin Chubanshe, 1993): 350.

8. Jiang Zemin, *Jiang Zemin Wenxuan* (Selected works of Jiang Zemin), vol. 1 (Beijing: Renmin Chubanshe, 2006): 203, 312.

9. Evan Medeiros, *Reluctant Restraint: The Evolution of China's Nonproliferation Policies and Practices, 1980-2004* (Stanford: Stanford University Press, 2007): 165-166.

10. U.S. Secretary of the Treasurer Henry M. Paulson, Jr. argues that prosperity of the United States and China depends on helping China further integrate into the global economic system. Paulson believes that engagement with China is the only path to success. See Paulson, "A Strategic Economic Engagement," *Foreign Affairs* (Sept/Oct. 2008): 59-77.

11. Andrew B. Kennedy, "China's perceptions of U.S. intentions toward Taiwan." *Asian Survey* (47, 2008): 268-287.

12. Kenneth Waltz, "Structural realism after the Cold War," in G. John Ikenberry, ed., *America Unrivaled: The Future of the Balance of Power* (Ithaca: Cornell University Press, 2002): 29-67.

13. John J. Mearsheimer, *The Tragedy of Great Power Politics* (New York: W. W. Norton, 2003): 2, 401.

14. Zbigniew Brzezinski, "Make money, not war," *Foreign Policy* 146 (January-February): 46-47. *Foreign Policy* 146 (January-February 2005) contains a debate "Clash of the Titans." It examines critical questions such as "is China more interested in money than missiles? Will the United States seek to contain China as it once contained the Soviet Union?" Brzezinski and John Mearsheimer go head-to-head on whether China and the United States are destined to fight it out. For more in depth analysis of strategic situation in East Asia with a focus on China, see Zbigniew Brzesinski, *The Choice: Global Domination or Global Leadership* (New York: Basic Books, 2004): 107-123.

15. Henry Kissinger, "Universal values, specific policies—A conversation with Henry Kissinger," *The National Interest* (Summer 2006): 13-15.

16. For analysis of China's military power, see Wei-chin Lee, "Long shot and short hit: China as a military power and its implications for the USA and Taiwan," *Journal of Asian and African Studies* (43, 2008): 523-539; and U.S. Department of Defense, *Military power of the People's Republic of China 2009*. Washington, DC: Office of the Secretary of Defense. See http://www.defenselink.mil/pubs/pdfs/China_ Military_Power_ Report_2009.pdf, accessed August 30, 2009.

17. Quansheng Zhao, "America's response to the rise of China and Sino-US relations," *American Journal of Political Science* (14, 2005): 1-27.

18. David Shambaugh, "Sino-American Relations since September 11," *Current History* (September 2002): 243-249.

19. For an overview of Chinese foreign policy, see Robert G. Sutter, *Chinese Foreign Relations: Power and Policy since the Cold War* (Lanham: Rowman and Littlefield, 2008).

20. For a theoretical analysis of China's grand strategy, see Avery Goldstein, *Rising to the Challenge: China's Grand Strategy and International Security* (Stanford: Stanford University Press, 2005). For a theoretical and empirical analysis of Chinese foreign policy, see Alastair I. Johnston and Robert Ross, eds. *New Directions in the Study of China's Foreign Policy* (Stanford: Stanford University Press, 2006).

21. David Kang makes a thought provoking argument that a strong China is a stabilizing force in Asia. David Kang, *China Rising: Peace, Power, and Order in East Asia* (New York: Columbia University Press, 2008).

22. Quansheng Zhao, "Beijing's Dilemma with Taiwan: War or Peace?" *The Pacific Review* (vol. 18, no. 2, 2005): 230.

23. Hu Jintao, "Hand in Hand to Advance Peaceful Development of Cross-strait Relations, Achieve Great Revitalization of the Chinese Nations," see *Renmin ribao* (*People's Daily*), (January 1, 2009): 1.

24. Wayne M. Morrrison, *China-U.S. Trade Issues*. Washington, D.C.: Congressional Research Service. http://www.fas.org/sgp/crs/row/RL33536.pdf, accessed July 5, 2009.

25. Data obtained from http://www.treas.gov/tic/mfh.txt, accessed August 21, 2009.

26. For China's growing role in the global economy, see Doug Guthrie, *China and Globalization: The Social, Economic, and Political Transformation of Chinese Society* (New York: Routledge, 2006). For a comprehensive analysis of China's power, see David M. Lampton, *The Three Faces of Chinese Power: Might, Money, and Minds* (Berkeley: University of California Press, 2008).

27. Henry Paulson, "A Strategic Economic Engagement," *Foreign Affairs* (Sept/Oct. 2008): 59-77.

28. C. Fred Bergsten, Bates Gill, Nicholas R. Lardy, and Derek Mitchell, *China: The balance sheet: What the world needs to know now about the emerging superpower* (New York: PublicAffairs, 2006): 160.

29. Allison Kaufman, "U.S.-China Economic Relations: Issues and Prospects" Conference Report (September 1): vii-viii. http://www.cna.org/documents/D0018855.A1.pdf, accessed May 30, 2009.

30. See CRS Report RL34742, *The Global Financial Crisis: Analysis and Policy Implications*, coordinated by Dick K. Nanto.

31. U.S. Census Bureau, Foreign Trade Division, Data Dissemination Branch, Washington, D.C. 20233. http://www.census.gov/foreign-trade/balance/c5700.html #2008, accessed August 22, 2009.

32. "American and Chinese Companies Sign Deals," *New York Times*, April 28, 2009, http://dealbook.blogs.nytimes.com/2009/04/28/american-and-chinese-companiessig ndeals/?scp=1&sq=U.S.%20Trade%20Representative%20Ron%20Kirk%20said%20in% 20a%20statement%20after%20meeting%20with%20Chinese%20Minister%20of%20Co mmerce%20Chen%20Deming&st=cse, accessed August 30, 2009.

33. See *Xinhua*, "China, US firms sign $10b deals," http://www.chinadaily.com.cn/china/2009-04/28/content_7724271.htm, accessed April 28, 2009.

34. Denny Roy, "New Circumstances Strain Old Arrangement," *Taiwan Journal*, April 24, 2009, p. 7.

35. National Bureau of Statistics of China 2006. For analysis of China's economic rise, see Ted Fishman, *China, Inc.: How the Rise of the Next Superpower Challenges America and the World* (New York: Scribner, 2005). For a contending perspective, see Minxin Pei, "The Dark Side of China's Rise," *Foreign Policy* 153 (March/April 2006): 32-42.

36. *Xinhua*, "China, U.S. to build positive, cooperative and comprehensive relationship in 21st century," April 2, 2009, http://news.xinhuanet.com/english/2009-04/02/content_111 16139.htm, accessed May 1, 2009.

37. Quansheng Zhao, "Moving toward a Co-management Approach: China's Policy toward North Korea and Taiwan," *Asian Perspective* (vol. 30, no. 1, 2006): 39-78.

38. Paul Richter, "U.S. Appeals to China to Help Stabilize Pakistan," *Los Angeles Times*, May 25, 2009. http://www.latimes.com/news/nationworld/nation/la-fg-us-china-pakistan 25-2009may25,0,6047766.story, accessed June 10, 2009.

39. Peter Foster and Malcolm Moore, "China Threatens Death Penalty for Xinjiang Rioters," *Telegraph*, July 9, 2009. http://www.telegraph.co.uk/news/worldnews/asia/ china/5783263/China-threatens-death-penalty-for-Xinjiang-rioters.html, accessed August 2, 2009.

40. For a thought provoking article, see Bruce Gilley, "Not So Dire Straits: How the Finlandization of Taiwan Benefits U.S. Security," *Foreign Affairs* vol. 89, no. 1 (January/February 2010): 44-60. If Gilley is right, the decline of the strategic significance of the issue of Taiwan for Washington could lead to greater cooperation between China and the United States and more stability in Asia-Pacific.

41. Chen Changying, "Why is U.S. ready to recognize China's market economy status?," *People's Daily Online*, August 14, 2009. http://english.people.com.cn/ 90001/90778/908 57/90861/6728731.html, accessed August 22, 2009.

42. Niall Ferguson, "Team 'Chimerica'," *The Washington Post*, November 17, 2008: A19; and Niall Ferguson, "'Chimerica' Is Headed for Divorce," *Newsweek*. August 19, 2009. http://www.newsweek.com/id/212143, accessed August 20, 2009.

43. Zakaria also discussed that China might have other options. "People often say that China and America are equally dependent on each other," says Joseph Stiglitz, winner of the 2001 Nobel Prize in Economics. "But that's no longer true. China has two ways to keep its economy growing. One way is to finance the American consumer. But another way is to finance its own citizens, who are increasingly able to consume in large enough quantities to stimulate economic growth in China. They have options, we don't. There isn't really any other country that could finance the American deficit." http://www. newsweek.com/id/170357/page/1, accessed August 21, 2009.

44. Henry Kissinger, "Rebalancing Relations with China," *The Washington Post*, August 18, 2009. http://www.washingtonpost.com/wp-dyn/content/article/2009/08/18/AR 20090 81802850.htm, accessed August 21, 2009.

45. The lack of mutual understanding and cooperation between the two sides resulted in the Hainan Incident in April 2001 in the form of the U.S. EP-3 spy plane collision with a Chinese fighter jet. See Dennis C. Blair and David V. Bonfili, "The April 2001 EP-3 Incident: The U.S. Point of View," in *Managing Sino-American Crises: Case Studies and Analysis* edited by Michael D. Swaine and Zhang Tuosheng (Washington D.C.: Carnegie Endowment for International Peace, 2006): 377-390. The two sides must work to prevent such dangerous incidents from happening in the future.

46. See Zachary Karabell, *Superfusion: How China and America Became One Economy and Why the World's Prosperity Depends on It* (New York: Simon & Schuster, 2009).

Chapter 7

Chinese Mainland-U.S.-Taiwan Triangular Relations since 2000: A Perspective of Complex Interdependence

Dennis Hickey and Yiran Zhou

Since the beginning of the twenty-first century, relations between the People's Republic of China (PRC or Chinese mainland), Republic of China (ROC or Taiwan) and the United States (U.S.) have witnessed a series of dramatic twists and turns.[1] Initially, Washington stepped up its support for Taipei. But following the sneak terrorist attacks on September 11, 2001, the U.S. declared its intention to pursue a "cooperative, constructive, and candid" relationship with the PRC. During the final years of the Jiang Zemin presidency, Beijing released a series of documents and "white papers" that seemed designed to discourage the Taiwan independence movement. Perhaps the most sensational of these was "anti-secession law" that was passed by the National People's Congress (NPC) on March 14, 2005. But on March 4, 2005—ten days *before* the law was passed—President Hu Jintao issued a "four-point opinion" outlining ways to promote the peaceful development of cross Taiwan-Strait relations "under the new circumstances."[2] Since that time, Beijing has continued to soften its rhetoric and employ economic and cultural instruments to promote ties with the island. As for Taipei, it appeared determined to provoke the Chinese mainland and march boldly toward *de jure* independence under the leadership of the Democratic Progressive Party (DPP). However, after Ma Ying-jeou's landslide victory in the island's historic 2008 election, these controversial policies were junked. Taipei now seems determined to improve relations with Beijing.

This chapter employs the theory of complex interdependence in an effort to help explain the dynamics of the trilateral relationship between Beijing, Taipei and Washington over the past eight years. It evaluates the levels of their mutual dependence, analyzes considerations contributing to these fluctuations, and predicts the possible trajectory of future relations. The authors suggest that it appears likely that long-term mutual engagement and cooperation will prevail over political containment, armed confrontation and military rivalry, although differences and problems will undoubtedly occur from time to time.

COMPLEX INTERDEPENDENCE

The concept of complex interdependence first gained widespread attention during the 1970s in the context of growing economic globalization and the burgeoning technological revolution. The politics of interdependence may be characterized as the existence of multiple channels connecting diverse societies with no hierarchy existing among interstate issues and the use of military action as a last resort to resolve disputes.[3] In other words, no single issue stands atop the agenda of governments and political areas, and a set of interrelated issues must be handled simultaneously with the same level of importance. No longer are all issues subordinate to military security, and the distribution of power resources within issues is differentiated; the interrelation of issues gives space for negotiation and cooperation among actors.

Complex interdependence emphasizes the role that international institutions may play in coordinating states' actions through established rules and procedures. Intergovernmental, transnational and other networks associated with these formal institutions "bring officials together on a regular, face-to-face basis," and create "a sense of collegiality" that helps create an environment conducive to problem solving.[4] Among the core ideas associated with complex interdependence is the establishment of cross-cutting ties between non-state actors (nongovernmental organizations and transnational organizations) as well as between state actors, propelled by rapidly developing economic exchanges and technological communication, which interlinks domestic and foreign policies with a variety of actors engaged in activities that cross borders.[5]

Although complex interdependence is often considered a challenge to neo-realism, this is an exaggeration because it does not deny all of the propositions of realism. Rather, it recognizes the relevance of power and security interests under specific conditions and does not dispute the relevance of coherent state actors as units within the global system. Of course, military force may remain an effective tool in solving disputes when they encroach upon any given state's core interests. But many international relations theorists now contend that "a differentiated, sophisticated approach" is needed rather than application of a simplified approach to all domains of the field regardless of differences.[6]

It is noteworthy that some—not all—theorists argue that complex independence may lead eventually to sustained peace and cooperation among the states and actors in the international system. According to this view, as the global system becomes increasingly interdependent, the "incentive to wage war is absent."[7] Leaders recognize eventually that their respective societies gain more from peaceful commerce than conflict. As Richard Rosecrance observed, actors recognize that "they can do better through internal economic development sustained by a worldwide market for their goods and services than by trying to conquer and assimilate large tracts of land."[8]

In the discussion below, this study employs complex interdependence to analyze and evaluate recent trends and characteristics in relations between the PRC, ROC and U.S. It examines major variables—economic, security and communication mechanisms—in measuring the interdependence levels of their relations. The study suggests that these developments bode well for the prospects for peace and stability in global politics.

U.S.-CHINA INTERDEPENDENCE

During the administration of President George W. Bush (2000-2008), relations between the U.S., the Chinese mainland and Taiwan experienced dramatic changes, with the tragedy of 9/11, serving as a watershed. Before the terrorist attack, it appeared that Washington's policy leaned toward an accommodation of Taiwan's interests. In a sharp departure from past policy, Bush proclaimed that the U.S. would do "whatever it takes" to assist in Taiwan's defense.[9] This statement prompted Beijing to accuse Washington of interfering in the country's internal affairs, which brought their bilateral relations to a low point.[10] By the time Bush left office, however, the PRC press described him as a "true friend" of the Chinese people.[11]

The terrorist attacks of 9/11 proved to be a turning point in U.S.-PRC relations. Beijing quickly signaled its support for the war on terrorism. But other issues also helped push the two nations together. Both states realized that they needed to cooperate with each other to help resolve a host of complicated international issues including the proliferation of weapons of mass destruction, health emergencies (a point driven home by the SARS epidemic), environmental degradation, dwindling energy supplies and the nuclear stand-off on the Korean peninsula. It is likely that China's rise as an economic superpower also played a role in both countries' calculations. According to some estimates, China will overtake Japan as the world's second largest economy in 2010.[12] Other studies suggest the PRC will become the world's largest economy in 2020.[13] To state it succinctly, the U.S. and the PRC—the world's largest economies—need each other.

In 2005, Robert Zoellick, then U.S. Deputy Secretary of State, introduced a new concept to characterize Sino-American relations. He described both countries as "responsible stakeholders," and pointed out that the two nations shared many common interests in international affairs.[14] On his trip to the U.S. in April 2006, President Hu Jintao claimed that the two states were more than "stakeholders." He declared that the two governments enjoy a "constructive and cooperative partnership."[15] In addition, President Bush repeatedly stressed the importance of China as an America's partner. In August 2008, he proclaimed that "U.S.-China relations are good and important," and, "China and the United States have become *increasingly interdependent* as their relationship is becoming more and more interwoven, particularly in the economic field [emphasis added]."[16] Against this backdrop, cooperation between the two countries in economic and international matters began to develop even further, and military ties grew.

Economic Ties

Sino-American economic ties have expanded substantially since 2000. As illustrated in Table 7.1 below, between 2002 and 2006 the average growth rate in trade was roughly 33 percent. Furthermore, in 2008, the volume of U.S.-China trade reached $409 billion (as compared to only $5 billion in 1980).

Table 7.1 Sino-U.S. Trade, 2002-2006 (USD millions)

	2002	2003	2004	2005	2006
U.S. Exports to China	22,053	28,418	34,721	41,837	55,224
U.S. Imports from China	125,168	152,379	196,699	243,462	287,773

Source: International Trade Administration, U.S. Department of Commerce, "TradeStats Express—National Trade at http://tse.export.gov/MapFrameset.aspx?MapPage=NTD MapDIsplay.aspx&UniqueURL=nwwwck55dk2051iyovmwp455-2009-1-27-13-18-49 (accessed 27 January, 2009).

As a rapidly-developing economic entity with an enormous population, China constitutes an alluring export market to American firms. In fact, China already is the third largest importer from the U.S. as well as the largest exporter to the U.S.[17] Additionally, the U.S. plays an important role in Foreign Direct Investment (FDI) in China. Taking advantage of lower labor costs, many American plants have relocated from Taiwan and Japan to the PRC. Not surprisingly, American FDI in China now outpaces investment in Taiwan by a substantial margin.

Propelled by the increasingly close economic interdependence, the voices in favor of maintaining steady progress in bilateral relations are gaining support in the political spheres of the U.S. and China. In recent years, the American government, lobbied by business interests, has taken into consideration U.S. economic stakes in China while crafting its policy toward that country. Some U.S. officials also believe that economic exchanges will promote political reform within China.   As for China's political elites, many of them—particularly well-educated technological bureaucrats—hope that the explosion in economic linkages will provide them with the skills required to enable the country to continue to compete in the global market economy.

Politically sensitive issues between the U.S. and China—for example, the Taiwan issue—have been put on the table for direct communication and interactive negotiation. In fact, the U.S. has attempted to strike a more even-handed balance in its relations with the mainland and Taiwan, and now listens to voices from both sides.   Indeed, in some instances, it appeared that the U.S. was standing on the side of the PRC, rather than the ROC, in recent years. The Bush administration issued clear and repeated warnings opposing Taipei's moves toward *de jure* independence on numerous occasions during the Chen Shui-bian era. For example, in 2003, President Bush publicly rebuked Chen and warned that "we oppose any unilateral decisions by either China or Taiwan to change the status quo. And the comments and actions by the leader of Taiwan indicate that he may be willing to make decisions unilaterally to change the status quo, which we oppose."[18] Some foreign policy analysts trace Washington's vocal and public opposition to Chen's policies directly to requests (or pressure) exerted by Beijing.

To be sure, economic cooperation alone cannot generate a harmonious relationship. The contradictions revolving around issues such as the continuing trade imbalance and the revaluation of the *renminbi* generate strains in the relationship. Nevertheless, it is noteworthy that close economic interaction intertwines mutual interests; there are many issues of equal importance, not merely security issues as in the past, which occupy agendas for negotiation. In this process, mutual accommodation, and to some extent trust, are being established. Although the two countries still possess distinctive political systems and ideologies, it is clear that economic interdependence has played a critical role in shaping the current period of their relations.

International Cooperation

Among the major characteristics of post-2000 U.S.-China relations is the bilateral and multilateral cooperation that both sides engage in with unprecedented frequency. These cooperation mechanisms offer a broad platform on which the two countries can have direct face-to-face negotiations on issues concerning their interests, thus boosting mutual accommodation and ensuring trust. A typical example of a bilateral communication mechanism is the Sino-U.S. Economic Dialogue (SED), initiated in 2006 and held twice a year, with the purpose of jointly discussing and solving problems arising in economic exchanges, such as RMB revaluation, technology transfers, and the growing trade imbalance. Recalling the six rounds of talks that were implemented by the end of 2008, both sides concurred that "the mechanism had become an effective framework to resolve disputes and react to challenges in the rapidly growing bilateral trade and investment, which could promote the fundamental interests of people of the two countries."[19] Simultaneously, the intertwined interests in international affairs brought them together in international consultation regimes such as the ASEAN+3 Summit, G8+Summit, G20, and the Asia-Pacific Economy Cooperation (APEC), which enhanced their understanding of the benefits of communication and cooperation with each other (and other countries) regarding international political and economic issues concerning their shared interests.

One of the most striking cases of multilateral dialogue in which both countries have cooperated to achieve a win-win outcome is the six-party talks on the North Korean nuclear program, which has achieved some degree of success in stabilizing the Northeast Asian security equation. The Bush administration was satisfied that this mechanism helped curb North Korea's growing appetite for nuclear weapons. Although officials in Washington steadfastly deny any linkage, some suspect that Beijing benefited from this mechanism by asking Washington to restrain Taiwan independence activities in exchange for help in resolving the Korean peninsula issue. In short, these bilateral and multilateral cooperative mechanisms have promoted mutual understanding and trust between the two sides. More important, in this process, a sense has been shaped between Beijing and Washington that when interests collide, the disputes will first be brought to the negotiating table for resolution.

When seeking to explain why the two countries have moved closer in recent years, interconnected economic interests constitute an indispensable variable. Of course, another critically important factor is the global anti-terrorist war that has bound the two countries together in maintaining interlocked security interests. The terrorist groups "replaced China as America's World Enemy Number 1," and China "became a close partner in the anti-terrorism campaign."[20] These interdependent relations have extended from the economic arena into the security arena, enriching the meaning of U.S.-China mutual dependence which originally entailed economic ties and linkages only.

Military Ties and Cooperation

Since 2000, U.S.-China military engagement has accelerated, although primarily in symbolic ways. Some of the most visible events between the two powers were the mutual visits of their respective state defense leaders. In 2002, Cao Gangchuan, then China's Defense Minister, journeyed to the United States and met with senior leaders. During his stay, President Bush informed Cao that Washington would "continue to enthusiastically show concern for and support the development of U.S.-China military ties."[21] In 2005, Donald Rumsfeld, then U.S. Secretary of Defense, visited Beijing, where he agreed to restore military exchanges with China. Following this visit, consultations on security affairs (defense consultations are held on an annual basis), as well as port calls and other practical exchanges, have accelerated noticeably. [22] In June 2006, a Chinese military delegation was invited to observe a U.S. military exercise in Guam, the first time this liaison had occurred since the founding of the PRC.[23] Cooperation in a number of non-traditional security areas—including public health, humanitarian relief efforts and the environment—helped to pave the way toward increased cooperation, if only symbolically.

It should come as little surprise that mutual suspicion still looms large in the two countries' defense sectors due to a long-standing historical differences and a series of unfortunate post Cold War incidents. Too much ink already has been spilled describing these problems, but suffice it to say that they include the 1989 Tiananmen Square Incident, the 1995-1996 missile tests in the Taiwan Strait, the 1999 Belgrade embassy bombing, and the 2001 EP-3 spy plane incident.[24] This might help explain why U.S.-China military exchanges remain more symbolic than functional and seem to be limited largely to dialogue and ritual visits. It is expected that this suspicion would continue to shackle progress in military ties during the short to medium-term future. A recent example is provided by the incident in the South China Sea on March 8, 2009, when an American surveillance ship was blocked by Chinese vessels; and this happened only a week after China and the U.S. renewed consultations that had been suspended for five months as a response to the Bush administration's approval of a major arms sales package to Taiwan.[25]

Despite their differences, the two countries have recognized that developing cooperation in military affairs will not only bring benefits to themselves, but will also make the world more secure, prosperous, and stable. The increasingly interconnected domestic economic sectors and societal forces also create a strong demand for a bilateral military détente. Continuing military engagement corresponds to U.S.-China strategic and security considerations; hence, it cannot be ruled out that the relationship will evolve gradually from the present level of "limited cooperation" to "complex engagement," premised on mutual trust being established.[26] In fact, it is quite possible that the U.S. and PRC already cooperate in numerous ways that remain unclear to the press and the public in both countries. This was certainly the case when both nations teamed up to combat Soviet expansionism during the cold war, and it is likely that the full extent of the present military relationship today is also intentionally obscured.

Summary

In the beginning of the twenty-first century, increasing economic and security ties have promoted interdependent relations between the U.S. and PRC. In fact, Washington found itself in need of Beijing's cooperation in handling a variety of global problems, including the financial crisis, the anti-terrorism war, environmental degradation, health issues, and dwindling energy supplies, to name just a few. China also needs access to American markets, American investment and technology, as well as support in restraining Taiwan's moves toward independence. The deepening U.S.-China mutual dependence has helped advance the momentum in bilateral relations.[27] In 2003, Colin Powell, then U.S. Secretary of State, declared that "U.S.-China relations are the best" since President Nixon's visit to China in 1972.[28] During an interview with one of the authors in January, 2007, Dr. Lin Chong-pin, then president of the Foundation on International and Cross-Strait Studies and former ROC Vice Minister of Defense, opined that Sino-American relations are at their best since the Qing dynasty.[29]

To be sure, the lingering distrust that exists between the U.S. and PRC will not disappear overnight. A risk of political confrontation—perhaps even military conflict—still remains. However, in the long term, the likelihood of either side resorting to armed conflict has declined steadily with the passage of time due to deepening economic ties and shared international concerns.[30] The increasingly intertwined interests in the areas of economy, finance, security, and regional politics have put the two countries on the road toward an enduring peace and constructive partnership.

CHINESE MAINLAND-TAIWAN INTERDEPENDENCE

Relations across the Taiwan Strait have witnessed dramatic changes in recent years that few could have predicted. At the beginning of his first term in office (2000-2004), Chen Shui-bian "sought to reassure both Washington and Beijing that he was not going to rock the cross-Strait boat by declaring independence or even taking any of several steps short of that to which the PRC had exhibited extreme neuralgia."[31] During his inaugural address, Chen pledged to abide by the "Five-no's" (i.e., no declaration of independence, no referendum on independence, no change in the ROC title, no reference to the "state to state" formula in the constitution, and no change in the Guidelines for National Unification).[32] After some time, however, Chen delivered a series of "surprises" that outraged the PRC authorities (and the U.S.). These moves included changing the name of Taiwan's state corporations, shelving the National Unification Guidelines and National Unification Council, holding a series of controversial referendums, and making repeated calls for a new Taiwan constitution.[33] Perhaps most provocative was the noisy 2008 campaign to join the UN and other international government organizations (IGOs) as a new country (Taiwan), an initiative that squarely put Taipei on a collision course with both Washington and Beijing.[34]

During Chen's administration, Taipei's relations with Washington and Beijing sank to new lows. The controversial leader ignored America's repeated warnings not to provoke the Chinese mainland or destabilize world politics. He came to be described as President Bush's "least favorite" democratically elected leader. Moreover, Chen rejected all olive branches extended by Beijing. During an interview with one of the authors, he blasted President Hu's calls for a new approach to cross-strait relations as "sugar coated poison."[35]

The Chen administration's actions contributed to a tense atmosphere across the Taiwan Strait. However, the situation was reversed following the 2008 election of Ma Ying-jeou. Ma responded positively to changes in Beijing's stance toward sensitive issues and initiated a package of policies aimed to relax cross-strait relations. In his inaugural address, Ma clearly indicated that things had changed in Taipei. In addition to outlining his "Three-no's" principle ("no unification, no independence, no use of force), the new president pledged to return to the "1992 consensus," and work toward the normalization of economic, cultural and other relations.[36] The possibility of a peace agreement was raised.

Beijing responded favorably to Ma's initiatives. In June and November 2008, a series of landmark agreements were signed, covering direct passenger and cargo charter flights, direct mail, direct shipping and food safety as well as the opening of Taiwan as a destination for Chinese tourists. In April 2009, representatives from the two sides signed a series of accords designed to fight crime, establish a financial cooperation mechanism and more than double the number of cross-strait passenger flights. That same month, Beijing agreed to Taipei's participation in the World Health Assembly (WHA) as an observer that would use the designation "Chinese Taipei."

One cannot deny that political factors—particularly the personalities and characteristics of key political leaders and political parties in Taipei and Beijing—played a large role in influencing the recent dynamics across the Straits. After all, both Ma and Hu are dynamic leaders who have charted a new direction for cross-strait relations. And both the Kuomintang (KMT) and Chinese Communist Party (CCP) embrace the concept of a shared destiny and membership in "greater China." However, empirical evidence also points to the likelihood that one of the driving forces behind the recent political warmth derives from the closely-knit economic ties between Taiwan and the Chinese mainland.

Economic Ties

Cross-Strait economic integration has grown steadily in recent years irrespective of political ups-and-downs. Trade volume jumped from under US$1 billion in 1986 to over US$46 billion in 2003 (see Figure 7.1)—it soared to $129.2 billion in 2008,[37] representing a growth of roughly 128 times more trade than occurred in 1986. From 2001 to 2007, the accumulated trade surplus Taiwan enjoyed was more than $200 billion; in 2008 alone, the trade surplus with the mainland reached $77.5 billion.[38] In 2007, 40.7 percent of Taiwan's exports consisted of goods shipped to the mainland, a growth of 1.7 times over that in the year 2000.[39]

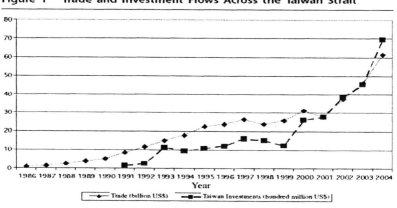

Figure 1   Trade and Investment Flows Across the Taiwan Strait

Figure 7.1 Trade and Investment Flows Across the Taiwan Strait

Source: Scott Kastner, "Does Economic Integration across the Taiwan Strait Make Military Conflict Less Likely?" *Journal of East Asian Studies*, 2006, 6, pp. 319–346.

Taiwan's accumulated investment in the mainland surged from $17.1 billion in 2000 to $64.9 billion in 2007.[40] The Chinese mainland has become Taiwan's largest export market,[41] trading partner and trade surplus contributor.[42] Taiwan is the mainland's seventh largest trading partner, ninth largest export market, and fifth largest import area.[43] According to statistics from Taiwan, in 2004, Taiwan's degree of dependence on exports to the mainland is 25.9 percent—if Hong Kong is included, 37 percent—and on imports from the mainland, 9.7 percent.[44] Not surprisingly, over one million Taiwanese compatriots now live and work in the Chinese mainland—many of them located near Shanghai.

Recognizing the reality of economic exchanges and the benefits to Taiwan, the Ma administration has implemented a series of policies aimed at promoting cross-strait economic cooperation. After relaxing restrictions on the "Mini Three Links" in June 2008,[45] the "Big Three Links" (direct trade, transportation, and postal exchanges between Taiwan and the Chinese mainland) were realized at the beginning of November 2008. As described, three agreements were signed regarding mail and air and sea transportation across the Straits—a momentous breakthrough after several decades of efforts on both sides (this initiative was proposed in the Letter to Taiwan's People in 1979 by the mainland).[46] In the meantime, other economic activities that signaled an increase in the momentum of bilateral exchanges include: resuming the joint prospecting for oil and gas resources by the mainland's China National Offshore Oil Company (CNOOC) and the Taiwan's China Petroleum Company (CPC) in mid-April; Taiwan's establishment of financial institutions to handle the exchange between New Taiwan Dollar (TWD) and Chinese yuan (*renminbi*) on June 30, which would facilitate capital flowing across the Straits, propelling economic integration; the Taiwan administration's mulling over an array of plans to promote commercial exchanges, such as opening of Taiwan's stock market, banks, and real estate to the mainland.[47] At the present moment, the two sides are hammering out the terms of an Economic Cooperation Framework Agreement (ECFA)—a free trade agreement.

The positive economic policies and measures that the two sides are taking will inject new vitality into the ever-developing economic integration, bringing mutual gains to each other. The economies of the Chinese mainland and Taiwan are increasingly interdependent and intertwined. This fact reduces the chances for cross-strait conflict. As one U.S. military report acknowledged, any military clash could "wreck" the economies of both the PRC and ROC and "trigger domestic unrest on the mainland."[48]

International Space and Military Relations

The warming cross-strait relationship—a rapprochement steered, in part, by expanded economic cooperation—has helped open up communication channels to resolve thorny issues such as Taiwan's international space and the relaxation of military tensions. Beijing had long implemented a strategy designed to restrain Taiwan's international space. At first, this tactic was intended to reduce international support for the ROC as the legitimate government of all China, while enhancing support for the PRC. As the years passed and the KMT lost power, however, Beijing's focus changed and it sought to cut off international support for Taiwan's independence. With the thaw in cross-strait relations, the mainland has softened its attitude toward this issue.

It appears that both Taipei and Beijing may have agreed to a "diplomatic truce." For decades, outsider observers criticized both sides for allegedly engaging in "dollar diplomacy." This was a practice whereby the ROC and the PRC "bribed" small and relatively insignificant states to switch recognition to one regime or the other (in keeping with the "one China" policy, states cannot recognize both). Some countries profited handsomely by the rivalry and switched recognition back and forth numerous times. The practice has been criticized as a colossal waste of the taxpayer's money. Since the election of Ma Ying-jeou, however, no countries have switched recognition from Taipei to Beijing or vice versa.

Another example is provided by the November 2008 APEC summit in Peru. During that meeting, both Hu Jintao, PRC president, and Lien Zhan, a former ROC vice president, were in attendance. Lien was "the most senior Taiwan official accepted since the summit was first organized in 1993."[49] Yet another breakthrough occurred in August, 2008, when mainland and Taiwan international trade experts were both were selected as members of the Committee on Subsidies and Countervailing Measures of the World Trade Organization (WTO), a move that signaled the reduced antagonism between both sides.

In December 2008, in his speech commemorating the 30th anniversary of China's "Message to Compatriots in Taiwan," President Hu Jintao reiterated that "China was willing to reasonably discuss with Taiwan about its concern in its international activity space, on the precondition of one China principle being followed."[50] As described, the mainland helped Taiwan enter the World Health Assembly (WHA)—the steering body of the World Health Organization (WHO)—as an observer in April 2009. [51]

It is not an exaggeration to suggest that the increase in economic interaction and political détente has relaxed—to some degree—the military antagonism between the two rivals. Beijing and Taipei have begun to adopt measures to ease military tensions that escalated during Chen's administration. Ma Ying-jeou has ordered the ROC military to halt production of a new generation of Hsiung-feng 2E cruise missiles capable of hitting Shanghai and other high-profile mainland targets. There are reports that the mainland has hinted to KMT officials that it could consider the issue of removing the 1,500 missiles it has deployed directly opposite Taiwan. [52] With respect to confidence building measures (CBMs), President Hu has expressed his support for exploring the possibility of establishing military exchanges and increasing other forms of military cooperation.[53] Perhaps this helps explain why in January 2009, the Chinese navy escorted a Taiwan ship in waters off Somali to protect it from pirate attacks. In the latest development, it has been confirmed that "servicemen from the mainland and Taiwan will meet for the first time during a security forum held in Hawaii this August, 60 years after the civil war."[54]

In short, the tense atmosphere of military confrontation that characterized relations during the Chen Shuibian era has been eased. As Hong Kong commentator Yangda observed, with the positive change of the island's political situation, the growing Beijing-Taipei détente, as well as an the interdependent international system, the risk of military conflict across the Straits has been reduced to the lowest levels since 1949.[55]

Summary

Increasing economic integration across the Taiwan Strait is playing a positive role in improving the relations of these two old foes. Some might argue that the asymmetry of their economic interdependence—Taiwan is more economically dependent on China than vice versa—functions as a stabilizer in the cross-Strait relations. According to the theory of complex interdependence, the difference in the level of mutual dependence is "most likely to provide sources of influence for actors in their dealing with one another" because "less dependent actors can often use the interdependent relationship as a source of power in bargaining over an issue and perhaps to affect other issues."[56] If this mutual dependence is evenly balanced, each side would be in the position of employing economic leverage to rival the other—the conflicts could conceivably escalate. Moreover, economic tools such as economic sanctions might offer Beijing another chance (in addition to military means) to express its firm attitude in holding back Taiwan independence movement regardless of any economic costs, thus alleviating the likelihood of military conflicts sparked by Taiwan's underestimating Beijing's true resolve in restraining provocative actions.[57]

Economic interdependence is becoming an important factor in preventing a cross-strait conflict. However, it would be an exaggeration to suggest economic interaction is an effective solution to the six-decade feud across the Straits. There are still a host of uncertainties in the road ahead. Particularly worrisome are the nationalist sentiments on both sides—instigated readily by misunderstandings and/or mischief—that pose a potential risk to the enduring peace across the Straits.[58]

Economic interdependence might not be a decisive variable in shaping bilateral relations; but it goes a long way in creating an atmosphere in which both sides can communicate and negotiate issues of mutual concern. If the current momentum of economic interaction and political detente proceeds smoothly, it is not beyond realm of possibility that some form of enhanced integration—in a way that both sides would be willing to explore and accept—could take shape someday in the future. Numerous ideas are being explored, debated and discussed in universities, think tanks and governmental agencies in both Taiwan and the Chinese mainland.[59]

U.S.-TAIWAN INTERDEPENDENCE

The U.S. no longer recognizes the ROC as the legitimate government of China. Washington broke its "formal" diplomatic relations with Taipei thirty years ago when it recognized Beijing. But the U.S. and Taiwan remain linked by political, economic and security considerations. In fact, U.S. officials often claim that Washington's "unofficial" relations with Taipei are closer than its "official" ties with most other countries.

Political Ties

The year 2000 proved to be a politically significant year for both Taiwan and the U.S.. In Taiwan, the KMT—which had governed the island for five decades— lost a landmark election. The election of an opposition candidate as the island's leader was viewed by many as a successful test of Taiwan's democratization, and strengthened America's determination to protect and promote Taiwan "as a model for democratization in China and East Asia."[60] The democratic ties built on shared values appeared to consolidate and enhance the U.S.-Taiwan bonds. George W. Bush, in his 2000 presidential campaign, "openly questioned the policy of strategic ambiguity toward Taiwan's defense," and favored a clear policy supportive of Taiwan.[61]

In 2001, President Bush proclaimed that he would do "whatever it took to help Taiwan defend theirself [sic]."[62] Following this declaration, American policy continued to tilt toward Taiwan. Perhaps the apex was reached in 2003 when Chen Shuibian traveled to the U.S. and was "allowed to give speeches in public venues, to entertain American politicians in grand style, and to greet his supporters in downtown New York streets."[63]

During Chen's second term in office (2004-2008), U.S.-Taiwan relations suffered. As described, Washington opposed Chen's moves toward *de jure* independence from China. But the Bush administration remained resolute in its support for Taiwan's democratization. In 2005, President Bush visited Japan. During his stay, the president urged Beijing to follow the model of Taiwan's political reform, saying "by embracing freedom at all levels, Taiwan has delivered prosperity to its people and created a free and democratic Chinese society . . .," and "as China reforms its economy, its leaders are finding that once the door to freedom is opened even a crack, it cannot be closed. The freer China is at home, the greater the welcome it will receive abroad."[64]

Taiwan's continued peaceful evolution from a staid authoritarian regime into a multi-party democracy conforms to America's overarching foreign policy goal of spreading democratic values worldwide. Many American officials— including President Bill Clinton and President George W. Bush—contend that democratization yields "practical" benefits for American interests. This is because they support the central propositions of "democratic peace theory." Those who embrace this position believe that democracies "are more likely than those with other governments to be reliable partners in trade and diplomacy, and less likely to threaten the peace."[65] Moreover, when more states democratize throughout the world, "the safer and more prosperous Americans will be, since democracies are demonstrably more likely to maintain their international commitments, less likely to engage in terrorism or wreak environmental damage, and less likely to make war on each other."[66]

American officials recognize that Taiwan's democracy is far from perfect. But the island's democratization has stiffened America's resolve to protect it. As Peter W. Rodman, then Assistant Secretary for International Security Affairs in the U.S. Department of Defense, explained in 2004, "Taiwan's evolution into a true multi-party democracy over the past decade is proof of the importance of America's commitment to Taiwan's defense. *It strengthens American resolve to see Taiwan's democracy grow and prosper* [emphasis added]." [67] It is noteworthy that President Barack Obama shares these sentiments. After Ma Ying-jeou won Taiwan's 2008 election, Obama sent him a message expressing his support for Taiwan's democratization while affirming its implications for regional stability and the world democratic movement. The charismatic candidate declared that "your election on March 22nd and your inauguration on May 20th were good days for the people of Taiwan, for the forces of democracy around the world, and for peace and stability in the Taiwan Strait and western Pacific. I will do all that I can to *support Taiwan's democracy in the years ahead* (emphasis added)."[68]

Economic Ties

Although only a fraction of the size of the Chinese mainland (which considers the island to be the nation's smallest province), Taiwan is one of the world's largest traders. As one of the America's largest trading partners, the ROC is of unquestionable economic importance to Washington. The U.S. presently conducts more trade with Taiwan than it does with Australia, Italy or any country in the Middle East, Africa, Eastern Europe or South America. Contrary to the popular misconception, Taiwan sells more than what critics once derided as "Taiwanese junk" (footwear, textiles and knick-knacks) to its trading partners. By 2007, Taiwan led the world in the manufacture of large-size Thin-Film Technology—Liquid Crystal Display (TFT-LCD) panels (49 percent of global market share) and integrated circuit chips (68.1 percent of global market share), while it enjoyed the position as the world's second largest manufacturer of Dynamic Random Access Memory (DRAM) chips (22.4 percent of global market share) and Organic Light-Emitting Diode (OLED) flat panels (39 percent of global market share).[69] Moreover, Taiwan corporations manufacture roughly "82 percent of notebook computers, 98 percent of motherboards, and 72 percent of LCD monitors."[70]

In addition to serving as a source for critical materials, Taiwan's "economic miracle" serves American interests in other ways. Perhaps most important, it serves as a model of modernization and development for much of the world. The island has long been an embarrassment to those governments that promote a totalitarian road to development, while serving as an inspiration to countries hoping to avoid such a path. As Representative Henry Hyde (R.-IL) observed, "Taiwan's economic success was essential in convincing Beijing that a Western, market-oriented economic model would work in China."[71]

Military Ties

The U.S. and Taiwan have been military partners for more than five decades. In 1954, Taipei and Washington concluded a mutual defense treaty that "bolstered the KMT regime's security and enhanced its legitimacy both at home and abroad."[72] In 1979, the U.S. terminated the defense treaty when it switched recognition to the PRC. That same year, however, the U.S. Congress passed the Taiwan Relations Act (TRA), a highly unusual piece of legislation that outlines the terms of Washington's "unofficial" political and military relations with Taipei. According to the law, the U.S. "will make available to Taiwan such defense articles and defense services in such quantity as may be necessary to enable Taiwan to maintain a sufficient self-defense capability." With respect to America's security guarantee to Taiwan, the TRA warns that the U.S. will consider any hostile actions directed against Taiwan as "a threat to the peace and security of the Western Pacific area and of grave concern to the U.S." In other words, it provides a U.S. administration with the *option* to go to war to protect the island.

Operating within this legal framework, U.S.-Taiwan military relations have remained largely intact. The security arrangement, albeit unusual, has benefited both sides—particularly Taipei. Taiwan receives both a critical boost to its defensive capabilities (American arms and technology) and a "tacit" alliance that helps deter potential aggression. As for Washington, some contend that Taiwan helps it pursue a 'hedging strategy" against the PRC and that the island would be a trustworthy partner during an emergency. Others point to the economic benefits accrued by large arms sales to the island. Still others point to less visible benefits. For example, despite American pledges to the contrary, it is clear that bilateral strategic cooperation did not end with the abrogation of the U.S.-ROC defense treaty and the switch in diplomatic relations to Beijing. There is much more to the military relationship than the highly visible and much-publicized American arms sales and technology transfers to Taiwan. For example, the two militaries share intelligence on the PRC and the U.S. reportedly operates a top-secret signals intelligence facility in Taiwan's Yangmingshan Mountain.[73] According to some accounts, Taiwan's human intelligence operations (HUMINT) in China are unparalleled by any other spy network.[74]

After 2000, Washington's military ties with Taipei became even closer. In 2001, President Bush announced that the "once-a-year bilateral military sales discussions" between the U.S. and Taiwan would be scrapped. Rather, the annual talks would be replaced by "normal, unscheduled military discussions to be convened *based on need*" [emphasis added].[75] The level of bilateral military exchanges was elevated and the U.S. began to deploy defense personnel to

Taiwan in order to observe military exercises and offer advice on improving the strength of Taiwan's armed forces. Moreover, high-level military officers and defense officials from Taiwan began to travel to the U.S. to attend short-term training sessions or semi-official meetings.[76] Furthermore, while the *quantity* of military weapons sold to Taiwan after 2000 remained roughly the same (see Table 7.2) as the 1990s,[77] the *quality* improved.[78] Perhaps most significant, in 2001, the Bush administration approved the sale of submarine-killer aircraft and diesel submarines "that had been denied to Taipei for decades."[79] In September 2008, Bush announced plans to sell more than $6.4 billion worth of such equipment to Taiwan (submarines were not included in this deal). The move signaled Washington's willingness to continue to sell arms to Taiwan. Obama supported the sale, while his opponent in the 2008 presidential election, Senator John McCain (R.-Arizona), argued for a larger package.

Table 7.2 Comparison of Values of U.S. Arms Sales to Taiwan between 1999-2002 and 2003-2006

	1999-2002 Period	2003-2006 Period
U.S. Agreements	$1.1 billion	$1.1 billion
U.S. Deliveries	$5.8 billion	$4.1 billion

Source: Shirley Kan, *CRS Report for Congress, Code RL30957, Taiwan: Major U.S. Arms Sales Since 1990*, (Washington, D.C.: *Congressional Research Service*, September 25, 2008).

Summary

U.S.-Taiwan interdependence, based on political, economic and security interests, constitutes an unusual phenomenon in the landscape of international politics. Although friendly China-U.S. interactions are increasing steadily, America's commitment to help Taiwan's security, which was further promoted by Taiwan's progress in democratization, remains steadfast. This type of interdependence—two governments linked by shared political values and security needs—was analyzed by Keohane and Nye, who pointed out the continuities between realist and interdependent politics. According to these prominent theorists, the "traditional politics of military security" also embodies the relations of mutual dependence, and "military allies actively seek interdependence to provide enhanced security for all."[80]

Looking ahead, the Obama administration has reaffirmed that the policy of providing military support for Taiwan will not change. As Hillary Clinton observed during her recent visit to four Asian countries (Japan, Indonesia, South Korea, and the PRC), "under the Taiwan Relations Act, there is a clear provision that the United States will provide support for Taiwan's defense. And that is why there has been, over the many years, the sale of defensive materials to Taiwan."[81] Consequently, it is possible that the issue of arms sales to Taiwan will remain as an irritant to U.S.-China relations, like an entangled knot, without prospects of being easily resolved in the near future.

CONCLUSION

Since the year 2000, the trilateral relationship between the U.S., PRC and ROC has become increasingly interdependent; although, the spheres and levels of interdependence vary (see Figure 7.2). Suffice it to say that the interdependent politics among the three have played a large role in creating the current dynamics in their mutual interaction. The economic interdependence between the PRC and the U.S. as well as Taiwan has helped promote a reconciliation of longstanding political and military problems, while China's weak military ties with the other two actors remain a potential threat to the peace and stability across the Straits. Strong U.S.-Taiwan security relations have remained intact against the backdrop of the U.S.-China economic partnership, while the U.S. explored a role for Taiwan in demonstrating the "fruits" of Western democracy planted in the soil of a traditional Asian culture. In short, one point is clear: economic considerations have gained an important position of influence with regard to the three actors' political and security agendas.

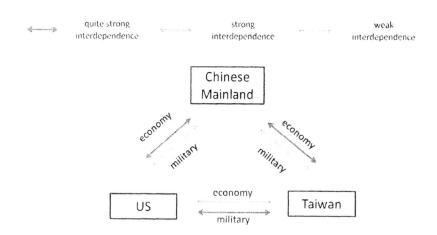

Figure 7.2 Chinese mainland-U.S.-Taiwan Interdependence Status

The rising trend of economic interdependence, wherein various interests become co-mingled, is projecting these relationships in the direction of mutual accommodation and cooperation. The three sides, however, each has its own political bottom-line that cannot be infringed upon. For Beijing, Taiwan is an inalienable part of China. For the U.S., Taiwan's feisty democracy must not be threatened by external forces, primarily the Chinese mainland. As for Taiwan, its absolute leadership over the island's destiny and future association with the mainland cannot be impaired. In other words, Beijing cannot expect the U.S. to abandon a democratic friend (Taiwan), while the U.S. must make an effort to understand and appreciate the importance that Taiwan holds for the Chinese mainland. Likewise, Beijing cannot expect Taipei to agree to all of Beijing's unification policies, while Taiwan should not underestimate the mainland's resolve to stymie moves toward *de jure* independence (and Washington's opposition to unilateral changes in the status quo). Any miscommunication and/or misunderstanding could reignite tensions among the three.

To forecast the trajectory of this trilateral relationship, it is probable that the economic linkages between the Chinese mainland, Taiwan and the U.S. will play an increasingly critical role in shaping their ties with one another, especially given the context of a close-knit, globalized world. Indeed, the scope and speed of the recent economic crisis underscores the interconnected characteristics of the entire global community. Economic considerations will carry more weight, not less, when Washington, Beijing and Taipei craft their respective policies toward one another. The recent Hu-Obama summit in London provides an example. The two leaders brokered an agreement to establish a mechanism, the "China-U.S. Strategic and Economic Dialogue," in an effort to "build a positive, cooperative, and comprehensive U.S.-China relationship for the 21st century and to maintain and strengthen exchanges at all levels"[82]; Beijing and Taipei have achieved consensus that they will improve their relations by starting with relatively easy economic issues and then moving on to tough political problems (*xianjingji houzhengzhi*). There is no telling how the Taiwan issue, which remains at the core for each side, can be resolved—but it can be said that a peaceful solution of this issue will have a win-win-win consequence to this trio that is bound by shared economic and security interests.

NOTES

1. The authors recognize that these national titles are considered sensitive. In keeping with the "1992 consensus," however, people from the Chinese mainland and Taiwan may hold differing views and interpretations of the meaning of China—whether it is the PRC or ROC. Mr. Zhou may believe it's the PRC. Taiwan compatriots may believe it's the ROC. And as an American, Dr. Hickey believes that both sides are correct—there is one China with two political entities.
2. See "President Sets Forth Guidelines on Taiwan," *China Daily* (Beijing), March 4, 2005. www.chinadaily.com.cn/english/doc/2005-03/04/content_421902.htm (accessed April 1, 2009).
3. Robert Keohane and Joseph Nye, *Power and Interdependence* (New York: Pearson Longman, 2000), p. 21.
4. Ibid., pp. 210-211.
5. Ibid., p. 22.

6. Ibid, p. 211.

7. See Richard Rosecrance, *The Rise of the Trading State: Commerce and Conquest in the Modern World* (New York: Basic Books, 1986), pp.13-14, 25-26.

8. Ibid.

9. See Kerry Dumbaugh, *Taiwan: Recent Developments and U.S. Policy Choices, CRS Brief for Congress, Foreign Affairs, Defense, and Trade Division*, Code IB98034, (Washington, D.C: Congressional Research Service, July 1, 2002.)

10. Steve Tsang, ed., *Peace and Security across the Taiwan Strait* (New York: Palgrave Macmillan, 2004), p.126.

11. See Barbara Demick, "In China, Bush Remains A Popular President," *Los Angeles Times*, January 15, 2009, in *Lexis/Nexis*.

12. See Si Tingting and Fu Jing, "China May Top Japan as World's Second Largest Economy," *China Daily*, March 10, 2009, http://www.chinadaily.com.cn/china/2009-03/10/content_7559222.htm (accessed on March 6, 2009).

13. See Gregory C. Chow, *China's Economic Transformation, 2nd edition* (Oxford: Blackwell Publishers, 2007), pp.107-108.

14. See Graham Webster, "Zoellick on China: The Washington Consensus?" *Transpacifica*, May 29, 2007. http://transpacifica.net/2007/05/29/zoellick-on-china-the-washington-consensus/ (accessed March 8, 2009).

15. See Hu Jintao, "Constructive and Cooperative China-US Relationship," *Speech at Dinner Hosted by Friendly Organizations in the United States*, April 20, 2006. http://www.asiasociety.org/speeches/06dc_Hu.html (accessed March 8, 2009).

16. See "Bush: U.S.-China Relations 'Good' and 'Important'," *People Daily*, August 1, 2008. http://english.peopledaily.com.cn/90001/90776/90883/6464276.html (accessed March 8, 2009).

17. See Wayne Morrison, *China-U.S. Trade Issues, CRS Report for Congress*, (Washington, D.C.: Congressional Research Service, January 2008).

18. Shirley Kan, *China/Taiwan: Evolution of the 'One China' Policy—Key Statements from Washington, Beijing and Taipei, CRS Report for Congress*, (Washington, D.C.: Congressional Research Service, December 13, 2007), p.78.

19. See Hongjiang Wang, "Commentary: Sino-U.S. Economic Dialogue Finish Sends Strong Signals to Future," *XinHuaNet*, December 5, 2008. http://news.xinhuanet.com/english/2008-12/05/content_10462771.htm (accessed on March 15, 2009).

20. Willy Lam, *Chinese Politics in the Hu Jintao Era: New Leaders, New Challenges* (Armonk, N.Y.: M.E. Sharpe, 2006), p. 183.

21. Ibid, p.185.

22. Dennis Hickey and Kelan Lu, "The Future of Sino-US Military Cooperation," in Sujian Guo, ed., *China in Search of a Harmonious Society* (Lanham: Lexington Books, 2008).

23. See "China to Observe Joint Drill in Guam," *China Daily*, June 9, 2006. http://www.chinadaily.com.cn/china/2006-06/09/content_612355.htm (accessed January 30, 2009).

24. See, Hickey and Lu, "The Future of Sino-US Military Cooperation."

25. See "U.S. Protests Chinese Harassing of Naval Ships," *USA Today*, March 20, 2009, p. 8A.

26. See, Hickey and Lu, "Future of Sino-US Military Cooperation."

27. President George W. Bush, in commenting on Ma Ying-jeou's victory in Taiwan's election, said that it "provides a fresh opportunity for both sides to reach out and engage one another in peacefully resolving their differences." See Charles Snyder, "Bush urges Hu to reach out to Taiwan," *Taipei Times*, March 28, 2008, p. 1.

28. Willy Lam, "The End of the Sino-American Honeymoon?" *China Brief*, Volume 4, Issue 13, July, 2004.

29. Dennis Hickey's interview with Dr. Lin Chong-pin, president of the Foundation on International and Cross-Strait Studies, Taipei, Taiwan, ROC, January 5, 2007.

30. Huiyun Feng and Kai He, "If Not Soft Balancing, Then What? Reconsidering Soft Balancing and U.S. Policy Towards China," paper presented at the annual meeting of the American Political Science Association, Marriott, Loews Philadelphia, and the Pennsylvania Convention Center, Philadelphia, PA, Aug 31, 2006.

31. See Tsang, *Peace and Security across the Taiwan Strait*, p. 122.

32. Derek McDougall, *Asia Pacific in World Politics* (Boulder, CO.: Lynne Rienner, 2007), pp. 170-174.

33. Dennis Hickey, "Friction Between Friends: US Policy and Taiwan's United Nations Campaign," *Tamkang Journal of International Affairs*, Volume 11, Number 4, April 2008, p. 22.

34. Ibid.

35. Author's interview with Chen Shui-bian, Taipei, November 21, 2007. For a text with highlights of the interview, please see Dennis V. Hickey, "Reading China's 'Peace' as 'Sugar Coated Poison'": Interview with President Chen Shui-bian," *Chicago Tribune*, January 6, 2008, Section 2, p. 4.

36 . Those in the Chinese mainland refer to Mr. Ma as a "leader," and Mr. Hu as a "president." But those in Taiwan do the opposite. One of the authors, Mr. Zhou, prefers to call Mr. Ma a "leader," while Dr. Hickey prefers to call both leaders "president." For these reasons, the term "president" is used very sparingly in this study, but it is used occasionally. The two authors have "agreed to disagree" on this point (one paper, two opinions).

37 . See "The Trade Volume Across the Straits in 2008 Exceeding $129 Billion (2008 nian liangan maoyi e yu 1290 yi meiyuan)," *GOV.CN*, February 4, 2009. On the World Wide Web http://www.gov.cn/jrzg/2009-02/04/content_1221481.htm (accessed April 10, 2009).

38. See Ming Yang, "Economic and Trade Relations across the Straits after Taiwan's General Election (Taiwan daxuan hou de jingji he liangan jingmao guanxi)," *VOAnews.com*, March 22, 2008. http://www.voanews.com/chinese/archive/2008-03 (accessed April 2, 2009).

39. See Shufang Huang, "Taiwan's Exports Increasing 10% Annually in 2007 (2007 nian Taiwan chukou nian zeng yu 10%)," *Epoch Times*, January 7, 2009.

40. See Mainland Affairs Council, *The Significance of the Second 'Chiang-Chen Talks'*, October 27, 2008. http://www.gio.gov.tw/ct.asp?xItem=43950&ctNode=4505 (accessed April 15, 2009).

41. Yang Ming, "Cross-Straits Economy and Trade Relations after Taiwan's Election," *VOAnews.com*, March 22, 2008. http://www.voanews.com/chinese/archive/2008-03/ (accessed February 22, 2009).

42 . Scott Kastner, "Ambiguity, Economic Interdependence, and the U.S. Strategic Dilemma in the Taiwan Strait," *Journal of Contemporary China*, Volume 15, Issue 49, November 2006, pp. 651-669.

43. See Taiwan Affairs Office of the State Council of the P.R.C., Information on Cross-Straits Economy and Trade, February 4, 2009. http://www.gwytb.gov.cn/lajmdt/ lajmdt0.asp?lajmdt_m_id=1475 (accessed February 25, 2009).

44. See "Cross-Strait Economy and Trade Relations in 2004 (2004 nian liangan jingmao guanxi)," *XinHuaNet*, April 3, 2006. http://news.xinhuanet.com/tai_gang_ao/2006-04/03/content_4378490.htm (accessed February 25, 2009).

45. Mini Three Links referred to the postal, transportation, and trade links between Chinese mainland's cities of Xiamen, Mawei and Quanzhou, and the Kinmen and Matsu islands of Taiwan. Originally, Taiwanese that could use the mini links were limited to the two islands' residents and the businessmen who invested in the mainland. On June 19,

2008, with the passing of an Implementation Plan for Normalization of Exchanges between Mini Links People, the mini links were applied to all Taiwanese.

46. See "Looking Back Cross-Straits Economy and Trade Relations in 2008 and Looking it Ahead in 2009," *China.com,cn*, January 9, 2009.   http://big5.china.com.cn/overseas/txt/2009-01/09/content_17079814.htm (accessed March 10, 2009).

47. Xitang Pan, "Cross-Straits Economic and Trade Relations Facing the Test of Transformation," *HongKong Business Newspaper*, October 8, 2008.

48. Office of the US Secretary of Defense, US Department of Defense, *Annual Report to Congress, Military Power of the People's Republic of China, 2008* (Washington, D.C.: US Government Printing Office, 2008), p.43.

49. See "YEARENDER: Taiwan-China Relations Thaw, But Real Truce Difficult."

50. See "China Will Allow Taiwan to Participate in International Events," *The China Post*, January 21, 2009. http://www.chinapost.com.tw/taiwan/china-taiwan-relations/2009/ 01/21/192958/China-will.htm (accessed March 3, 2009).

51. Yu Xie, "Beijing May Help Taipei in WHO Role," *China Daily*, March 26, 2009. http://www.chinadaily.com.cn/china/2009-03/26/content_7618267.htm (accessed April 10, 2009); see "WHO Invites Taiwan to Attend World Health Assembly as Observer," People's Daily   Online, April 30, 2009. http://english.peopledaily.com.cn/ 90001/90776/90883/ (accessed on May 1, 2009).

52. Dennis Hickey, "President Ma's Chief Challenges: Taiwan, the Chinese mainland and America," paper delivered at the conference Taiwan's New Approach: Opportunities and Challenges for President Ma Ying-jeou's Government, University of Chicago, October 24, 2008, p. 21.

53. Li Chuan, "Chinese Navy Improves its Impression on Taiwan People: First Time Escorting Taiwan Ships in Six Decades (Zhongguo haijun liushi nian lai shoudu huhang gaishan Taiwan minzhong yinxiang)," *China News*, January 13, 2009.   http://www.chinanews.com.cn/tw/lajl/news/2009/01-13/1525938.shtml (accessed March 4, 2009).

54. Xiaohuo Cui, "Mainland, Taiwan Servicemen to Meet in Hawaii," *China Daily*, March 30, 2009. http://www.chinadaily.com.cn/china/2009-03/30/ (accessed on April 10, 2009).

55. See "It's of Far-reaching Implication that the PLA Navy Escorted Taiwan Ships First Time during Six Decades (Zhongguo haijun liushi nian lai shoudu huhang taichuan You shenyuan yiyi)," *Xinhua News*, January 13, 2009, http://news.xinhuanet.com/mil/2009-01/13/content_10651780.htm (accessed on April 16, 2009).

56. Keohane and Nye, *Power and Interdependence*, p. 9.

57. Scott Kastner, "Ambiguity, Economic Interdependence, and the U.S. Strategic Dilemma in the Taiwan Strait," *Journal of Contemporary China* 15, November 2006, Number 49, pp. 651-669.

58. McDougall, *Asia Pacific in World Politics*, p. 176.

59. Some scholars have proposed a Commonwealth Model or a Union Model to be applied to China Mainland-Taiwan integration. See Tai-chun Kuo and Ramon Myers, "Peace Proposal One: The China Commonwealth Model," and Steve Tsang, " Peace Proposal Two: The Chinese Union Model," in Steve Tsang, ed., *Peace and Security Across the Taiwan Strait* (New York: Palgrave MacMillan, 2004), pp. 192, 203.

60. Dennis Hickey, "Strategic, Economic or Political Partner: Understanding the Basis of America's Continuing Commitment to Taiwan," paper delivered at the international conference, *Taiwan's Search for Democratic Partners: Workshop at St. Anthony's College, Oxford University*, Oxford, United Kingdom, June 15-16, 2007. p.10.

61. Dennis Hickey, *Foreign Policy Making in Taiwan: From Principle to Pragmatism*, (London: Routledge, 2007), p. 35.

62. Ibid., p. 36.

63. Lam, "The End of the Sino-American Honeymoon?" p. 186.

64. Erick Johnson, "Be More Like Taiwan, Bush Urges Beijing," *The Guardian*, November 17, 2005. http://www.guardian.co.uk/world/2005/nov/17/usa.china (accessed March 20, 2009).

65. Strobe Talbott, "Democracy and the National Interest," *Foreign Affairs*, November/ December 1996, pp.47-63.

66. Ibid.

67. See Prepared Statement of Peter W. Rodman, Assistant Secretary for International Security Affairs, US Department of Defense, in *The Taiwan Relations Act: The Next Twenty-Five Years*, Hearing Before the Committee on International Relations, One Hundred Eighth Congress, Second Session, April 21, 2004 (Washington, D.C.: US Government Printing Office, 2004), p.23

68. See "Letter from Barack Obama to Ma Ying-jeou," *USC US-China Institute*, May 22, 2008. http://www.china.usc.edu/ShowArticle.aspx?articleID=1066 (accessed March 22, 2009).

69. See Government Information Office, *Republic of China Yearbook, 2008*, http://www.gio.gov.tw/taiwan-website/5-gp/yearbook/ch9.html (accessed May 1, 2009).

70. See Jorge Liu and Deborah Kuo, "China May Destroy World's Chip Supply if It Attacks Taiwan," *Central News Agency*, February 1, 2007, in *Lexis/Nexis*.

71. See Remarks of the Honorable Henry J. Hyde before the Chinese National Association of Industry and Commerce, August 24, 2001   http://house.gov/hyde/ statements2001/ TaipeiSpeech.htm (accessed on May 2, 2009).

72. Hickey, *Foreign Policy Making in Taiwan: From Principle to Pragmatism*, p. 9.

73. For more information, see Brian Hsu, "Taiwan and US Jointly Spying on China: Report," *Taipei Times*, January 30, 2001, p.3, http://taipeitimes.com/news/archives/2001/ 01/30/0000071597/print (accessed on April 20, 2009).

74. See Wendell Minnick, "The Men in Black: How Taiwan spies on China," *Asia Times Online*, February 26, 2004, http://www.atimes.com/atimes/China/FB26Ad05.html (accessed on April 28, 2009).

75. Su Chi, *Taiwan's Relations with Mainland China: A Tail Wagging Tow Dogs* (New York: Routledge, 2009), p. 155.

76. Ibid., p. 156.

77. Among worldwide U.S. weapon customers, Taiwan ranked 2nd (behind Saudi Arabia) in 1999-2002 and 4th (behind Israel, Egypt, and Saudi Arabia) in 2003-2006.

78. Weixing Wang, "Historical Evolution of American Arm Sales to Taiwan (Meiguo duitai junshou de lishi yange)," *Taiwan Week*, November 2008, Number 41.

79. Hickey, *Foreign Policy Making in Taiwan*, p. 35.

80. Keohane and Nye, *Power and Interdependence*, p. 9.

81. Chiehyu Lin and Y.F. Low, "U.S. to Continue Arms Sales to Taiwan: U.S. State Secretary," *The China Post*, February 17, 2009.

82. See Foon Rhee, "Obama Meets Chinese, Russian Leaders," *Boston.Com*, April 1, 2009.http://www.boston.com/news/politics/politicalintelligence/2009/04/obama_meets_c hi.html (accessed April 10, 2009).

Chapter 8

The Role of American Business in Sino-American Normalization

Kailai Huang

This study examines the entanglement of politics and trade in the tortuous journey toward the normalization of US-China relations in the 1970s. The fluctuation of U.S.-China trade correlated closely with the development, or the lack of it, in Sino-American political relations. When US-China reconciliation made progress, trade experienced rapid growth. Both Beijing and Washington considered growing economic ties would broaden the basis of the political relationship and generate the perception of momentum. When normalization stagnated, trade suffered sharp decline and American business felt pressured by China to lobby Washington for political concessions. Caught in the crosscurrents of international and domestic politics, American business had to carefully navigate the uncharted water in the China market and to be mindful of the conservative, pro-Taiwan sentiment at home. Even more challenging was the dynamics in China's foreign trade policy that was guided more by political usefulness than by economic rationality. While generally supportive of the diplomatic recognition of China, American business refrained from playing a vigorous role in Sino-American normalization due to the political complications and the moderate assessment of the China market.

CORRELATION BETWEEN NORMALIZATION AND TRADE

The resumption of trade between the U.S. and China was the direct result of two countries' political rapprochement. In 1971 Washington lifted the embargo imposed on China trade since the Korean War as one of the conciliatory overtures to Beijing. China however waited until after Nixon's visit in February 1972 to respond. In the Shanghai Communiqué the two countries committed themselves to a "one China" principle and agreed to "facilitate the progressive development of trade" based on equality and mutual benefit. Thus, for the first time in over two decades Americans could legally engage in direct trade with China, and in Spring 1972 the first group of American business people were invited to attend the biannual Guangzhou (Canton) Export and Import Trade Fair, the most important venue where China's trade negotiations and deals were made.

Despite the excitement following the reopening of the China trade and some impetuous remarks about the teeming million Chinese consumers, American business was cautious about the trade prospects. China, after all, was a poor developing country and its import-substitute trade regime allowed only capital-good and grain imports to accelerate industrialization and relieve food shortage. Exports, under this regime, were employed as means to finance imports. China's refusal to seek foreign credits and lack of marketable goods in U.S. market further limited its buying power.[1]

Another uncertainty was the political aspect of China's foreign trade—the ramifications of China's internal politics and foreign policy issues. Considering China's long-held position that the settlement of Taiwan question was the precondition for trade relations, also considering the recent extremism during the Cultural Revolution, many were wondering what political conditions might be attached to U.S.-China trade.

The past patterns of China's foreign trade had the faces of Janus. On the one side, the Chinese were practical, holding commercial competitiveness above ideology and not letting politics dictate whenever a better deal was available. In fact, China was doing most of its foreign trade with non-socialist countries and had no formal diplomatic relations with the largest trade partners such as Japan and West Germany. With the other face, however, China never hesitated to lecture foreign businessmen on the "inseparability of trade and politics," and expected from them at least lip service to the "five principles of peaceful coexistence" and China's claim over Taiwan. It had made breaking commercial ties with Taiwan a precondition for Japanese companies trading with China and blacklisted those who did not comply. There was little doubt that China's intention was to use business as leverage to press the Japanese government on the issue of diplomatic recognition of Beijing. With Japanese precedent in mind, some American business people feared that the similar precondition would be laid down for them.[2]

To the surprise of American businessmen and women visiting China in 1972, their Chinese hosts—government officials from the state trading corporations—showed little interest in discussing political issues. In business negotiations, product and right price, not correct political attitudes, were primary concerns. Gone were the frenetic days of the Cultural Revolution when foreign traders were lectured, admonished and harangued by the Red Guards; gone also were some companies classified as "friendly firms" and granted preferential treatment because of their expressed sympathy for China's policies. In several cases when some Americans quoted Mao's little red book and professed support to Beijing's political line in business negotiations, the Chinese officials, instructed to treat "foreign friends" with unfailing politeness, would just "listen patiently and [were] exceedingly bored."[3] Premier Zhou Enlai once expressed his "disdain" for those who would exploit Chairman Mao's writings in such a utilitarian way.[4] Whereas not a few Americans found the Chinese way of doing business frustratingly time-consuming and even the most basic information was often kept by the Chinese as a state secret, few complained about any political strings attached to business deals. Instead, the Chinese lavished on Americans with endless banquets and cared only talking about how trade would strengthen Sino-American friendship.[5]

The disarming cordiality and absence of political lectures were actually an integral part of a well choreographed Chinese public-relation offensive aimed to project an image of a new China and to court American goodwill. China hoped that American business people—the "72-style Marco Polos"—well treated and benefited from China ties, would influence American public opinion to China's favor. Actually both Beijing and Washington considered promoting trade an important means to create a warming-up atmosphere in the new Sino-American detente.[6] In Chinese political parlance and news media diplomacy was often referred as *waijaozhanxian*, diplomatic battle line, foreign trade therefore was an important front.

The development of Sino-American trade after Nixon's visit manifested the correlation between the progress of political reconciliation and trade growth. U.S. exports to China shot up from zero in 1971 to $806.9 million in 1974, with 80 percent of them agriculture commodities. And during the same period, U.S. imports from China increased at a spectacular rate from an insignificant $4.7 million to $114.7 million. In 1974, the two-way trade almost hit the $1 billion mark. Although the amount of Sino-American trade was still relatively small compared with both U.S. foreign trade and China's national income, the U.S. became China's second largest trading partner after Japan in less than three years. Contrary to many early expectations, China was willing to tolerate an 8:1 trade imbalance in favor of the U.S.

The surprising surge of bilateral trade was closely tied to the rapid development of political relations. The high point of this "honeymoon" phase was Kissinger's visit to Beijing in February 1973, when the U.S. and China agreed to establish de facto embassies in each other's capital under the name of Liaison Office. The momentum in Sino-American rapprochement apparently convinced the Chinese government that Nixon was going to carry out his commitment to establishing full diplomatic relations with Beijing before the end of his second term. In the trade field, the government-blessed National Council of U.S.-China Trade was inaugurated in May 1973 in Washington and sent a delegation to China in October. American business people visited China in increasing numbers and found their hosts always eager to emphasize how trade contributed to the friendship between two great peoples. As the rapid growth of U.S.-China trade proved most early pessimistic forecasts wrong, Americans were optimistic about the future.[7]

Sino-American political relations began to cool off in 1974, however. Domestic politics in both countries contributed to the loss of momentum toward normalization. Vulnerable to criticism from the radicals, Zhou Enlai and his pragmatist colleagues found it difficult to show more flexibility in dealing with the U.S., especially on the issue of Taiwan. Doubting U.S. sincerity in abiding by a promised "One China" policy, China hardened its position by laying down the three conditions for normalizing relations: a U.S. breaking of diplomatic relations with the Nationalist government; the withdrawal of U.S. troops from Taiwan; and the abrogation of the mutual defense treaty.

U.S. internal politics, nevertheless, hampered Washington from accepting such conditions, even if the White House so desired. The Watergate scandal devastated the Nixon Administration and cramped his leverage in initiating any new moves on China, especially since he had to depend on the Republican right wing to save his skin in Congress. Similarly, Nixon's successor, President Ford, could not afford to be accused of abandoning Taiwan by his conservative Republican challenger Ronald Reagan. Polls also showed the public opposed to recognizing the People's Republic at the cost of breaking ties with Taiwan. Ford's trip to Beijing in December 1975 achieved no breakthrough. As 1976 was an election year in the U.S. and political turmoil erupted once again in China, the process of Sino-American normalization stuck in an impasse.

The political stagnation coincided with the unexpected slump of U.S.-China trade. Defying all optimistic projections, total trade in 1975 declined to $461.6 million, just about half of the 1974 volume. It reached a new low of $335.9 million in 1976 and only slightly increased to $372 million in 1977. Although there were apparent economic reasons for the decline, such as China's good harvests that reduced buying U.S. grain and import cuts to redress the large trade deficit, many American businessmen worried that the overall U.S.-China commercial relationship was being impeded by interference from both China's internal political campaigns and the outstanding issue of Sino-American normalization.

POLITICAL CAMPAIGNS AND FOREIGN TRADE

Visitors to China during the early and mid 1970s could not miss two slogans: "Political work is the life-blood of all economic work," and "Building our country independently and with the initiative in our own hands through self-reliance." These two quotations from Chairman Mao were ubiquitous—in the media as well as posted with large characters in offices, factories, schools, and communes. To China watchers in the West, the constant challenge was to determine how these Mao's tenets were interpreted and applied in making China's economic policies, including those for foreign trade.

The history of China's erratic economic development since 1949 showed the policy-pendulum swinging between propelling economic growth and stressing ideological purity, between accepting foreign aid and promoting autarky. In the 1960s, after the Sino-Soviet split, China became increasingly inward-looking and foreign trade stagnated. Ideology, rather than technology, was regarded as more vital to the Chinese model of modernization. During the Cultural Revolution the economy as a whole suffered serious setbacks and foreign trade evidenced a three-year decline (1967-1969). The principle of "self-reliance" was lauded with feverish enthusiasm, and many officials in charge of economy lost their jobs for the alleged crime that they had practiced "productionism " and "worship of things foreign"—code words for emphasizing production and supporting import of foreign equipment and technology.

The policy pendulum seemed to swing to the moderate end when U.S.-China trade was resumed in 1972. The madness of the Cultural Revolution was over and the shattered economy, under the leadership of the pragmatic premier Zhou Enlai, began to pick up. Along with the major breakthrough in China's foreign relations was a new policy in foreign trade. With the approval of Mao and Zhou, the State Planning Committee began in January 1973 to implement the so-called "4.3 Plan": importing machinery and complete plants from the West at the value of $4.3 billion.[8] Though China did not officially announce this plan, foreign businessmen could hardly miss it because substantial import contracts were signed between China and Western firms. Among them was Pullman Kellogg, a Texas-based company, whose sale of 8 ammonia plants to China came to $200 million dollars.

While the general view was that foreign advanced technology and equipment were indispensable for China's modernization, and price and quality weighed more than anything else in making a sale, few were so naive to exclude the possibility of political interference in China's foreign trade. It was no secret that the two factions inside the Communist party leadership, often labeled as "moderates" and "radicals," were divided and debating on what should be the correct strategy for the nation's economic development. On the issue of foreign trade, the moderates advocated importing foreign machinery and technology to accelerate China's industrialization. They supported expanded foreign trade on the basis of "equality and mutual benefit." But the radicals were suspicious of even the partial opening to the West and fanatically emphasized "self-reliance." They proposed that, rather than depending on machinery, technology and professionals, the development of a socialist economy should rely on the "masses' wisdom and strength," as well as "revolutionary spirit."[9] In the history of the People's Republic such debates almost always led to political campaigns with disruptive impact on economy. There was good reason for U.S. China traders to be increasingly concerned about China's political stability and consistency of foreign trade policy.

Without many portents, in early 1974 China plunged into another political storm—a campaign called "criticize Lin Piao, criticize Confucius." On appearance, the campaign focused on attacking the "philosophy of restoring the old order" of Confucius, the sagacious philosopher of the fifth century B.C., and his alleged twentieth-century disciple Lin Piao, the former designated successor to Mao reportedly dead in a plane crash in 1971 after an aborted coup. But the essence of the campaign was a power struggle in which the radicals, led by Mao's wife Jiang Qing, tried to ouster Premier Zhou Enlai and other moderate leaders. The current economic policy's emphasis on production and the importation of technology and whole plants from abroad were under severe attacks by the radicals who controlled the propaganda apparatus. The media barrage lauded China's achievements under "self-reliance" and accused the capitalist countries of being based their development on "exploiting their own people, and plundering people of the other countries." The justifications for whole plant imports—technological edge and reliability—were vilified as the "blind worship of things foreign" and "the traitorous philosophy of slavish mentality." And the moderates who supported increased foreign trade were labeled as modern compradors who had no basic patriotism.[10]

Such venomous attacks with their anti-foreign tone, along with mass rallies and wall posters across the country, looked like a rerun of the Cultural Revolution. To many people's relief, however, the movement appeared to be under control by the summer of 1974 and Premier Zhou and other moderates retained power. In a bid to alleviate foreign business people's anxiety, Chinese trade officials went out of their way to reassure them that it was business as usual, and that the on-going campaign would not be allowed to hurt the country's burgeoning foreign trade.[11]

China's economy was not greatly disrupted, but American traders nevertheless felt the impact of the campaign. The accusation of "slavish comprador philosophy" and the glorification of "self-reliance" apparently forced Chinese trade officials to recoil, for their own political safety, from new initiatives.[12] One example was China's rigidity on the issue of labeling exported foodstuffs. Despite U.S. importers' suggestions that private labels of major American wholesalers or retailers would enable Chinese canned food to sell better, Chinese officials refused to make the change, in large degree out of fear of being criticized for allowing China to be debased by the capitalists as just an anonymous supplier.[13] China also cancelled a scheduled visit to the U.S. in the summer of 1974 by a high-level trade delegation including representatives from all eight state trading companies.

Another area of possible U.S.-Chinese economic cooperation blocked by the ideological campaign was joint exploitation of China's offshore oil reserves. Indeed, what American companies most hoped—direct investment through "joint ventures"—was politically unthinkable even to the pragmatists at that time, but other forms of cooperation were possible, such as long-term credits for China to import U.S. drilling equipment and later repay them with oil products. The political campaign, however, made certain that such deals would be denounced as a sellout of the nation's resources. As a result, negotiations between China and American oil companies led to no concrete outcomes.[14]

The campaign of 1974 set the pattern of political jockeying for succession. The radicals, with Mao's backing, saw a convenient target in the pragmatists' foreign trade policy and hoped to discredit their rivals by the charge of betraying Mao's sacrosanct principle of "self-reliance." The moderates, often on the defensive, had to postpone their more outward-looking economic plan, waiting for the aging Chairman to pass away. The ouster of Deng Xiaoping in 1976 rekindled the criticism of expansive foreign economic relations. Deng's alleged support for expanding exports, including oil and mineral products, in order to increase imports of foreign equipment and technology, was labeled a "national betrayal." Beyond propaganda, China cut back its imports and exports. The 1976 Spring Guangzhou Trade Fair suffered from a scarcity of goods and Chinese officials revealed that production was down 10 percent to 15 percent because of the campaign. China returned to the early inflexible position regarding labeling and trade officials were reluctant to enter into long-term contracts. U.S. business totaled only $23 million in the spring fair, nearly 50 percent below the previous fall's 40 million.[15]

In the first half of 1976, almost all nations' two-way trade with China was down. Foreign trade, as *The China Letter* reported, "is the area that is feeling the greatest immediate impact of recent political developments and natural disasters in the People's Republic."[16] Like China traders from other countries, Americans resigned themselves to the reality that economy and politics were intertwined in China and could only hope that the periodic political campaigns would not disrupt their business with the country too much.

THE OBSTACLE OF SINO-AMERICAN NORMALIZATION

Many Americans involved in China trade only belatedly began to realize that what affected their business more than China's internal turmoil was the overdue American diplomatic recognition to the People's Republic. In the mid 1970s, the U.S. was the only major Western country that had not established full diplomatic relations with Beijing. The recognition, or normalization as the Chinese preferred to call it, was more complex than just switching the embassy from Taipei to Beijing, for the U.S. had also committed to Taiwan's security by a mutual defense treaty of 1955. As Washington was unwilling to abandon its Nationalist allies by abrogating the treaty, the negotiation for normalization stalemated. The political difficulty inevitably affected every aspect of Sino-American relations; hence it became the ultimate obstacle in further development of U.S.-China trade. And American China traders experienced an increasing pressure from the Chinese to become actively involved in pushing Sino-American normalization.

Before 1975 few Americans seemed to give much thought that trade between the two countries existed not for its own sake but as an integral part of the whole process of Sino-American rapprochement. The rapid growth of commercial exchanges should not obscure the fact that political relations did not catch up. Even the commercial relationship itself was not fully normalized in terms of China's lack of most-favored-nation status for tariffs and the unresolved issue of frozen claims and assets, which prohibited the establishment of direct banking, aviation, and shipping links between China and the U.S. Many Americans, believing that blocked assets and discriminatory tariffs were major obstacles in U.S.-China trade, strongly supported MFN for China and a fast settlement on frozen claims and assets. They did not realize, at least for a period of time, that the solutions of those issues hinged on the progress of normalization which was stuck with the thorny Taiwan question.

Not abruptly but still unmistakably, China let American businessmen know, through words and action, its evident discontent with the deadlock in normalization. Previously, the favorite topic in Chinese trade officials' conversations with Americans had been how trade would strengthen the people-to-people friendship. Now the Chinese would lose no opportunity to point out that without normalization there was little prospect for trade to increase. Whereas some Americans tried to explain the sharp decline of trade since 1975 as caused by economic factors, the Chinese were blunt as to what should be blamed:

> The prospect of trade growth can't be decided solely by economic factors . . . If the relations and pace of normalization accelerate politically, trade growth will reflect this. If relations remain stagnant, trade growth will be at a slow pace.[17]

Lest someone might get the wrong idea that U.S-China trade had developed because of economic necessities rather than political needs, the Chinese told the Americans in unambiguous language:

> As regards political considerations, since the Shanghai Communiqué, we really feel we should import something from the U.S. and increase the volume of our trade . . . (however), the theory that we will import the best needs at the best prices irrespective of political considerations is not true.[18]

From 1975, many Americans believed that U.S. business was relegated to a residual-supplier status, both in agricultural products and non-agricultural goods. There were reports that China imported manufactured goods, including American-made goods, from third-country traders just to avoid buying directly from the U.S., even American companies could offer better deals. The intended message was clear: the major barrier to U.S.-China trade was political, not economic.

China's increasingly vocal and critical concern for the absence of MFN also demonstrated the political implications of U.S.-China trade. Having indicated only general interest in MFN status, Beijing had not pressed the issue even when the 1974 Trade Act disqualified China for MFN because of the "Jackson-Vanik free emigration amendment." But as its impatience with the slow pace of normalization growing, China now saw the issue as just another irritate symbol that Washington was dragging its feet. Not caring for MFN per se, the Chinese declared, they just wanted to be dealt with "on the basis of mutual benefit and equality." To China, the MFN status was not the major issue here:

> MFN treatment would expand trade but the key factor in normalization does not lie here, and, therefore, the MFN question is not the major factor. If you do away with the discriminatory measure, trade could increase, but increased trade between China and the U.S. does not hinge on the MFN treatment question.[19]

China also balked at reaching any final settlement on the Chinese assets frozen in the U.S. after the outbreak of the Korean War and American claims to properties confiscated in China after the communist takeover in 1949. It adopted the same position that was to tie the issue to normalization. Previously, China and the U.S. reached an agreement in principle on settlement in 1973. But since then Beijing stalled on a final accord. Despite realizing that a settlement would bring the benefits of direct air links and trade exhibitions in the U.S., China saw the assets question a "minor issue" compared with the major issue of normalization. "As long as we continue normalization," the Chinese liked to say, "this question is bound to be resolved."[20]

From a legal perspective, the assets and claims issue was the most significant impediment to further development of economic ties. And, again legally, the issue could be settled on its own, independent of the question of diplomatic recognition. But China was in no hurry to reach a deal unless such act would also result in political gains. Commercial normalization—a trade agreement that would settle the assets and MFN issues, could be used as an inducement that would motivate American business to press on Washington to accomplish the political normalization with China.

THE TAIWAN CONTROVERSY

By careful management, U.S.-China trade was not disrupted by the politically charged Taiwan issue for several years. In general, China tolerated U.S. companies' ties with Taiwan, so long as these companies did not support the Nationalist government politically. Yet the PRC remained very sensitive to any activities of U.S. firms that appeared to advocate a "two-China policy." When Sino-American relations were relatively warm, China reacted to such incidents with moderation.[21] But when relations stagnated, China would play up its displeasure. Such was the controversy over the formation of the U.S-Republic of China Economic Council (USROCEC) in 1976. The Council was promoted by a former U.S. cabinet member and a high-ranking Nationalist official. A number of major American corporations joined the Council and nine members of the Board of Directors were also members of the National Council for U.S.-China Trade (NCUSCT), the pro-Beijing trade organization.[22] Beijing reacted strongly, stating: "The companies that have joined seem to believe there are two Chinas. It constitutes an unfriendly act."[23] Therefore relations between China and those companies with dual membership would be impossible not to be affected. China backed its words with action. American Express, for example, found that China refused to honor its traveler's checks; two other companies, Union Carbide and General Electric, were passed over for invitations to the fall 1976 Guangzhou Trade Fair. China did not try to conceal that these moves were retaliation against firms enrolled in USROCEC.

China's strong reaction caught many American businessmen by surprise, even though the consequent punishments were little more than a slap on the wrist. There was a certain amount of naivete on the part of American companies, which considered their action of joining the pro-Taiwan council no more than a commercial decision. As Beijing was concerned, its goal was not to punishing any individual firms, but to send a message to the profit-minded-only

Americans. Without U.S. recognition of the People's Republic as the only China, it was unrealistic to count on business as usual in trade relations.

Many got the message. "Two years ago, I was not convinced that prospects for U.S.-China trade were firmly tied to diplomatic recognition," an American banker said in 1976. "But since then, I've seen this thing swing around."[24] Few Americans had envisioned that the lack of diplomatic relations would become a major obstacle to the growth of bilateral trade; many had believed the most urgent issues were granting China MFN and settling the assets and claims questions. Only now it became abundantly clear that China viewed U.S.-China trade not just as economic exchanges which benefited both sides, but more as a means to multiply its strategic ties with the U.S. Beijing's rhetoric and acts with respect to trade were aimed at pressing Washington to quicken the pace of normalization. The Chinese hoped that American business, presumably to benefit from better relations, would help by lobbying the U.S. government, influencing public opinion and contributing to a domestic consensus supportive of diplomatic recognition of Beijing.

However despite Beijing's insistence on the linkage between trade and normalization, the limited China market and its unpredictable future gave few incentives to American business community to lobby for China's cause. The low-key posture of American business during the whole process of normalization reflected the conservative assessments of China's trade potential and the awareness of public opposition to breaking ties with Taiwan. As Sino-American normalization followed a slow and zigzag path, U.S.-China trade continued to twist in the uncertain political wind.

NORMALIZATION AND THE SURGE OF U.S.-CHINA TRADE

Prospects for U.S.-China trade turned decidedly brighter in 1978. After the purge of the radical Gang of Four and the return of Deng Xiaoping to the power center, China embarked on a path of economic reform and open-up. Shelving Mao's self-reliance principle, China was willing to import foreign goods and technology in an unprecedented scale. To finance such massive importation, China decided to increase its exports, especially oil, and for the first time to ask for direct foreign credits. To American business, even more important than China's domestic changes was that the long, strenuous journey of Sino-American normalization finally approached the end. In May 1978, Washington informed Beijing that it would accept China's three conditions for normalization: breaking U.S. official ties with Taiwan, withdrawing U.S. troops and abrogating the mutual defense treaty. Although such a breakthrough and the ensuing negotiations were tight secrets, trade with China immediately benefited from the regained momentum in Sino-American relations.

Realizing that the recognition of the People's Republic at the cost of Taiwan would provoke domestic controversy, the Carter Administration tried to solicit the widest possible support, including that from the business community. The Administration encouraged American business to get more involved in

China and pledged to facilitate processing export license applications. [25] Washington lifted an earlier ban on selling China advanced equipment for geological and earthquake research. The flocking of U.S. business people to China was matched by a parade of government officials, among them Agriculture Secretary Bob Bergland and Energy Secretary James Schlesinger, on missions to promote opportunities for American business.

China also did its best to help build favorable public opinions in the U.S. "Both before and after normalization," as Carter later wrote with appreciation, "the Chinese exhibited a fine sensitivity about my other duties, and also about our domestic political realities." [26] The Chinese understood that purchasing American products and receiving hundreds of American business people, among them top men from the *Fortune* 500, would definitely have a positive impact on American public perception of China. The attraction of the lucrative China market would motivate many Americans to support better relations with the mainland. In business negotiations the Chinese replaced their past "no greater trade without normalization" theme with a new familiar refrain of trade promoting friendship, and more contracts than ever were signed with American firms. The adjusted estimation for the 1978 U.S.-China trade was over $1 billion, doubling the earlier prediction. As the clock set for normalization ticked away, both Washington and Beijing hoped that a booming trade could reduce, if only partially, the expected negative reactions to such a dramatic development.

The active courting of business support paid off when business opinions responded favorably to President Carter's announcement on December 15, 1978, that the United States and the People's Republic of China would officially establish diplomatic relations on January 1, 1979. [27] On December 17 Energy Secretary James Schlesinger declared that diplomatic recognition could benefit American oil companies' on-going talks with China. On the same day, Li Qiang, China's Foreign Trade Minister, announced that henceforth American companies could trade on an equal footing with traders from countries with established diplomatic relations, thus ending the U.S. "residual supplier" status. Furthermore, Li said that China would consider a long term trade agreement with the U.S. along the lines of those signed with Japan and European countries.

Sino-American normalization triggered a wave of "euphoria" that swept over the business community. The outpouring interest in China trade was fueled to the boiling point by well-publicized multimillion dollar "contracts galore" with China. [28] The most conspicuous event among the feverish China gold-rush was Coca-Cola Company's announcement that it would begin to sell its soft drink in China on January 1, 1979, the official day for diplomatic relations. Despite the denial of direct link with the normalization by Coca-Cola and several other companies also concluding big deals with China, the timing could hardly be interpreted as mere coincidence. With Deng Xiaoping's scheduled visit to Washington for late January 1979 promised to contribute toward favorable American public response, China had been trying to show U.S. business that the China market was for real. [29] With all their economic merits, the accelerated trade activities since the December 15 announcement were no doubt part of the preparation for Deng's visit to cement the embryonic political ties.

Also, the more American business got involved in trading with China, the more leverage Beijing would have in the upcoming negotiations on the issues of frozen assets and MFN.

On the eve of Deng's visit, China upgraded its banking relationships with many big U.S. banks to that of full correspondent banking relationship, a move it had dodged for years. Smelling politics in such a change, one banker noted: "They may have wanted these banks to put pressure on Washington to settle the remaining problems between the two countries."[30] Whatever China's true consideration, such development was good news to the Carter Administration. It needed immediate evidence that closer political ties with China would bring economic benefits. With political relations normalized and the solutions of other trade related issues put on fast track, U.S.-China trade entered a new era.

CONCLUSION

Sino-American trade from 1972 to 1978 demonstrates that economy in China was inescapably entangled with politics. The ups and downs of U.S.-China trade were affected more by the politicized nature of China's foreign trade, which was to use trade as a chip in the game of international politics. The fluctuation of US-China trade correlated closely with the development, or the lack of it, in Sino-American political relations. When reconciliation between the U.S. and China made rapid progress after Nixon's visit in 1972, trade with China experienced unexpected growth. Both Beijing and Washington considered growing economic ties would broaden the basis of the political relationship and generate the perception of momentum. When normalization stagnated, trade suffered sharp decline and American business felt pressured by China to lobby Washington for political concessions. Beijing repeatedly stated that in making trade decisions political considerations outweighed economic benefits. Caught in the crosscurrents of international and domestic politics, American business had to carefully navigate the uncharted water in China and to be mindful of the conservative, pro-Taiwan sentiment at home. The moderate assessment of the China market provided few incentives for a vigorous campaign. Therefore the business community, while in general supporting a better relationship with China, was conspicuously absent in lobbying for the normalization. Only when the U.S. and China resolved the diplomatic recognition problem, trade began to climb up again in faster pace and other economic barriers melted away rapidly. Closer commercial ties were regarded as important to strengthen the new political partnership. After all, trade and politics, as China always proclaimed, were inseparable and politics should always take the command.

NOTES

1. Robert F. Dernberger, "Prospects for Trade Between China and the United States," in Alexander Eckstein (eds.), *China Trade Prospects and U.S. Policy*(New York: Praeger, 1971), 185-319. Also see William R. Galeota, "Trade with China, Long A Dream of Americans, Remains Only a Mirage," *Wall Street Journal*, February 29, 1972, 1; "Chemical Men Skeptical About Red China Trade," *Oil, Paint and Drug Reporter* 199 (April 19, 1971): 3; Leonard S. Silk, "Nixon, China and Wall St.," *New York Times*, July 21, 1971, 4; "China Shows Little Trade Potential: McQuade," *Advertizing Age* 42 (November 15, 1971): 64; "Despite 'Thaw,' No Bonanza in U.S.-China Trade," *U.S. News & World Report*, February 14, 1972, 30.

2. See Lawrence C. McQuade, Najeeb E. Halaby, *Vital Speeches of the Day* 38 (December 15, 1971): 148-152; *New York Times*, January 24, 1971, 12; *Burroughs Clearings House* 56 (February 1972): 62.

3. "Trade with China," *China News Analysis*, July 13, 1973, 6. Also see Nicholas C. Chriss, "Chinese Trade—Little Red Book Points the Way," *Los Angeles Times*, April 26, 1974, sec.1, 10.

4. "China Trade Won't Give Quick Fillip to Exports, U.S. Business Is Told," *Wall Street Journal*, October 10, 1972, 13.

5. *New York Times*, May 18, 1972, 42; *Los Angeles Times*, June 11, 1972, sec. E, 1; December 17, 1973, sec. III, 13.

6. See "U.S. Trade Prospects with the P.R.C.: A Realistic Assessment," a speech delivered by Marshall Green, Assistant Secretary of State for East Asian and Pacific Affairs, *Current Foreign Policy*, Department of State Publication 8687, East Asian and Pacific Series 207, December 1972. Also, Steven W. Mosher, *China Misperceived: American Illusions and Chinese Reality* (New York: Basic Books, 1990).

7. Edward Neilan and Charles R. Smith, *The Future of the China Market* (Washington D.C.: AEI-Hoover Policy Studies, 1974). Also see *Wall Street Journal*, June 4, 1974, 22; Chin-Yuen-Chen, "U.S.-China Trade Prospects," *Columbia Journal of World Business* 9 (Fall, 1974): 80-86.

8. Fang Weizhong et al., eds., *Zhonghuarenmingongheguo Jingji Da Shi Ji: 1949-1980 (Economic Chronicle of the People's Republic of China: 1949-1980)* (Beijing: Chinese Social Sciences Publishing House, 1984), 505.

9. Li Hsin, "Self-Reliance Is a Question of Line," *Peking Review*, August 8, 1975, 14-23.

10. *Red Flag*, no. 1 (January 1974): 85-88. Also see, *Xuexi yu Pipan (Study and Criticism)* 3 (1974): 39-41.

11. *Far Eastern Economic Review*, April 8, 1974, 38-39; *US-China Business Review* 1 (May-June 1974): 42-45; and 3 (November-December 1974): 33-37.

12. John Sharkey, "China Debate Seen Limiting U.S. Contacts," *Los Angeles Times*, February 19, 1974, sec. I, 7.

13. *Los Angeles Times*, February 19, 1974, sec. I, 7.

14. *Los Angeles Times*, January 10, 1974, sec. I, 14.

15. *US-China Business Review* 3 (May-June 1976): 47-48. Also see *New York Times*, May 24, 1976, 45; *China Trade Report* (August 1976): 25; *Industry Week*, September 6, 1976, 26.

16. *The China Letter* no. 58 (1976): 4.

17. China Trip Diary, 1975, folder John Knowles, box 5, The University of Michigan National Archive on Sino-American Relations (Hereafter cited as Michigan Archive).

18. Ibid.

19. Knowles folder, box 5, Michigan Archive.

20. Ibid.

21. For example, when a major U.S. ship-chartering firm listed Taiwan as "Republic of China" in its printed materials sent to PRC, the mainland Chinese expressed its objection by telling the U.S. firm that Taiwan was "an inalienable part of China." Then, they added diplomatically: "We believe your careless printer will withdraw such mistakes in the future." See *Christian Science Monitor*, December 5, 1975, 28.

22. *The China Letter* no. 55 (May 1976): 1-2.

23. Barry Wain, "Numerous Major U.S. Firms Are Caught in Middle of China-Taiwan Trade Row," *Wall Street Journal*, January 25, 1977, 17.

24. Jacques Leslie, "U.S.-China Trade Hinges on Diplomatic Relations," *Los Angeles Times*, September 12, 1976, sec.VI, 1.

25. *China Business Review* 5 (July-August 1978): 17.

26. Jimmy Carter, *Keeping Faith, Memoirs of a President* (Toronto: Bantam Books, 1982), 211.

27. For supportive business opinions, see "Special Message to National Council Members," *China Business Review* 5 (November-December 1978): back to the cover; Peter T. Kilborn, "Trade with China: High Hopes in U.S.," *New York Times*, December 19, 1978, sec. d, 1; Karen Elliott House and Robert Keatley, "U.S.-China Ties Likely to Lead to More Trade, Closer Political Contact," *Wall Street Journal*, December 18, 1978, p. 1.

28. See, for examples, *Business Week*, January 8, 1979, 16; Hobart Rowen, "That Euphoria Over Chinese Trade," *Washington Post*, January 11, 1979, sec. A, 23; William H. Miller, "China Trade: Euphoria Now and Big Dollars Later," *Industrial Week*, January 8, 1979, 17; H. J. Maldeabert, "Trade-Offs in China Trade, US Business Sees an Opportunity—and Peril," *Christian Science Monitor*, January 8, 1979, 16.

29. Besides Coca-Cola, for example, Boeing announced on 19 December 1978 that it would sell three Boeing 747SP jumbo jets to China costing $156 million. In early January, U.S. Steel announced it would build a huge iron-ore processing plant worth about $1 billion. The Flour Corp., also in January, signed a $10 million agreement to plan a copper mine for China.

30. Karen W. Arenson, "Bank Links with China Upgraded," *New York Times*, January 24, 1979, sec. D, 1.

Chapter 9

From Pragmatism to Morality: The Changing Rhetoric of the Chinese Foreign Policy in the Transitional Period

Dominik Mierzejewski

INTRODUCTION

Since 1978, China has been enjoying rapid economic growth. The new strategy that has embraced the global processes has been beneficial for China. Because of taking this initiative, China's international activities, for the first time in its history, were framed on a big scale. Beijing's interaction with the outside world has helped to find a proper way to communicate with the world in terms of its intentions and projection of her future role in international politics. China perceives its foreign policy as a program of actions chosen to achieve particular goals during a particular period, which consists of six basic elements: goals and objectives, perceived capabilities, identity and image of foreign actors, identity and definition of prevailing and dependent situations, identity and status of decision making individuals or institutions, actual conducts.[1] To the author, one of the most interesting problems in the contemporary international relations is building the identity through the usage of a proper rhetoric and framing that would convince others of our rightfulness.

Is the vocabulary hollow? —the question put by Jean Luc Domenach is still more than topical today. In politics and foreign affairs, language has never been innocent. It conceals, but it also reveals and maintains the convictions of the actors.[2] As the primary system of communication in human society, language makes us understandable to other people and, thus, we possess the power to communicate. Moreover, if used with skill and deliberation, words offer us the power of persuasion. Such power enables us to move and influence others, even to their detriment. Special words in certain contexts have an extraordinary ability to structure beliefs and emotions in a particular way.[3] Political rhetoric creates the arena of political reality within which political thought and action take place.[4] These are not only words that matter, however. As Lloyd F. Bitzer notes, rhetorical constraints are "made up of persons, events, objects, and relations

which are parts of the situation because they have the power to constrain decision and action." Sources of such a constraint might include "beliefs, attitudes,
documents, facts, tradition, images, interests, motives and the like."[5] In this particular case, China is not an exception.

Regarding Chinese ancient philosophers, moral and ethical issues have been
a central theme throughout the representative Chinese rhetorical text. As Confucius advocated, being a moral person was considered the most essential trait for
speakers and rulers alike. Notions like: *tian ming*—mandate of heaven, *jun zi*—
noblemen, *zheng ming*—rectification of names, were ethically correct language
used for the purpose of establishing order and stability in society. For Confucius,
every name or term prescribed a concept and a pattern of behavior. Through the
rectification of names, the leader has been predestined to amend the way of
thinking and the patterns of behavior and, thus, to build societal norms. In Confucius's words: "when names are not correct, speech will not be appropriate;
when speech is not appropriate, tasks will not be accomplished."

The earliest examples of Chinese rhetoric are the "instructions," especially
those concerning the ways in which a minister of state should address the ruler.
For it is here that the speaker is expected to be honest, sincere and forthright, to
preserve his own dignity, to avoid flattery and, at the same time, to show respect
for the ruler and keep from antagonizing him.[6] As John Makeham explains,
Confucius did not regard names as mere passive labels, but rather as social and,
hence, political catalysts. In the sense *zheng ming* aimed at transforming Chinese society and its people through advocacy of certain terms or concepts. In
Chinese rhetorical tradition, thinkers were very much aware of the power of
symbols in human motivation, in the perception of reality, and in control of human action.[7]

A most practical piece of advice was provided by Han Feizi of the legalist
school. In "*The Difficulties of Persuasion*" he persuaded as follows:

> On the whole, the difficult thing about persuading others is not that one lacks the
> knowledge needed to state his case nor the audacity to exercise his abilities to the
> full. On the whole, the difficult thing about persuasion is to know the mind of the
> person one is trying to persuade and to be able to fit one's words to it.[8]

Like his predecessors, Han Feizi advocated that the speaker must know the
"soul" of the listener and adapt the message to his understanding. What Han
Feizi had in mind, however, was something more sophisticated and manipulative.
Rhetoric was conceptualized in ancient China and terminology was created to
describe features of invention and style, but speech was not studied as a separate
discipline; it was always thought of as a part of political and moral philosophy.[9]

By means of describing the rhetoric of pragmatism and morality, this chapter aims to analyze and find a proper answer to two basic questions: why Chinese policy makers in the 1980s and 1990s followed a rather pragmatic rhetoric,
while after Hu Jintao took over power, China started to use moral language to
describe its actions in the international arena. The second basic question revolves around the meaning of China's pragmatism vs. moral rhetoric for the rest

of the big powers. As it was mentioned above, to the author, not only material issues play an important role in international relations, but so does rhetoric (understood as diplomatic language) in shaping the understanding of foreign policy motivations, especially in relations between big powers.

BEING PRAGMATIC AND INDEPENDENT

Having learned from Mao Zedong's international relations thoughts, which might be described as "revolutionary romantic," Deng Xiaoping was more realistic in his calculations. While Mao Zedong's policy was idealistic (*lixiang zhuyi*), Deng Xiaoping provided China with pragmatic and realistic foreign policy (*shixian zhuyi*). As Zi Jichen remarked, in Deng's foreign policy periods one could distinguish two "leaps forward" (1985 and 1989), and "three stages," namely: 1977-1984, 1985-1989 and 1989-1992.[10]

In 1980s, the international problems in China were described in a rather clear-cut way. What might be interesting, during the Party Congresses (12th in 1982 and 13th in 1987), the Secretary Generals of the Chinese Communist Party did not mention the international problems in their reports. In 1982, Hu Yaobang referred only to the international market (*guoji shichang*). Five years later, Zhao Ziyang spoke highly of the international situation that benefited China's economic development.[11]

Deng Xiaoping pragmatism was based on the assumption that only practice determines the truth. Working rules of *shishi qiushi* were made up of four general instructions:

1. Identify the desired results and goals, then find the appropriate method to achieve these results and goals;

2. Be realistic in choosing the method; if the method chosen can lead to the desired goals, then adopt it no matter whether it is ideologically correct or not, do not let the ideology stand in the way;

3. Based on the above, get rid of ignorance and poverty and adopt methods to get rich and become economically developed;

4. If the method is capitalist by definition, then so be it as long as it produces results.[12]

In the 1980s, Deng stated that China's role in international affairs depended on the level of economic success of the country:

> If our country developed and became more prosperous, we would play a larger role in international affairs. Our current role in international affairs is not small, but if our material basis and material capabilities are enhanced, our role will be even larger. [13]

Having a realistic approach, Chinese authorities declared an independent foreign policy. China was afraid that Ronald Reagan would play the *China card* in the ongoing game with the Soviet Union. Deng Xiaoping calculated: "We do not want you Americans to stand on our shoulders to fight the Russians."[14] During his visit to the US in 1984, Zhao Ziyang argued that China would stand for normalizing relationships under the five principles of peaceful coexistence. This new shape of China's foreign policy was determined by two major factors: Ronald Reagan's pro-Taiwan stance and the domestic leadership shakeup in June 1981. The newly stated rhetoric of independent policy was a vital dissociation from the past.[15]

The period between 1984 and May 1989 was one of the most productive eras in Chinese foreign relations. The approach to foreign policy became less ideological and more pragmatic as it sought friendly relations with all states based on the five principles of peaceful coexistence. China strived for a status quo between major powers and herself, the US and USSR, and, what was most important for the Chinese reforms, China entered negotiations with GATT to rejoin the organization.[16]

A serious situation in the Soviet Union and in the East European countries, such as Poland or Hungary, caused by insufficient material basis, was the impulse for Deng Xiaoping to set up the concept of *taoguan yanghui*. After the Tiananmen Incident, in 1989, the international community criticized the Communist Party of China. The problem of China's reaction to the first ever bold words of criticism arose. Chinese authorities were not accustomed to the criticism of other states, even more so since it came from its former ideological rival —Soviet Union. Their first reaction was to stop the reforms and the opening-up process. In September 1989, the announced strategy included the following phrases: watch and analyze calmly (*leng jing guan cha*), secure the position (*wen zhu zhen jiao*), deal with confidence (*chen zhe ying fu*), conceal capabilities (*tao guan yang hui*) and be good at keeping a low profile (*shan yu shou zhuo*).[17] The *taoguan yanghui* might be understood as it had been in *Sanguo Yanying— yangjing xurui*—to hone one's ability and strength for a big push.[18] On the one hand, the rhetoric of *tao guang* articulated the passive posture of China in international relations but, on the other, Deng Xiaoping put forward the concept of "active promotion of the new world political and economical order."[19] This, after two years of a closed-door policy, brought the Chinese policy makers and intellectuals to a broader analysis. For the first time ever, in 1992, Jiang Zemin discussed the international situation in a separate paragraph of the Party's report. He advocated that in the new international situation there was still a chance to avoid the next world war. Jiang Zemin also stressed the importance of the Five Principles of Peaceful Coexistence in the Chinese foreign policy.[20]

The discussion on the passive posture in international affairs has been driven by both internal and external affairs. The major internal factor was the "patriotic education" and new "middle class," and the major international affairs were: the Taiwan crisis in 1995/1996, the Kosovo crisis of 1999, and EP-3 Spy Plane Collision incident of 2001. To the author, the most important as well as influential was the NATO intervention in Yugoslavia.

The Kosovo crisis and bombing of the Chinese Embassy in Belgrade were interpreted in terms of China's need to participate actively in forming the international norms. For Yan Xuetong, the conflict was driven not by the contradictions between cultures or nationalities, as Samuel Huntington claimed, but because of the contradiction between American concept of the new international order and that of the other states–unipolarity versus multipolarity. The war in 1999 was not a turning point but it made for a better understanding of contemporary international relations.[21] Moreover, the US led NATO coalition was construed as a manifestation of the new unilateral world order in the twenty-first Century. First, the Americans would like to lead Europe, next, the whole world. President Kennedy and, later, President Carter equated absolute freedom values with American security. For China, as strengthened by Deng Xiaoping, the most important in international relations was the state's sovereignty as the superior value. All interventions and interference in sovereign issues equaled the breaking of the UN Charter.[22] It meant a challenge to the rise of China. Since the end of the Cold War, China has been talking very optimistic on the peace and development and creation of a multipolar world. The posture of passive adjustment (*beidong tiaozheng*) in face of crisis (*shushou wuce*) should be replaced by active policy. For Li Yihu, the best way of playing an important role by China was to restore the triangle policy (*san jiao*) between Beijing, Moscow and Washington. In fact, the War of 1999 called China up to the plate because the international order should have been revised.[23] Chinese scholars started a discussion on China's foreign behavior using the quotation of John Mearsheimer, in which he stated that:

> Great powers behave aggressively not because they want to or because they posses some inner drive to dominate, but because they have to seek more power if they want to maximize their odds of survival.[24]

The following proposals made by Yan Xuetong were an important signal to offensive realists:

1. To use China's limited force on issues directly relevant to China and to put pressure on Taiwan separatism;

2. The replacement of the four modernizations program with anti-hegemony as the highest goal of the foreign policy does not meet China's strategic interests;

3. To maintain the independent, autonomous and peaceful diplomacy, avoiding a full scale confrontation with the US not to rally support from the middle zone (because China will be pushed to a leading role); and to a build anti-hegemonic united front with other powers when developing partnership with the latter, and not to implement the SIR Alliance.[25]

International issues have played an important role in China's foreign policy. Chinese intellectuals and policy makers have understood that along with economic growth, Beijing should have taken a more active role on the international arena. This fact should be perceived as a major condition for China's rising.

RISING WITHOUT UNDERSTANDING

The concept of rising expressed via rising rhetoric has been discussed since the mid 1990s, when Beijing-based scholars used the term "peaceful rise" for the first time in order to justify China's foreign policy activities. During the 80th anniversary of the CCP in July 2001, Jiang Zemin officially presented a new concept of China's development—"three represents" (*san ge daibiao*). He admitted that from 1949 until the first half of twenty-first century, the Chinese nation would strive for a motherland of "power and wealth," people's prosperity, and "the great renaissance of the nation"(*minzu weida fuxing*).[26] The consecutive symptom of the coming concept of rising was a focus of Jiang Zemin's report delivered during the 16th Party Congress in 2002. He also related to "the great renaissance of the Chinese nation" (*Zhonghua mingzu weida fuxing*).[27] This should be interpreted as China's decision to open up an important chapter in its own perception of the international relations.

In 2003, the international environment was very much in favor of Chinese diplomatic initiatives—the U.S. war in Iraq, the Korean Peninsula controversy over the nuclear program in the North Korea, The six-Party Talks, the first document on the policy towards the EU. From the end of 2003 onward, senior Chinese leaders and prominent analysts have been promoting the notion of "peaceful-rise" (*heping jueqi*) as "the new pathway" (*xin daolu*) of China's foreign relations and the strategic choice for China in the coming decades. In November 2003, in his speech entitled *A New Path for China's Peaceful Rise and the Future of Asia*, Zheng Bijian introduced a new concept in international relations, which he called China's "peaceful rise":

> In the 25 years since the inception of its reform and opening up, China has blazed a new strategic path that not only suits its national conditions but also conforms to the tide of the times. This new strategic path is China's peaceful rise through independently building socialism with Chinese characteristics, while participating in, rather than detaching from, economic globalization.[28]

The next step in promoting the new concept was taken by Prime Minister, Wen Jiabao, during his visit to the United States. In his speech at Harvard University, he tried to explain the concept of "peaceful-rise" with Chinese traditional values of peace. He mentioned positive values such as benevolence (humanity) and love (*ren ai*), collectiveness (*juti*)⊓unity in diversity (*he er bu tong*) ⊓common world (*tianxia wei gong*). Moreover, he used Chinese proverbs that are difficult to interpret: *tianxian xinwang, pifu you ze* (the world rises and falls, everyone has responsibilities), used by the late Ming and early Qing Confucian philosopher Gu Yanwu in the "Record of Daily Studies," or *jisuo buyi wushi yiren* (do not do to others what you would not have them do to you) that comes from Confucius *Analects*. On the other hand, however, the Chinese Prime Minister was conscious of the internal situation and he finally realized that China's rise would be limited by its internal problems. This time the Chinese government would have to ensure labour law, property law, private rights and achievements inside society developed on equal terms.[29]

Shortly after Wen's speech at the Harvard University, during the workshop celebrating the 110th anniversary of the birth of Mao Zedong, Hu Jintao mentioned the term "peaceful-rise." Hu Jintao supported his words with evidence of "the great renaissance of the Chinese nation" and principles of peaceful coexistence.[30] In the months to follow, Hu reiterated the term many times on different occasions, at home and abroad, also during his visit to France in January 2004, and at a Politburo meeting in February.

In March 2004, contrary to Western politicians and scholars, the Prime Minister, Wen Jiabao, put an emphasis on peace rather than rising in the Western sense. The Chinese elites admitted that China would not constitute a threat, but rather an opportunity for other states. Wen Jiabao pointed out five "essentials" (*yaoyi*) of China's peaceful rise:

1. being involved in taking advantage of the world's peace to promote China's development, and safeguarding the world's peace through China's development;

2. basing the peaceful rise on China's own strength and independent hard work;

3. it should not be achieved without continuing the "opening-up policy," an active set of international trade and economic exchanges;

4. it is likely to take several generations;

5. "not to stand in the way of any other country or pose a threat to any other country, or be achieved at the expense of any particular nation."[31]

CRITICS OF RISING RHETORIC

On the one hand, the concept of "peaceful rise" caused positive feelings and some policy makers and academics tried to substantiate the thesis with Chinese cultural values. Taking the newly announced concept, a group of scholars expressed their serious doubts about China's future foreign policy. Wang Yizhou and Wang Jisi from the Chinese Academy of Social Science urged further discussion on the inconsistencies and theoretical problems inherent in the concept. Next, Shi Yinhong from the People's University of China raised the question of the Taiwan issue as a potential complicating factor for China's rise.

Furthermore, sceptics' voices brought up the issue of "rising" itself. To them, a noun "rising" would create problems with Chinese relations with neighbours, fear and opposition in Asia. The semantic problems were mentioned e.g., by Pan Wei, the chair of the China-World Forum at the Beijing University, in an article entitled "Another Discussing on 'Peaceful-rise' (*ye tan heping ju-eqi*)." In his opinion, China's rise should not cause astonishment because it arose from 1949 and all the issues in Chinese foreign policy like Nixon's visit and becoming a permanent member of the Security Council in 1971 were the significant signs of rising. During the last decade, China has become the second largest economy and by this means, China's rise is an incontrovertible fact. Some scholars admitted that the peaceful-rise concept was a continuation of the *tao guan yanghui you suo zuo wei* but this time the Party leadership put the accent rather on "potential achievements" than on "hiding intentions."[32] The term "rise" indicates being strong (*qiang da*) and this means to be in opposition. This realistic paradigm indicates that there are four major situations when "rising" might be implemented:

1. Rising does not mean becoming a superpower rather a regional power (*qiquxing qiangguo*);

2. In the world there are certain super powers (*chaoji qiangguo*) or several regional powers that try to counterbalance (*ping qi ping zuo*) a certain number of superpowers;

3. In the world there are two superpowers or several regional powers to counterbalance two superpowers;

4. In the world there is one superpower and several rising powers to countermeasure the superpower hegemony.

In the opponents' view, China's rising is to counterbalance the U.S. hegemonic power but in fact, China is still a "backward country" (*luohou guojia*) and still a developing country (*fazhang zhong guojia*). In fact, the new concept has created an unfavorable atmosphere about China's intentions. Furthermore, all rising powers do not intend to use "the gun" but rather use peace as a method of rising. But if, after all, the international situation turns out to be more difficult than the elites had dreamt about—peace is only a desire and a beautiful dream (*yiwang he meili de mengxiang*).[33]

To some extent, the "peaceful-rise" concept was only empty rhetoric, which did not correspond with reality. Pan Yue argued that the process of rising itself must lead to the revision of contemporary international relations and at best would contribute to the balance of power. The major task for the "rise" problem was how to maintain the peaceful status in international relations. The history of the world's major powers' rise and fall did not yet have a "peaceful-rise precedent" (*heping jueqi de xianli*). Powers like Spain, Portugal, Britain, France, Germany, Italy, Japan, Russia, the United States and other countries has not been based on the same case. In this regard, it would be a difficult task to convince the international community of the "Chinese characteristic rise" (*Zhongguo tese de jueqi*) and will ruin the "peaceful image" of China. For Huang Aiping, both the concepts of "peaceful-rise" as well as "peaceful development" had the same meaning. He posed a rhetorical question: Why did Chinese propaganda strongly promote the concept that raised objections and with which other states disagreed. Such propaganda should consider not only rhetoric but also the reality inside the country (*guoqing*) as well as the international situation (*qiuqing*). The "peace and development," contrary to the "peaceful-rise," has helped China to present itself as a benign, peaceful and contractive actor.[34] In this regard, China should have taken actions instead of dwelling on "empty rhetoric" to demonstrate to its neighbors that it adhered to the existing rules and would not be a revisionist power.[35]

This leads to the conclusion of Pan Zhongying that its national reputation has been as important as military and political power. The problem of assuring the others of China's peaceful intention has also been raised by military circles. Pan Zhengqiang from China's National Defense University, as well as Yan Xuetong, have pointed out that the most difficult problem for China decision makers was to convince international public opinion that Beijing has no aggressive intentions but, on the contrary, it intends to follow the path of cooperation and economic development. China should have the power to let others accept its status without using the military force.[36] This remark fits Yan Xuetong's definition of "soft power" and the fact that China should have paid attention to its international image. On the other hand, the politicians admitted that a cooperative approach, which has been the best way to reduce the risk of international reaction, could lead to domestic political turbulences. [37]

Taking a realistic view, which was unquestionably more important, was the negative impact of the "peaceful-rise" concept on Sino-US relations in the context of neo-conservatism in America. The "peaceful-rise" rhetoric has been recognized as a mistake. Scholars from the Central Party School, in an article *Zhongguo heping jueqi shi fou keneng?* published in *Study Times* (August 2004), asked whether a peaceful-rise was achievable. They concluded by identifying the Taiwan issue and the United States as the major obstacles preventing China's rise. They implied that the Chinese have a "holy right" to reunification with Taiwan and in a dead-end situation; China could use a "no-peaceful" measures. The second problem related to US domination and interference in China's domestic problems, e.g., *zu guo tongyi*. In this case, China would be obliged to have a realistic view and "peaceful-rise" might not fit the contemporary international situation. In the 21st century, not only would China rise but some other nations (*daguo jueqi jun*–the group of rising powers) would also become powers, basically sharing the same values as China. In that situation, Chinese diplomacy should carefully observe international relations and learn lessons from the current situation.[38] Otherwise, China's growth might face challenges it would not be able to overcome. Historically, the word "rise" is associated with the rise of military powers, such as Germany and Japan, or the Roman Empire and, of course, is invariably followed by the "fall." *The Global Times* also published an anti-US commentary by Zhou Jianming entitled *"[We] must consider our country's national security strategy from the worst possible [scenario]: observe closely the American strategic trends."* Zhou criticized pro-American officials and scholars who have misjudged and underestimated the administration of President George W. Bush's determination to move the centre of American strategic policy, increase the level of US military assistance to Taiwan, and adjust its strategic arrangements with China as the major competitor.[39]

The "threat perception" of China in Asia might be the first step to a disruption of Asian integration (ASEAN, ASEAN+3 and ASEAN-China FTA). If China's neighbors consider that the Middle Kingdom's intentions are going too far, they will rethink the cooperation process and obstruct the decision implementation process. Furthermore, "rise" corresponds with "Asian values," China becoming one of "traditional Asian values" holders. This, as a final consequence, might ruin China's attempts to build its positive image in, e.g., South-east Asia. The insistent promotion of China's rising might also change the atti-tude of world public opinion towards China. In the West, China will still be la-beled as a "threat," "communist regime" and "the Tibetans' torturer." The ma-jority of Americans "do not trust China at all," but, on the other hand, Asian nations like Malaysia or Indonesia have started to perceive China as an entirely friendly nation.[40]

MORAL DIMENSIONS OF NEW DIPLOMATIC LANGUAGE

At the beginning of 2004, the Chinese leadership started to promote the "recov-ery of national morale." The basis for further campaigns was created in *2001 Action Plan for the Development of Civic Morality* and five years after—in *2006 Plan for Cultural Development,* that figured in the five-year plan 2006-2010. In the context of a new harmonious society as well as harmonious world, the Con-fucian revival (*rujia fuxing*) was a turning point. The Chinese PDC admitted that:

> Chinese culture, with over five thousand years of brilliance, has contributed im-mensely to the progress of human civilization. It is the spiritual bond of our na-tional heritage, of our unceasing dynamism, the source of our power of resistance in the face of difficult challenges and a complex world.[41]

The processes that took place in the 1990s resulted in a transition of the way in which China presented itself: from the victim (*shouhaizhe*) to the power (*da-guo*). The intellectuals rejected the persistent emphasis on China's "150 years of shame and humiliation" as the main lens through which Chinese view their place in the modern international affairs. The "patriotic education" and "the great re-naissance of the Chinese nation" (*Zhonghua minzu weida fuxing*) were signs of the new era in Chinese foreign relations.[42]

This has been the major issue discussed by Chinese scholars. The aforemen-tioned Wang Jisi says that, as a result of a gradual process of de-Marxization in Chinese society, there is a general tendency towards seeking an explanation of the Chinese theory and practice of international relations in traditional culture. Wang Huning of Fudan University thinks that culture is a dimension of national strength but they still took the Marxist approach, i.e., only a state economically and politically strong could use culture as a tool in soft power policy.[43] To the author, the most important remark considering China's future status was made by Yan Xuetong, who maintained that status depends on international accep-tance.[44] Seeking the acceptance of the international community, China has made considerable progress, but still not sufficient for its foreign partners.

In this context, Chinese authorities decided to invoke China's ancient tradi-tion of peace. As Samuel Kim states:

While Chinese image of world order cannot be construed as containing either a crusading or a colonial doctrine, it represented a formidable barrier against the thought of external policy in terms of mutually beneficial interactions between or among equal sovereign states.[45]

The legitimacy of the Sino-centric world order rested more on moral virtue than military power. It is clear that the traditional Chinese worldview left no room for egalitarianism in international relations. The Confucian, Sino-centric concepts of morality and ethics, which dictated both domestic and international policy, maintained that through good government, internal peace and prosperity China would play a leading role in the world and serve as a universal paradigm for other nations. Only moral individuals can create a moral order at every level of society and therefore a moral world with China at its center. As Feng Huiying admits:

Confucius scholars differed most with their opponents in their view that the universalized order of the Chinese world should be a cultural order and that the only way to accommodate an expansion should be by means of an outward radiation of cultural influence.[46]

Harmony might be provided only by a nobleman (*junzi*) that is ready for self-cultivation (*xiuji*). The *he er bu tong* concept arose from the earlier concept of the *tian ren he yi* (unity between the universe and the mankind). In Confucian philosophy it was described as *jun he er butong* (unity between nobleman and the universe). This, as put in the context of international relations indicates that there are no equal partners in foreign affairs.[47] The second important value is *zhongyong*—the Doctrine of Mean. As Li Jianchang argues, the Doctrine of the Mean fails to be understood as a compromise, but rather as the ability to find a proper way of dealing with problems in society.[48]

In the modern history of China, the first reformist that took *datong* (the great unity) seriously was Kang Youwei, in a book published seven years after his death.[49] In his *Book of Datong* he argued:

States should be abolished, so that there would be no more struggle between the strong and the weak. Families should also be done away with, so that there would no longer be inequality of love and affection. And finally, selfishness itself should be banished, so that goods and services would not be used for private ends.[50]

On the other hand, some scholars mentioned the major argumentation of Mencius: "to seek domination by force will simply turn the world against you."[51] Taking a foreign policy rhetoric as an example, the author argues that on the one hand materialism plays an important role in shaping external affairs, but also the non-material aspects like culture, identity, ideas or even rhetoric play crucial roles in foreign affairs. Social constructivism argues that the ideal structure shapes the identity of the agent, structure in Wendt's constructivism is not material but cultural, defined by the distribution of ideas. The essence of international politics, in the view of Wendt, is ideas rather than material capabilities.[52]

Concerning the "soft-power" notion, a deep discussion has been held by scholars mainly from Beijing and Shanghai academic circles. The linkage between rhetoric and power leads to the conclusion that rhetoric itself has become an important component of soft-power. The concept of Joseph Nye has been both challenged and developed. Nye concentrated on the potential of arguments to move people, and their ability to attract (*xiyin li*) and shape preferences of others. Moreover, as Joseph Nye argues, the current leadership should be based on institutions, values, culture and politics in order to shape other people's needs.[53] If that is the case, this, according to Aristotle, is a major task for rhetoric. Moreover, to the author, rhetoric plays an important role in shaping the image of the country. Portraying itself as a moral, good and reliable partner, any country might be able to win the trust of a third party and built its position in international relations. All the values have been articulated via language, and, what goes with it, the rhetoric is considered, as was mentioned above, an important component of contemporary diplomacy. Foreign policy discourse is rhetorical, in the sense that it attempts to reconstruct a desired, practical, or normative framework from inconsistent and often competing assumptions that underlie the institutional inertia of a nation-state's foreign policy.

For Chinese authorities, soft-power might be a kind of leverage and agency used in order to exercise political objectives, with the additional dimension of being both derived from and contributing to domestic stability and the internal strength of the state. Wang Huning's thesis on soft power from 1993 identifies the basic elements of the principle, including the historical texts and ideas related to Confucian, Taoist and Buddhist thoughts. These represent the Chinese conceptions of winning respect through virtue (*yi de fu ren*), benevolent governance (*wang dao*), peace and harmony (*he*), and, finally, harmony without suppressing differences (*he er bu tong*).[54] Leading Chinese scholars: Meng Honghua, Yan Xuetong or Kang Xiaoguang tried to adapt the foreign concept of "soft-power" to the Chinese realities. The first scholar has admitted that China's definition of "soft power" should include culture, concepts, a model of development, international system, and international image of China.[55] Yan Xuetong, contrary to Yu Xitian and Liu Gang, says that political power (*zhengzhi shili*) is the most powerful element in the "soft power" concept. The Culture has been very closely associated with politics. Yu Xitian has considered the ideas, international and domestic system, strategy and politics as deeply rooted in culture, which is the core of any "soft actions" on the international arena.[56] Li Mingjing builds an argument based on evidence from leaders and media-reports in China, that soft power is perceived as a "tool for defensive purposes"—an instrument to create a better image for China, to influence perceptions, and to defend China from Western culture and ideology.[57] According to Pang Zhongying, the concept of Nye failed to be accepted in China. Chinese authorities could not differentiate between soft and hard power. He advocated for comprehensive power (*zonghe de guojia nengli* or *zonghe guojia li*), where the soft and hard power intertwine. The Chinese definition of "soft power" should be made up of economy, education, culture, human resources, political system, diplomacy, international political participation and resolutions of international problems.[58] The differences in the understanding of power usage between the West and China have played an important role in shaping China's "soft power" definition. For the Chinese, the clear differentiation between hard (*ying*) and soft (*ruan*) has been difficult to render because, as they have argued, sometimes hard becomes soft and soft becomes hard.[59] Zhang Jianjing says:

> The competition among nation-states appears to be a rivalry of hard power, but behind such rivalry is the competition between institutions, civilizations, and strategies, which are essentially the rivalry of soft power.[60]

Without promoting Chinese culture and history, since there has been little knowledge about the country across the world, China was unable to convince the rest of its positive intentions. This issue has been pointed out by a scholar from Fudan University—Ni Jianping. Instead of great progress, Chinese authorities have been making plenty of errors (*bu shao wuqu*) while building up the Middle Kingdom's image in the foreign media. Aware of foreign countries reality, culture, politics and economy, the decision makers should have applied the methods that suit local circumstances (*yin di zhi yi*). In other words, if something is controversial for the target audience (*shou zhong*), it should be modified and announced in a way that would limit any controversies and strengthen Chinese persuasive power (*shuofu li*).[61]

BEING LIKE MAO, DENG AND WOODROW WILSON

In July 2005, at the Meeting of Leaders from China, India, Brazil, South Africa and Mexico in Gleneagles, Hu Jintao presented his view on globalization. In his speech one can easily notice similarities to Mao Zedong's idea of the rich North and poor South. The problem of global injustice was broadly discussed, and the Chinese leader presented China's view on the issue:

> In order to seize the opportunities and rise to the challenges, developing countries should, on the one hand, rely on themselves to grow the economy through reform, innovation and persistent efforts to emancipate and develop the productive forces, and on the other, create a favorable environment for development by opening up to the outside world and actively participating in economic and technological competition and cooperation with other countries.[62]

The final result was that Hu Jintao presented the *hexie shijie* concept during his speech to the General Assembly of the United Nations. He made a 4-point proposal that guaranteed the world's safety and stability. In his opinion, there were four major conditions to "uphold a lasting peace" (*chijiu heping*). The first is múltilateralism (*duobian zhuyi*) that should be upheld to achieve common security. In the contemporary world the international community should abandon the "cold war mentality" and, instead, create a collective system of global security based on the UN Charter and basic values. The international community should oppose any interference in the sovereignty of independent states, internal affairs, arbitrary use of military forces, and together fight against terrorism and prevent nuclear weapons proliferation. The second point was the common development (*pubian fazhan he gongtong farong*) which should be promoted in cases when the world is not developing simultaneously. Globalization should be a mechanism used for common benefits (*pubian shouyi*), especially for developing countries. Still, the world's peace would be endangered because of the rich-poor polarization and lack of a fair multilateral world trade system (*duobian maoyi zhidu*). The international community should prepare a common health system, emphasize the importance of equal rights for women and worldwide development and, finally, reduce disparities between North and South. The third point mentioned by Hu Jintao was the spirit of tolerance (*baoyi jinsheng*) as the basis for building a harmonious world. In his opinion, diversity is a characteristic point in the history of humankind and development, and the world needs cross-cultural exchanges between people. The different ways of development, diversity and different historical backgrounds should not affect international cooperation. The international community should make up for the deficiency, as Mencius proverb *quchuang buduan* indicated, to seek common ground for cooperation while avoiding differences (*qiutong cunyi*), eliminate mutual reservations and distrust, promote more peaceful relations (*he mu*) as well as democracy in international relations. The fourth point encouraged the implementation of the UN reform that would ensure the healthy development of international relations and benefit all the people around the world. The UN and the Security Council need to proceed step by step, gradually (*xunxu jianjin*) introducing reforms, and should consider allowing small and medium developing countries, mainly African states, to have an influence on the UN's decisions. It is on this matter that the world needs an extensive consensus (*guangfan gongzhi*).[63]

In his speech on *hexie*, in October 2006, Hu Jintao explained the notion of harmony using a variety of cultural dimensions coming from Confucius's *datong* and *xiaokang*, through Universal Harmony, Marxism, Maoism or Ideology of Deng Xiaoping and Jiang Zemin. What might be interesting, is that the external concept has not been far different from the internal concept of a harmonious well-off society. Hu Jintao promotes six qualities: the rule of law, fairness and justice, honesty and fraternalism and harmony with nature.[64] Using a Confucian moral tone, China portrays itself as a moral power, according to ancient philosophy: if someone is moral himself, he has the character to serve others (*yi de fu ren*). The ruler should self-cultivate (*xiuyang*) and, thanks to this, he can rule the people (*xiu ji zhi ren*). In "Liji," the logic of relations in the family correlated with the relations within the society and between states. In this context, the correlation between internal and external languages of harmony should not be disrupted (see Table 9.1).[65]

On the other hand, all these Chinese political declarations, apart from promoting a very idealistic vision of the world, might be compared with Woodrow Wilson's concept of developing peace. In comparison with the original concept of Confucius's harmony, this presented by Hu Jintao seemed to be more Wilsonian than Confucian. Wang Yiwei claims that the concept of harmony differs from the original Chinese world view (*tianxia guan*). The concept of *tianxia* was linked not to the idea of assimilation to or integration with the world (*rongru* means assimilate the minority), but of being the center (*zhongxin*), being the world itself (*zhongguo jiu shi shijie*).[66]

At the same time, Lucien Pye has pointed out that the *ti-yong* essence and utility formula had it the wrong way around in that modernization calls for the acceptance of universal values associated with the world's culture, adapted to local parochial conditions. The *ti* should stand for the universal values and it is the *yong* that should be related to the Chinese realities.[67] The Chinese side might combine the achievement of the West with Chinese positive traditional values.

Table 9.1 The Similarities between "Harmonious Society" and "Harmonious World" (Chinese and English)

Harmonious society concept 和谐社会 02/2005	Harmonious world concept 和谐世界 09/2005
公平正义 *gongping zhengyi* equality	开放、公平、非歧视的多边贸易体制，人人享有平等追求全面发展的机会和权利 fair, equal and non-discriminatory world's trade system, the opportunity for a full scale development
民主法治 *minzhu fazhi* democracy and the rule of law	联合国宪章, 国际关系基本准则 UN Charter as a basic rule of IR 促进国际关系民主化 democratization of IR
诚信友爱 *chengxin youai* honesty and friendship	各种文明相互借鉴、共同提高 multicultural exchange, growing together
安定有序 *anding youxu* stability and order	努力普及全民教育，实现男女平等，加强公共卫生能力建设 striving for common education, to achieve equal rights for women and to improve public health care system
人与自然和谐相处 *renyizhiran hexie xiangchu* harmony with nature	清洁的能源环境 a clean natural environment

Source: from two Hu Jintao's speeches: *Nuli jianshe tejiu heping, gongtong farong de hexie shijie*, Sept. 16, 2005. http://www.southcn.com/news/china/china05/hjtfbm/hbmzx/200509160019.htm (accessed on May 15, 2009) and *Ri tigao goujian shehuizhui de hexie shehui nengli (quan wen)*, Feb. 9, 2005. http://www.southcn.com/nflr/llzhuanti/hexie/ldls/200506270097.htm (accessed on May 15, 2009)

Before he presented the fourteen points in April 1917, Woodrow Wilson suggested three times the ways to have a peaceful resolution in the affairs of the then contemporary world. In mid 1914, he proposed that, for example, small nations should be equal with the great nations, and the world should have "some sort of association of nations wherein all small guarantee the territorial integrity of each." In 1916, in his address, he postulated establishing the League of Enforced Peace. Furthermore, on January 21, 1917, a further idea was presented that all nations should take the Monroe Doctrine as the World's doctrine and, thus, they should not interfere with other nations' affairs. To sum up, Woodrow Wilson's points were derived from four cardinal rules: a mutual guarantee of political independence, mutual guarantee of territorial integrity, mutual guarantee against economic warfare and limitation of armaments.[68] After the World War I, Wilson and his administration prepared a variety of solutions for Europe's future, having the preservation of peace between France and Germany in mind as one of the major issues.[69] Because of its peaceful, non-confrontational significance, Wilsonism might, as Hu Rongrong states, serve as a model for Chinese policy makers.[70]

Behind the peaceful rhetoric, the whole team of advisors worked for future objectives. One might compare the crisis that ended in 1918 with the economic, global crisis of 2008. The nature of both is very different, but the world needs solutions in any case. The question is about the substations of the "harmonious world" in the days after economic crises. On the other hand, the "harmonious world" might only serve building a positive Chinese image in the global arena.[71]

CONCLUSION

Using different types of languages: moral, soften or aggressive, about both the domestic and international scene, politicians would like to achieve their goals and priorities. In this chapter, the author has tried to prove the view that rhetoric, especially in diplomacy, does matter. The non-material factors play an important role in shaping international relations, and, to some extent, in checking the reactions of other actors. In China, using the pragmatic rhetoric by the policy makers means that they are not mentally and materially prepared to take the responsibility for international order. On the other hand, to the author, by speaking in a moral tone, the politicians have indicated their readiness to stand up and be responsible stakeholders. In the context of the harmonious world rhetoric, language plays an important role in shaping China's image. Contrary to the "rising" rhetoric, China presents itself as an important player not only by saying it, but also by managing or trying to manage both, regional and the global affairs.

They claim that, for a country like China, the long-term goal (*yuanqi mubiao*) is to establish a fair and reasonable (*gongzheng heli*) new, international order, which might be achieved by China's "peaceful rise."[72] China has advocated that to build new international political and economic structures, there is no need to challenge or overthrow the present international order with revolutionary methods. The international community, in particular, should strengthen its ability to support the interests of developing as well as developed countries. The Chinese system of values has underpinned China's attempts to organize international politics according to its own notion of justice. This enables China to safeguard its strategic opportunity (*zhanlue jiyu*) and strengthen China's confidence in international relations, particularly on the international market.[73]

Finding a proper way to be understood and to play a responsible role might be a difficult task for China. One argument behind this is that the "Westphalia system" was imposed upon the Middle Kingdom by the Western powers. In Chinese philosophy, however, it is important to be responsible for the world as a whole, not just for one's own state—*tianxia*. In this respect, to understand Western thinking based on the nation-state's analytical unit and to assume a sense of responsibility for the world (for constructing theories and the system of global dimension) will be a difficult but not impossible task.[74]

Having analyzed the international situation in 1990s, which has been the background for China's decision of "rising" and, next, of "the harmonious world" as a negative evaluation of the rising rhetoric, Yan Xuetong states that the only choice for China in the current situation would be to support independent, peaceful diplomacy of *heping waijiao*, and to keep or protect the world's morality and justice (*weihu shijie dayi*).[75] It might be an interesting general conclusion that China's use of its moral diplomatic language means that it would shape the future of international relations and play an active role in general. Unlike the US, Britain or France, China's history of the last 200 years does not offer a set of foreign policy traditions—such as the Jeffersonian, Jacksonian, Hamiltonian and Wilsonian, detected in US foreign policy by Walter Russell Mead—that are reference points for the future actions of a great power.[76]

The pragmatic rhetoric was addressed to the superpowers and it expressed China's independent foreign policy. Deng Xiaoping experiences based on the revolutionary rhetoric and actions motivated him to "seek the truth from the facts" and have revealed China's intentions in international politics. The tactics of "tao guan yang hui" was appropriated in the 1980s and early 1990s. Along with the US domination, China tried to balance American influence and put itself in a favorable position. Contrary to Deng's times, the fourth generation of the leadership, with Hu Jintao, also used moral language but more gentle than the previous one. The language of Confucian morality also shows the injustice, difference and anguishes of the South when compared to the North. At the present stage, while using an instructive tone, China intends to take on the role of the "creator" of international reality. Using moral language in its foreign policy, China has put itself forward as a candidate to be one of an extremely important nation in the world dominated by other powers.

NOTES

1. D. Bobrow, S.Chan, "On a Slow Boat to Where? Analyzing Chinese Foreign Policy," in *China and the World, Chinese Foreign Policy in the Post-Mao Era*, ed. by Samuel S. Kim (Boulder: Westview Press, 1984), p. 36.

2. J. Luc Domenach, "Ideological Reform," in *Chinese Politics and Foreign Policy Reform*, ed. by Gerald Segal (London, New York: Kegan Paul International, 1990), pp. 31-32.

3. Zongli Lu, *Power of the Words, Chen Prophecy in Chinese Politics, AD 265-618* (Oxford, Bern, Berlin: Peter Land, 2003), p. 111.

4. T. O. Windt Jr., *Presidents and Protesters: Political Rhetoric in the 1960s* (Tuscaloosa, AL: University of Alabama Press, 1990), p. 3-4.

5. M. J. Medhurst, "Rhetoric and Cold War: A Strategic Approach," in *Cold War Rhetoric: Strategy, Metaphor, and Ideology*, Martin J. Medhurst, ed. (East Lansing, MI: Michigan State University Press, 1997), pp. 19-20.

6. G. A. Kennedy, *Comparative Rhetoric: An Historical and Cross-Cultural Introduction* (Oxford, UK: Oxford University Press, 1998), p. 158.

7 Xing Lu, "The Influence of Classical Chinese Rhetoric on Contemporary Chinese Political Communication and Social Relations," in *Chinese Perspectives in Rhetoric and Communication*, edited by D. Ray Heisey (New York: JAI Press, 2000), pp. 5-7.

8. Ibid, pp. 163-164.

9. Ibid, pp. 165-166.

10. Zi Jichen, *Xin Zhongguo Waijiao Sixiang: Cong Mao Zedong dao Deng Xiaoping* [The New China's Diplomatic Thoughts: from Mao Zedong to Deng Xiaoping] (Beijing: Beijing University Press, 2001), p. 49.

11. Hu Yaobang, *Quanmian kaichuang shehuizhuyi xiandaihua jianshe de xi jiumian* [New phase in the comprehensive building of the socialist modernization], Xinhua News Agency, September 1, 1982, http://news.xinhuanet.com/ziliao/2003-01/20/ (accessed on December 1, 2007); Zhao Ziyang, *Yanzhe you Zhongguo tese de shehui zhuyi daolu qianjin* [we go forward along the road of the Socialism with Chinese characteristic] Xinhua News Agency, January 20, 2003, http://news.xinhuanet.com/ziliao/2003-01/20/content_697061.htm (accessed on December 7, 2007)

12. Gerald Chen, *Chinese Perspective on international Relations, A Framework for Analysis* (Hampshire, London, New York: MacMillan Press and St. Martin Press, 1999), p. 23.

13. Fei-Ling Wang, "Self-Image and Strategic Intentions: National Confidence and Political Insecurity," in *In the Eyes of the Dragon, China Views the World*, ed. by Yong Deng and Fei-Ling Wang (Lanham, Boulder, New York: Rowman & Littlefield, 1999), p. 35.

14. J. C. Hsiung, "Challenge of China's Independent Foreign Policy," in *Beyond China's Independent Foreign Policy, Challenges for the US and Its Asian Allies,* ed. by James C. Hsiung (New York: Praeger Special Studies, 1985), p. 166.

15. J. C. Hsiung, *op.cit.*, p. 167.

16. R. Foot, "China's Foreign Policy in the Post-1989 Era," in *China in the 1990s*, ed. by R. Benewick, R. Wingrove (London: McMillan, 1999), p. 235.

17. Quansheng Zhao, *Interpreting Chinese Foreign Policy* (Oxford, UK: Oxford University Press, 1996), p. 53.

18. Wan Xuefei, *Taoguang yanghui: Weihu Zhonggguo guojia anquan de youxiao waijiao zhanlue!* [Taoguang yanghui: the Effective Strategy for Preserving China's national Security], *Hebei Shehui Kexue*, no. 1, (2003), p. 56.

19. Zhao Mingliang, *Deng Xiaoping "taoguang yanghui, you suo zuo wei" xisiang yu Xin Shiji Zhongguo Waijiao* [Deng Xiaoping concept of "taoguang yanghui, you suo zuo wei" and Chinese Diplomacy in the New Century], *Nanjing Shifan Daxue Bao*, no. 5, (2002), p. 13.

20. Jiang Zemin, *"Jiakuai gaige kaifang he xiandaihua jianshe bufa, duoqu you Zhongguo tese shehuizhuyi shiye de genda shenli"* [Accelerating the Reform, the Opening to the Outside World and the Drive for Modernization, so as to Achieve Greater Successes in Building Socialism with Chinese Characteristics], Xinhua New Agency, January 20,

2003, http://news.xinhuanet.com/ziliao/2003-01/20/content_697148.htm (accessed on December 6, 2007).

21. Yan Xuetong, *"Kesuowo zhanzheng bu shi lishi de zhuanxidian"* [The War in Kosovo is not a Turning Point], *Liaowang*, no. 25, (1999), p. 12.

22. Wang Fuchuan, *"Kesuowo zhanzheng yu Zhongguo waijiao zhanlue"* [War in Kosovo and China's foreign policy strategy], *Guoji Guanxi Yanjiu*, no 4, (1999), p. 22.

23. Ibid, p. 23 and Li Yuhu, *"Kesuowo zhanzheng suo dailai de sikao"* [The Reflection on the International Relations after the Kosovo War], *Shijie Jingji yu Zhengzhi*, no. 7, (1999), p. 18.

24. Simon Shen, *Redefining Nationalism in Modern China, Sino-American Relations and the Emergence of Chinese Public Opinion in the 21st Century* (New York, NY: Palgrave Macmillan, 2007), p. 55.

25. Ibid, p. 56.

26. Jiang Zemin, *"Zai qungzhu Zhongguo Gongchan dang chengli le bashi zhou nian dahui shang de jianghua"* [the speech at the 80th anniversary of the establishment of the CCP] Xomhua News Agency, July 1, 2001, http://news.xinhuanet.com/ziliao/2001-12/03/content_499021.htm (accessed on December 12, 2007).

27. Jiang Zemin, *"Quanmian jianshe shehuizhuyi, kaichuan Zhongguo tese shehui zhuyi shiye xin jumian"* [Build a well-off society in an all-round way and create a new situation in building socialism with Chinese characteristics], Xinhua News Agency, November 17, 2002, http://news.xinhuanet.com/ziliao/2002-11/17/content_693542.htm (accessed on December 12, 2007).

28. Zheng Bijian, "China' s 'Peaceful Rise' to Great-Power Status," *Foreign Affairs*, vol. 84, no. 5, (2005), pp. 18-24.

29. "Turning Your Eyes to China," Speech by Premier Wen Jiabao at Harvard University), http://www.people.com.cn/GB/shehui/1061/2241298.html and *China premier comes to Harvard*, online http://www.hno.harvard.edu/gazette/2003/12.11/01-china.html (accessed on July 4, 2007).

30. Hu Jintao, *Zai nianji Mao Zedong tongzhi danchen 110 zhou nian zuotan hui shang de jiang hua* (The speech in the commemoration of Comrade Mao Zedong's 110th birthday's anniversary), *Renmin Ribao*, December 27, 2003.

31. Wu Guoguang, "The peaceful emergence of a great power?" *Social Research*, Spring 2006, online, http://findarticles.com/p/articles/mi_m2267/is_1_73/ai_n26878481/ (accessed on May 16, 2009)

32. In the article, he quoted one of Mao Zedong's paper on war preparation. See: Mao Zedong, "Cast away illusion, prepare for struggle," in *Selected works of Mao Zedong*, available online: http://www.marxists.org/reference/archive/mao/selected-works/volume-4/mswv4_66.htm (accessed on May 17, 2009).

33. Pan Wei, "Another discussion of the "peaceful-rise," online: http://www.tecn.cn/data/detail.php?id=12361 (accessed on May 18, 2009).

34. Huang Aiping, "Guanyi heping jueqi yu heping fazhan de sikao" [To consider the peaceful-rise and peaceful development], online: http://www.tecn.cn/ (accessed on May 25, 2009).

35. S. L. Shirk, *China: Fragile Superpower* (New York: Oxford University Press, 2007), p. 129.

36. Yan Xuetong, "Heping jueqi tiaojian yu yiyi" [Conditions and meaning of "peaceful rise'], *Zhongguo Shehui Kexue*, no 4, (2004), online: http://www.cqvip.com/QK/81431X/2005001/11818663.html (accessed on May 15, 2009).

37. S. L. Shirk, *op.cit.*, pp. 106-107.

38. Chen Xiankui & Xin Xiangyang, *"Zhongguo heping jueqi shi fou keneng?"* [Is China's peaceful rise possible, or not?], *Xuexi Shibao*, no. 250, August, 20, 2004, online:

http://www.china.com.cn/xxsb/txt/2004-08/30/content_5648323.htm (accessed on 19 August 2008).

39. H. Yee, Zhu Feng, *op. cit.*, p. 31.

40. A 2007 Pew Research poll found that only 29 percent of Indonesians and 27 percent of Malaysians polled had a favorable view of the United States as opposed to 83 percent of Malaysians and 65 percent of Indonesians who had favorable views of China. Americans themselves are more popular than their country, with 42 percent of Indonesians having a favorable view towards Americans in 2007. The figure for Indonesia is up slightly from a favorable view of only 15 percent in 2003 but remains well below the 2000 rate of 75 percent. See T. Lum, W. M. Morrison, B. Vaughn, "China's 'Soft Power' in Southeast Asia," CRS Report to Congress, January 2008, CRS-2, online. Compare also Susan L. Shirk, *op. cit.*, p. 252 and Sun Jing, "Tipping the Balance–China's 'Peaceful Rise' in the Eyes of Japanese Press," *P*aper presented at the annual meeting of the International Studies Association 48th Annual Convention, Hilton Chicago, CHICAGO, IL, USA, February 28, 2007, online: http://www.allacademic.com/meta/p180078_index.html (accessed on July 2, 2009).

41 Sebastian Billioud, "Confucianism, 'Cultural Tradition' and Official Discourse in China at the Start of the New Century," *Asian Perspective*, no. 3, (2007), p. 53.

42. E. Medeiros, M. Fravel, "China's New Diplomacy," *Foreign Affairs*, no. 6, (2003), pp. 32-33.

43. G. Chen, *op. cit.*, pp. 57-58.

44. Yong Deng, "Better than Power: "International Status" in Chinese Foreign Policy," in *China Rising, Power and Motivation in Chinese Foreign Policy*, ed. by Yong Deng & Fei-Ling Wang (Lanham, Boulder, New York: Rowman & Littlefield Publishers, 2005), p. 160.

45. S. S. Kim, *China, the United Nations, and World Order*, *op.cit.*, p. 46.

46. Huiying Feng, "Chinese Strategic Culture and Foreign Policy Decision-Making, Confucianism, Leadership and War," *ASIAN Security Studies* (London, New York: Routledge, 2007), p. 20.

47. Chai Jia, Li Jianchang, "Rujia sixiang dui goujian hexie shehui de xianshi yiyi" [The Practical Dimensions of Confucianism in Building Harmonious Society], *Liaoning Xingzheng Xueyuan Xuebao*, no. 1, (2009), p. 168.

48. Ibid, p. 169.

49. J. Delury, " 'Harmonious' in China," *Policy Review*, issue 148, (2008), p. 36.

50. Hua Shiping, *"Inside the Chinese Mind,"* The Wilson Quarterly, vol. 29, no. 4, (2005) (accessed via the Questia Library on May 15, 2009).

51. Huiying Feng, *op. cit.*, p. 21.

52. Qin Yaqing, Wei Ling, "Structure, Processes, and the Socialization of Power, East Asia Community-building and the Rise of China," in *China's Ascent, Power, Security, and the Future of International Politics*, ed. by R. S. Ross & Zhu Feng (Ithaca, CT, Cornell University Press, 2008), pp. 121-124.

53. J. Nye, "Soft power. The Means to Success in World Politics," *Public Affairs*, 2004, pp. 11-15.

54. C. Hayden, "The Premises of Soft Power: A Comparative Analysis of Public Diplomacy Policy Rhetoric in China and Japan," paper presented to the International Studies Association Convention New York, New York. February 16, 2009, online: http://www.allacademic.com/ (accessed on 12 August 2009).

55. Meng Honghua, "Zhongguo ruan liliang pingu baogao (shang)" [the Evaluation Report on China's Soft Power), *Guoji Guancha*, no. 2, (2007), pp. 18-19.

56. Yu Xitian, *"Ruan liliang jianshe yu Zhongguo dui wai zhanglue"* [The Soft Power Building and China's Foreign Strategy], *Guoji Zhanwang*, 2007, *Shikan hao* (test edition), pp. 19-20.

57. Li Mingjian, "China Debates Soft-Power," *Chinese Journal of International Politics*, vol. 2, (2008), pp. 287-308.

58. Pang Zhongying, "Guanyu Zhongguo de ruan liliang wenti" [On the Chinese soft power], *Guoji Wenti luntan*, no. 42, (2006), pp. 8-9.

59. Pan Zhongying, "Zhongguo de ruan guoli de wenti" [the problem of China's soft power], *Nankai Daxue Xinwen*, September 3, 2006, online: http://news.nankai.edu.cn/gnjt/system/2006/09/14/000001399.shtml (accessed on May 16, 2009).

60. C. Hayden, *op. cit.*

61. Ni Jianping, "Dui wai chuanbo yu "heping jueqi": guojia xingxiang suzao de shijiao" [The Foreign Media and "Peaceful-rise": the perspective of the state's image model], online: http://media.people.com.cn/ (accessed on August 25, 2009).

62. *Address by President Hu Jintao of China at Meeting of Leaders from China, India, Brazil, South Africa and Mexico*, 2005/07/07, online: http://www.fmprc.gov.cn/eng/wjdt/zyjh/ (accessed on September 1, 2009)

63. Hu Jintao, "Nuli jianshe chijiu heping, gongtong farong de hexieshijie" [To hard build a listing peace, for common and prosperous harmonious world], September 16, 2005, online http://www.southcn.com/news/ (accessed on April 24, 2009).

64 Josef Gregory Mahoney, "On the Way to Harmony: Marxism, Confucianism and Hu Jintao's Hexie Concept," in *China in Search of a Harmonious Society*, ed. by Sujian Guo and Baogang Guo (Lanham: Rowman & Littlefield Publishers, 2008), p. 115.

65. Po Bingjiu, " 'Liji'de hexie shijie sixiang," *Guoji Zhengzhi Kexue*, no. 3, (2008), pp. 59-60.

66. Wang Yiwei, "Hexie shijie guan de san zhong neihang," *Zhexue yu Yanjiu*;, no. 2, (2007) pp. 67-68.

67. M. Yahuda, "How much has China learned about interdependence?" in *China Rising, Nationalism and Interdependence*, ed. by David S. G. Goldman and Gerald Segal (New York, Routledge, 1997), pp. 8-9.

68. A. S. Link; H. Davidson, *Woodrow Wilson: Revolution, War, and Peace*, pp. 74-75.

69. Ibid, pp. 90-92.

70. Hu Rongrong, "Huayun quan yu wenhua waijiao" [The Power of Language and the Cultural Diplomacy], *Shijie Jingji yu Zhengzhi Luntan*, no. 5, (2008), p. 66.

71. J. Ramo, *Brand China*, online: http://fpc.org.uk/fsblob/827.pdf (accessed on May 16, 2009)

72. Jiang Xiyuan & Xia Liping, *op. cit.* pp. 140-142.

73. Zou Xiaoming, "Heping jueqi jinfang 'guojia jihui zhuyi' " [The 'peaceful-rise' to guard 'national pragmatism'] online http://www.tecn.cn/ (accessed September 4, 2008).

74. Yu Bin, "China's Harmonious World: Beyond Cultural Interpretation," in *China in Search of a Harmonious Society*, ed. by Sujian Guo & Baogang Guo (Lanham: Rowman & Littlefield Publishers, 2008), pp. 77-78.

75. Yan Xuetong, "Meiguo baquan yu Zhongguo anquan" [American hegemony and China's security], *Tianjin Renmin Chubanshe*, 2000, p. 15.

76. T. G. Ash, "China arrives as a world power today—and we should welcome it," *Guardian*, April 2, 2009, online: http://www.almendron.com/tribuna/24520/ (accessed on May 10, 2009).

Chapter 10

Explanations of China's Compliance with International Agreements: Configuring Three Approaches to Institutional Effects on State Behavior

Albert S. Yee

INTRODUCTION

Beginning in the 1980s, China has steadily increased its presence in international institutions and participated more extensively in their activities. Today, it is a signatory to over three hundreds international treaties and a member of every major international and regional organization that it is eligible to join. By most scholarly accounts, China's compliance with the rules of these organizations and the provisions of these treaties has been generally "reasonable"[1] or somewhere in the "B" grade range[2] depending on the issue area. As a result, Chinese foreign policy has become increasingly cooperative, multilateral, and largely supportive of the "liberal world order"[3] built upon the intergovernmental organizations of the UN, the Bretton Woods economic institutions, and a slew of more recent international institutions covering numerous issue areas.

In assessing the effects of international institutions on state behavior, clear definitions of key terms are needed to minimize ambiguity and confusion. In this chapter, "institutions" are defined as the organizations and/or the rules that arrange or stipulate an activity.[4] "International institutions" refer to international and regional organizations and/or the rules that arrange or stipulate activities with international ramifications by nation-states. An "international regime" is a set of institutions (i.e., rules, norms, principles and procedures) arranging or stipulating activities by nation-states within a specified issue area of international relations.[5] Meanwhile, "compliance" is defined as behavioral conformity to the rules prescribing an activity.[6] More precisely, this chapter focuses on "decisional compliance," which refers specifically to the legislation and issuance of directives by political authorities to formally adopt international rules and laws. "Compliance capacity," in contrast, refers to the bureaucratic and administrative (i.e., "managerial") ability to adequately implement these rules and laws domestically.[7]

In analyzing decisional compliance with international rules and regulations, scholars of international relations and international law have pursued mainly three approaches to the effects of international institutions on state behavior. They have also acknowledged the existence of a separate realist approach that minimizes the significant independent effects of these institutions. Some analysts have combined the three institutional approaches in their empirical studies or have attempted theoretical syntheses. The first approach is based on rational calculations and has been labeled "rational functionalism," "neoliberal institutionalism," "rational institutionalism," etc. The second approach emphasizes the role of domestic politics, "domestic structure," domestic political process, etc. The third approach focuses on the effects of norms, learning, "cognitivism," socialization, etc. Finally, by emphasizing the pursuit of power and self-interests in an anarchic international system, the realist approach reduces international institutions to epiphenomena or as merely the instruments used by states to obtain power and self-interested objectives. Although they employ slightly different terminology, many analysts of international relations and international law have classified existing analyses of institutional effects into these three institutional approaches plus a separate realist approach.[8]

Analysts of China's decisional compliance with international rules and laws also have used variants of these three institutional approaches.[9] In different ways, they have explained Chinese compliance as the product of institutional effects on China's foreign policies. As a result, these analysts have countered realist explanations and delineated the institutional bases for continued Chinese adherence to international rules and laws.

Despite their many advantages, however, these existing analyses are hobbled by significant weaknesses. These flaws hinder more accurate explanations of institutional effects and impede efforts to develop more cogent syntheses of the three strands of institutional analysis. Moreover, existing analyses lack a comprehensive framework to organize and differentiate variations in institutional effects on state behavior across issue areas. Not only are integrations of existing approaches needed, their varying salience on different issues also need to be examined and prioritized.

This chapter examines the effects of international institutions on China's (non)compliance with international agreements. Part One delineates the three main analytical approaches to the effects of international institutions on state behavior. For each approach, representative studies are presented from existing institutional analyses of international relations and Chinese foreign policy. The limitations and weaknesses of each approach are then identified and critiqued.

The drawbacks of the three major existing approaches to institutional effects have led some analysts to combine them in different ways. These attempts at analytical integration, however, have been haphazard theoretically and inductive empirically. In addition, there have not been attempts to differentiate these three explanations, and the integrations of them, across issue areas. Hence, Part Two of this chapter seeks to provide a more theoretically coherent conceptualization of the three existing approaches and their possible integrations for different issues. It begins by identifying and configuring three important factors that are significant in explaining institutional effects. These are 1) policy elite cohesion and insulation; 2) domestic mobilization; and 3) issue evolution. By positing alternative configurations of these three factors, different types of institutional effects are delineated in terms of a series of explicit propositions. Four of these propositions succinctly characterize the core properties of the three major approaches to institutional effects. These are rationalist institutionalism (P1), domestic process institutionalism (P2), and adaptive learning (P3b)/normative socialization (P3a) institutionalism. In addition, five integrative propositions delineate possible combinations of the three major explanations. These are rationalism/domestic process (P4), domestic process/adaptive learning (P5b), domestic process/normative socialization (P5a), rationalism/adaptive learning (P6b), and rationalism/normative socialization (P6a).

In Part Three of this chapter, these possible explanations of institutional effects are used to examine China's (non)compliance with international institutions across issue areas since the 1980s. Specifically, different explanations are used to illuminate the effects of international institutions on the compliance decisions of Chinese policymakers with regard to international agreements on issues of security, economics, environment and human rights. For each of these four issue areas, primary explanations are identified and then supplemented with relevant secondary explanations. The result is a more precise and differentiated overall explanation of China's compliance with international agreements across issue areas.

PART ONE

RATIONALIST INSTITUTIONALISM

The first approach to institutional effects is based on rational calculations and can be divided into "rational-functionalist institutionalism" (or "contractual institutionalism") and instrumental "rational institutionalism."[10] In this type of analysis, international institutions provide functional and/or instrumental (dis)advantages that can render (non)compliance with international agreements (un)desirable in the rational calculations of state actors. "Rationalist institutionalism" posits the existence of rational state actors that engage in cooperative foreign policy behavior as a result of the instrumental and/or functional benefits provided by international institutions.

Institutionalist Proposition #1:

International institutions provide functional or instrumental costs and benefits that affect the utility maximizing calculations of rational state actors to (not) comply with international agreements.

Rational-Functionalist Institutionalism

Beginning in the early 1980s, advocates of "rational-functional" institutionalism argued that "international regimes" enabled rational state actors to overcome collective action problems by focusing on expectations, reducing transaction costs, providing information, enhancing transparency, linking issues, and harnessing reputational concerns. By performing all these functions, international "regimes" remove (or reduce) impediments to cooperation and supply conditions that render states more likely to cooperate.[11] Due in large part to its encompassing ambiguity and its fundamental compatibility with realist explanations, rational-functional analyses of international regimes became a very influential approach during the 1980s.

Although not widely influential among China scholars, some analysts have acknowledged some aspects of these rational-functionalist arguments in their studies of recent Chinese foreign policy behavior. Although not a proponent of this approach, Pearson briefly discussed the effects of reputation and the roles of information and transparency in reducing uncertainty.[12] Similarly, Johnston and Evans briefly cited the reputational effects of "social opprobrium" and "social backpatting."[13] Meanwhile, Hempson-Jones noted the role of international regimes in "reinforcing reciprocity between states and making defection from the norms easier to punish." As China becomes "further bound into the norms and conduct of international society," he concluded, "constraints on Chinese behavior have been accepted in exchange for gains for the state."[14]

Despite its popularity among international relations analysts, however, there are numerous problems associated with the rational-functionalist approach to international institutions. First, there has been so little supporting evidence and so much conceptual confusion surrounding the analysis of international regimes that "the word 'institution' has now largely replaced 'regime' in the scholarly IR literature."[15] As realists have pointed out and some institutionalists have acknowledged, there has been very modest empirical evidence to support the rational functionalist arguments.[16] Second, definitional confusion arising from a convoluted multi-part understanding of "regimes" as "rules, norms, principles and procedures around which expectations converge"[17] has reduced the usefulness of the concept. In particular, this "consensus definition" conflated widely disparate phenomena and asserted their focalizing capabilities as part of the defined properties already possessed by the regimes.[18] Third, as Simmons and Martin observed, many standard definitions fail to "separate the definition of an institution from behavioral outcomes that ought to *be explained*" and hence "makes it impossible to test for the impact of institutions on activities and expectations."[19] (Emphasis original)

Rational Institutionalism

In contrast, "rational institutionalists" focus more simply on the instrumental benefits and costs supplied by institutions to explain the compliance of rational states. In these analyses, instrumental states embark upon cooperative foreign policies because they derive more benefits than costs from participating in and complying with the rules and/or norms of international institutions. This compliance occurs through "calculations of advantage" made by "self-interested, goal-seeking" states maximizing their individual utilities.[20] In other versions of rational institutionalism, compliance stems from the rational calculations of self-interested states acting within their strategic (i.e., game theoretic) interactions.[21]

Existing rational institutionalist analyses of China's compliance with international agreements focus mostly on these instrumental, rather than the functional, benefits of international institutions. As Oksenberg and Economy reported, "Our study stresses the essential rationality of China's leaders. Within the context of their domestic political situation and their perceptions of the international context, they seek to maximize their benefits and minimize costs."[22] At the simplest level, rationalist institutionalists explain Chinese participation in and compliance with international institutions by citing the many material benefits received by China. These concrete payoffs include financial resources, technology transfers, equipment, technical expertise, personnel training, etc.[23] More broadly, these instrumental benefits can also include acquiring new knowledge, establishing connections, and securing a favorable international "image" or reputation.[24] Indeed, rational institutionalists view the acquisition of these non-material benefits as clearly part of a rational Chinese calculus of "free riding" and "extracting side payments."[25] At the broadest level, rational institutionalists explain China's participation in and compliance with international institutions as mainly rational means to achieve enduring national and strategic ends. Oksenberg and Economy, for example, listed "five objectives: protecting Chinese sovereignty, maintaining national security, eroding Taiwan's status, cultivating a favorable image, and promoting economic interests."[26]

Rational institutionalist analyses that emphasize the pursuit of instrumental benefits offer plausible explanations of China's (non)compliance with international agreements. Moreover, they avoid the definitional confusion that plague "rational functionalist" institutionalism as well as the resulting conflation of institutions with posited policy effects that make it difficult to ascertain "*whether* rules influence behavior."[27] Despite these advantages, however, instrumental versions of rational institutionalism also suffer from several major flaws.

First, by incorporating the benefits of participating in international institutions into the utility functions of rational state actors, rational institutionalists risk subsuming institutional analyses under rational choice theory. If the effects of institutions derive from their ability to supply benefits, then these effects become conditional to the balance of costs and benefits supplied by other factors. Under these circumstances, international institutions might (or not) have a non-epiphenomenal effect on state behavior, depending on how they operate in conjunction with myriad factors to affect the preference rankings of rational actors.

Second, by basing their analyses on rationalist foundations, rationalist institutionalists risk subsuming their analyses under rationalist versions of realism. Some realist analysts would readily concur that international institutions are merely one factor among many affecting the rational calculations of state actors. Among rationalist realist analysts of China's foreign policy behavior, for exam-

ple, Sutter explicitly argued that "Chinese leaders tended to approach each foreign policy issue on a case-by-case basis, each time calculating the costs and
benefits of adherence to international norms."[28] Likewise, rationalist realist analysts of Chinese grand strategy like Swaine and Tellis observed that

> The calculative strategy currently pursued by Beijing has resulted in China adopt-
> ing an "instrumental" attitude toward international regimes. This implies that
> China possesses neither an intrinsic commitment nor an intrinsic antipathy to the
> existing international norms and organizations but approaches these simply in
> terms of a pragmatic calculation centered on the benefits and losses of participa-
> tion and nonparticipation.[29]

Since both rationalist realists and rational institutionalists concur on such an
instrumental understanding of institutional effects, some analysts have sought to
synthesize them on the basis of their common rationalist foundations.[30]

DOMESTIC PROCESS INSTITUTIONALISM

A second major strand of institutionalism explains the policy effects of international institutions by examining their impacts on a state's foreign policy bureaucracy and domestic politics. In this type of "domestic process" institutionalism,
participation in international institutions entails the appointment of new government envoys, creation of new administrative staffs, and establishment of new
research departments. All of these personnel and knowledge requirements generate policy advocates and experts within the government seeking greater compliance with the rules and norms of international institutions. At the same time,
other bureaucrats and policy experts that oppose compliance would be mobilized
to block or impede the implementation of these rules and regulations.

Concurrently, participation in international institutions also generates new
domestic constituencies and experts outside of the government with knowledge,
interests and stakes in the state's responses to international rules and norms.
Domestic groups and civil society policy advocates that favor or benefit from
these rules and norms would use their political and informational resources to
press for government compliance. In contrast, domestic groups and policy experts within civil society that oppose or are harmed by these rules and regulations would deploy these resources to lobby for non-compliance by the government.[31]

These domestic groups and societal policy advocates can forge informational and political linkages with like-minded bureaucratic players and expert policymakers to facilitate or hinder the state's compliance with international agreements. By generating new political participants, necessitating new expertise, and
mobilizing domestic groups and policy advocates, international institutions can
alter the configuration of policy preferences within both the policymaking bureaucracy and the wider domestic political process. As a result of these bureaucratic and political changes, the policy preferences of political leaders can be

influenced and state actors can pursue more cooperative foreign policies. In particular, the extent of government's decisional compliance with international agreements will depend upon the political strengths of pro-compliance vs. anti-compliance forces within the policymaking bureaucracy and domestic civil society.

This domestic process approach to the effects of international institutions on state behavior can be formulated succinctly as a basic proposition.

Institutionalist Proposition #2:

Participation in international institutions generates and/or mobilizes bureaucratic personnel and societal groups that prompt political leaders to (not)comply with international agreements.

Some institutionalist analysts of recent Chinese foreign policy have pursued variants of this second strand of institutionalism to explain China's (non)compliance with international agreements. For example, Johnston and Evans investigated the domestic political ramifications of China's participation in international security institutions. "As the agenda of these institutions becomes more technical," they reported, "China is compelled to develop expertise to handle the complexity of the issues at stake. This expertise requires organizational and bureaucratic resources. This emergent constituency of experts has a normative or organizational interest, or both, in preserving and expanding participation."[32] Similarly, with regard to international economic institutions, Pearson extensively examined how they exerted effects on a state's cooperative foreign policy by becoming "entangled" with the domestic political process. As she cogently observed,

> International norms and rules might influence the beliefs and behavior of domestic decision makers, the positions articulated in the domestic policy debate, and, ultimately, their policies. Yet international influences must also be channeled through domestic actors and institutions, a process that may enhance or thwart external influence. In other words, the norms and rules of international institutions are made influential through their "entanglement" with the domestic political process.[33]

"Domestic process" analyses of the foreign policy effects of international institutions offer plausible explanations with rich empirical case study evidence. By departing from the rational and unitary assumptions of rationalist institutionalism, they avoid analytical subsumption to realism and rational choice theory. No doubt, "domestic process" institutionalists are correct that foreign policy decisions to comply with international institutions, like all government policies, are the products of a domestic political process. However, by attributing compliance with international agreements to a domestic political process, "domestic process" institutionalism risks being mainly a domestic politics explanation, albeit with important indirect effects by international institutions.

INSTITUTIONAL LEARNING AND NORMATIVE SOCIALIZATION

A third major approach to the effects of international institutions on state behavior emphasizes the role of "learning" and "socialization." By participating in international institutions, states apparently "learn" or are "socialized" to comply with the rules and norms of these institutions and consequently become more cooperative in their foreign policy behavior. This institutional learning and socialization approach can be formulated succinctly as a basic proposition.

Institutionalist Proposition #3a, 3b:

Participation in international institutions prompts member states a) to learn or b) to become socialized to (not) comply with their norms and rules.

Institutional Learning

The concept of "learning" is often invoked by myriad analysts to explain the evolution of new thinking and the resulting new behavior by state actors.[34] In the study of international relations, some analysts explain the effects of international institutions on foreign policy behavior by arguing that participation in international organizations prompts members to "learn" to comply with their rules and norms. As actors acquire more knowledge about relevant issues and their institutional context, they adjust their thinking and behavior in accordance with the rules and norms of their international institutions. Some analysts have identified the existence or emergence of international norms, traced their transmission through international organizations to state actors, and attributed normative compliance to state actors learning these norms.[35]

Similarly, in explaining China's recent cooperative foreign policy, some scholars have emphasized the learning of new norms by Chinese leaders. By participating in international institutions, they gradually learned to abide by their rules and norms. As Pearson explained, "domestic policy-makers *learn* new ideas. The concept of learning suggests that genuine (if often incremental) transformation of elite perceptions occurs as a result of exposure to international economic norms or rules."[36] (Emphasis original) These ideational and normative changes lead states to view compliance with international rules and norms as compatible with their national self-interests. According to Cui Tiankai, the director general of Asian affairs in China's Ministry of Foreign Affairs, "It was a gradual learning process for us, as we needed to become more familiar with how these [international] organizations worked and to learn how to play the game."[37]

Analyses of institutional learning, however, contain several weaknesses. First, the plausibility of "learning" stems apparently from its commonsensical familiarity. Drawing on their personal everyday or classroom experiences, analysts readily invoke this concept to explain changes in state behavior. Yet the phenomenon of how actors actually "learn" is highly complex and contingent. New thinking has to be transmitted by international institutions, accepted by state actors, and enacted into congruent policies. As Pearson elaborated:

> To show that learning has occurred, we would need to show first that new ideas about economic integration have been transmitted to a country. This can happen through the business community or through agents of the multilateral institutions. This transmission of ideas through these linkages would need to lead to a shift in the dominant thinking among elites about the value of integration into the world economy, a shift that ideally leads to policy change in a direction that is consistent with the new ideas, but which can also be blocked by bureaucratic or other factors.[38]

Second, "learning" brackets exceedingly complex processes of post-transmission ideational change, normative internalization, and policy adoption. Instead of one omnibus opaque concept, "learning" actually consists of many interrelated "microprocesses" of persuasion, internalization, etc. Yet proponents of institutional learning have not adequately analyzed these microprocesses between the transmission of new ideas and the adoption of new policies. Yet without explicating these microprocesses, analyses of institutional learning encounter difficulties explaining how new thinking prompts state actors to adopt, internalize, and comply with international norms.

Institutional Socialization

Cognizant of the problems plaguing analyses of institutional learning, some analysts have advanced another approach to institutional effects that emphasizes the socialization of states within international organizations. By participating in these institutions, state actors become socialized into embracing and complying with their norms and rules. Unlike rationalist compliance based on "strategic calculations," this socialized compliance occurs through the social effects of participating in group activities. According to Checkel, these social effects operate mainly through "role playing" and "normative suasion." Role playing entails "noncalculative behavioral adaptation" to "environmental triggers" within an organization or group which entails the "agent's passive, noncalculative acceptance of new roles" that are "appropriate in that particular setting." Meanwhile, "normative suasion" occurs when arguments and persuasion prompt agents to "actively and reflectively internalize new understandings of appropriateness" and thereby to act accordingly.[39]

In explaining China's recent cooperative foreign policy, some analysts have also emphasized the effects of institutional socialization on state behavior.[40] For example, Johnston views institutions as "social environments" within which "state behavior changes . . . in the presence of the endogenous 'social' effects of institutions."[41] This institutional socialization occurs through three "microprocesses": mimicking (or role playing), social influence, and persuasion. As Johnston explained,

> Mimicking explains pro-group behavior as a function of borrowing the language, habits, and ways of acting as a safe, first reaction to a novel environment. . . . Social influence explains pro-group behavior as a function of an actor's sensitivity to status markers bestowed by a social group, and requires some common understanding in the social value the group places on largely symbolic backpatting and opprobrium signals. . . . Persuasion explains pro-group behavior as an effect of the internalization of fundamentally new causal understandings of an actor's environment, such that these new understandings are considered normal, given, and normatively correct.[42]

These three "microprocesses" of socialization help illuminate how international institutions exert social effects that prompt their members to comply with their rules and norms. Like institutional "learning," however, analyses of institutional socialization also encounter difficulties explaining how new thinking prompts state actors to adopt, internalize, and comply with international norms. For example, Johnston's analysis of "persuasion" does not explain how ideational and normative internalization actually occurs within the thinking of state actors. Instead of ascertaining the actual operation of internalization, he relies on a methodological procedure to determine simply the occurrence of persuasion.[43] With his usual rigor and clarity, he proposed four sequential steps to serially examine various empirical "indicators," followed by the use of "critical tests" of competing explanations. As Johnston explained,

> How would one know if persuasion had led to prosocial/pronormative behavior in international institutions? First, . . . one would have to show that social environments in institutions are conducive to persuasion. Second, one would have to show that after exposure to or involvement in a new social environment, attitudes or arguments for participation have indeed changed, converging with the normative/causal arguments that predominate in a particular social environment. Third, one would have to show that behavior had changed in ways consistent with prior attitudinal change. Finally, one would have to show that material side payment or threats were not present, nor were they part of the decision to conform to prosocial norms.[44]

INTEGRATING INSTITUTIONAL APPROACHES TO DECISIONAL (NON)COMPLIANCE

The three major approaches to the effects of international institutions on state behavior present analytically distinct explanations. All three illuminate aspects of the decisional (non)compliance of states to international agreements. However, since they also contain some weaknesses and limitations, some analysts have integrated two or more of them in order to "triangulate" institutional effects.

Integrating Rationalist and Domestic Process Approaches (P4)

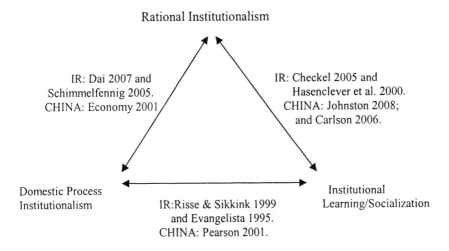

Figure 10.1 follows:

Rational Institutionalism

IR: Dai 2007 and
Schimmelfennig 2005.
CHINA: Economy 2001

IR: Checkel 2005 and
Hasenclever et al. 2000.
CHINA: Johnston 2008;
and Carlson 2006.

Domestic Process
Institutionalism

IR:Risse & Sikkink 1999
and Evangelista 1995.
CHINA: Pearson 2001.

Institutional
Learning/Socialization

Figure 10.1 Integrations of Three Approaches to Institutional Effects

Some international relations scholars have combined rationalist and domestic process approaches in their analysis of the effects of international institutions.[45] Building upon a "rationalist framework," for example, Dai argued that "a government's compliance is determined not only by the electoral leverage of domestic constituencies but also by how much information they have" about the policy process. International institutions "alter the strategic environment that governments face domestically" because they "can employ victims of noncompliance and empower domestic pro-compliance constituencies to monitor and enforce national compliance."[46] Similarly, Schimmelfennig advanced a "rationalist approach to the study of international socialization based on strategic calculation." In his version of rational institutionalism, "socialization works through reinforcement. International organizations reward norm-confirming behavior and punish norm-violating behavior; target states conform with the norms and rules in order to avoid punishment and gain rewards."[47] In the long-term, however, "the most important factor for successful international reinforcement is the constellation of [political] parties" within nation-states (i.e., all liberal, all anti-liberal, or mixed).[48]

Some institutionalist analysts of recent Chinese foreign policy have also combined rationalist and domestic process explanations of China's compliance with international agreements.[49] For example, Economy argued that China's adherence to international regimes is governed by a "maxi-mini principle" (i.e., maximize rights, minimize responsibilities), but participation in international institutions has affected decisional compliance by generating new bureaucrats, new domestic actors, and new domestic institutions and laws. As she argued, "international regimes spur the emergence of new bureaucratic arrangements to manage China's involvement in the regimes and encourage the introduction of new actors from the scientific and expert communities into prominent policy-making positions."[50]

Analyses that combine rationalist and domestic process approaches can be formulated succinctly as a basic proposition about the dual bases of institutional effects on (non)compliance with international agreements:

Institutionalist Proposition #4:

Participation in international institutions generates and/or mobilizes bureaucratic personnel and societal groups that affect the utility maximizing calculations of rational state actors to produce (non)compliance with international agreements.

Integrating Learning/Socialization and Domestic Process Approaches (P5a, P5b)

Some international relations scholars have integrated learning/socialization and domestic process approaches in their analyses of state (non)compliance with international norms. In their study of human rights norms, for example, Risse and Sikkink delineated a five-stage "spiral model" of normative compliance. Through the efforts of "transnational advocacy networks," international norms are transmitted to states and eventually incorporated into domestic legislation and discourse.[51] Similarly, in his study of Soviet security policy in the 1980s, Evangelista combined the transmission of transnational security ideas with an analysis of different types of "domestic structures" derived from the varying character of political institutions, society and policy networks.[52]

Some institutionalist analysts of recent Chinese foreign policy have also combined learning/socialization and domestic process approaches in their explanations. For example, in her highly nuanced study of China's GATT/WTO accession, Pearson emphasized the "learning" of international economic ideas by Chinese leaders and the "pluralization" and "internal lobbying" by "domestic actors" within China's policymaking process. According to her, "Perhaps the most significant role of outside influences has been that ideas and norms of the market and the GATT/WTO system have both been adopted by Chinese policymakers and reflected in policy reforms. . . . Learning occurred directly through channels of influence . . . and indirectly as more and more Chinese officials became convinced that deeper economic integration was both beneficial and necessary." At the same time, "policy changes occurred in large part, and perhaps predominantly, as a result of domestic forces."[53]

Analyses that integrate learning/socialization and domestic process approaches can be formulated as two basic propositions about the dual bases of institutional effects on (non)compliance with international agreements.

Institutionalist Proposition #5a:

Participation in international institutions mobilizes domestic actors to influence the policymaking process and prompts member state policymakers to become socialized to (not) comply with their norms and rules.

Institutionalist Proposition #5b:

Participation in international institutions mobilizes domestic actors to influence the policymaking process and prompts member state policymakers to learn to adapt in (not) complying with their norms and rules.

Integrating Rationalist and Learning/Socialization Approaches (P6a, P6b)

Some scholars of international relations have also combined rationalist and learning/socialization approaches in their analyses of international institutions. For example, Hasenclever, Mayer and Rittberger relied on a sequential procedure to synthesize rationalist explanations of international regimes with "weak cognitive" learning by state actors.[54] Meanwhile, Checkel posited the existence of multiple mechanisms of socialization and explored synergies between them. In particular, he combined rationalist "strategic calculation" with noncalculative "role playing" that relies on adaptive learning and "normative suasion" that leads to the internalization of new thinking.[55] All existing attempts to juxtapose or sequentially combine rationalist and learning/socialization approaches, however, have not produced any actual theoretical synthesis.

Some institutionalist analysts of China's compliance with international agreements have also combined rationalist and learning/socialization approaches in their explanations. According to Oksenberg and Economy, for example, "The Chinese have learned how to extract the benefits that international regimes offer and minimize the costs they impose."[56] Similarly, Carlson's explanation of Chinese foreign policy behavior "combines elements of rationalist and ideationalist arguments." As he argued, "Chinese behavior has been informed by cost-benefit calculations . . . but Beijing's perception of Chinese interests was framed by both old ideas . . . and new norms . . . International norms have mattered, but their influence was only felt through the prism of older, more deeply entrenched, and largely domestic normative constructs . . . and was offset by more utilitarian considerations."[57]

Meanwhile, Johnston's analysis of institutional socialization also combined rationalist and learning/socialization approaches to China's compliance with international agreements. Indeed, two of his three "microprocesses" of socialization rely at least partly on rationalist calculations. "Mimicking" (or role playing) and "social influence" are rational adaptations to social contingencies. So long as the utilities being maximized are broadened to include social benefits such as group acceptance and group esteem, these two "microprocesses" are compatible with the rationalist approach to international institutions. In contrast, the microprocess of "persuasion" entails the internalizations of social norms. As Johnston recognized:

> Two of the socialization microprocesses . . . could fall within the "rationalist" paradigm (mimicking and social influence)—an actor is, roughly speaking, maximizing some utility by choosing alternatives that appear to increase the probability of meeting some goal. In the case of mimicking, survival is being maximized by copying the group. In the case of social influence, self-perceptions of status are being maximized through interaction with other humans . . . . Only persuasion entails . . . the logic of appropriateness, where socialization leaves actors with new definitions of self that provide self-evident and normal notions of expected behavior.[58]

Analyses that integrate rationalist and learning/socialization approaches can be formulated as two basic propositions about the dual bases of institutional effects on (non)compliance with international agreements.

Institutionalist Proposition #6a:

Participation in international institutions prompts member state actors both to rationally decide and to become socialized to (not) comply with their norms and rules.

Institutionalist Proposition #6b:

Participation in international institutions prompts member state actors both to rationally decide and to learn to adapt to (not) comply with their norms and rules.

PART TWO

FOUR HYPOTHESES ON CONFIGURING INSTITUTIONAL EFFECTS

The three major approaches to the effects of international institutions on state behavior posit four analytically distinct explanations of the decisional (non)compliance of state actors with international agreements (P1, P2, P3a and P3b). In additions, combinations of these explanations produces five additional integrated explanations (P4, P5a, P5b, P6a and P6b). All of these distinct and integrated explanations are plausible and have some empirical support. As delineated in Part One of this chapter, they can be formulated succinctly as propositions about the effects of international institutions on state (non)compliance with international agreements. With adaptive learning and normative socialization considered as one approach, these propositions are depicted in Figure 10.2.

Although they offer plausible explanations of China's decisional (non)compliance with international agreements since the 1990s, these propositions about distinct and integrated explanations are viewed usually as competitors that require adjudication or as coexisting explanations that require an "eclectic" approach.[59] Unfortunately, empirical adjudication is inconclusive because all of these propositions are plausible and have some empirical support. Meanwhile, "eclecticism" is theoretically underspecified and risks producing comprehensively non-coherent explanations. To better specify the circumstances under which particular institutional propositions are operative, this section pursues an alternative approach to decisional (non)compliance by extracting three sets of factors from the three major approaches and configuring them in multiple ways to more precisely ascertain the applicability of distinct and integrated institutionalist propositions across issue areas in different nation-states.

The first set of factors concerns the internal and external characteristics of the state apparatus needed for rationalist institutionalism explanations. In order for states to make rational calculations about (non)compliance with international agreements, they have to be largely "unitary" internally and relatively "insulated" externally from societal pressures. This "unitary" requirement presupposes that the policymaking elite is mostly cohesive, rather than divided and conflictual.[60] The societal "insulation" requirement, meanwhile, assumes that "state autonomy,"[61] rather than the influence of civil society groups, largely determines foreign policy decisions. For heuristic purposes, policy elite "cohesion/insulation" can be conceptualized on a high-low, increasing-decreasing, continuum. In the case of China, this continuum delimits a narrower range that is operationally conceivable for authoritarian political systems. Specifically, "low" amounts of elite cohesion/insulation also refers to high contestation at the ministerial and local/provincial levels of government, rather than exclusively within the politburo.

The second set of factors concerns the characteristics of the societal influences that operate in domestic process explanations. In order for domestic groups to influence (non)compliance with international agreements, they have to be mobilized and possess the capacity to affect the decisions of foreign policymakers. Policy elites still make the actual policy decisions, but they do so because of the actual and contemplated influence of mobilized domestic constituencies. Unless policy unanimity among state and civil society exists, this domestic mobilization usually cannot coexist with state autonomy without generating state-society tensions over foreign policies. For heuristic purposes, "domestic mobilization" can be conceptualized on a high-low, increasing-decreasing, continuum. In the case of China, this continuum delimits a narrowed range within the limits of what is possible for authoritarian political systems. Specifically, "high" levels of domestic mobilization refer to extensive amounts of public NGO activity, spontaneous local popular protests, and active lobbying by domestic non-governmental groups through formal and informal channels.

The third set of factors concerns whether learning and socialization can occur on particular issues. In order for learning/socialization explanations to be applicable to (non)compliance with particular international agreements, the issues involved must be susceptible to interpretive evolution. If understandings of issues are stable and rigid, then routine calculations of costs/benefits are possible, and rational institutionalism explanations would be more applicable. For heuristic purposes, this "evolutionary susceptibility" of issues can be conceptualized on a high-low, increasing-decreasing, continuum.

The continuums of these three sets of factors are depicted in Figure 10.3. Depending on the different configurations of these three factors within particular nation-states, different explanations of state (non)compliance with international agreements across issue areas are more applicable. For example, in nation-states with high policy cohesion/insulation, low domestic mobilization, and low issue evolution, (non)compliance with international agreements accords with rationalist institutionalism explanations (P1). This occurs because cohesive policy elites insulated from un-mobilized domestic groups and adhering to stable understandings of issues, possess the "unitary" attribute and "state autonomy" needed to rationally evaluate the costs and benefits of (non)compliance with international agreements.

In contrast, in nation-states with low policy cohesion/insulation, high domestic mobilization, and high issue evolution, "domestic process" institutionalism explains more accurately (non)compliance with international agreements (P2). This occurs because non-cohesive policy elites that are not insulated from mobilized domestic groups and confronting issues with evolving meanings are influenced by domestic pressures to entertain new understandings of national interests in deciding to (not) comply with international agreements.

Meanwhile, in nation-states with low policy cohesion/insulation, low domestic mobilization, and high issue evolution, (non)compliance with international agreements accords with institutional socialization explanations (P3a). This occurs because non-cohesive and un-insulated policy elites facing evolving issues, but not subject to pressure from mobilized domestic groups, are primed to become socialized into accepting new institutional norms. Since a lively policy debate is occurring within the policy elite, understandings of national interests on particular issues are more likely to evolve away from the status quo ante and toward greater compatibility with international norms.

Finally, in nation-states with high policy cohesion/insulation, low domestic mobilization, and high issue evolution, (non)compliance with international agreements occurs in accordance with adaptive learning explanations (P3b). This occurs because cohesive policy elites facing evolving issues, but insulated from un-mobilized domestic groups, have the policy autonomy to rationally learn or adapt to institutional norms. For these unitary and autonomous policymakers, procedural compliance and tactical concessions are low cost options that constitute the path of least cognitive and bureaucratic resistance.

The effects of these four configurations of factors on (non)compliance with international agreements can be formulated succinctly as 4 hypotheses:

H1:   In nation-states where
        a) policy elite "cohesion/insulation" is high,
        b) "domestic mobilization" is low, and

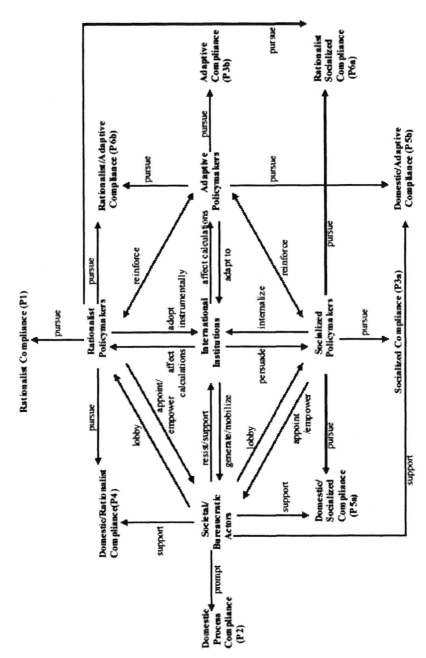

Figure 10.2 Institutional Propositions on Decisional Compliance with International Agreements

c) "evolutionary susceptibility" of the issue is low,
rationalist institutionalism explanations (P1) are most applicable.

H2:   In nation-states where
a) policy elite "cohesion/insulation" is low,
b) "domestic mobilization" is high, and
c) "evolutionary susceptibility" of the issue is high
domestic process institutionalism explanations (P2) are most applicable.

H3a: In nation-states where
a) policy elite "cohesion/insulation" is low,
b) "domestic mobilization" is low, and
c) "evolutionary susceptibility" of the issue is high,
institutional socialization explanations (P3a) are most applicable

H3b: In nation-states where
a) policy elite "cohesion/insulation" is high,
b) "domestic mobilization" is low, and
c) "evolutionary susceptibility" of the issue is high,
institutional adaptive learning explanations (P3b) are most applicable.

In addition to these four hypotheses, there are also five possible integrations of these configurations of institutional effects. Combinations of rational institutionalism explanations (P1) and domestic process explanations (P2) yield integrated P4 explanations. Meanwhile, combinations of domestic process explanations (P2) and institutional socialization explanations (P3a) produce integrated P5a explanations. Similarly, combinations of domestic process explanations (P2) and adaptive learning explanations (P3b) generate integrated P5b explanations. Finally, combinations of rational institutionalism explanations (P1) and institutional socialization explanations (P3a) yield integrated P6a explanations. Similarly, combinations of rational institutionalism explanations (P1) and adaptive learning explanations (P3b) produce integrated P6b explanations. These five integrated explanations (P4-P6), along with the four hypotheses about the configurations of P1-P3 are depicted in Figure #3. In the next five sections, these four hypotheses and their five possible integrations are used to assess China's (non)compliance with international agreements across issue areas since the 1990s.

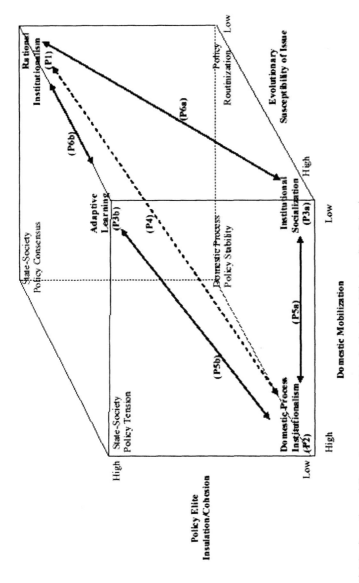

Figure 10.3 Configurations of Three Approaches (P1–P6) to Institutional Effects on State Behavior

PART THREE

EFFECTS OF CONFIGURATIONS OF THREE FACTORS ACROSS ISSUE AREAS

In China, policy elite cohesion/insulation, domestic mobilization, and issue evolution vary across issue areas in particular ways. This section posits some plausible variations across security, economic, environmental and human rights issues. In four subsequent sections, these hypothesized variations are assessed using evidence from China's decisional (non)compliance with international agreements in these four issue areas. The effects of these international institutions on Chinese foreign policy decision-making are examined using the four hypotheses about configurations of P1-P3 and the five potential integrations of institutional explanations (P4-P6).

Policy Elite Cohesion/Insulation Across Issue Areas

Although China has an authoritarian political system, Chinese political elites do not possess policy cohesion and insulation across all issue areas. On security and human rights issues, they have enormous "state autonomy" to (not) comply with international agreements due to traditional concerns about national security, regime survival, and social stability. For reasons of state, military and security issues are cloaked in secrecy and tightly controlled by top leaders and the military. Meanwhile, human rights issues are also tightly controlled by the state due to fears about social stability and unwanted popular challenges to authoritarian rule.

In contrast, policymakers have less cohesion and insulation on economic and environmental issues. This occurs because these issues generate cross-cutting preferences among policy elites, and diffuse and disparate material effects on individuals and localities. Since international economic and environmental agreements benefit some sectors and firms, while hurting other sectors and firms, they all have strong incentives to mobilize and influence the (non)compliance of policymakers.

Domestic Mobilization Across Issue Areas

In China's authoritarian political system, domestic mobilizations generally do not occur without official state sponsorship due to the lack of formally institutionalized channels for unfettered popular expression and political participation. Nevertheless, some domestic groups do become mobilized in some issue areas. In particular, they are more mobilized on economic and environmental issues because their material interests are affected directly and on a daily basis. Depending on their strength and preferences, these mobilized groups are likely to affect China's (non)compliance on economic and environmental issues.

In contrast, domestic groups are not affected on an individual and daily basis by security issues. Although they are affected daily and directly on human rights issues, domestic groups are politically demobilized due to active state repression and passive traditional habits. Accordingly, they are not likely to affect (non)compliance on security and human rights issues.

Issue Evolution Across Issue Areas

Finally, some issues are more susceptible to evolutionary interpretation in China than other issues. As understandings of economic and environmental interests evolve under conditions of globalization, Chinese policymakers increasingly learn or become more socialized to comply with international agreements in these issue areas.

In contrast, they are less likely to alter their understandings of security issues due to the persistent condition of anarchy in the international system and the tangible materiality of military capabilities. Meanwhile, Chinese leaders continue to view human rights issues in terms of the need for social stability and regime survival. As a result, they are likely to have a mixed record of decisional compliance with international agreements on security and human rights issues.

Four Configurations of Factors Across Issue Areas

Different configurations of policy elite cohesion/insulation; domestic mobilization; and evolutionary susceptibility of issues operate in China for different issue areas. Table 10.1 summarizes these varying configurations for economic, security, environmental, and human rights issues. In the next four sections, these configurations are examined with regard to China's decisional (non)compliance with international institutions in each of these four issue areas.

ARMS CONTROL AND WEAPONS PROLIFERATION AGREEMENTS (P1, P3B)

On national security issues, China's decisional (non)compliance with international security agreements is characterized by high policy elite cohesion/insulation, low domestic mobilization, and low issue evolution. As one would expect from an authoritarian political system, Chinese policymakers possessed a high amount of "state autonomy" and exhibited a high degree of unity with regards to the military requirements for the country's security. Although "fractious internal debate"[62] can occur over an issue such as the Comprehensive Test Ban Treaty (CTBT), Chinese leaders were internally cohesive and politically insulated in their decision-making. Domestic groups were not mobilized on issues of nonproliferation and arms control. Despite bureaucratic disagreements between the Ministry of Foreign Affairs on the one hand and the PLA and military-owned industries on the other,[63] Chinese leaders rationally weighed the costs and benefits and decided to accede to the CTBT in September 1996. These benefits included enhancing China's international stature and image as a responsible great power, obtaining concrete security benefits of reduced armaments worldwide, creating more peaceful international conditions for Chinese economic development, and contributing to further disarmament in the future.[64] "In the end," as Gill argued, "the Chinese leadership was convinced by the MFA argument and decided against the military's recommendation of continued testing."[65] On stable security issues involving arms control and nonproliferation, therefore, China's decisional (non)compliance occurred in accordance with Hypothesis #1 and generally as depicted in "rationalist institutionalism" explanations (P1). However, although they concur that rational calculations explain China's decisional (non)compliance with international security agreements, scholars differ with regards to the specific content of the costs and benefits. For example, Swaine and Johnston argued that "China's greatly increased involvement in arms control regimes consists primarily of realpolitik adaptation to a changing security environment" by a militarily weak state.[66] More recently, Gill

Table 10.1 Configurations of Factors Across Issue Areas

	Policy Elite Cohesion /Insulation	Domestic Mobilization	Issue Evolution	Primary /Secondary Explanations
Security Issues	High	Low	Low	Rationalist (P1) /Learning (P3b)
Economic Issues	Low	High	High	Domestic Process (P2) /Learning (P3b) Socialization (P3a)
Environmental Issues	Low	Increasing	Increasing	Rationalist (P1) Domestic Process (P2) /Socialization (P3a) Learning (P3b)
Human Rights Issues	High	Low	Increasing	Rationalist (P1) /Learning (P3b)

concluded that China's "more constructive approach toward nonproliferation and arms control" stems from Beijing's efforts to "reduce tensions and instabilities in its external security environment," project its "influence in a more reassuring way," and "quietly balance against American influence while defusing overt confrontation with Washington."[67] Meanwhile, Medeiros emphasized U.S. China policy as the "one dominant relationship [that] explains much of the change in China's nonproliferation policies and practices." As he elaborated, "U.S. policy intervention played a significant and enduring role in fostering China's increasing commitment to nonproliferation. America's use of rewards and sanctions repeatedly led China to expand its commitments and to comply with them."[68] Similarly, Chan also pointed to the effects of external pressures on Chinese rational calculations about (non)compliance with international security agreements. "China's increasing compliance with the MTCR [Missile Technology Control Regime]," he argued, "was the result of a successful application of a combination of political pressures and economic sanctions by the US and, to a certain extent, of coordinated efforts taken by the US and its allies." In addition, Chinese compliance was "also the result of China's rational calculation of its national interests based on an increasing engagement with the outside world, and on its increasing awareness of the dangers posed by the proliferation of nuclear weapons in neighboring countries. . . ."[69]

Although "rationalist institutionalism" explanations appear to dominate analyses of China's decisional (non)compliance with international security agreements, some scholars have also emphasized the role of adaptive learning. According to Johnston, "Chinese decision makers were well aware" of the "moral norms of a putative international community" and "of the backpatting benefits and opprobrium costs involved in the CTBT process."[70] Despite initially opposing the treaty, they eventually adapted to the social pressures of the international community and learned to value the image and status benefits of complying with the CTBT. Similarly, due to an "intricate web of international dependencies, commitments, status relationships, and security realities," Yuan argued that "the imperative to 'learn' becomes more pressing for Chinese national interests. This process of both adaptation and learning has set China on a path toward nonproliferation and arms control policies more consistent with broader international norms and practices."[71] Meanwhile, Kent emphasized the role of the Conference on Disarmament (CD) in "promoting discussion, disseminating information, and applying multilateral pressures." As she concluded, "Interaction with other states members, and the expertise it has required, have persuaded China to ratify treaties that in turn have generated arms control activities and stimulated domestic legislation and institution building to harmonize with its international obligations."[72] As Chinese leaders adapt to social pressures and learn to reap the benefits of adjusting their understanding of national security, rationalist institutionalism explanations must be supplemented with adaptive learning explanations (i.e., P6b integrations). As security issues become more susceptible to evolutionary interpretation, the basis of China's decisional (non)compliance with international security agreements increasingly shift from rationalist institutionalist calculations (P1) to adaptive learning within international institutions (P3b).

INTERNATIONAL ECONOMIC AGREEMENTS (P2, P3A, P3B)

Within an authoritarian political system, Chinese decision-making with regards to international economic agreements also can be explained by "rationalist institutionalism." With a cohesive and insulated policy elite, low domestic mobilization, and wide support for Deng's economic reforms, decisional (non)compliance with the Bretton Woods institutions (IMF, WB and GATT/WTO) occurred through the calculation of costs and benefits by top leaders.[73] "In joining the World Bank, International Monetary Fund (IMF), and GATT," explained Pearson, "reformers stood to gain funds, advice, and (through GATT) reciprocal MFN treatment that would enhance China's exports."[74] In addition, China would also obtain technical training, infrastructure building, poverty reduction, technology transfer, managerial expertise, and other "less-tangible" benefits such as international prestige and legitimacy.[75]

As China's integration into the liberal global economy deepened, however, changes occurred in the character of Chinese decision-making on international economic issues. By the late 1990s, policy elite cohesion/insulation decreased, domestic mobilization increased, and elite understanding of China's economic interests in the global economy evolved beyond simply material benefits. Within the government, more central ministries and local/provincial governments became involved in national economic policymaking.[76] Meanwhile, a "pluralization of domestic actors" occurred as more domestic firms and groups exerted greater influence in the policymaking process.[77] Particularly with regards to China's WTO accession, industrial interests (e.g., machinery, automobiles) and service sectors (e.g., financial services, insurance) that feared greater international competition mobilized to thwart government concessions in the negotiations.[78] Fears of rural unrest, similarly, drove policymakers in their treatment of agricultural issues. Post-accession, large state-owned enterprises (SOE) in import-competing industries such as steel and chemicals continued to press government policymakers to use WTO rules for economic protectionism. In lobbying for government assistance, these SOEs were assisted by the national China Chamber of Commerce and their sectoral business associations (e.g., China Iron and Steel Association or CISA, China Chamber of Commerce of Metals, Minerals and Chemical Importers and Exporters or CCCMC, and China Association of Textile Industry or CATI).[79] For example, when the U.S. imposed safeguard measures on 14 imported steel products in March 2002, Chinese steel companies and CISA lobbied the Chinese government for protection. "These actors were able to influence China's trade policy-making process," reported Zeng, and in May 2002 the Chinese government invoked the WTO's Safeguard Agreement in announcing retaliatory measures against the U.S.[80]

As a result of this "pluralization of domestic actors," China's decisional (non)compliance with international economic agreements began to shift toward the pattern posited in Hypothesis #2 and in increasing conformity with "domestic process institutionalism" explanations (P2). As Zeng and Mertha reported, "domestic political forces not only drive the outcome of China's bilateral trade negotiations, but they are also increasingly important in shaping China's approach toward the WTO's rules-based international trading system."[81] More elaborately, Pearson argued that the "norms and rules of the international economic regime" must be "channeled through domestic actors and institutions" and "made influential through their 'entanglement' with the domestic political process." To "align China with international regime norms," she concluded, "require[s] a supportive—or at least acquiescent—domestic political constituency.[82]

Although "domestic process institutionalism" explanations offer persuasive accounts of China's decisional (non)compliance with international economic agreements since the 1990s, some scholars have also emphasized the role of adaptive learning and institutional socialization. For example, Liang explained China's resolution of the 2004 semiconductor trade dispute with the US at the consultation stage of the WTO dispute settlement process by emphasizing the role of "institutional learning" and the concerns of Chinese leaders about the country's political image and reputation.[83] Similarly, Pearson noted the "extensive adoption by China of the norms and rules of the international economic regime" and concluded that "genuine learning has occurred" on the part of Chinese leaders and "significant portions of the Chinese economic policy community."[84] Indeed, during its first two years of membership, China has been a "system maintainer" and "has not challenged the rules and norms of the WTO" except in "sovereignty-regarding areas."[85] Meanwhile, China's membership in the World Bank and the IMF has led apparently to some socialization into the rules and norms of these institutions. According to Kent,

"Through its ongoing interaction with other states in these multilateral institutions, through repeated admonitions and recurring pressures having a feedback effect into the domestic polity, China has come to a gradual acceptance of the need to comply with their norms, principles, and rules. Negotiation, persuasion, and modeling, rather than . . . coercive sanctions, have been the medium of norm internalization."[86]

As Chinese policymakers learn or become socialized to embrace new understandings of their national interests in the global economy, domestic process explanations must be supplemented with adaptive learning and normative socialization explanations (i.e., resulting in P6a and P6b integrations). By participating in international economic institutions, Chinese policymaking elites developed new interpretations of economic issues separate from the narrow material interests of domestic producer groups. As a result, China's decisional (non)compliance with international economic agreements increasingly integrates domestic processes (P2) with adaptive learning and normative socialization within the Bretton Woods international economic institutions (P3a, P3b).

INTERNATIONAL ENVIRONMENTAL AGREEMENTS (P1, P2, P3A, P3B)

Since the 1970s, China has signed or ratified about 50 international environmental treaties and in 1994 adopted the comprehensive Agenda 21 program of the UN Environment Programme (UNEP).[87] These Chinese policy decisions can be analyzed using rationalist institutionalism explanations (P1). In an authoritarian political system, policy elites have a high degree of internal cohesion and insulation from external forces. Domestic mobilization is low due to the diffuse effects of many environmental issues and their generally lower salience for people in less developed countries. Some issue evolution occurs, but for political leaders, environmental concerns do not trump economic, security and social stability considerations.

Under these circumstances, Chinese decisional (non)compliance on international environmental agreements occurred as posited by rationalist institutionalism explanations (P1). For example, Oksenberg and Economy argued that China signed and ratified five treaties between 1981-1991 "to secure access to hard currency and technology" and avoid "possible international penalties." In all these agreements (i.e., Convention in Trade in Endangered Species or CITES, London Convention against Ocean Dumping or LC, World Heritage Convention or WHC, International Tropical Timber Agreement or ITTA, and Montreal Protocol or MP), Chinese policymakers utilized a "calculus of cost and gain" at both the accession and implementation stages.[88] With regard particularly to the Montreal Protocol on atmospheric ozone depletion, the "dominant incentive" and "driving force" prompting China's decisional compliance was the 1990 London Amendments to this Protocol. Ratified by China in 1991, these amendments created a Multilateral Fund (MLF) to provide financial and technological assistance to enable MP signatory developing countries to reduce their use of chlorofluorocarbons (CFCs), halons and other ozone-depleting industrial chemicals.[89] As Economy tartly concluded, "the key to Chinese accession and compliance was the international community's willingness to finance its implementation efforts."[90]

Yet once China began contemplating these international environmental agreements and particularly after accession, their administrative and implementation requirements necessitated the development of substantive expertise and administrative positions within the government bureaucracy. After the 1972 UN Conference on the Environment in Stockholm, China established a small Environmental Protection Office within the State Council to address environmental issues. By the early 1980s, a National Environmental Protection Bureau was established, but located bureaucratically within the Ministry of Construction. In 1988, this primary government agency for addressing environmental issues was upgraded to an independent government department and renamed the National Environmental Protection Agency (NEPA). A decade later, in response to growing environmental problems and the need to strengthen administrative capabilities, this agency was upgraded to an independent ministry with increased funding and staffing and renamed the State Environmental Protection Administration

(SEPA).[91] In recent years, SEPA has stepped up inspections of possible polluters and enforcement of environmental laws and regulations.[92]

Prospective and actual accessions to international environmental treaties also prompted the development of substantive experts and knowledgeable environmental NGOs outside of the government. In China, the first ENGO, Friends of Nature, was formally registered with the Ministry of Civil Affairs in 1994, followed by Green Volunteer League in 1995, and Global Village of Beijing in 1996. Today, there are an estimated 1,000-2,000 registered ENGOs in China. Including rural grassroots and student groups, the All-China Environment Federation tabulated 2,768 ENGOs in China by the end of 2005 with a total membership of 224,000 people. Although most of these are small and poorly funded, the larger and better-known ENGOs with government subsidies or foreign foundation funding (from Ford, Rockefeller Brothers Fund, and Winrock International) have become increasingly active in publicizing environmental issues.[93]

As China's economic development accelerated, industrial pollutions of air and waterways have also expanded alarmingly. According to Pei, seven of the world's ten most polluted cities are now in China, while 50 percent of Chinese rivers and 75 percent of Chinese lakes are polluted.[94] As a result, there have been rising numbers of citizen complaints and local protests about pollution. In 2005, there were 51,000 pollution-related disputes in China, while the government received 1,814 petitions from citizens seeking a cleaner environment.[95]

This growing nexus of ministerial activity, ENGO activism, and popular protests has led to greater mobilization of domestic forces on environmental issues. In a virtuous circle of publicity, incidents of pollution, ENGO activism, and SEPA's informational, ceremonial, and regulatory activities combined to generate greater public awareness of environmental problems.[96] In some cases, citizens and/or ENGOs complained about specific incidents of environmental degradation, ENGOs then publicized these problems, and finally SEPA organized public hearings and invited citizens, experts, company executives, and environmentalists to testify.[97] As a result, growing public consciousness and demands regarding environmental issues placed greater pressure on policymakers to legislate and enforce environmental laws and regulations. Accordingly, "domestic process institutionalism" (P2) becomes more salient in explaining China's decisional compliance with international environmental agreements.

Nevertheless, as long as Chinese leaders prioritized economic growth over environmental protection, rationalist institutionalism (P1) continued to provide the more accurate explanation of their decision-making. Yet Chinese understandings of environmental issues and their impacts on economic development and social stability were slowly evolving. By the mid-1990s top Chinese leaders recognized that environmental degradation in fact diminished economic growth and incited local protests that undermined social stability. At the 1996 National Environmental Protection Conference, Jiang announced that environmental concerns cannot be subordinated to economic development.[98] Institutional learning (P3b) and normative socialization (P3a) were becoming increasingly salient in accounting for China's decisional compliance with international environmental agreements.

Even with regard to the Montreal Protocol, adaptive learning has always been an important factor in prompting Chinese policymakers to accede to the treaty. With regard to numerous international environmental agreements, concerns about China's international image, status, and identity as a responsible international actor influenced the compliance decisions of Chinese leaders.[99] Yet as their understanding of environmental issues evolved, they also began to reconceptualize their national interests and to gradually internalize international environmental norms.[100] As Kent observed,

> as a result of its ongoing participation in international environmental forums, China's own views of the impact of environmental problems on its economic future were changing. Under the socializing influence of interaction and the exchange of ideas with other member states, as well as its own scientific observation, it was finally beginning to redefine its interests in terms that corresponded with [international environmental] regime norms.[101]

INTERNATIONAL HUMAN RIGHTS AGREEMENTS (P1, P3B)

There exist over forty international human rights treaties and protocols, of which twenty-three are sponsored by the UN General Assembly. Of these, the Office of the UN High Commissioner for Human Rights (OHCHR) has designated thirteen as core instruments of international human rights law. Since the early 1980s, China has acceded to eight of these thirteen core international human rights treaties and protocols, including the ICCPR, ICESCR and the CAT.[102] In explaining Chinese decisional (non)compliance on these international human rights agreements, most scholars have advanced "rationalist institutionalism" explanations (P1).

In an authoritarian political system, the Chinese government possesses high levels of internal cohesion and external insulation. It clings insistently to a "Westphalian definition of state sovereignty" and has a "strong attachment to state autonomy."[103] As a "strong state," China's "response to international human rights pressures demonstrated strategic consistency, central co-ordination, realism and tactical flexibility."[104] Since full compliance with international human rights treaties would threaten an authoritarian government by implicitly limiting its authority and ending its political monopoly, the Chinese party-state resists adopting international human rights norms and fails to fully implement international human rights agreements.[105]

Meanwhile, there is little domestic mobilization of citizens and groups on human rights issues for two main reasons. First, there is sufficient satisfaction with the current state of human rights in China to discourage popular protests and demands for change. In stark contrast to the Maoist era, the human rights conditions of ordinary Chinese people have improved markedly since the initiation of Deng's economic reforms.[106] As long as the CCP successfully promotes economic growth, ensures social stability, and defends the nation's territorial integrity, Chinese citizens are apparently content to support or tolerate the CCP's monopoly of political power.[107] Second, the Chinese government has been very active and vigilant in squashing and preempting organized popular protests. In the case of democracy activists (e.g., Wei Jingsheng, Wang Dan, etc.) and religious groups (e.g., Falun Gong), state security forces have repressed them through detention, imprisonment and exile. Although small "spontaneous" riots and protests against local governments (e.g., for corruption, land, etc.) and factories (e.g., over jobs, pollution, etc.) occur regularly in rural and semi-urban areas, Beijing authorities have acted swiftly to control and defuse these outbreaks of social unrest.

With high levels of state autonomy and unencumbered by domestic mobilization, the Chinese government makes rational decisions about (non)compliance with international human rights agreements based on its self-interests. In making these cost/benefit calculations, Chinese leaders are willing to make concessions and compromises in order to maintain their international reputation and status as a responsible member of the international community.[108] However, their fundamental commitments to maintaining "the CCP's monopoly on political power" and preventing "widespread social unrest" prompt them to "override all other considerations, including those of reputation and image."[109]

Although their fundamental views about human rights remained consistent and stable, Chinese policymakers nevertheless learned to adapt to international human rights institutions. First of all, they engaged in "tactical learning" whereby "highly specialized Chinese human rights diplomats have learned how to work the UN system to China's advantage." In addition, they also engaged in "adaptive learning" to minimally comply with international human rights agreements. "What stands out in China's multilateral human rights diplomacy," Wan ruefully observed, "is that its participation has so far only led to adaptive learning about how to defend its sovereignty and national interests, rather than a change of heart about the importance of safeguarding human rights at home."[110] Similarly, although China has complied procedurally with conventions of the International Labor Organization (ILO) and the UN Committee against Torture (CAT), "it has resisted the internalization of their core values" and "participation in these organizations has not had the effect of encouraging China to redefine its interests in terms that correspond with organizational rules and treaty norms."[111] As Kent lamented, "in critical instances affecting sovereignty or state security, the state's self-interest will prevail over organizational norms. . . . A significant aspect of self-interest remains exogenous to the participation process."[112]

Given the high policy cohesion/insulation of Chinese policymakers, the stability of their understanding of human rights issues, and the low levels of domestic mobilization, China's decisional (non)compliance with international human rights agreements occurs mainly in accordance with rationalist institutionalism (P1) explanations. Over time, however, Chinese policymakers have learned to adapt and comply procedurally and tactically with international human rights institutions (P3b). Nevertheless, although normative socialization (P3a) has not occurred, some scholars have noted the "normative enmeshment"[113] and discursive "lock-in" of Chinese policymakers through their participation in international human rights institutions. "Having begun to debate the concept of human rights in global and domestic arenas," observed Foot, "Chinese officials tended to become locked into particular discursive formulations, not irrevocably, but to a degree sufficient to show that ideas were being shaped and developed."[114] The "language of rights" placed constraints on Chinese policymakers, while "international human rights law" set "standards and frames of reference for Chinese legal debates."[115] In turn, "China's international discourse and growing international commitments" provided a "political space" that allowed domestic groups to advocate legal and political reforms.[116] Over time, this human rights discourse was legitimized and allowed "to move in a more liberal and legalistic direction consistent with China's legal process and social progress."[117]

CONCLUSION

This chapter examined three major institutional approaches to the effects of international institutions on the foreign policy behavior of state actors. The first is "rationalist institutionalism" consisting of "functionalist" and "instrumental" variants. The second strand can be labeled "domestic process institutionalism." The third might be called "adaptive learning/normative socialization institutionalism." All three approaches illuminate aspects of institutional effects on state behavior. However, since they also contain various drawbacks and limitations, many scholars have advanced various integrations of these approaches. These existing integrated explanations, however, have been theoretically ad hoc and empirically inductive. Moreover, they have not addressed the variations in institutional effects across issue areas.

To improve upon these existing attempts at explanatory integration, this chapter advanced a more analytically explicit framework for identifying and integrating explanations of institutional effects on state behavior. By combining policy elite cohesion/insulation, domestic mobilization, and issue evolution, configurations of these three factors generate four different types of institutional effects (P1, P2, P3a and P3b). In addition, these different configurations also can be combined to generate five possible integrations (P4, P5a, P5b, P6a and P6b). After delineating these types of institutional effects, the chapter then examined China's decisional (non)compliance with international agreements using these propositions.

This empirical investigation showed that the effects of international institutions on state behavior varied across issue areas. On security issues, rational institutionalism (P1) explanations provided the most accurate account of China's decisional (non)compliance with arms control and nonproliferation agreements. Over time, however, Chinese policymakers also engaged in some adaptive learning. They did not internalize the norms of these security agreements, but they did learn to adapt to them for practical, tactical and other reasons. Adaptive learning institutionalism (P3b), therefore, provides an important supplementary explanation of China's (non)compliance with international security institutions.

On economic issues, meanwhile, domestic process institutionalism (P2) offered the most accurate explanations of China's decisional (non)compliance with the Bretton Woods institutions. Chinese policymakers still made decisions about (non)compliance, but they did so with significant inputs by bureaucratic and societal forces. The content of their (non)compliance decisions reflected the compromises and trade-offs made to appease competing ministerial and societal interests. Yet over time, Chinese policymakers also learned to adapt to these institutions and to perhaps even to internalize some of their liberal economic norms. Accordingly, adaptive learning (P3b) and (some) normative socialization (P3a) explanations complement the basic domestic process institutionalism analysis of China's (non)compliance with international economic institutions.

On environmental issues, all three of the major approaches to institutional effects illuminated aspects of China's decisional (non)compliance with various environmental treaties. Unsurprisingly, since environmental issues impinge on economic issues, domestic process explanations are needed to analyze the contestation between environmental and economic interests within the bureaucracy and civil society. Similarly, as the detrimental effects of pollution become starkly visible, policymakers inevitably engage in adaptive learning and some normative internalization of environmental norms. As a result, integrations of rationalist institutionalism (P1), domestic process institutionalism (P2), and adaptive learning (P3b)/normative socialization (P3a) institutionalism are needed to adequately explain China's (non)compliance with international environmental agreements.

Finally, on human rights issues, rationalist institutionalism (P1) most accurately explained the decisional (non)compliance of Chinese policymakers. However, over time, Chinese leaders also learned to adapt to international human rights institutions. They did not internalize international human rights norms, but they did learn to tactically adapt to them procedurally and through minor concessions. Accordingly, adaptive learning institutionalism (P3b) helps supplement the basic rationalist institutionalism explanations of China's (non)compliance with international human rights institutions.

These variations in China's (non)compliance on different international agreements suggest that the analytical configurations presented in this chapter can help illuminate the effects of international institutions on state behavior across issue areas. They can also be useful in mapping the potential directions of future Chinese (non)compliance with international agreements on different issues.

NOTES

1. Ann Kent, *Beyond Compliance: China, International Organizations, and Global Security* (Stanford, CA: Stanford University Press 2007), pp. 226-28.
2. Gerald Chan, *China's Compliance in Global Affairs: Trade, Arms Control, Environmental Protection, Human Rights* (Singapore: World Scientific 2006), pp. 204-06.
3. G. John Ikenberry, "The Rise of China: Power, Institutions, and the Western Order," in Robert S. Ross and Zhu Feng, eds. *China's Ascent: Power, Security, and the Future of International Politics* (Ithaca, NY: Cornell University Press 2008).

4. Peter Hall, *Governing the Economy: The Politics of State Intervention in Britain and France* (New York: Oxford University Press 1986).

5. Stephen D. Krasner, "Structural Causes and Regime Consequences: Regimes as Intervening Variables," in Stephen D. Krasner, ed. *International Regimes*, (Ithaca, NY: Cornell University Press 1983), p. 2; Robert O. Keohane, *After Hegemony: Cooperation and Discord in the World Political Economy* (Princeton, NJ: Princeton University Press 1984); Robert O. Keohane, *International Institutions and State Power: Essays in International Relations Theory* (Boulder, CO: Westview Press 1989), p. 4.

6. Beth A. Simmons, "Compliance with International Agreements," *Annual Review of Political Science* 1998:75-93, p. 77.

7. On a "managerial" approach to international institutions, see Abram Chayes and Antonia Handler Chayes, "On Compliance," *International Organization* 47, 2, Spring 1993, pp. 175-205. With regard specifically to China's compliance capacity, see Dali M. Yang, "Can the Chinese State meet its WTO Obligations? Government Reforms, Regulatory Capacity, and WTO Membership" *American Asian Review* 20, 2, Summer 2002, pp. 191-216; Margaret M. Pearson, "China's WTO Implementation in Comparative Perspective: Lessons from the Literatures on Trade Policy and Regulation," *The Review of International Affairs* 3,4 Summer 2004, pp. 567-83; Paul Thiers, "Challenges for WTO Implementation: Lessons from China's Deep Integration into an International Trade Regime" *Journal of Contemporary China* 11, 32, 2002, pp. 413-31.

8. Andreas Hasenclever, Peter Mayer and Volker Rittberger, *Theories of International Regimes* (Cambridge, UK: Cambridge University Press 1997); Xinyuan Dai, *International Institutions and National Policies* (Cambridge, UK: Cambridge University Press 2007); Andrew Walter, *Governing Finance: East Asia's Adoption of International Standards* (Ithaca, NY: Cornell University Press 2008); and Simmons, "Compliance with International Agreements."

9. E.g., Kent, *Beyond Compliance.*

10. For "contractual institutionalism," see Alastair Iain Johnston, "Socialization in International Institutions: The ASEAN Way and International Relations Theory," in G. John Ikenberry and Michael Mastanduno, eds. *International Relations Theory and the Asia-Pacific* (New York: Columbia University Press 2003), pp. 111-12. For "rational functionalist institutionalism," see Beth A. Simmons and Lisa L. Martin, "International Organizations and Institutions," in Walter Carlsnaes, Thomas Risse, and Beth A. Simmons, eds. *Handbook of International Relations* (Thousand Oaks, CA: Sage 2002), pp. 195-97.

11. Keohane, *After Hegemony.*

12. Margaret M. Pearson, "The Major Multilateral Economic Institutions Engage China," in Alastair Iain Johnston and Robert S. Ross, eds. *Engaging China: The Management of an Emerging Power* (London: Routledge 1999), p. 212.

13. Alastair Iain Johnston and Paul Evans, "China's Engagement with Multilateral Security Institutions," in Alastair Iain Johnston and Robert S. Ross, eds. *Engaging China: The Management of an Emerging Power* (London: Routledge 1999), pp. 237, 252-53.

14. Justin S. Hempson-Jones, "The Evolution of China's Engagement with International Governmental Organizations: Toward a Liberal Foreign Policy?" *Asian Survey* 45, 5, 2005, p. 704.

15. Arthur A. Stein, "Neoliberal Institutionalism," in Christian Reus-Smit and Duncan Snidal, eds. *The Oxford Handbook of International Relations* (New York: Oxford University Press 2008), pp. 203-04; Simmons and Martin, "International Organizations and Institutions," p. 194.

16. John J. Mearsheimer, "The False Promise of International Institutions," *International Security* 19, 1994/95, pp. 5-49.

17. Krasner, "Structural Causes and Regime Consequences"; Keohane, *After Hegemony.*

18. Hasenclever, Mayer and Rittberger, *Theories of International Regimes*, pp. 10-14.

19. Simmons and Martin, "International Organizations and Institutions," p. 194.

20. Hasenclever, Mayer and Rittberger, *Theories of International Regimes*, p. 23.

21. Lisa L. Martin, "The Rational State Choice of Multilateralism," in John Gerard Ruggie, ed. *Multilateralism Matters: The Theory and Praxis of an Institutional Form* (New York: Columbia University Press 1993); Hasenclever, Mayer and Rittberger, *Theories of International Regimes*, pp. 44-53.

22. Michel Oksenberg and Elizabeth Economy, "Introduction: China Joins the World," in Elizabeth Economy and Michel Oksenberg, eds. *China Joins the World: Progress and Prospects* (New York: Council on Foreign Relations 1999), pp. 36-7, cf. 23-4.

23. Elizabeth Economy, "The Impact of International Regimes on Chinese Foreign Policy-Making: Broadening Perspectives and Policies . . . But Only to a Point," in David M. Lampton, ed. *The Making of Chinese Foreign and Security Policy in the Era of Reform* (Stanford, CA: Stanford University Press 2001), pp. 236-37.

24. Economy, "The Impact of International Regimes on Chinese Foreign Policy-Making," p. 235; Oksenberg and Economy, "Introduction: China Joins the World," p. 21.

25. Oksenberg and Economy, "Introduction: China Joins the World," pp. 21-22, 25; also Economy, "The Impact of International Regimes on Chinese Foreign Policy-Making," p. 232.

26. Oksenberg and Economy, "Introduction: China Joins the World," p. 20; cf. Marc Lanteigne, *China and International Institutions: Alternate Paths to Global Power* (London: Routledge 2005).

27. Simmons and Martin, "International Organizations and Institutions," p. 194.

28. Robert G. Sutter, *China's Rise in Asia: Promises and Perils* (Lanham, MD: Rowman & Littlefield 2005), p. 45.

29. Michael Swaine and Ashley Tellis, *Interpreting China's Grand Strategy: Past, Present and Future* (Santa Monica, CA: RAND Corporation 2001), p. 133.

30. Andreas Hasenclever, Peter Mayer and Volker Rittberger, "Integrating Theories of International Regimes," *Review of International Studies* 26, 2000, pp. 12-19.

31. Dai, *International Institutions and National Policies*; Walter, *Governing Finance.*

32. Johnston and Evans, "China's Engagement with Multilateral Security Institutions," p. 237. For examples of institution-building and research development requirements of the Conference on Disarmament (1980) and the Chemical Weapons Convention, see pp. 240-44.

33. Pearson, "The Major Multilateral Economic Institutions Engage China," p. 212.

34. For a survey, see Jack S. Levy, "Learning and Foreign Policy: Sweeping a Conceptual Minefield," *International Organization* 48, 2, Spring 1994, pp. 279-312.

35. E.g., Martha Finnemore, *National Interests in International Society* (Ithaca, NY: Cornell University Press 1996).

36. Pearson, "The Major Multilateral Economic Institutions Engage China," p. 212.

37. Quoted in David Shambaugh, "China Engages Asia: Reshaping the Regional Order," *International Security* 29, 3, Winter 2004/05, p. 70.

38. Pearson, "The Major Multilateral Economic Institutions Engage China," p. 212.

39. Jeffrey T. Checkel, "International Institutions and Socialization in Europe: Introduction and Framework," *International Organization* 59, Fall 2005, pp. 810-12.

40. E.g., Ann Kent, "China's International Socialization: The Role of International Organizations," *Global Governance* 8, 3, July-Sept. 2002, pp. 343-64.

41. Johnston, "Socialization in International Institutions," p. 108.

42. Alastair Iain Johnston, *Social States: China in International Institutions, 1980-2000* (Princeton, NJ: Princeton University Press 2008), pp. xxv-vi.

43. Johnston, "Socialization in International Institutions," pp. 126-27 for "indicators"; for "critical test," see p. 119.

44. Johnston, "Socialization in International Institutions," pp. 122; 126-27.

45. Lisa L. Martin and Beth A. Simmons, "Theories and Empirical Studies of International Institutions," *International Organization* 52, 4, Autumn 1998), pp. 752-57.

46. Dai, *International Institutions and National Policies*, pp. 3-8, 71, 142, quotes on pp. 3 and 71.

47. Frank Schimmelfennig, "Strategic Calculation and International Socialization: Membership Incentives, Party Constellations, and Sustained Compliance in Central and Eastern Europe," *International Organization* 59, Fall 2005, p. 830; Frank Schimmelfennig, "International Socialization in the New Europe: Rational Action in an Institutional Environment," *European Journal of International Relations* 6, 1, 2000, pp. 116-19.

48. Schimmelfennig, "Strategic Calculation and International Socialization," pp. 828-29, 835-36.

49. E.g., Oksenberg and Economy, "Introduction: China Joins the World," p. 24.

50. Economy, "The Impact of International Regimes on Chinese Foreign Policy-Making," pp. 236-38, quotes on pp. 232 and 251.

51. Thomas Risse and Kathryn Sikkink, "The Socialization of International Human Rights Norms into Domestic Practices," in Thomas Risse, Stephen Ropp, and Kathryn Sikkink, eds. *The Power of Human Rights: International Norms and Domestic Change* (Cambridge, Eng.: Cambridge University Press 1999).

52. Matthew Evangelista, "The Paradox of State Strength: Transnational Relations, Domestic Structures and Security Policy in Russia and the Soviet Union," *International Organization* 49, 1995, pp. 1-38.

53. Margaret M. Pearson, "The Case of China's Accession to GATT/WTO," in David M. Lampton, ed. *The Making of Chinese Foreign and Security Policy in the Era of Reform* (Stanford, CA: Stanford University Press 2001), pp. 367-69.

54. Hasenclever, Mayer and Rittberger, "Integrating Theories of International Regimes," pp. 25-30.

55. Checkel, "International Institutions and Socialization in Europe," pp. 808-13.

56. Oksenberg and Economy, "Introduction: China Joins the World," p. 29.

57. Allen Carlson, "More Than Just Saying No: China's Evolving Approach to Sovereignty and Intervention since Tiananmen," in Alastair Iain Johnston and Robert S. Ross, eds. *New Directions in the Study of China's Foreign Policy* (Stanford, CA: Stanford University Press 2006), p. 235.

58. Johnston, *Social States*, p. xxvii; cf. Michael Zürn, and Jeffrey T. Checkel, "Getting Socialized to Build Bridges: Constructivism and Rationalism, Europe and the Nation-State," *International Organization* 59, Fall 2005, pp. 1052-53.

59. E.g., J. J. Suh, Peter Katzenstein, and Allen Carlson, eds. *Rethinking Security in East Asia* (Stanford, CA: Stanford University Press 2004).

60. Cf. Joseph Fewsmith and Stanley Rosen, "The Domestic Context of Chinese Foreign Policy: Does 'Public Opinion' Matter?, in David M. Lampton, ed. *The Making of Chinese Foreign and Security Policy in the Era of Reform* (Stanford, CA: Stanford University Press 2001), p. 174; Oksenberg and Economy, "Introduction: China Joins the World," p. 24.

61. Stephan Haggard, *Pathways from the Periphery: The Politics of Growth in Newly Industrializing Countries* (Ithaca, NY: Cornell University Press 1990); Peter B. Evan, Dietrich Rueschemeyer and Theda Skocpol, eds. *Bringing the State Back In* (New York: Cambridge University Press 1985).

62. Bates Gill and Evan S. Medeiros, "Foreign and Domestic Influences on China's Arms Control and Nonproliferation Policies," *The China Quarterly* 161, March 2000, pp. 68 and 87.

63. Gill and Medeiros, "Foreign and Domestic Influences on China's Arms Control and Nonproliferation Policies," pp. 87-90; Bates Gill, "Two Steps Forward, One Step Back: The Dynamics of Chinese Nonproliferation and Arms Control Policy-Making in an Era

of Reform," in David M. Lampton, ed. *The Making of Chinese Foreign and Security Policy in the Era of Reform* (Stanford, CA: Stanford University Press 2001), pp. 263-64.

64. Kent, *Beyond Compliance*, pp. 83-84.

65. Gill, "Two Steps Forward, One Step Back," p. 265; Gill and Medeiros, "Foreign and Domestic Influences on China's Arms Control and Nonproliferation Policies," p. 90.

66. Michael D. Swaine and Alastair Iain Johnston, "China and Arms Control Institutions," in Elizabeth Economy and Michel Oksenberg, eds. *China Joins the World: Progress and Prospects* (New York: Council on Foreign Relations 1999), p. 118.

67. Bates Gill, *Rising Star: China's New Security Diplomacy* (Washington, DC: Brookings Institution 2007), pp. 84, 98-102.

68. Evan S. Medeiros, *Reluctant Restraint: The Evolution of China's Nonproliferation Policies and Practices, 1980-2004* (Stanford, CA: Stanford University Press 2007), p. 13.

69. Chan, *China's Compliance in Global Affairs*, p. 140.

70. Johnston, *Social States*, pp. 113-15; cf. Kent, *Beyond Compliance*, p. 76.

71. Gill, "Two Steps Forward, One Step Back," p. 280.

72. Kent, *Beyond Compliance*, p. 101.

73. Margaret M. Pearson, "China's Integration into the International Trade and Investment Regime," in Elizabeth Economy and Michel Oksenberg, eds. *China Joins the World: Progress and Prospects* (New York: Council on Foreign Relations 1999), pp. 182-83; Pearson, "The Major Multilateral Economic Institutions Engage China,"p. 220.

74. Pearson, "China's Integration into the International Trade and Investment Regime," p. 165.

75. Kent, *Beyond Compliance*, p. 142; Pearson, "China's Integration into the International Trade and Investment Regime," p. 165.

76. Pearson, "The Case of China's Accession to GATT/WTO," pp. 350-51; Pearson, "China's Integration into the International Trade and Investment Regime," pp. 186-88; Pearson, "The Major Multilateral Economic Institutions Engage China," pp. 221 and 228.

77. Pearson, "The Case of China's Accession to GATT/WTO," p. 338.

78. Pearson, "The Major Multilateral Economic Institutions Engage China," p. 221; Pearson, "The Case of China's Accession to GATT/WTO," p. 361; Wei Liang, "Bureaucratic Politics, Interministerial Coordination and China's GATT/WTO Accession Negotiations," in Ka Zeng, ed. *China's Foreign Trade Policy: The New Constituencies* (London: Routledge 2007), pp. 26-28; Albert S. Yee, "Domestic Support Ratios in Two-Level Bargaining: The US-China WTO Negotiations," *The China Review* 4, 2, Fall 2004, pp. 129-163.

79. Ka Zeng, "State, Business Interests and China's Use of Legal Trade Remedies," in Ka Zeng, ed. *China's Foreign Trade Policy: The New Constituencies* (London: Routledge 2007), pp. 126, 133 and 135.

80. Zeng, "State, Business Interests and China's Use of Legal Trade Remedies," pp. 126-27, 137.

81. Ka Zeng and Andrew Mertha, "Introduction," in Ka Zeng, ed. *China's Foreign Trade Policy: The New Constituencies* (London: Routledge 2007), p. 10.

82. Pearson, "The Major Multilateral Economic Institutions Engage China," pp. 227-28 and 212.

83. Wei Liang, "China's WTO Commitment Compliance: A Case Study of the US-China Semiconductor Trade Dispute," in Ka Zeng, ed., *China's Foreign Trade Policy: The New Constituencies* (London: Routledge 2007), p. 113.

84. Pearson, "The Major Multilateral Economic Institutions Engage China," pp. 222-23; Pearson, "The Case of China's Accession to GATT/WTO," pp. 367-68.

85. Margaret M. Pearson, "China in Geneva: Lessons from China's Early Years in the World Trade Organization," in Alastair Iain Johnston and Robert S. Ross, eds. *New Di-*

rections in the Study of China's Foreign Policy (Stanford, CA: Stanford University Press 2006), pp. 242 and 266.

86. Kent, *Beyond Compliance*, pp. 139-40.

87. Gerald Chan, Pak K. Lee and Lai-Ha Chan, "China's Environmental Governance: the Domestic-International Nexus," *Third World Quarterly* 29, 2, 2008, p. 295.

88. Michel Oksenberg and Elizabeth Economy, "China: Implementation Under Economic Growth and Market Reform," in Edith Brown Weiss and Harold K. Jacobson, eds. *Engaging Countries: Strengthening Compliance with International Environmental Accords* (Cambridge, MA: MIT Press 1998), p. 389.

89. Jimin Zhao, "Implementing International Environmental Treaties in Developing Countries: China's Compliance with the Montreal Protocol," *Global Environmental Politics* 5, 1, February 2005, pp. 66 and 72; Jimin Zhao and Leonard Ortolano, "The Chinese Government's Role in Implementing Multilateral Environmental Agreements: The Case of he Montreal Protocol," *The China Quarterly* 175, September 2003, p. 714.

90. Economy, "The Impact of International Regimes on Chinese Foreign Policy-Making," pp. 252 and 242.

91. Chan, *China's Compliance in Global Affairs*, p. 151.

92 . Chan, Lee and Chan, "China's Environmental Governance: the Domestic-International Nexus," pp. 303-04.

93. Kent, *Beyond Compliance*, p. 153; Chan, *China's Compliance in Global Affairs*, p. 159; Chan, Lee and Chan, "China's Environmental Governance: the Domestic-International Nexus," pp. 299-300 and 310.

94 . Minxin Pei, "China's Governance Crisis," *Foreign Affairs* 81, 5, September/October 2002.

95 . Chan, Lee and Chan, "China's Environmental Governance: the Domestic-International Nexus," p. 298; Ross 1998, 812.

96. Lester Ross, "China: Environmental Protection, Domestic Policy Trends, Patterns of Participation in Regimes and Compliance with International Norms," *The China Quarterly* 156, December 1998, pp. 819 and 834; Zhao and Ortolano, "The Chinese Government's Role in Implementing Multilateral Environmental Agreements," p. 717.

97. Chan, *China's Compliance in Global Affairs*, pp. 152-53.

98. Ross, "China," p. 813.

99. Zhao and Ortolano, "The Chinese Government's Role in Implementing Multilateral Environmental Agreements," pp. 715-16 and 724; Zhao, "Implementing International Environmental Treaties in Developing Countries," pp. 72-73; Kent 2007, 167.

100. Kent, *Beyond Compliance*, pp. 146 and 160.

101. Kent, *Beyond Compliance*, p. 167.

102. Ming Wan, "Human Rights Lawmaking in China: Domestic Politics, International Law, and International Politics," *Human Rights Quarterly* 29, 2007, p. 729; Chan, *China's Compliance in Global Affairs*, p. 184. The eight core treaties and protocols signed by China are: International Covenant on Civil and Political Rights (ICCPR) in 1998; International Covenant on Economic, Social and Cultural Rights (ICESCR) in 1997, ratified in 2001; Convention against Torture and Other Cruel, Inhuman or Degrading Treatment or Punishment (CAT) in 1986, ratified in 1988; International Convention on the Elimination of All Forms of Racial Discrimination (ICERD) in 1981; Convention on the Elimination of All Forms of Discrimination against Women (CEDAW) signed and ratified in 1980; Convention on the Rights of the Child (CRC) in 1990 and ratified in 1992; CRC Optional Protocol on the Involvement of Children in Armed Conflict (OP-CRC-AC) in 2001; and CRC Optional Protocol on the Sale of Children, Child Prostitution and Child Pornography (OP-CRC-SC) in 2000 and ratified in 2002.

103. Rosemary Foot, *Rights Beyond Borders: The Global Community and the Struggle over Human Rights in China* (Oxford, Eng.: Oxford University Press 2000), p. 2.

104. Andrew J. Nathan, "Human Rights in Chinese Foreign Policy," *The China Quarterly* 139, September 1994, p. 638; Andrew J. Nathan, "China and the International Human Rights Regime," in Elizabeth Economy and Michel Oksenberg, eds. *China Joins the World: Progress and Prospects* (New York: Council on Foreign Relations 1999), p. 148.

105. Jeremy Paltiel, "Peaceful Rise? Soft Power? Human Rights in China's New Multilateralism," in Guoguang Wu and Helen Lansdowne, eds. *China Turns to Multilateralism: Foreign Policy and Regional* Security (London: Routledge 2008), p. 202; Foot, *Rights Beyond Borders*, p. 2; Ming Wan, *Human Rights in Chinese Foreign Relations: Defining and Defending National Interests* (Philadelphia, PA: University of Pennsylvania Press 2001), pp. 9 and 138; Kent, *Beyond Compliance*, pp. 218-19.

106. Alan M. Wachman, "Does the Diplomacy of Shame Promote Human Rights in China?, *Third World Quarterly* 22, 2, 2001, pp. 265-66.

107. Wan, *Human Rights in Chinese Foreign Relations*, pp. 139-40.

108. Kent, *Beyond Compliance*, pp. 218-19; Wan, *Human Rights in Chinese Foreign Relations*, pp. 125-26.

109. Foot, *Rights Beyond Borders*, pp. 26 and 258; Yong Deng, *China's Struggle for Status: The Realignment of International Relations* (Cambridge, Eng.: Cambridge University Press 2008), p. 87.

110. Wan, *Human Rights in Chinese Foreign Relations*, pp. 126, 127, cf. 2, 11.

111. Kent, *Beyond Compliance*, p. 218.

112. Kent, *Beyond Compliance*, p. 219.

113. Foot, *Rights Beyond Borders*, pp. 24 and 260.

114. Foot, *Rights Beyond Borders*, p. 260.

115. Wan, "Human Rights Lawmaking in China," p. 753; Foot, *Rights Beyond Borders*, p. 253.

116. Foot, *Rights Beyond Borders*, pp. 260 and 253.

117. Wan, "Human Rights Lawmaking in China," p. 745.

Chapter 11

Searching for a New Cultural Identity: China's Soft Power and Media Culture Today

Liu Kang

INTRODUCTION

On January 13, 2009, the Hong Kong-based English newspaper, *South China Morning Post,* reported a 45 billion RMB or 6.6 billion US dollar Chinese government program to fund international ventures undertaken by state media.[1] *International Herald Leader*, a Chinese-language newspaper of the official Xinhua News Agency, retold the story from the Hong Kong newspaper in Xinhua's website xinhuanet.com on February 3, with the headline of "China Launches National Publicity Campaign to Improve Its International Image."[2] It was reported that the plan will target global audiences by constructing the multi-lingual versions of the China Central Television (CCTV), Xinhua and the *People's Daily*. China wants its own CNN or Al-Jazeera. The news drew immediate worldwide attention. And not surprisingly, some sharp criticism from the West, too. *Wall Street Journal Asia* on January 30 carried an editorial "China's New Propaganda Machine" by Nicholas Bequelin, a researcher at the international NGO, Human Rights Watch, which is one of China's most vocal critics. "Can state-run broadcasters, whose traditional role is to be the 'throat and tongue' of the Communist Party, really turn into competitors for the likes of CNN and the BBC?" the author asked rhetorically. In conclusion, the author lectured the Chinese that "the soft and persuasive power that can only come with a free, unbiased media that informs rather than misleads."[3]

A well-known Chinese journalist and popular columnist, Yan Lieshan, senior editor at the *Southern Weekend,* wrote in his Hong Kong-based blog in March, commenting on the grand state PR campaign, or so-called "external propaganda": "If you want European viewers to abandon CNN and watch the TV channel run by Xinhua News Agency, the first thing you need to do is to establish credibility and win trust. In my opinion, if foreigners believe that foreign and Chinese reporters are not free to report the truth in China, our new "great external propaganda" drive will not fare any better than the overseas edition of the *People's Daily* and the English-language *China Daily*."[4] To return to the beginning of the story, it's interesting to note that the story at the Xinhua official website vanished two days after its first appearance. Only two months later on April 14, did the *International Herald Leader* online version mention the news again, in a story entitled "Foreign Media Concerned about China's Deliberations of National Publicity."

Those familiar with Chinese political delicacies will note the intricate twists and turns in the above narrative. It can be understood as a meta-commentary on media and publicity or propaganda, since different kinds of media and news professionals got involved in the circulation and attendant commentaries of the purported major international media campaign by the Chinese state. The news itself should have come from one source in Beijing, particularly from the meeting of the Chinese propaganda administrators held on January 4-5, in which Li Changchun, China's highest official in charge of "propaganda work" publicly announced that "enhancing our communication capacity domestically and internationally is of direct consequence to our nation's international influence and international position." The news of the 4.5 billion RMB plan, however, took a detour by way of Hong Kong media, as an unofficial leakage to "test the water," so to speak. Yet the criticism from the western media is unanimous, and some liberal-leaning, outspoken Chinese intellectuals such as Yan Lieshan did not hesitate to voice their skepticism (again via Hong Kong-based internet blog), if not outright opposition. Guangzhou-based *Southern Weekend* is a popular herald for liberal-minded Chinese intellectuals and a weekly paper of investigative news that boldly exposes official corruption and other social ills. Guangzhou's proximity to Hong Kong and Shenzhen, Special Administrative Region and Special Economic Zone respectively, makes it a haven for Chinese print media, enjoying a degree of press freedom unmatched by any other Chinese press. Yet Yan Lieshan's commentary could not possibly appear in the newspapers, as the topic he touched was of high political significance and sensitivity. The thriving internet blogs, however, gives Yan a less restrained venue raising a critical question of free press and propaganda, external or otherwise.

We detect several threads in the above-mentioned communicational loop, first the print media of state-run Chinese newspaper, and the Hong Kong newspaper, then the American media (also published in Hong Kong), and finally the Chinese journalist's internet blog, concentrated on the three locales, i.e., Beijing, Hong Kong, and Guangzhou. Several layers of meanings can be construed from the narrative, too. Instead of dwelling on the political hermeneutics of the news story and the story of its transmission and circulation, suffice it to mention here that the story-within-story is indicative of the dilemma that China faces now in terms of its soft power or the arena of culture and media.

The sharply divided line between the western liberal views of free press and what is being practiced in China's news media and cultural arena has not been easily crisscrossed, and as a legacy of the cold war, western liberal ideology as proselytized by western media is not well received in China, and challenged by an increasingly assertive and "nationalistic" Chinese public, consisting largely of young internet users or "netizens." Within the great wall of China, and more recently within the so-called "great firewall of China," i.e., the Chinese cyber space policing, tensions are brimming and "sectarian wars" are highly visible in different media forms and sectors, though fought mostly in economic terrain. Entertainment-driven media, especially television, are vying for a market with an enormous population, which nonetheless has a decreasing appetite for the consumer cultural products that media have tirelessly fed them. Aloft and cynical, Chinese intellectuals, particularly those self-styled crusaders of high culture, tend to further distance themselves from both the state ideology and the consumer popular culture, whereas not a few of them managed to break the academic cocoons and become media celebrities, thanks to the consumer culture. Those once high-brow professors of literature and history such as Yu Qiuyu, Yu Dan, and Yi Zhongtian now enjoy popular icon status by giving CCTV lectures popularizing Confucian classics and traditional literature, along side with popular-elected Super Girl singers, or more lately, Happy Girl singers, in addition to the ever-expanding host of Hong Kong and Taiwan-based, commercially manufactured pop stars.

Out of the tug of wars of consumer popular culture and intellectual elite, the state has seemed little disturbed, remaining in firm control over the "propaganda work," or anything related to ideology, culture, and media. In China, all media organizations are state-run "public service units" (*shiye danwei*, a peculiar Chinese social entity created from era of the command economy) while their operation and management are more like "corporate units" (*qiye danwei*) in market economy after the reform. This split character of Chinese news media (as both the CCP's political mouthpieces and profit-driven businesses) spawns tension and contradiction in practicing professional journalism and business operations. Providing the public with balanced and independent news is often at odds with the dictates of the CCP, while the profit-driven business interests result in entertainment-oriented programs targeting at higher viewers ratings as its foremost objective, rather than serving the public good. The Internet media are more complicated, as many privately owned Internet businesses such as Sina, Tengxun-QQ, Sohu, and Netease and more blog sites and BBS (popular online discussion forums) have now become the most powerful alternative media with its newscast constantly breaking the state media's boundaries.

Underneath sometimes anarchic and schizophrenic appearance of the Chinese media is a social reality that cannot be adequately covered or represented by the media and the ideological state apparatuses in general. Revolutionary ideology has legitimated the rule of the CCP for sixty years, but it becomes increasingly at odds with the rapid socio-economic development that began thirty years ago. The crisis of representation, or the discrepancy between the state ideology and China's socio-economic reality, is reaffirmed paradoxically by the "external propaganda" or "China's CNN/Al-Jazeera" campaign as an urgent call to revamp the propaganda machinery, only from the "external" rather than "internal" necessity. It's all too obvious that what the Chinese critic Yan Lieshan calls to "establish credibility and win trust" applies to both "internal" and "external" media.

In the following pages, I will first gauge the representational crisis at the current conjuncture. Then I shall discuss the fragmentation and separation of the state, the intellectual elite and the grassroots population in terms of cultural expressions, forms, and underlying values. Thirdly, I will address briefly the prevalence of entertainment-centered consumer culture, which unleashes individualistic and materialistic desires at the expense of social cohesiveness and pursuit of public good, while serving to reinforce a facile political stability. Finally I shall try to outline a few features of an emergent cultural formation amidst these tension and contradictions. This rising "post-80s" generation urban youth culture will inevitably become a dominant cultural formation in China in the years to come.

THE CRISIS OF REPRESENTATION AT THE NEW PHASE OF THE PRC HISTORY

The current conjuncture can be seen as the beginning of a new phase of PRC history. The first phase of thirty years from 1949 to 1979 or the Mao era (even though Mao died in 1976, his immediate successor Hua Guofeng did little to change his policy), leaves a controversial legacy. Notwithstanding the historic milestones of national independence and establishment of the Communist state, the Soviet-style command economy and the culminating Cultural Revolution, the Mao era or the first thirty years passed on its posterity a revolutionary culture or ideological legacy with an enduring, significant impact on China today. "Revolution" is now a passé word in China and elsewhere, except in phrases such as "information revolution," "digital revolution," or "velvet revolution" referring to the pro-western political movements in the former Soviet republics. However, revolution and liberation are fundamental precepts in the CCP's eighty-eight years history, and despite numerous revisions since Deng Xiaoping's *gaige kaifang* (reform and opening-up), revolution, or at least the revolutionary wars, has still been the legitimating, if no longer the ruling, ideology of the CCP. The recent upsurge of popular books and TV dramas and films about the revolutionary wars prior to the founding of the People's Republic testifies to the powerful presence of revolution as the lasting political unconscious or cultural imagining. These new cultural products are supposed to celebrate the PRC's 60th anniversary. Ironically, the celebrated images arise largely from the pre-PRC years or earlier period of the Korean War, rather than from the three decades of the 1950s-1970s.

The Deng era from 1979, known otherwise as the *gaige kaifang* or the New Era, has set in motion China's modernization and globalization, turning China into an economic giant and a significant player in the world affairs today. The second phase of thirty years of PRC history both fascinates and puzzles the world for an obvious reason: the transformation of China's economy from an agrarian and command economy of scarcity to an industrial and market economy of relative affluence in merely thirty years has been led by the Chinese Communist Party in a one-party state, without going through any significant reform in the political system. Set against the worldwide backdrop of the political seismic waves in these same decades that have ended communism in Russia and Eastern Europe, and fundamentally changed the global political landscape, the "Chinese model" or the so-called "socialism with Chinese characteristics" is all the more "anomalous" to our common sense, which is shaped largely by the Western model of modernization that lines up market economy and multi-party electoral democracy as inseparable twins. Is China's way a viable alternative, or at least a challenge to the accepted, western model of modernization? This question now acquires new potency as the West is plunged into a deep economic crisis, while China's relatively strong growth pushes it into the limelight of the world stage.

Now in hindsight, the Deng era began as a fierce denouncement of the radical ideology of the Cultural Revolution. During his reign, Mao launched incessant radical ideological campaigns to maintain revolutionary zest from the populace, in a belief that those immaterial, moral and semi-religious forces of loyalty, purity and altruism would pave a way for fast regeneration of the Chinese nation. Such a hubris and fanaticism ended up in political chaos and opposition of both bureaucratic and intellectual elite. Deng's *gaige kaifang* reversed virtually everything that Mao's radicalism embodied, replacing the pursuit of moral purity with that of material wealth. However, Deng insisted that "Mao's banner" should never be abandoned, and with his astute pragmatic wisdom, Deng managed to salvage China from one after another political and ideological crises, particularly the 1989's Tiananmen event. The "banner of Mao" thus remains an ambiguous and ambivalent icon ever since the *gaige kaifang*, providing a legitimating rhetoric and cultural imagining on the one hand, and serving as a reminder of the CCP's ideological legacy on the other. The Mao banner that Deng and his successors have held on, however, has resulted in sustained attacks by China's foes or befuddlement by its friends.

As one may recall, the split character of Chinese media, that is, as both CCP's mouthpiece and profit-driven business, showcases the ideological dilemma in an institutional sense. The media in Mao's time were nothing but the CCP's propaganda machinery. During the *gaike gaifang*, media's ideological function is retained by the institutional structure under the CCP's propaganda department, whereas in reality or in substance, the media are nothing if not corporate businesses. The institutional arrangement is meant to guarantee the ideological content that media produce. However, as one looks at the newspaper or watches TV news, it only takes one a little more than a few minutes to note the vast difference between the front pages and headlines of the official news and editorials on the one hand, and the rest of media programs on the other, dominated by entertainment products and other programs concerned with everyday reality.

The headlines and editorials of the *People's Daily* and its local counterparts conform to the CCP ideological guidelines minutely, in both rhetoric and content. The front page headline news on August 20, 2009, for instance, begins with these lines over the news of Taiwan's typhoon disaster: "We share the same feeling with Taiwan compatriots, especially the ethnic minorities, who suffered serious life and property loss in the recent disaster. We are very much concerned," said Hu, general secretary of the CPC Central Committee." Glancing the same day's *People's Daily* online, one finds under the section of People's Op-Ed such titles as "Why the Police Car Dare to Escort the Pop Star Fan Bingbing" and "Warning for the Rip-off Ploys Japanese Businessmen Set up for the Chinese Nouveau Riche Tourists" and so forth. While the variety of the "non-stately" media content reflects a vigorous and complex social life, the political speeches and editorials of the CCP leadership can hardly respond to such a plurality of values and issues in a non-formulaic and plain language. Important messages are usually conveyed through often highly abstract and ceremonial rhetoric of the political discourse, and those coded messages can only be understood by the well-informed insiders. It is thus little wonder that a major task of Western China hands is to decipher the meaning of Chinese political speeches filled with ideological platitudes.

Over the years, the CCP leadership has tried to revitalize its ideology in several theoretical formulations, such as the ex-CCP General Secretary Jiang Zeming's theory of "Three Represents" and the current General Secretary Hu Jintao's "scientific concept of development" and "harmonious society" as the "core socialist values." At the 17th Congress of the CCP in 2007, Hu Jintao for the first time called for enhancing "soft power" of Chinese culture, elevating culture to a high status of an "important source of national cohesion and creativity and a factor of growing significance in the competition in overall national strength." [5] My previous study of the theory of Three Represents suggests that the theory does not resolve the dilemma of how the CCP can represent itself, both politically and symbolically, as it faces these vexing contradictions in China. [6] Hu Jintao's effort in the "scientific concept of development" is to re-channel his predecessor's economist or developmentalist policy that focused solely on the growth of GDP to a more balanced reform to address the mounting social disparity, injustice and popular resentment. In so doing, issues of culture, ideology or "soft power," a concept loaded with global strategic implications, return to the CCP political agenda with a new urgency.

A popular saying circulating in China now is that "in the first thirty years China under Mao rid itself of the military threat; in the second thirty years China under Deng rid itself of poverty; now in the third thirty years, China will have to rid itself of all blames!" Now the blames or disapproval of what China does circulate and transmit globally in a matter of seconds both inside and outside China, thanks to the rapidly growing and ubiquitous media technology. We live in a world of media culture. Denying or relegating culture's role to the periphery is only a wishful-thinking, however powerful that skewed view of culture has dominated the Deng era. Avowedly pragmatic, Deng's *gaige kaifang* strategy is largely one dimensional modernization in the economic sector, at the expense of other equally important areas of the political, social, and cultural. Granted, culture is a highly charged, politicized zone in the PRC history, from Mao's Cultural Revolution to the Cultural Reflection of the late 1980s culminating in the 1989s Tiananmen Incident.

The post-Deng CCP leadership, consisting mostly of technocrats and engineers, continued to defer indefinitely modernization efforts in other areas, political and cultural in particular. Yet modernization never occurs according to a state policy. The past three decades of *gaige kaifang* only shows that Chinese culture has transformed beyond any CCP policymakers could have imagined, in spite of the often repressive measures. The recent "soft power" policy initiatives by the CCP leadership is primarily reactive, too. With its growing importance in the global affairs, China is under more rigorous scrutiny, particularly by ideologically opposed, skeptical and wary western media. Faced with the pressures both internationally and domestically, the CCP leadership only reluctantly begins to address the question of its global image and soft power as an integral part of modernization, or in Hu Jintao's vocabulary, "scientific concept of development."

FRAGMENTATION AND SEPARATION: THE STATE, THE INTELL-ECTUAL AND THE POPULAR

A serious predicament for the current CCP leadership is the disenfranchisement and fragmentation of the intellectual elite. What the western media focus on the political oppositions or dissent of the Chinese intellectuals, represented by such figures as Liu Xiaobo, whose political prominence rose during the 1989 Tiananmen Incident, and some exiled human rights activists and lately the signatories of the Charter 08, are only a few extreme cases. The majority of Chinese intellectuals, which can hardly be named "silent" for their active public roles today, remain nonetheless deeply divided and fragmented. Furthermore, because of the professionalization and corporatization of China's education for the last decade or so, Chinese intellectuals view themselves more as professional or academic elite than the public conscience. While the debate about a burgeoning civil society or public sphere had caught the public attention in the last two decades, such topics seem no longer able to arouse popular enthusiasm now. The esteem and moral authority that the Chinese intellectuals once earned from the general populace, particularly in the early 1980s Cultural Reflection period, seem to have all but vanished. As some critics point out, the critical spirit and social responsibility, autonomy and independence of Chinese intellectuals have been seriously eroded by the market forces of China's social life.[7]

It should be noted that Chinese intellectuals are mostly the beneficiaries of the *gaike kaifang*, contrary to the claims made by some leading oppositional figures. The intellectuals during the Cultural Revolution were subjected to re-education campaigns led by radical revolutionaries and a significant number of them were humiliated and victimized, together with many bureaucrats, labeled as "capitalist runners," with Deng Xiaoping as the arch villain. A main motivation of *gaige kaifang* is to redress the wrongs wrought on the bureaucrats and intellectuals, who then assembled under Deng as the most devoted supporters of the reform. The decade of the 1980s saw the ascendance of the intellectuals to the center stage of China's social life, leading the socio-political movements of the so-called Emancipation of Minds, the Second Enlightenment or Cultural Reflection (also known as the "Cultural Fever") respectively. These intellectuals, mostly in the humanities of literature, history and philosophy, invoked the passion and idealism of the May Fourth Cultural Movement of 1919 as the precursor to China's modern culture, and in the meantime embraced liberal ideas from the West as China's new direction of modernization. However, cultural movements in China inevitably fall prey to politics, and the turmoil and the ensuing bloody crackdown at Tiananmen in 1989 ended in another round of political repression. But contrary to the widespread apocalyptic prediction in the West of the return of Maoist radicalism, the 1990s China witnessed much accelerated economic reform. During his Southern Tour in the Spring 1992, Deng Xiaoping declared a ban on any ideological debate while encouraging privatization and marketization in economic sectors.

Consequently, division and fragmentation among Chinese intellectuals intensified, as the green light now was turned on for economists and business professionals, whereas the red light firmly blocked any motion of the humanists and other carriers of the Cultural Fever "viruses." Deng's successors from Jiang Zemin to Hu Jintao consisted primarily of technocrats with almost exclusive engineering backgrounds. And those working in engineering and natural sciences in China were much less affected by the ideological and political turmoil of the late 1980s than the humanists. Once again, their importance in building the scientific-technological infrastructure was highlighted in Deng's new economic initiatives. In the later half of the 1990s and early years of the new century, China began to increase the educational and research funds and expenditures, in an effort to make up the vast deficiency in the educational sector, the universities in particular. The reform priority was driven by pragmatic demands of immediate outcome from education and research. Hence the American style corporatization of higher education and research was implemented by the state, resulting in nationwide mergers of smaller colleges into mammoth universities such as Zhejiang University and Wuhua University, and the Ministry of Education's annual research fund saw astronomical increase in less than ten years span.

However, the casualty in such corporatizing drive was the humanities as the backbones of liberal arts education. Under such circumstances, Chinese intellectuals in the humanities were devastated not only by the political stalemate that deprived their high social status they began to enjoy only a few years in the 1980s, but also by the economic and material disadvantage, when the university administrators now distributed funding only by the utilitarian and quantitative calculations of academic production. All of a sudden, the Chinese intellectuals were faced with an identity crisis: the corporatization of education called for swift professionalization of the academics. The notion of being a "professional" rather than "intellectual" in the changing social and academic environment is deeply alien to the Chinese humanists, whose historical lineage is traceable from the more modern period of the May Fourth Movement of 1919 to the Confucian scholar or literati in antiquity. If the Cultural Revolution and other political campaigns during Mao era often targeted at the intellectuals, they were at least "respected" by society and even by their persecutors, who acknowledged the significant symbolic power vested in the intelligentsia class. The marketization of Chinese society and the corporatization of education of the 1990, however, simply denied them that symbolic aura, reducing or repositioning their status according to the logic of the market, rather than by the exclusive cultural upbringing and prestige.

It was now difficult for the humanists to reinvent their self-esteem by having recourse to the Enlightenment philosophy of subjectivity, as they did in the early 1980s. For one thing, while in the early 1980s, millions of young students embraced grand ideas and knowledge with passion, the young enthusiasts in the 1990s were attracted to the more tangible and material wealth than ephemeral ideas. The philosophical propositions of Hegelian subjectivity gave way to the success stories of a Bill Gates or his sizable Chinese replicates. Moreover, the triumphant ideology or non-ideology in the age of globalization was that of neoliberalism, which substitutes a flexible, mobile, business executive or CEO as the prototype of postmodern agency for the now "out-dated," class-based notion of the proletarian or bourgeois subjectivity. Neoliberalism in China was endorsed in the academia by a majority of economists and social scientists, who have now taken over the academic central stage, and popularized by the media with great interests in consumerism and marketization. The CCP's position towards such western trends was always cautious and ambivalent, assimilating tacitly its market logic of efficiency and profitability without any public acknowledgement of its ideology of individual freedom and market capitalism.

Neoliberalism and its variants have met with some resistance. The Chinese New Left, a very loosely defined and controversial cohort of intellectuals, has been at the forefront of critiquing the dominant neoliberal ideology both domestically and internationally. And their voices sometimes reach beyond China's academic circles and arouse interests by their western counterparts. However, their often jargon-ridden and complex academic discourse cannot be accessible to the general public, and indeed, the Chinese populace have hardly heard of, let alone being persuaded, by those self-styled defenders of the disempowered, thanks to the mainstream media's reluctance to grant them access and their own sectarianism and proclivity to high-sounding abstraction. The media publicity and controversy of Chinese "public intellectuals" generated more confusion and aversion from the populace than admiration, since the media's parading of the "public intellectuals," as shown by the naming of China's "Top 50 Public Intellectuals" by *Southern People's Week*, a popular magazine in Guangzhou, was largely commercially motivated and the list was produced quite indiscriminately, including such figures as rock pop star Cui Jian and Harvard professor Wei-ming Tu, an American neo-Confucian crusader. It eventually became a media event after the CCP leadership reportedly made a "gray list" of those prominent figures who often voiced opposition and dissent to the CCP policies. As usual, it came to the attention of Western media. Robert Marquand, staff writer of *The Christian Science Monitor,* wrote on November 30, 2004: "In a move intended to muffle the voices of some of China's most prominent and independent scholars and activists, hard-line elements in the new Hu Jintao government are seeking to eradicate the concept of "public intellectuals" in China."[8]

It should be noted, however, that those "independent scholars" or "public intellectuals" with media publicity in both China and abroad were mostly liberal or pro-liberals with very few exceptions, especially among the academics mentioned in the so-called "Top 50 Public Intellectuals" controversy. These liberal intellectuals are usually very active online, but in traditional media outlet they are covered only by Guangzhou newspapers. Their proselytizing of Western style liberal democracy is considered by most Chinese media as abstract high-sounding at the best, and politically dangerous at the worst.

The Chinese version of "political correctness" in popular media can best be represented by Yu Qiuyu, Yu Dan and Yi Zhongtian, who as media celebrities lecture the Chinese populace about classical Confucian values and historical anecdotes on highly-rated TV talk shows and in their bestsellers, in highly entertaining and accessible manners. The two Yus and Qi serve the public with their wisdom of Chinese tradition in keeping with the state mission of building a "harmonious society," by turning the classics of high-culture into profitable products of consumer popular culture. No where in their speeches and books can one find commentaries on current affairs, yet one can always learn some good lessons about meaning of life and society metaphorically and even poetically. Metaphor being the most influential figure of speech in China, especially in political discourses, one learns to be "politically correct" by speaking and reading metaphorically all the time. The two Yus, Yi and their likes live in a world widely apart from those neoliberal "Public Intellectuals" or New Left academics. It's the world of consumer popular culture and popular media, in which these "Popular Intellectuals," so to speak, find their new identity in the consumer society Chinese style.

The neoliberal or neoconservative "public intellectuals" in the U.S. have constructed a "market populism" by equating democracy and freedom with consumption.[9] In China, however, to publicly advocate Western ideas of democracy and freedom is certainly unwise. It's nonetheless propitious and appropriate to promote ideas of social harmony and cohesion in China's market-consumption-centered society. One cannot equate Chinese popular intellectuals with the American neoconservative market populism in terms of their strategies and objectives, yet it is necessary to question the social agendas of the intellectual trends in terms of their relevance to the compelling issues of justice, rule of law and civil rights in either China, the U.S. or elsewhere. The "politically correct" popular intellectuals of the Yu Qiuyus remain completely silent on these issues, while the pro-western, liberal public intellectuals' critical voices reach out to only a small fraction of the intellectual elite in China and mostly to their outside sympathizers, leaving the concerns of the Chinese populace mostly unattended.

ENTERTAINMENT: CELEBRATION OF INDIVIDUALITY AND FACILE STABILITY

The fragmentation and separation of Chinese intellectuals should be understood in the context of media culture in which relationship between the intellectuals and media has become more complex and intertwined than ever before. Apart from the sizable media professionals and executives who now consider themselves a distinct species of *zhishi fenzi* or intellectuals, the popular intellectuals of the Yu Qiuyus have become an integral part of consumer popular culture as media celebrities. Indeed, Yu Dan, whose astounding rise from an obscure academic to a media super star or "the Most Famous Woman in China" on CCTV's talk show of *baijia jiangtan*, Lecture Room Forum, is a perfect example of media packaging, or *meiti baozhuang*. Yu Dan has been an associate professor of film and television at Beijing Normal University before and after her rise to stardom, with little scholarly credentials in classical Chinese studies.

However, since the 2006 CCTV talk show and the publication of the collection of her lectures, *Yu Dan's Insights into the Analects*, i.e., her personal and popular readings of the classics by Confucius, the book has sold millions of millions copies and Yu Dan, according to the portrayal of the *L.A. Times* reporter, "has been racing from college lectures to book signings, TV appearances and speaking engagements. The public can't seem to get enough of this overnight sensation who has turned dusty old Confucian teachings into a Chinese version of 'Chicken Soup for the Soul.'"[10] The American media hail her instant success as a modern fashionable way to fill the moral and ideological vacuum in China today by "making Confucius cool again."[11] By the account in *Guardian*, a British media outlet, "the Chinese government is now reviving Confucianism as part of its strategy to promote the "harmonious society," establishing Confucian MBA courses for the new rich and even setting up Confucian institutes around the world. It has distributed Yu Dan's book to teachers, students and civil servants." The *Guardian* book reviewer continues, "Classical scholars, though, feel no such reverence. They have called her "an illiterate with a higher degree who takes pleasure in castrating traditional Chinese culture"; one turned up at a book-signing wearing a T-shirt that read: 'Confucius is deeply worried'."[12]

Yu Dan, and Yu Qiuyu, a male professor of Chinese literature at Shanghai Institute of Theater, and Yi Zhongtian, a male professor of Chinese literature at Xiamen University, take the same trail to media success. They all started out in some TV talk show forums, ultimately the CCTV Lecture Room, and then published their lectures on classical Chinese literature by Yi Zhongtian and prose essays and travelogues by Yu Qiuyu, and their books were packaged, promoted by an enormous publicity campaign launched by the CCTV media chain and other media outlets, publishers, etc. Of course these campaigns were not political tasks ordered by the CCP propaganda departments. They were primarily commercial advertizing campaigns promoting the consumer products—their books. Yu Dan's surprising success owed to a great extent to her role as a program consultant for the CCTV talk shows, an insider or designer who ultimately designed herself to become a media star. As a consultant and designer, Yu Dan knows perfectly all the gimmicks of entertaining the audience. Television as the most popular media outlet in China today depends almost entirely on its audience—the viewer's ratings are the vital indices for advertisement, and the advertising revenue determines the fate of TV station as a business entity. Entertainment, more than anything else, then becomes the most important and perhaps the only viable way to raise the viewer's ratings, since the news programs at the state-run media are exclusively controlled by the CCP propaganda departments, and consequently can contribute almost nothing to boost the ratings, unless the news of the Sichuan earthquake or events of such a magnitude break out.

It should be added here that entertainment does not merely serve the commercial purposes. Being didactic and aesthetic—the age-old universal wisdom, especially valued by Confucian tradition, is now reinforced with a modified version of both entertaining and edifying in today's media culture. The popular intellectuals of the Yus and Yis fulfill such dual mission of both the media and CCP propaganda departments, serving as entertainers as well as proselytizers of the dominant ideology in media age. Undoubtedly, turning the classics and traditional values into entertainment products reduces the richness and complexity of tradition, and flattens the historical context in which traditional values were engendered and evolved, a deficiency readily recognized by both the intellectual and political elites.

Critical intellectuals from both the New Left and liberal camps unanimously denounce such trends to succumb intellectual values to pure entertainment in their assault on the dominance of consumer popular culture. Much worse than those "vulgarizing" attempts at high cultural values made by the Yus and Yis, now widespread violence, sexual irresponsibility and criminality in video games, TV reality shows, the internet pornography, and in pirated DVDs of Hollywood films, in pop music and in tabloid stories of celebrity scandals are now the main villains attacked by the government, educators and parents alike, held responsible for the widespread moral degeneration. What is been widely criticized is the prevalence of entertainment-centered consumer culture, which unleashes individualistic and materialistic desires at the expense of social cohesiveness and pursuit of public good. However, entertainment in China is Janus-faced, both as the espousal of individual wish-fulfillment, and reinforcement of a facile political stability and public satisfaction with the present life.

Entertainment is now the single most important program in Chinese television, garnering more than 50 percent of viewer's ratings. Television dramas (*dianshi ju*), a unique form of television serial, have consistently garnered the highest share of ratings of all television programs since 2000. In 2004, television drama accounted for 29.4 percent of all program ratings, followed by news programs (16.8 percent), variety shows (7.9 percent), special features (7.7 percent), sports (7.0 percent) and films (5.6 percent). Today not only does television drama boast the highest ratings, it also covers a rich diversity of subject matter and genres: romance, domestic drama, martial arts, romantic and youth idol drama, crime, revolutionary drama, history, and so on. A great deal of TV dramas deal with the emperors, especially the glory of the Han, Tang Dynasties, and mostly the Qing Dynasty (1640-1911), the last imperial era before the modern time. Crime and revolutionary dramas are always popular, blending plots of anti-corruption, spy, gangsters and revolutionary wars including the Sino-Japanese War and the Chinese civil wars, the Korean War. One gets a glimpse of the revolutionary idealism and heroism amid highly entertaining ingredients of violence, espionage, conspiracy, and love affairs. It is interesting to note that in the past months of 2009, revolutionary themes tend to dominate the scene.

There has been an outburst of spy stories based on the history of Communist versus the Guomindang (Nationalist) that spanned a significant portion of the first half of the twentieth century. The biggest hit this year was the spy thriller *Lurk* (*Qianfu*), which depicts a spy's dangerous "lurking" as double agent for both Communist and the Guomindang during the civil war period. The spy-hero forges a chameleon-like persona with everyone surrounding him—his Guomindang military spy colleagues and his faked wife, a communist guerilla leader dispatched to be his assistant. But the drama singles out his loyalty—loyalty to the CCP and its cause, of course—as its central motif, taking pains to portray the hero and his comrades, including his lover and wife, first "faked" then "real," as a noble, dedicated, and selfless cohort. Such a task to reinvent revolutionary idealism under the current circumstances is quite thankless, as the rampant individualism and materialism in Chinese society easily sweep away any high-sounding idealistic preaching. Chinese viewers love the spy-hero for his multifaceted persona and his dignified yet very amiable personality, and critics hail the success of the drama as innovative representation of the revolutionary motifs. As the 60th anniversary of the founding of the People's Republic comes close, a profusion of television drama and other cultural products celebrates the glory of the nation and its historical journey.

Amid the media blaze celebrating the anniversary, there is a peculiar imbalance of cultural representations. Take the TV drama for instance. While an outpouring number of dramas focus on pre-1949 revolutionary wars, the history of the sixty years of the PRC is hardly mentioned. Such an absence is striking, but mostly unnoticed by the media and the populace, who have been braced for a more stringent economic downturn yet to come, despite the upbeat, festive atmosphere the Chinese media and the CCP propaganda departments have pumped up. The year 2009 is for China a year of high hopes and deep worries. Its global presence and importance is bolstered in no small way by the global economic recession. And at the same time the rising social discontent is affected by China's own lopsided, GDP-only development and by the worldwide economic woes. The legitimation crisis lurking behind the astonishing economic growth ever since the *gaike kaifang* has resurfaced over and again. The collective aphasia or loss of speech on precisely what should be mostly talked about at the time of commemoration, namely the entire span of the sixty years from 1949 to the present, strikes one as symptomatic of a deep-seated identity crisis, that an entertainment-driven media and popular culture is by no means capable of unraveling and analyzing, let alone remedying.

The entertainment's use value in China is now seriously challenged, as the discrepancy between its own dual functions, that is, gratification of individual wish-fulfillments on the one hand, and promotion of political stability and public support on the other, is widening. However, it would be too simplistic to condemn it as a irredeemable sin, citing the popular dictum of "amusing ourselves to death," a convenient dismissal now as popular in China as the popular culture it is intended to castigate.[13] Indeed, in the world of media culture, or the consumer popular culture, no one is "dead" or dying; quite on the contrary, it's all thriving and lively. China's hosting of the 2008 Beijing Olympics is an enormous boost to the "creative industry" or "cultural industry," now widely celebrated as a powerful opportunity for the next round of economic growth and GDP increase.

And in China's consumer popular culture, the passion for catching up with the latest chic or coolness is endemic and relentless. Suffice it to mention in brief the two uniquely Chinese events in show business: the CCTV Chinese New Year Gala and the Super Girl Singing Contest at Hunan Satellite TV. If there is a single television entertainment program that can attract the largest audience in the world, it is CCTV's Spring Festival Gala or celebration show (*chunjie lianhuan wanhui*). The Gala debuted in 1983. A spectacular variety show filmed in CCTV's giant studio that includes dance and musical performance, sketch comedy, and cross talks with appearances by national celebrities, it is broadcast live on Chinese New Year's Eve, the traditional time for family reunions, from 8:00 pm till after midnight—New Year's Day. In the 26 years since its debut, the program has boasted ratings of more than 90 percent, or approximately 1 billion viewers. It has now become part of the Chinese New Year celebrations—a new custom. No other entertainment program embodies the mainstream ideology of "harmonious society" better than the Gala, as the four-hour long show tries most painstakingly to include all the hot and chic in pop culture and the current CCP propaganda outlines.

Compared to the CCTV New Years Gala, the Super Girl Contest is a grassroots product with much less pomp than the CCTV show, but no less popular in the numerous teenage fans with a fanaticism unmatched by any other groups, unless one wants to draw an uncanny parallel with that of their parents in teenage years as Red Guards, dated back some forty years ago during the height of the Cultural Revolution. Revolutionary passion being long gone, the new fanaticism is aroused by the instant success of stardom and the fanfare, vanity, and promise of immense material benefit as media celebrity. Modeled after the popular US television show American Idol, Super Girl is a blend of reality show, singing and dancing contest, beauty pageant as well as incorporating popular votes from viewers through cellular phones (over 300 million viewers cast their votes by cell phone in 2005), attracting thousands of millions of young teenage girls and their families to apply, participate, and vote for their favorite singers. However, because of the scandals and "vulgarity" it involves, the Hunan Satellite TV finally canceled the show in 2007 after its three years existence. Now after two years lapse, the Super Girl made a comeback this year, changing its name to Happy Girl. As it turns out, the Happy Girl's "happiness" is much scaled down, as too many restrictions on the participation and broadcasting of the program, as well as the viewer's fatigue, now is taking a toll on the program. Yet a veritable "Super Girl culture" with its fans, rituals and coded language has become widely accepted by the urban youth, the generation known as the "Post-80s" *baling hou* and now the "Post-90s" *jiuling hou.* Entertainment has become an integral part of the experience of growth of this younger generation. The consumer popular culture's impact on changing social values and lifestyles is most visible in China's urban youth, born at the early *gaige kaifang* years of the 1980s.

THE POST-80 GENERATION: EMERGENT CULTURAL FORMATION

Chinese youth, mostly those born since the 1980s, are the main beneficiaries of reform in terms of material and economic prosperity, but they also bear the brunt of the social transition—confusion and the loss of values and ethical norms, as the revolutionary idealism of Mao's era has been rapidly replaced by consumerism and egotism. The beginning of the twenty-first century marks the coming of age of the new generation. A distinct urban youth culture is taking shape, nurtured largely by an electronically-based consumer culture. As such, this youth culture is the embodiment of globalization: it draws its icons, styles, images and values mainly from the "global" (read: Western) consumer culture and entertainment industry. In the meantime, the younger generation has a much stronger desire for a distinct cultural identity and marking their individual differences than did their parents' generation, who were Mao's children, born in the 1950s.

The internet serves as an interface between the self-identities of urban youth, consumer culture, global fashions and cultural trends. Urban youth today are much more inclined to pleasure-seeking, sensuous or aesthetically pleasing lifestyles and self-expression. The internet hence provides these techno-savvy youth, who sometimes label themselves Newer New Humanity (*xinxin renlei*), with a much freer and trendier (or "cooler") venue for self-expression in artistic and literary forms. At the turn of the century, the so-called beauty-baby authors (*meinu zuojia)* are the products of the Internet and the consumer bestselling market. Wei Hui's novel *Shanghai Baby* (*Shanghai baobei,* 2000) is generally considered the most well-known work of the "beauty-baby writers." The novel depicts sex, lust and drugs among contemporary young Shanghai women who have both leisure time and money, creating a subgenre of "body writing" (*shenti xiezuo)*—i.e., writing about feminine bodies or using (displaying) feminine bodies as tools for writing. Since then, numerous post-80s writers, pop singers and other media celebrities have emerged, including the writers such as Han

Han, Guo Jingming, the Super Girl singer Li Yuchun, etc., who take the multimedia channels such as the internet, television and printed books, magazines, and others to write and perform, with strong corporate supports from the information and communication industries and show business.

A distinct feature of the the post-80s generation is their internet language. In 2001, the e-fiction *The First Intimate Touch* (*Di yici qinmi jiechu*) by Taiwanese cyber writer Bum Cai (Pizi Cai) marked the beginning of vibrant online writing filled with internet slang and "cool" language invented by young internet users. The cyber writing that Bum Cai's e-fiction initiated has since created a "liberating" language that mixes English acronyms with Chinese shorthand and swear words, and even obscenity with high-tech jargon. The interactive nature of the Internet allows young users to experiment freely with newly invented cyber slang or colloquialisms. [14] Blogs have thus gained tremendous popularity in China, as blog (*boke*) provides users with a space in which to freely write and post multi-media materials (photos, sound bites and other forms) through hyper links about their personal experiences and opinions in diary form. Blogs are more personalized or customized than BBS or public forums. As a media form, blogs in China also tend to focus on individual experiences and feelings of love, romance, leisure and entertainment, as opposed to BBS and chat rooms, which primarily deal with issues of public interest. Another powerful telecommunication tool is cell phones. The rapid development of cellular phones provides thousands of millions of Chinese with an instant, flexible and affordable means not only of communication but also of entertainment, which allows the not simply to call each other, but to exchange a good deal of information and entertainment. Cellular phones can be connected to the internet, to allow the users to download popular music as ring tones, flashes from the web, and, above all, text messages.

The digital network of communication, information, news and entertainment has opened up not only a market with staggering economic potential but also a formidable social space especially for the post-80s generation of urban use. Compared to all the preceding generations the post-80s urban youth in China marks a distinct new cultural formation and values. Their parents, born in the 1950s, grew up during the Cultural Revolution and shared an unbroken chain of cultural heritage and values in Mao's revolutionary era. Chinese culture in most part of the twentieth century can be described as a revolutionary, radical culture in the throes of China's modernity, Only after the *gaike kaifang* of the late 1970s did Chinese culture begin to move into a post-revolutionary phase, marked by a series of fundamental displacements, discontinuities, ruptures and breakthroughs. Maoist collective idealism gradually gave way to individualism and pragmatism.

The coming of age of the post-80s generation coincided with this fundamental cultural change, and their cultural formation embodies this historical cultural transformation by its own historical vision deeply rooted in contemporary media culture. History is "liberated" from history textbooks and integrated into the everyday life by way of popular media culture: films, television dramas, talk shows and bestsellers of biographies, historical anecdotes. History appears as nostalgia, as entertainment, as consumer popular cultural products. The historical vision of the post-80s is thus much pluralistic, and paradoxically non-historic, in the sense of denial of history as continuous and unbroken lineage governing the ways to think and to live, or history serving as dominant social values. To the post-80s generation, history, modern Chinese history in particular, is nothing more than any other histories, American, Japanese, or French, as entertaining stories with little practical relevance or implications to their life today.

However, "history" as one of the primary figure of speech in Chinese culture, or a central metaphor in China's social life is still dominant, and the post-80s generation's patriotic pride or nationalistic sentiment, largely derived from China's fast growth into a world power, are registered in a historical narrative of modernity of development and progress, from the humiliations and backwardness of the 1840s Opium War to China's rise as a significant player in the world today. A surprising show of social and political activism of the post-80s generation appeared in the aftermath of the 2008 April Tibet riots and the disruptions of the 2008 Olympic torch relays in Paris, London, Los Angeles and other Western cities. Hundreds of thousands of Chinese students studying in western countries were mobilized by the internet, rallied to protest what they conceived as the distortion and demonization of China by western media. And in the Sichuan earthquake of May 2008, the post-80s youth became a major force of volunteers for rescue and charity work. The display of strong public sentiment of the post-80s generation this time is fundamentally different from that of the earlier years of the 1980s, culminating in the political upheavals of the 1989 Tiananmen Incidents. History was a latent cause this time, as the young generation's sensitivity to the western biases in the protests and the public volunteerism in the earthquake are in a large measure aroused by historical sense of responsibility, not imposed by the CCP propaganda departments or by the schools, but by a volunteerism with a historical understanding of progress.

Perhaps the post-80s generation's often contradictory and paradoxical sense of history of China as progress and history as entertainment, linked with their national and personal identities and delinked at the same time with their everyday life styles and their individual dreams, can offer us some clue to the understanding of their searches for a new cultural identity, a search for each concrete individual as well as for China as a nation. Amidst all the tension and contradictions, however, a "post-80s" generation urban youth culture emerges and will inevitably becomes a dominant cultural formation in China in the years to come. It is media-driven, globalized, and in the meantime more inclined towards its own cultural heritage, should be understood as the core of China's soft power competing in a global new order.

NOTES

1. "China Launches Publicity Campaign," *South China Morning Post,* Jan. 13, 2009.
2. "China Launches National Publicity Campaign to Improve Its International Image," *International Herald Leader*, Feb. 3, 2009.
3. Nicholas Bequelin, "China's New Propaganda Machine," *Wall Street Journal Asia,* Jan. 30, 2009.
4. Yan Lieshan, "When in Rome—A Few Thoughts on "External Propaganda," http://blog. ifeng.com/article/2427560.html
5. "Hu Jintao Calls for Enhancing 'Soft Power' of Chinese Culture," Xinhua newswire (English), Oct 15, 2007.
6. Liu Kang, "Emergent Globalism and Ideological Change in Post-Revolutionary China," Manfred Steger, ed., *Rethinking Globalism* (Boulder, CO: Rowman and Littlefield, 2004), 188.
7. For a critical assessment of Chinese intellectuals, see Edward Gu and Merle Goldman eds., *Chinese Intellectuals between State and Market* (New York: RutledgeCurzon, 2004).
8. Robert Marquand, "China 'Gray Lists' its Intellectuals," *The Christian Science Monitor,* Nov. 30, 2004.
9. For critical analysis of the neoliberal and neoconservative "market populism" in the U.S., see Thomas Frank, The Rise of Market Populism," *Nation,* 30, 2000, 13-19; and Lawrence Grossberg, *Caught in the Crossfire: Kids, Politics, and America's Future* (Boulder, CO: Paradigm Publishers, 2005), especially Chapter 4 and 5 on neoliberalism and neoconservatism in the U.S.
10. Ching-Ching Ni, "She makes Confucius Cool Again," *Los Angeles Times,* May 07, 2007.
11. Ibid.
12. Sun Shuyin, "Chicken broth for the soul? No thanks," *Guardian*, May 7, 2009, http://www.guardian.co.uk/books/2009/may/17/confucius-from-the-heart-yu-dan
13. Neil Postman, *Amusing Ourselves to Death: Public Discourse in the Age of Show Business* (New York: Penguin, 1986). This book is a bestseller in itself, and its Chinese 2004 translation is frequently cited by Chinese scholars and students of media and cultural studies.
14 Liu Kang, *Globalization and Cultural Trends in China* (University of Hawaii Press, 2004), p. 154.

Chapter 12

Obama's China Policy

Bo Zhiyue[*]

A descendent of a Kenyan father and a white American mother, Barack Hussein Obama II (born August 4, 1961) was elected president of the United States on November 4, 2008. He was sworn in on January 20, 2009 as the first African American president in the history of the United States. "Change" was the main theme of Obama's presidential campaigns. Now as a president, will he introduce any radical change to U.S. China policy?

In the early days of his administration, Bush attempted to shift the U.S. China policy from the engagement policy of the Clinton administration to a containment one. After the 9/11 terrorist attacks on the U.S., however, Bush administration reversed his policy from containment to cooperation. During the Bush administration, U.S.-China relations were substantially improved. Economic interdependence was deepened, and leadership diplomacy enhanced. The two sides were able to work together on major bilateral as well as international issues.

Barack Obama began to formulate his policy toward China in 2008 while he was still a presidential candidate. In the first ten months in office, the Obama administration has adopted a more cooperative approach in its relations with China. Politically, the new administration has deemphasized the importance of human rights in the bilateral relations, made significant unilateral concessions on the Tibet issue, and accepted the new development across the Taiwan Strait. Economically, the new administration has twice refused to brand China a currency exchange manipulator and made efforts to increase the bilateral trade. Nevertheless, the Obama administration has yet to make substantial progress in its policies in the areas of military cooperation. It should also curb its protectionist urge in its trade with China.

THE LEGACIES OF BUSH'S CHINA POLICY

In general, what George W. Bush passes on to Obama are mostly "negative assets"—two wars and an economy in recession. Nevertheless, Bush's China poli-

cy has proved to be successful and fruitful. Despite his initial adventurous overtures along China's coast, George W. Bush quickly learned to work with the
Chinese in the aftermath of the September 11 Incident. In the subsequent seven
years, the Bush administration cooperated with the Chinese over a number of
regional and global issues.

Bush's Policy Reversal

A little over two months after George W. Bush was sworn in as the forty-third
president of the United States on January 20, 2001, an American Navy spy plane
(EP-3) clashed with a Chinese Air Force plane over South China Sea, causing it
to crash and killing its pilot, Wang Wei.

Soon after the United States was attacked by terrorists on September 11,
2001, however, Chinese President Jiang Zemin wrote to President Bush, expressing condolences and condemning terrorism the very next day.[1] In the face
of terror, the United States changed its confrontational policy toward China. The
People's Republic of China was accepted into the World Trade Organization
(WTO) on November 11, 2001, and President Bush granted China permanent
trade status on December 27, 2001, ending a long history of an annual review in
the United States Congress of China's "most favored-nation treatment."

The Bush administration worked with China over a number of regional and
global issues, and the bilateral relations were institutionalized in the course of
subsequent seven years. First, the United States worked with China to prevent
Taiwan from rushing into independence. During Premier Wen Jiabao's visit to
the White House on December 9, 2003, President Bush made it clear that the
U.S. government opposed Taiwan independence.[2]

Second, the United States cooperated with China over trade and currency
issues. During President Hu Jintao's visit to Washington, D.C., George W. Bush
defended China's policy on its currency and explained U.S.-China trade as
something beneficial to Americans as well. At the press conference on April 20,
2006 along with President Hu Jintao, it was Bush who reminded the American
audience that the Chinese had made a major decision in July 2005 to appreciate
the Chinese currency and that the U.S. trade with China also meant jobs for
Americans.[3]

Third, the U.S. government was a strong supporter of the Beijing 2008
Olympic Games. In spite of domestic and international pressures, President
Bush refused to link his attendance to the opening ceremony of the Beijing
Olympics either to the genocide in Darfur, Sudan or to the dialogue with the
Dalai Lama.

U.S.-China Interdependence

Partly because of Bush's China policy, government officials from the United
States and China had a lot to celebrate on the thirtieth anniversary of the U.S.-

China diplomatic normalization in January 2009.[4] In the span of three decades, the two countries have become mutually dependent economically, financially, politically, and diplomatically.

Economically, the United States and China have become partners in many areas. The bilateral trade expanded from merely US$2.5 billion in 1979[5] to US$333.7 billion in 2008.[6] The United States was China's No. 1 trade partner in 2008, and China became the United States' No. 2 trade partner with a total trade of US$407.5 billion in that year.[7]

In particular, China has emerged as one of the most important sources of goods and products in the world for the United States (Figure 12.1). In 1987, Japan exported the most to the United States; in 1997, Canada became the largest supplier for the United States; and in 2007, China surpassed Canada as the No. 1 provider of goods and products for the U.S. consumers.[8] In contrast, U.S.'s imports from Germany (the largest exporter of the world) were less than 30 percent of those from China; and the share of India's exports to the United States in 2007 was less than that of China's exports to the U.S. in 1987.

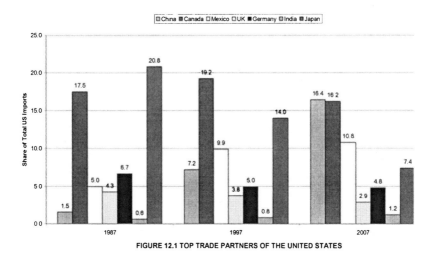

FIGURE 12.1 TOP TRADE PARTNERS OF THE UNITED STATES

Source: U.S. Census Bureau, http://www.census.gov/foreign-trade/balance/c5700.html

Although U.S. trade deficit with China was an issue of contention over the years,[9] it was no longer a major issue in the U.S.-China relations under the Bush administration. Many Americans have gradually realized that China is not an economic competitor of the United States. Instead, China has been a major contributor to the welfare of the Americans. "China is large enough and competitive enough to cause economic problems for the United States," advisors from two major think tanks in Washington, D.C. (the Center For Strategic and International Studies and the Institute for International Economics) pointed out in 2006, "but it has neither derailed our economy nor been the chief cause of our difficulties, any more than were Japan in the 1980s or other Asian countries in the early 1990s."[10]

More importantly, China has been rapidly becoming an important market for American products in the past twenty years (Figure 12.2), expanding from US$3.5 billion in 1987 to US$69.7 billion in 2008.[11]

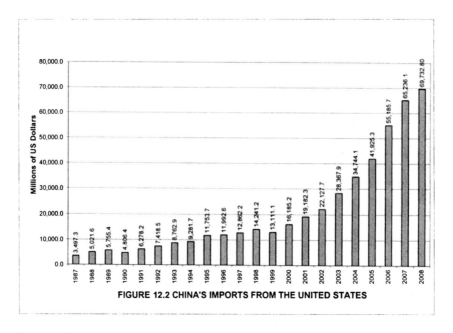

FIGURE 12.2 CHINA'S IMPORTS FROM THE UNITED STATES

Source: U.S. Census Bureau, http://www.census.gov/foreign-trade/balance/index.html#C

Financially, the United States has become increasingly dependent on China. Over the past 30 years, China's foreign reserve skyrocketed from US$167 million in 1978 to US$1,945,985 million in 2008, becoming No. 1 holder of foreign reserve in the world.[12]

In the meantime, China also surpassed Japan and became the largest holder of U.S. treasury securities in 2008 (Figure 12.3). Within twelve months from October 2007 to October 2008, China's holdings of U.S. treasury securities expanded from US$459.1 billion to US$652.9 billion, by a net of almost US$200 billion. In particular, after Lehman Brothers went bankrupt in September 2008, China acquired an additional US$66 billion worth of U.S. treasury securities in October 2008 as a show of its support for the U.S. government.

Politically, China and the United States collaborated over issues of regional and global significance. Both made efforts to become "responsible stakeholders" (as Robert Zoellick put it in 2005)[13] in international affairs. The two countries worked together to promote peace and stability in Asia, especially in the Six-Party Talks on the North Korea nuclear weapons program.

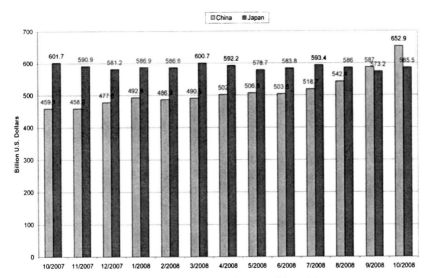

Figure 12.3 Holdings of U.S. Treasury Securities: China and Japan

Source: U.S. Department of Treasury. http://www.treas.gov/tic/mfh.txt

Most importantly, Sino-U.S. relationship has become institutionalized. President Hu Jintao met President Bush nineteen times on various occasions since 2002; the military-to-military hotline was opened on April 10, 2008; and the two sides completed the fifth round of the Strategic Economic Dialogue (SED) in Beijing (see Appendix 1) and the sixth round of the Senior Dialogue in Washington, D.C. in December 2008 (see Appendix 2).

Diplomatically, the bilateral relations expanded so much in the previous three decades that the two countries built new embassies in each other's capitals. In January 1979 when the United States Liaison Office (No. 1 Office) was transformed into the U.S. Embassy in Beijing, there were about sixty American and Chinese employees on the staff. In October 2008 when the embassy moved into its new complex, it had a staff of 1,100 from twenty six different U.S. government agencies. "In only three decades," as Clark Randt. Jr., the then U.S. Ambassador to China, commented, "the U.S.-China relationship has burgeoned into the most important bilateral relationship in the world, one that touches the lives of not only every American and Chinese citizen but also of almost every person in the world."[14] In August 2008, a new U.S. Embassy in Beijing was open for business. Located on a ten-acre site, the U.S. Embassy in Beijing is the second-largest U.S. embassy in the world.[15]

In general, the Bush administration welcomed the peaceful rise of China, and China was prepared to accept the United States as a leader in a new world political, economic, and financial order. As a result, "China" was no longer an issue in the 2008 U.S. presidential campaigns.

OBAMA'S CHINA POLICY: A PRELIMINARY REVIEW

The Obama administration had three major options in its China policy. First, the new administration might adopt a containment policy toward China. Along the line of a "league of democracies" as suggested by John McCain during his presidential campaign, Obama might very well attempt to strengthen the United States' ties with democracies in Asia such as Japan, India, South Korea, and Taiwan at China's expense. By continuing arms sales to Taiwan and upgrading arms sales to Japan (e.g., F-22 fighters) (as suggested by Dan Blumenthal, a resident fellow of the American Enterprise Institute and John McCain's advisor on Asia policy),[16] for instance, Obama might jeopardize his relations with Chinese leaders and change the nature of current bilateral relations from being essentially cooperative to basically confrontational.

Second, Obama could follow the footsteps of George W. Bush's China policy. He would work with China on a number of issues such as the North Korean nuclear issue, the Taiwan issue, and in particular, the global economic crisis.

Third, the Obama administration could significantly upgrade U.S.-China relations and make them the core of his global diplomacy. During his presidential campaigns, Obama called for "fresh thinking" and "a change from the US policy approach of the past eight years" in terms of U.S. China policy.[17] He expressed his willingness to develop "a strong foundation for a long-term positive and constructive relationship with an emerging China" in general and cooperating with China over regional issues such as the North Korean nuclear issue in the Six Party Talks and the improvement of relations across the Taiwan Strait in particular.

Hillary Clinton, Obama's Secretary of State and his former political rival, shares Obama's foreign policy orientation. In her confirmation speech, she indicated that the new administration would use "smart power"—the full range of tools including diplomatic, economic, military, political, legal, and cultural and picking the right tool or combination of tools for each situation—to reestablish America's leadership in the world.[18] She also indicated her willingness to cooperate with China. "China is a critically important actor in a changing global landscape," she said. "We want a positive and cooperative relationship with China, one where we deepen and strengthen our ties on a number of issues, and candidly address differences where they persist."

In its first 10 months in office, the Obama administration went through a fundamental shift in its foreign policy in general and significantly upgraded its China policy in particular. Obama's foreign policy in general shifted from unilateralism to multilateralism; from relying on hard power to replying on soft power; from using primarily military power to using "smart power"; from focusing on Middle East to concentrating on Asia. Its policy toward China was more than simply a continuation of the Bush administration's policy. The Bush administration was mostly passive toward China, while the Obama administration is more engaging. Obama's China policy is based on cooperation instead of confrontation and communication instead of criticism.

Political Orientation

Under the Obama administration, the United States takes China seriously. The United States and China, as Zbigniew Brzezinski (President Jimmy Carter's National Security Advisor) suggested in January 2009, might form a "G-2" with regular, informal, and "truly personal" discussions of foreign policy. The two countries might build "a truly comprehensive, global partnership" over such issues as India-Pakistan and Israeli-Palestinian conflicts as well as the Iran nuclear issue and the issue of failed states.[19] Although the Obama administration has not acknowledged the G-2 as its official policy toward China,[20] it indeed deems the relations with China as the most important bilateral relationship in the twenty-first century. In the past ten months, the new administration has downplayed the importance of human rights in the bilateral relations and made significant unilateral concessions on the Tibet issue. Most importantly, the United States has taken China as a partner on a series of world issues such as the climate change, global financial and economic reforms, and nuclear issues.

Hillary Clinton's China Visit: Global Crises vs. Human Rights

State Secretary Hillary Clinton changed the practice of her predecessors since the Kennedy years and chose Asia for her first trip abroad as the U.S. Secretary of State. She made her first stop in Tokyo but she had Beijing in mind as her top priority. As a presidential candidate in 2007, Clinton wrote that "our relationship with China will be the most important bilateral relationship in the world this century."[21] As the new Secretary of State in 2009, she matched her deeds with her words. In a speech in New York on February 13, 2009 before her Asia tour, Hillary Clinton used a Chinese idiom, "*tong zhou gong ji*" (working together in times of crisis), to describe U.S.-China relations. "When you are in a common boat," she said, "you need to cross the river peacefully together."[22]

During her three-day visit to Beijing from February 20 to 22, 2009, Hillary Clinton met with President Hu Jintao, Premier Wen Jiabao, State Councilor Dai Bingguo, and Foreign Minister Yang Jiechi.[23] The way she approached the Chinese leaders and the topics she chose to emphasize reflect the changing international context and the new diplomatic style. For Hillary Clinton, the world is faced with three crises: the global economic crisis, the global climate change crisis, and the security crisis. It is important that the United States and China work together to deal with these crises.

During her talks with the Chinese leaders, she paid more attention to cooperation on dealing with the global financial crisis, the global climate change, and the nuclear issue of North Korea. She urged the Chinese leaders to purchase more U.S. treasury securities,[24] discussed with them on venues of high-level dialogues, and visited a clean energy thermal power plant featuring equipment made by U.S.-based General Electric. She broached the issue of human rights with Chinese leaders but did not regard it as of higher priority than other more pressing issues such as the global financial crisis and climate change. During her stay in China, she was more of a listener than a lecturer; she sought common grounds instead of looking for problems; she was pragmatic instead of ideological; and she was cooperative instead of confrontational.

She told reporters in South Korea that the United States would continue to press China on such issues as Tibet, Taiwan, and human rights but in a new international context. "Successive administrations and Chinese governments have been poised back and forth on these issues, and we have to continue to press them," she said. "But our pressing on those issues can't interfere with the global economic crisis, the global climate change crisis, and the security crisis. We have to have a dialogue that leads to an understanding and cooperation on each of those."[25]

Nancy Pelosi's "Climate Change" Tour

Nancy Patricia D'Alesandro Pelosi (born March 26, 1940), the current Speaker of the House of Representatives (Democrat, California), has been a constant critic of China's policies, in particular its human rights violations. During her visit to China in May 2009, however, Pelosi became very subtle about her criticisms of the Chinese government.

In the past twenty years, no one has been more critical of the CCP regime than Pelosi, a crusader for human rights in China. After the Tiananmen Incident of 1989, she sponsored a bill to allow 40,000 Chinese students to remain in the United States after their visas expired. "Congress," she argued, "must send a very clear signal to the butchers of Beijing."[26] In September 1991, during her visit to Beijing, Pelosi unfurled a banner in the Tiananmen Square that read, "To those who died for democracy in China."[27]

A Democrat from San Francisco, California, she conflicted fiercely with both Republican President George Bush and Democrat President Bill Clinton over the extension of most-favored-nation status to China. "I am an enthusiastic Democrat," she explained. "But I cannot say one thing about George Bush's policy and another about Bill Clinton's when they are the same policy."[28] She was also critical of Bill Clinton over his decision to visit Beijing in the week of June 4 in 1998. President Bill Clinton, she said, would be "on the wrong side of history" for visiting Tiananmen Square during this sensitive time. For her, it is neither Ok for a Republican president nor Ok for a Democrat president to "coddle dictators."[29]

After the March riots in Tibet and Gansu, Pelosi criticized the Chinese government and called on "freedom-loving people throughout the world" to condemn China. If people do not speak out, she argued, then "we have lost all moral authority to speak on behalf of human rights anywhere in the world." To show her solidarity with Tibetan people, she traveled to the residence of the Dalai Lama in Dharamshala, India and appeared in public with the Tibetan spiritual and political leader in exile. She was the first foreign politician to meet with the Dalai Lama after the riots.[30] And she urged President George W. Bush to boycott the opening ceremony of the 2008 Beijing Olympics.[31]

On her visit to China from May 24 to 31, 2009,[32] however, Pelosi did not speak up against China at all. In her seven-day trip, Pelosi was accompanied by a delegation of four Democrats and one Republican, all members of the House Select Committee on Energy Independence and Global Warming (Rep. Ed Markey, a Democrat from Massachusetts and committee chairman; Rep. James Sensenbrenner, a Republican from Wisconsin and ranking committee member; Rep. Earl Blumenauer, a Democrat from Oregon; Rep. Jay Inslee, a Democrat from Washington; and Rep. Jackie Speier, a Democrat from California).[33]

The main purpose of her visit was on U.S.-China cooperation on energy policy and climate change.[34] Before the trip, she had highlighted the significance of her visit in terms of climate change. "The urgency of the global climate crisis requires that critical choices be made now that are bold and based on the clearest understanding of how to achieve our goals of preserving the planet and protecting the health of the world's people," she said. "Climate change provides a crucial opportunity for dialogue between our two nations."[35]

During her entire trip, she did not mention Tibet, Taiwan, and human rights. The only time she did use "human rights" was when she was talking about climate change and environment. In her speech at Qinghua University on May 28, 2009, Pelosi linked global warming to environmental justice and saw the right to a clean environment as a human right. "I do see this opportunity for climate change to be . . . a game-changer," she said. "It's a place where human rights—looking out for the needs of the poor in terms of climate change and healthy environment—are a human right."[36]

U.S.-China Strategic and Economic Dialogue

Only half a year after Obama took office, the United States and China conducted their first round of Strategic and Economic Dialogue in Washington, D.C. on July 27-28, 2009. Treasury Secretary Timothy F. Geithner and Secretary of State Hillary Rodham Clinton were representatives of the United States, and they were joined by their respective Chinese Co-Chairs, Vice Premier Wang Qishan and State Councilor Dai Bingguo.

In his remarks at the U.S.-China Strategic and Economic Dialogue on July 27, 2009, President Obama indicated his willingness to establish "a positive, constructive, and comprehensive relationship" with China.[37] He believed that "the relationship between the United States and China will shape the twenty-first century, which makes it as important as any bilateral relationship in the world." And he regarded China as a partner with the same responsibility for global affairs.[38] As he stated,

> My confidence is rooted in the fact that the United States and China share mutual interests. If we advance those interests through cooperation, our people will benefit and the world will be better off – because our ability to partner with each other is a prerequisite for progress on many of the most pressing global challenges.[39]

Obama then went on with a list of global challenges that the United States and China would face together. First, the United States and China need to work together to deal with the global financial and economic crisis. They need to promote financial stability through transparency and regulatory reform; to conclude a Doha Round agreement; to update international institutions with a greater role played by growing economies like China. Second, they need to cooperate on energy security and climate change. Third, they need to cooperate on stopping the spread of nuclear weapons. And fourth, they need to cooperate on confronting transnational threats.

As for his view on the rise of China, Obama made it clear that the United States will not try to contain China and instead welcomes "a future where China is a strong, prosperous, and successful member of the community of nations." The United States and China, as he characterized, "are partners out of necessity, but also out of opportunity."

Barack Obama: the Dalai Lama Meeting vs. Beijing Visit

President Obama also departed from a tradition of his predecessors since 1991 and decided not to meet the Dalai Lama in Washington, D.C. ahead of his scheduled visit to Beijing. The Dalai Lama made a major breakthrough in 1991 when the then President George Herbert Walker Bush (the father of George W. Bush) granted him a meeting in the White House. In the subsequent years, Presidents Bill Clinton and George W. Bush met the Dalai Lama every time when he was in Washington (see Appendix 3).[40]

Evidently, Barack Obama had never been a big fan of the Tibetan Buddhist monk. When he was a presidential candidate of the Democratic Party, he had a chance to meet the Dalai Lama. But he had apparently decided not to meet him. He wrote an open letter to the Dalai Lama instead. On July 24, 2008, one day before his opponent, Senator John McCain, the Republican candidate, met the Dalai Lama, Obama wrote a letter to the Dalai Lama explaining his inability to meet the Tibetan monk due to their different schedules.[41] Obama expressed his support for the Dalai Lama and the rights of Tibetans and indicated his willingness to meet him at another time. But the Dalai Lama stayed in the United States for more than two weeks (from July 11 to 27, 2008), and John McCain made a special trip to visit him on July 25, 2008.[42]

After having toyed with the idea for a while, Obama eventually again decided to go against seeing the Dalai Lama in Washington in October 2009 before his scheduled trip to Beijing. He sent a delegation to Dharmsala, India, the headquarters of the Tibetan exile government, to convey his message in September 2009. The delegation was led by Valerie Jarrett (born November 14, 1956), a senior adviser and assistant to the President, and Maria Otero, State Department Undersecretary for Democracy and Global Affairs and later special envoy for Tibet. The two must have explained Obama's decision not to meet him in Washington.[43] Yet the Dalai Lama was reported to have expressed his wishes to meet President Obama in his forthcoming trip to the United States in October 2009.[44] The Dalai Lama spent five days in the U.S.[45] However, President Obama did not see him.[46]

It is true that George W. Bush had met with the Dalai Lama in May 2001, ahead of his visit to China. Nevertheless, the circumstances before and after

September 11, 2001 were miles apart. Bush met with the Dalai Lama in defiance of China because he was adopting a confrontational stance against China before the 9/11. After the incident, the United States shifted its attention to terror and did not regard China as a competitor any longer.

It is also true that the Dalai Lama has met every sitting president in his Washington visits since 1991, but he has avoided Washington in some of trips to the United States. As mentioned above, the Dalai Lama spent more than two weeks in the United States in July 2008 but he did not visit Washington on this trip. President George W. Bush, therefore, did not meet with him in 2008. As Bush was planning to attend the opening ceremony of the Beijing Olympics, it was not convenient for him to meet with the Dalai Lama.[47] Apparently, the Dalai Lama was not happy about the arrangement. In a lecture in Philadelphia on July 17, 2008, he openly criticized George W. Bush for lack of understanding of reality.[48]

In the aftermath of the Sarkosy fiasco, Beijing's message was loud and clear. Tibet is a part of China, and Beijing would not hesitate to display its frustration over this issue. That is reflected in the fact that Premier Wen Jiabao skipped France in his trip to Europe in January 2009. Obama obviously would not want to run the risk of offending his host in Beijing.

Obama's China Trip: the Taiwan Issue and the Taiwan Relations Act

Obama has also accepted the recent development of cross-Strait relations. In his trip to China from November 15-18, 2009, he rarely mentioned the Taiwan Relations Act regarding the Taiwan issue. In his answer to an internet question on the improved relations across the Taiwan Strait and U.S. arms sales to Taiwan during the town-hall meeting with Chinese youth on November 16, 2009, Obama expressed his support for the one China policy based on the principles of the three joint communiqués between the United States and China without mentioning the Taiwan Relations Act.[49]

In the U.S.-China Joint Statement released on November 17, 2009, the Taiwan issue was addressed in Beijing's terms. After indicating each side's views on the issue, the document went on to elaborate Beijing's interpretation of the relations regarding Taiwan,

> The two countries reiterated that the fundamental principle of respect for each other's sovereignty and territorial integrity is at the core of the three U.S.-China joint communiqués which guide U.S.-China relations. Neither side supports any attempts by any force to undermine this principle. The two sides agreed that respecting each other's core interests is extremely important to ensure steady progress in U.S.-China relations.[50]

Apparently, this is not just about Taiwan but also about Tibet and Xinjiang. Through this statement, China wants to make sure that the United States would not support separatists such as the Dalai Lama and Rebiya Kadeer and would not harbor them on its soil. In the joint press conference with President Hu Jintao on November 17, 2009, Obama deviated from the joint statement regarding Taiwan and mentioned the Taiwan Relations Act orally.[51]

Political Relations: from "Responsible Stakeholder" to "Strategic Partner"

The political relations with China have apparently moved beyond holding China accountable as a "responsible stakeholder." In his interview with Reuters on November 9, 2009, a few days before his Asia trip, Obama described China as a "strategic partner." To a question about his opinion on whether China is a rival or an ally, Obama replied,

> Well, I see China as a vital partner, as well as a competitor. The key is for us to make sure that that competition is friendly, and it's competition for customers and markets, it's within the bounds of well-defined international rules of the road that both China and the United States are party to, but also that together we are encouraging responsible behavior around the world. And on critical issues, whether climate change, economic recovery, nuclear non-proliferation, it's very hard to see how we succeed or China succeeds in our respective goals without working together. And that is, I think, the purpose of the *strategic partnership* (italics added) and that is why this trip to China is going to be so important.[52]

Although the term "strategic partnership" did not appear in the joint statement, there is a major section on "building and deepening bilateral strategic trust." In this section, the two countries pledged to work together on issues concerning global stability and prosperity. "The United States and China," it is stated, "have an increasingly broad base of cooperation and share increasingly important common responsibilities on many major issues concerning global stability and prosperity." The two sides expressed their willingness to tackle regional and global challenges in economic recovery, security, climate change, and many other issues together. They are partners on an equal footing.

Economic Cooperation and Competition

Under the Obama administration, the bilateral economic relationship between the United States and China has become a bit complicated. On the one hand, the U.S. government is trying to ease tension with China over currency exchange issues. On the other hand, it is intensifying its pressure on China over trade issues. In other words, Obama treats China as a partner on currency issues and as a competitor on trade issues.

Tim Geithner's Slips of Tongue over Currency Issues

Apparently, the Obama administration was not prepared to confront China over currency issues. Timothy Franz Geithner (born August 18, 1961), Obama's Secretary of the Treasury, has stumbled over this issue twice.[53] In replies to questions from Senator Charles Schumer (Democrat, New York) and Senator Olympia Jean Snowe (Republican, Maine) of the Senate Finance Committee on January 21, 2009 as the Treasury Secretary designate, he wrote "President Obama— backed by the conclusions of a broad range of economists—believes that China is manipulating its currency." The new administration would "use aggressively all the diplomatic avenues" to change China's currency practices.[54]

The international media and the market read his replies as a signal that the Obama administration would adopt a confrontational approach toward China. *The New York Times* reported that the Obama administration would take "a more confrontational stance toward" China than the Bush administration.[55] *Guardian* of the United Kingdom believed that Tim Geithner "has fired the first shot in what could be a new protectionist battle between America and China."[56] Tim Geithner's accusation, *Guardian* predicted, is "likely to hurt relations between the two countries." The market reacted to his signal. The yield on the ten-year Treasury note, which moves inversely from the price, traded at 2.65 percent on January 23, up from 2.59 percent the day before. The yield on the thirty-year bond jumped to 3.36 percent, up from 3.26 percent.[57]

The Chinese government also reacted strongly. The Chinese Ministry of Commerce issued a statement saying that "the Chinese government has never used so-called currency manipulation to gain benefits in its international trade." The ministry also lashed out at "unsubstantiated criticism," saying it could risk a protectionist backlash in the United States.[58] The People's Bank of China, the central bank, also dismissed Geithner's allegation as "untrue and misleading." Su Ning, vice governor of the central bank, said that the allegation could sidetrack the effort to find the real cause of the financial crisis. He warned against possible reemergence of protectionism. "Also, we should avoid any excuse that might revitalize or fuel protectionism," he said. "Because it will do no good to the fight against the crisis, nor will it help the healthy and stable development of the global economy."[59] Subsequently, China purchased significantly less additional U.S. treasury securities than before. In the month of February 2009, China acquired US$4.6 billion more U.S. treasury securities, about seven percent of its additions in the peak month of October 2008 (US$65.9 billion).

However, as it has been revealed later, it was not Tim Geithner's intention to accuse China of manipulating its currency in the first place. According to Treasury officials, Geithner's written comment about China's currency was "mistakenly included in his responses to senators" and the Obama administration "was not signaling a more confrontational stance than the Bush administration had taken toward trade with China."[60]

In a statement on the U.S. Treasury Department's semi-annual report to the Congress on international economic and exchange rate policies on April 15, 2009, Tim Geithner determined that China was not a currency manipulator after all.[61] "Treasury did not find that any major trading partner had manipulated its exchange rate for the purposes of preventing effective balance of payments adjustment or to gain unfair competitive advantage," he stated. He provided a detail account for his determination regarding China.

With respect to China, which has been highlighted in the Report in recent years, our conclusion is based on the following factors. First, China has taken steps to enhance exchange rate flexibility. Chinese officials reaffirmed in January 2009 their commitment to greater flexibility and the need to allow the exchange rate to adapt to an equilibrium level. Second, the Chinese currency appreciated by 16.6 percent in real effective terms between the end of June 2008 and the end of February 2009. As the crisis intensified, the currency appreciated slightly against the dollar when most other emerging market and other currencies fell sharply against the dollar. Third, official statistics suggest the pace of China's foreign exchange reserve accumulation slowed in the fourth quarter of last year. Fourth, China has enacted a large fiscal stimulus package – second in size to that of the United States in the G-20 – which should help spur domestic demand growth and rebalance the Chinese economy. Even so, Treasury remains of the view that the *renminbi* is undervalued. Given China's large and rapid increase in its current account surplus, these steps should be just a beginning to a series of policy steps to rebalance the Chinese economy so that economic growth is more dependent on domestic demand, particularly private consumption.[62]

In other words, China is not a currency manipulator but Chinese currency remains undervalued. The apparent policy reversal, as a senior Treasury official explained at a briefing, was also due to the financial crisis. "The financial crisis has really changed the context. We're looking at a global recession," the official said.[63]

On the eve of the G-20 meeting, however, Tim Geithner had yet another slip of tongue, again on currency issues. On March 24, 2009, ahead of the G-20 summit in London on the global financial and economic crisis, Zhou Xiaochuan, governor of the Chinese central bank, published an article on the international monetary system and the global financial crisis. In the article, Zhou argued that the ongoing financial crisis was a reflection of the inherent weaknesses of the current international monetary system and called for a gradual move towards using IMF Special Drawing Rights (SDRs) as a centrally managed global reserve currency. He argued that this would address the inadequacies of using a national currency as a global reserve currency, particularly the Triffin dilemma—the dilemma faced by issuing countries in trying to simultaneously achieve their domestic monetary policy goals and meet other countries' demand for reserve currency. Zhou explained global currency diversification was needed because an over-concentration of foreign assets denominated in the dollar may bring about undesirable consequences. Zhou argued that it was regrettable that John Maynard Keynes's "farsighted" Bancor proposal was not adopted at Bretton Woods in the 1940s.[64]

Tim Geithner responded to the proposal positively initially. In response to a question on March 25, 2009, he said he had not read Zhou's proposal but was quite open to the suggestion of moving toward a currency system linked to the International Monetary Fund's Special Drawing Rights. "As I understand it, it's a proposal designed to increase the use of the IMF's Special Drawing Rights. I am actually quite open to that suggestion."[65]

Again, the international media was baffled by Geithner's comments. Why did he say he was open to a proposal without having read it in the first place? "US Treasury Secretary Tim Geithner confessed on Wednesday that he had not read the plans by China's central bank governor for a 'super-sovereign reserve currency' run by the International Monetary Fund," Ambrose Evans-Pritchard of *Telegraph* observed, "but nevertheless let slip that Washington was 'open' to the idea. Whoops."[66]

Clearly, currency traders did not think it such a good idea for the dollar. The dollar dropped by 4.2 percent against all major currencies in less than 10 minutes after his comments. Fifteen minutes later, Geithner backtracked. President Obama later reaffirmed the strength and long-term viability of the dollar as the global reserve currency.[67]

Yet in another semi-annual report to the Congress on international economic and exchange rate policies released on October 15, 2009, the Treasury Department again concluded that no major trading partner of the United States (including China) has manipulated its rate of exchange against the U.S. dollar.[68] The report noted that China returned to a policy of maintaining a largely stable renminbi-dollar exchange rate in the summer of 2008. As a result, China's real effective rate depreciated by 6.9 percent between February and August 2009 (along with the depreciation of the U.S. dollar), although it appreciated 13.3 percent between June 2008 and February 2009.[69]

One of the reasons why the Obama administration has been very careful about the currency issues with China is that China has been the largest holder of the U.S. treasury bills since September 2008 and China's holdings have been increasing. According to the U.S. Department of Treasury, foreigners purchased a total of US$760.4 billion of additional U.S. treasury securities (treasury bills, T-Bonds & Notes, and others) between August 2008 and August 2009 (Figure 12.4). In the meantime, China increased its holdings by US$223.4 billion, representing 29.4 percent of the total additional foreign holdings of the period. By the end of August 2009, China's holdings of U.S. treasury securities were US$797.1 billion, 23.1 percent of the total foreign holdings (US$3,448.8 billion).[70]

Trade Wars

However, protectionism has become more prevalent in the United States. Since January 2009, the U.S. Department of Commerce has initiated a series of trade subsidy investigations on imports from China. In the first three quarters, the United States launched 14 investigations against Chinese products worth US$5.8 billion (639 percent over the same period of 2008).[71] In particular, President Obama signed an order in September 2009 to impose a 35 percent tariff on Chinese-made tire imports over the next three years, in response to a petition from the U.S.

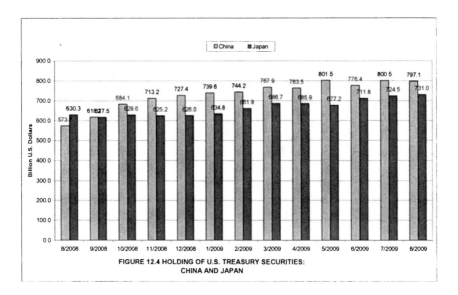

FIGURE 12.4 HOLDING OF U.S. TREASURY SECURITIES: CHINA AND JAPAN

Source: U.S. Department of Treasury, http://www.treas.gov/tic/mfh.txt

Steelworkers union. One week before Obama's trip to Asia, the United States also slapped preliminary anti-dumping duties ranging up to 99 percent on Chinese-made oil well pipe in the biggest U.S. trade action against China, risking a trade war with its largest supplier.[72]

It should be noted that in the time of the global economic crisis, professionalism has been on the rise. China has been a target of anti-dumping investigations since 1995. Between 1995 and 2008, WTO members initiated altogether 677 anti-dumping investigations against China. In the first three quarters, 19 countries launched 88 trade subside investigations against China.[73]

These investigations have occurred in the backdrop of the expansion of China's exports. In the first half a year of 2009, China overtook Germany as the largest exporter in the world by a small margin. For the first six months, China exported goods worth US$521.7 billion, and Germany, which had been the world's biggest exporter since 2003, exported goods worth US$521.6 billion.[74]

In 2008 as a whole, Canada was the largest supplier to the United States. The total exports from Canada to the United States were US$339,491.4 million, followed by China with US$337,772.6 million.[75] If we look at monthly data, however, we may find that China's export to the United States surpassed that of Canada in August 2008 and maintained its lead in every single month in the subsequent 12 months (Figure 12.5).

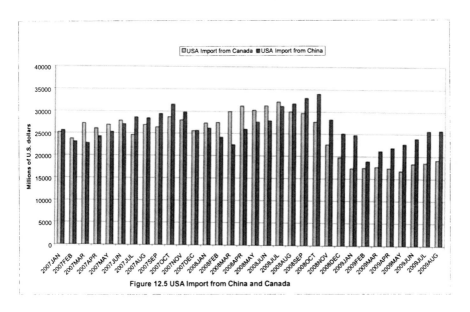

Figure 12.5 USA Import from China and Canada

Source: U.S. Bureau of Census (http://www.census.gov/foreigntrade/balance/index.html)

Military Interactions

The United States and China still need more communication and cooperation in the area of the military. The United States military still played some provocative moves along China's coast, and the United States continues to sell arms to Taiwan.

South China Sea Incident

In early March 2009, two weeks after Hillary Clinton left Beijing, the United States and China was involved in an incident in South China Sea. According to the United States, an American surveillance vessel, the Impeccable, was surrounded and harassed by five Chinese ships on March 8, 2009 while it was operating in international waters. Beijing asserted that the U.S. ship behaved "like a spy" and accused it of breaking international law by operating in its Exclusive Economic Zone (EEZ).[76] It is indisputable that the incident occurred 75 miles south of Hainan Island, in China's exclusive economic zone, but the two sides tried to interpret the international law in its own favor.

Under the United Nations Convention on the Law of the Sea (UNCLOS), which was concluded in 1982 and came into force in 1994, coastal states are entitled to a 200-nautical-mile (321 km) exclusive economic zone. According to Article 56, within the exclusive economic zone, coastal states enjoy: (1) sovereignty rights for the purpose of exploring and exploiting, conserving and managing the natural resources, whether living or nonliving, of the waters superjacent to the seabed and of the seabed and its subsoil, and with regard to other activities for the economic exploitation and exploration of the zone, such as the production of energy from the water, currents and winds; (2) jurisdiction as provided for in the relevant provisions of this Convention with regard to: the establishment and use of artificial islands, installations and structures; marine scientific research; the protection and preservation of the marine environment; (3) other rights and duties provided for in this Convention.[77]

In the meantime, the Convention also stipulates that in the exclusive economic zone, all states enjoy, "subject to the relevant provisions," the freedoms of navigation and overflight and of the laying of submarine cables and pipelines, such as those associated with the operation of ships, aircraft and submarine cables and pipelines (Article 58). The same article also makes it clear that other states "shall have due regard to the rights and duties of the coastal state and shall comply with the laws and regulations adopted by the coastal state" in accordance with the Convention.[78]

The People's Republic of China has signed and ratified the UN Convention and adopted a law on the exclusive economic zone and the continental shelf accordingly. Under the Law of the PRC on the Exclusive Economic Zone and the Continental Shelf adopted on June 26, 1998, the People's Republic of China exercises sovereign rights and management rights over its exclusive economic zone and continental shelf.[79]

The United States, on the other hand, signed the Convention but has not ratified it. Therefore it is not a state party to the Convention. "This puts the US in an awkward position," as Mark J. Valencia, a leading maritime expert, observed. "They are trying to interpret the terms of the Convention in their favor, which they are not a party to."[80]

USNS Impeccable (T-AGOS-23) is an Impeccable-class ocean surveillance ship acquired by the U.S. Navy in 2001 and assigned to the Military Sealift Command's special missions program. The mission of the Impeccable is to support the U.S. Navy by using SURTASS passive and active low frequency sonar arrays to detect and track undersea threats.[81]

Apparently, according to Hans M. Kristensen of the Federation of American Scientists, the incident is a part of "a wider and dangerous cat and mouse game between U.S. and Chinese submarines and their hunters."[82] The incident occurred seventy five miles south of a Chinese naval base near Yulin on Hainan Island from where the People's Liberation Army Navy was operating new nuclear submarines. "The U.S. Navy on its part," Kristensen wrote, "is busy collecting data on the submarines and seafloor to improve its ability to detect the submarines in peacetime and more efficiently hunt them in case of war." In other words, USNS Impeccable was asked to leave for good reasons because its activities were not entirely "innocent." This incident is a vivid reminder of a similar incident in April 2001 when a U.S. spy plane collided with a Chinese jet over the Chinese coast, killing a Chinese pilot.

The United States sent the guided missile destroyer USS Chung-Hoon (DDG-93) to the South China Sea to protect the Impeccable on March 12, 2009. In the meantime, China also dispatched its largest and most modern patrol ship, the Yuzheng 311, into the same general area. But two countries decided to put an end to the dispute ahead of the G20 Summit.[83]

Xu Caihou's U.S. Visit

To further communication and understanding between the militaries of the two countries, General Xu Caihou, vice chairman of the Central Military Commission, visited the United States in late October 2009. During his visit, he reached a seven-point understanding with his counterpart, Defense Secretary Robert Gates.[84] These are 1) increase high-level exchanges. Defense Secretary Robert Gates will visit China in 2010. General Chen Bingde, Chief of the General Staff of the People's Liberation Army and Admiral Michael Mullen, Chairman of the U.S. Joint Chiefs of Staff will exchange their visits. 2) expand cooperation in humanitarian assistance and disaster relief. Along with the exchanges of military ships, the two sides may conduct joint rescue exercises and disaster exchanges in air and water under complicated conditions. 3) deepen cooperation in the area of military medicine, especially on the prevention of epidemics. Specialists in this regard will focus on special themes in their exchanges. 4) expand exchanges of the army in all areas and start exchanges in military engineering. 5) increase exchanges of young and middle-aged officers, beginning in 2010. 6) promote exchanges in arts and sports of the two militaries. 7) promote Sino-U.S. maritime military safety, give a full play to the existing diplomatic and consultation channels, including the Sino-U.S. working meeting of the defense ministries and maritime military safety consultation mechanism meeting scheduled for December 2009.[85]

During the meeting on October 27, 2009, Xu indicated that to promote the healthy development of military-to-military relations, both sides need to eliminate some major barriers for their military-to-military relations, including the military relations between the United States and Taiwan, especially U.S. arms sales to Taiwan; the operation of U.S. military ships in China's exclusive economic zone; the legal barriers of military-to-military relations; and the U.S.'s lack of strategic trust of China.[86]

The joint statement commended the outcomes of Xu Caihou's visit and pledged to take "concrete steps" to advance "sustained and reliable" military-to-military relations in the future. The two militaries would make efforts to "improve their capabilities for practical cooperation and foster greater understanding of each other's intentions and of the international security environment," and the two countries agreed to build and deepen bilateral "strategic trust."[87]

CONCLUDING REMARKS

After its inauguration in January 2009, the Obama administration had three op-tions for its China policy. The first was to seek to contain China. But this would not bode well for either the bilateral relations or the world as a whole. The ond was to maintain a cooperative relationship with China, as George W. Bush had done in the previous seven years. And the third was to upgrade U.S.-China relations.

In his first ten months in office, President Barack Obama has adopted a pragmatic policy toward China. The new administration has taken China more seriously than any time in the history of the United States and is willing to build comprehensive, cooperative, strategic partnership with China on bilateral relations as well as on a host of world issues. In order to develop trust, American leaders made extraordinary efforts. Secretary of State Hillary Clinton was the first secretary of state in almost five decades to make her first visit abroad to Asia. President Obama was the first American president ever to make his first state visit to China within the first year in office. The first time in 18 years, President Obama did not see the Dalai Lama when he visited Washington. Both leaders deemphasized human rights issues in their visits and paid more attention to cooperation with China on dealing with global economic crisis, global climate change, and global security issues. Even Nancy Pelosi, a strong critic of China's policies, was "all smiles and handshakes" during her "climate change" tour of China in May 2009.[88]

In economic terms, the United States and China are both partners and competitors. On the one hand, China has continued its accumulation of U.S. treasury bills, which financed the economic recovery of the only superpower. In exchange, the United States has exercised self-restraints not to brand China as a currency exchange rate manipulator. On the other hand, the United States has intensified its protectionist measures against Chinese products. In the first three quarters of 2009, the United States launched fourteen investigations against Chinese products.

In military terms, the United States has been very suspicious of China's real intentions. Chinese leaders have been talking about a peaceful development strategy since 2003, but China's military build-up has also accelerated. In March 2009, an American surveillance vessel, the Impeccable, was involved in a dispute with several Chinese ships within the Chinese exclusive economic zone, south of the Hainan Island. In order to enhance mutual understanding and reduce mistrust, General Xu Caihou visited the United States in October 2009 and reached a seven-point understanding with his counterpart. The two countries have also made pledges to build "strategic trust," a term that has been written into the joint statement during President Obama's visit to Beijing.

In a word, the Obama administration has attempted to build a strategic partnership with China over a host of global issues but has yet to formulate a consistent policy regarding trade and security issues.

APPENDICES

No.	Date	Venue	Location	Chinese Leader
Appendix 1 George W. Bush's Meetings with Chinese Leaders			
1	19 October 2001	Asia-Pacific Summit	Shanghai	Jiang Zemin
2	21-22 February 2002	State Visit	Beijing	Jiang Zemin
3	25 October 2002	Working Visit	Crawford, Texas	Jiang Zemin
4	1-2 June 2003	G-8 Economic Summit	Evian-les-Bains, France	Hu Jintao
5	18-21 October 2003	APEC Summit Meeting	Bangkok, Thailand	Hu Jintao
6	19-22 November 2004	APEC Summit Meeting	Chile, Santiago	Hu Jintao
7	6-8 July 2005	G-8 Economic Summit	Gleneagles, UK	Hu Jintao
8	13 September 2005	Margins of UN General Assembly	New York	Hu Jintao
9	16-20 November 2005	APEC Summit Meeting	Pusan, Korea	Hu Jintao
10	20-21 November 2005	State Visit	Beijing	Hu Jintao
11	20 April 2006	State Visit	Washington	Hu Jintao
12	14-17 July 2006	G-8 Economic Summit	St. Petersburg, Russia	Hu Jintao
13	19 November 2006	APEC Summit Meeting	Hanoi, Vietnam	Hu Jintao
14	6-8 June 2007	G-8 Economic Summit	Heiligendamm, Germany	Hu Jintao
15	3-8 September 2007	APEC Summit Meeting	Sydney, Australia	Hu Jintao
16	6-9 July 2008	G-8 Economic Summit	Tokayo, Japan	Hu Jintao
17	10 August 2008	Beijing Olympics	Beijing	Hu Jintao
18	14-15 November 2008	G-20 Economic Summit	Washington	Hu Jintao
19	21 November 2008	APEC Summit Meeting	Lima, Peru	Hu Jintao

Sources:
1) http://www.abc.net.au/pm/stories/s395664.htm
2) http://www.state.gov/r/pa/ho/trvl/pres/5218.htm
3) http://georgewbush-whitehouse.archives.gov/news/releases/2002/10/20021025.html
4) http://www.state.gov/r/pa/ho/trvl/pres/5218.htm
5) http://www.chinadaily.com.cn/en/doc/2003-10/20/content_273702.htm
6) http://english.peopledaily.com.cn/200411/05/eng20041105_162946.html
7) http://www.china.org.cn/archive/2006-07/17/content_1174855.htm
8) http://georgewbush-whitehouse.archives.gov/news/releases/2005/09/20050913-8.html
9) http://www.china-embassy.org/eng/zmgx/zmgx/Economic%20Cooperation%20&%20Trade/t217107.htm
10) http://www.china-embassy.org/eng/zmgx/zmgx/Economic%20Cooperation%20&%20Trade/t217107.htm
11) http://georgewbush-whitehouse.archives.gov/news/releases/2006/04/images/20060420_v042006db-0222jpg-515h.html, http://georgewbush-whitehouse.archives.gov/news/releases/2006/03/20060322.html
12) http://english.people.com.cn/200607/17/eng20060717_283803.html
13) http://english.people.com.cn/200611/20/eng20061120_323348.html
14) http://en.wikipedia.org/wiki/33rd_G8_summit#Schedule_and_Agenda
15) http://news.bbc.co.uk/2/hi/asia-pacific/6981007.stm, http://georgewbush-whitehouse.archives.gov/news/release
16) http://georgewbush-whitehouse.archives.gov/news/releases/2008/07/images/20080709-4_d-0460-2-515h.html
17) http://georgewbush-whitehouse.archives.gov/news/releases/2008/08/20080810-3.html
18) http://georgewbush-whitehouse.archives.gov/news/releases/2008/11/20081114-5.html
19) http://georgewbush-whitehouse.archives.gov/news/releases/2008/11/images/20081121_p112108cg-0050-515h

Appendix 2 China-US Senior Dialogue				
Round	Dates	Location	US Representative	Chinese Representative
1	1-2 August 2005	Beijing	Deputy Secretary of State Robert Zoellick	Executive Vice Foreign Minister Dai Bingguo
2	7-8 December 2005	Washington, D.C.	Deputy Secretary of State Robert Zoellick	Executive Vice Foreign Minister Dai Bingguo
3	8 November 2006	Beijing	Undersecretary of State Nicolas Burns	Executive Vice Foreign Minister Dai Bingguo
4	20-21 June 2007	Maryland	Deputy Secretary of State John Negroponte	Executive Vice Foreign Minister Dai Bingguo
5	17-18 January 2008	Guizhou	Deputy Secretary of State John Negroponte	Executive Vice Foreign Minister Dai Bingguo
6	15 December 2008	Washington, D.C.	Deputy Secretary of State John Negroponte	State Councilor Dai Bingguo

Sources:
1) http://www.america.gov/st/washfile-english/2005/August/20050803180456TJkcolluB0.4520075.html
2) http://www.america.gov/st/washfile-english/2005/December/20051202181222ajesrom0.2403681.html
3) http://hongkong.usconsulate.gov/uscn_state_2006110801.html
4) http://www.state.gov/documents/organization/87271.pdf
5) http://hongkong.usconsulate.gov/ustw_state_2008011801.html
6) http://hongkong.usconsulate.gov/uscn_state_2008121602.html

Appendix 3 The Dalai Lama's Meetings with U.S. Presidents			
No.	Date	President	Location
1	16 April 1991	George H.W. Bush	Washington
2	27 April 1993	William J. Clinton	Washington
3	28 April 1994	William J. Clinton	Washington
4	13 September 1995	William J. Clinton	Washington
5	23 April 1997	William J. Clinton	Washington
6	10 November 1998	William J. Clinton	Washington
7	20 June 2000	William J. Clinton	Washington
8	23 May 2001	George W. Bush	Washington
9	10 September 2003	George W. Bush	Washington
10	9 November 2005	George W. Bush	Washington
11	16 October 2007	George W. Bush	Washington

Sources:
http://www.tibet.com/DL/leaders.html

Appendix 4 China-US Strategic Economic Dialogue				
Round	Dates	Location	US Representative	Chinese Representative
1	14-15th December 2006	Beijing	Treasury Secretary Henry M Paulson	Vice Premier Wu Yi
2	22-23rd May 2007	Washington, D.C.	Treasury Secretary Henry M Paulson	Vice Premier Wu Yi
3	12-13th December 2007	Beijing	Treasury Secretary Henry M Paulson	Vice Premier Wu Yi
4	17-18th June 2008	Annapolis, Maryland	Treasury Secretary Henry M Paulson	Vice Premier Wang Qishan
5	4-5th December 2008	Beijing	Treasury Secretary Henry M Paulson	Vice Premier Wang Qishan

Sources:
http://www.ustreas.gov/initiatives/us-china/

Office	Name	Tenure	Party Affiliation
Appendix 5 American Ambassadors to the People's Republic of China			
US Liason Office (Beijing)	David K.E. Bruce	14/05/1973 - 25/09/1974	Career Diplomat, Non Partisan
US Liason Office (Beijing)	George H.W. Bush	21/10/1974 - 7/12/1975	Republican
US Liason Office (Beijing)	Thomas S.Gates Jr	06/05/1976 - 8/05/1977	Republican
US Liason Office (Beijing)	Leonard F. Woodcock	26/7/1977 - 1/03/1979	Democrat
Ambassador	Leonard F. Woodcock	07/03/1979 - 13/02/1981	Democrat
Ambassador	Arthur W. Hummel, Jr	24/09/1981 - 24/09/1985	Career Diplomat
Ambassador	Winston Lord	19/11/1985 - 23/04/1989	Republican
Ambassador	James Roderick Lilley	08/05/1989 - 10/05/1991	Non-partisan, subsequently Republican
Ambassador	J. Stapleton Roy	20/08/1991 - 17/06/1995	Republican
Ambassador	Jim Sasser	14/02/1996 - 01/07/1999	Democrat
Ambassador	Joseph W. Prueher	15/12/1999 - 01/05/2001	Democrat
Ambassador	Clark T. Randt, Jr.	28/07/2001 - 20/01/2009	Republican
Ambassador	Jon Huntsman		Republican

Sources:
1) http://www.state.gov/r/pa/ho/po/com/10454.htm
2) http://www.trumanlibrary.org/oralhist/bruce.htm
3) http://www.nndb.com/people/934/000127553/

NOTES

* The author would like to thank Ms. Pan Rongfang and Mr. Desmond Chua for their research assistance.

1. *Renmin Ribao*, September 12, 2001, p. 1.
2. *Renmin Ribao*, December 11, 2003, p. 1. For the White House's record, see http://www.whitehouse.gov/news/releases/2003/12/20031209-3.html#3. In *Renmin Ribao*, Bush is quoted as saying "opposing" (*fandui*) Taiwan independence; in the press briefing released by the White House, the quote is "do not support" Taiwan independence. But in his remarks to the press, Bush did use the word "oppose" (see http://www.whitehouse.gov/news/releases/2003/12/20031209-2.html).
3. http://www.whitehouse.gov/news/releases/2006/04/20060420-1.html.
4. For a list of guests from the United States and China to the gathering in Beijing for the celebration of the thirtieth anniversary of the Sino-U.S. relations, see Edward Wong, "Former Carter adviser calls for a 'G-2' between U.S. and China," *International Herald Tribune*, January 12, 2009, http://www.iht.com/articles/2009/01/12/asia/beijing.php.
5. Figures for trade between China and the United States are not available for the period of 1979-1982. But Premier Wen Jiaobao used this figure for 1979 in his speech delivered at a luncheon hosted by the American Bankers Association in New York on 8 December 2003. See Wen Jiabao, "Work Together to Open a New Chapter in China-U.S. Trade and Economic Cooperation", December 8, 2003, http://www.for68.com/new/2006/7/wu1072 18362027760024180-0.htm.
6. In 2008, China's exports to the U.S. were US$252.3 billion (an increase of 8.4% over 2007) and China's imports from the U.S. were US$81.4 billion (an increase of 17.4% over 2007), with a trade surplus of US$170.9 billion. For details, see http://www.cacs.gov.cn/ zhongmeimaoyi/show.aspx?str1=&articleId=50011.

7. This figure comes from the U.S. Census Bureau, http://www.census.gov/foreign-trade/balance/c5700.html#2008.

8. Although Canada surpassed China in 2008 as the exporter to the United States, China caught up with Canada again in the first eight months of 2009. For details, see http://www.census.gov/foreign-trade/balance/index.html#C.

9. For a detailed analysis of this issue, see Wang Yong, *Zhongmei Jingmao Guanxi* (The Political Economy of China-U.S. Trade Relations) (Beijing: Zhongguo Shichang Chubanshe, 2007), pp. 123-136.

10. C. Fred Bergsten, Bates Gill, Nicholas R. Lardy, and Derek J. Mitchell, *China—The Balance Sheet: What the World Needs to Know Now about the Emerging Superpower* (Washington, D.C.: Public Affairs/IIE/CSIS, 2006), p. 10.

11. http://www.census.gov/foreign-trade/balance/c5700.html#2003.

12. For details, see http://www.safe.gov.cn; and http://finance.people.com.cn/.

13. For his original speech delivered on September 21, 2005 and some discussions of U.S.-China relations, see http://www.nbr.org/publications/analysis/pdf/vol16no4.pdf.

14. "Thirtieth Anniversary: A Message from Clark T. Randt, Jr., US Ambassador to China," *The China Business Review*, January 2009, http://www.chinabusinessreview.com/public/0901/randt.html

15. Lydia R. Goldfine, "A New U.S. Embassy—and a Chance to Look Back and to the Future," *The China Business Review*, January 2009, http://www.chinabusinessreview.com/ public/0901/last_page.html. The largest U.S. embassy in the world is the one in Bagdad. Known as "Fortress America," the embassy complex comprises 21 buildings on a 104 acre site—the size of Vatican City. It is 10 times as large as the US embassy in Beijing, and its staff is five times as many as in Beijing. For details, see http://en.wikipedia.org/wiki/Embassy_of_the_United_States_in_ Baghdad.

16. For a report on an American strategy for Asia written by Dan Blumenthal and Aaron Friedberg in January 2009, see http://www.aei.org/publications/filter.all,pubID. 29144/pub_detail.asp. For a report on Xinhuanet, see http://news.xinhuanet.com/ mil/2009-01/10/content_10634775.htm.

17. Barack Obama, "U.S. China Policy under the Obama Administration," *China Brief*, October 2008, p. 2.

18. For the full text of her confirmation speech, see http://www.observer.com/ 2009/politics/hillarys-secretary-state-speech.

19. Edward Wong, "Former Carter adviser calls for a 'G-2' between U.S. and China," *International Herald Tribune*, January 12, 2009, http://www.iht.com/articles/2009/ 01/12/asia/beijing.php.

20. With the exception of U.S. Ambassador to China, Jon Huntsman, who commented that China and the United States really are the "only two countries in the world that together can solve certain issues, whether they are clean energy, climate changes, regional security, or those dealing with the global economy." See Lee Davidson, "Huntsman pleased with Obama in China," *Deseret News*, November 17, 2009, http://www.deseretnews.com/article/705345147/Huntsman-pleased-with-Obama-in-China.html.

21. Hillary Clinton, "Security and Opportunity for the Twenty-first Century," *Foreign Affairs* (November/December 2007).

22. Hillary Rodham Clinton, "U.S.-Asia Relations: Indispensable to Our Future—Remarks at the Asia Society," New York, New York, February 13, 2009, http://www.state.gov/secretary/rm/2009a/02/117333.htm.

23. For a collection of reports on her Asia visit in Chinese, see http://news.sina. com.cn/z/xllfwyz/index.shtml.

24. http://news.sina.com.cn/c/2009-02-23/073217268886.shtml.

25. Jill Dougherty, "Clinton sets framework for U.S.-Asia relations," *CNN.com/Asia*, February 22, 2009, http://edition.cnn.com/2009/WORLD/asiapcf/02/22/clinton/index. ht ml.

26. Quoted in Keiji Nakatsuji, "Nancy Pelosi and Human Rights in China," *Limingguan International Studies* 12, no. 2 (December 1999), p. 12, http://www.ritsumei.ac.jp/ acd/cg/ir/college/bulletin/vol12-2/nakatsuji.pdf.

27. Robert Salladay, "Pelosi on China: A voice in the global wilderness?" *SF Gate*, June 29, 1998, http://www.sfgate.com/cgi-bin/article.cgi?file=/examiner/archive/1998/06/29/ NEWS2190.dtl.

28. Quoted in Keiji Nakatsuji, "Nancy Pelosi and Human Rights in China," *Limingguan International Studies* 12, no. 2 (December 1999), p. 21, http://www.ritsumei.ac.jp/acd/cg/ ir/college/bulletin/vol12-2/nakatsuji.pdf.

29. Robert Salladay, "Pelosi on China: A voice in the global wilderness?" *SF Gate*, June 29, 1998, http://www.sfgate.com/cgi-bin/article.cgi?file=/examiner/archive/1998/ 06/29/ NEWS2190.dtl.

30. Randeep Ramesh, Julian Borger, Angelique Chrisafis, Graham Keeley, Elana, Schor, and John Hooper, "Pelosi urges world to condemn China over crackdown," *Guardian.co.uk*, 22 March 2009, http://www.guardian.co.uk/world/2008/mar/22/tibet.china1.

31. "Pelosi calls on Bush to boycott Olympic opening ceremonies," April 1, 2008, *CNN*, http://edition.cnn.com/2008/WORLD/asiapcf/04/01/pelosi.olympics/index.html.

32. Li Zhaoxing, former Chinese ambassador to the United States and former foreign minister, accompanied her during the trip as her interpreter. http://www.cnsphoto.com/ NewsPhoto/ShowNewsDetail.asp?Flag=WN&ID=551065.

33. Elaine Kurtenbach, "Pelosi on China visit," *AP news*, March 25, 2009, http://www. google.com/hostednews/ap/article/ALeqM5hLcZ2jQ4mu4rd7XlB3hetiVn1qbAD98D5H 801.

34. For her meeting with President Hu Jintao, NPC Standing Committee Chairman Wu Bangguo, and Premier Wen Jiabao on May 27, 2009, see http://paper.people.com.cn/ rmrb/html/2009-05/28/content_262667.htm; http://paper.people.com.cn/rmrb/html/2009-05/28/content_262669.htm; http://paper.people.com.cn/rmrb/html/2009-05/28/content_2 62672.htm.

35. Walter Alarkon, "Pelosi to China kicking off recess Codels," March 24, 2009, *The Hill*, http://thehill.com/leading-the-news/pelosi-to-china-kicking-off-recess-codels-2009- 05-24.html.

36. Audra Ang, "Pelosi appeals for China's help on climate change," *AP news*, March 29, 2009, http://www.google.com/hostednews/ap/article/ALeqM5hLcZ2jQ4mu4rd7XlB3het iVn1qbAD98F32AG0.

37. http://www.whitehouse.gov/the_press_office/Remarks-by-the-President-at-the-US/C hina-Strategic-and-Economic-Dialogue/

38. In his interview with Reuters on November 9, 2009 before his Asia trip, Obama even characterized China as a "strategic partner." For the full text, see http://www.reuters. com/article/ObamaEconomy/idUSTRE5A902Q20091110?feedType=RSS&feedName=O bamaEconomy&virtualBrandChannel=10441.

39. http://www.whitehouse.gov/the_press_office/Remarks-by-the-President-at-the-US/C hina-Strategic-and-Economic-Dialogue/.

40. "No Time for the Dalai Lama: Obama is willing to anger China on tire tariffs but not on Tibet," *Wall Street Journal*, October 6, 2009, http://online.wsj.com/article/SB10001 424052748704471504574449420327844600.html.

41. "Barack Obama's letter to the Dalai Lama," July 24, 2008, http://www.scribd.com/ doc/4107352/Barack-Obamas-Letter-to-The-Dalai-Lama.

42. "McCain Meets Dalai Lama, Calls On China To Release Prisoners," http://www. dalailama.com/news.283.htm.

43. http://timesofindia.indiatimes.com/world/us/Obama-pilloried-over-ducking-Dalai-Lama-to-appease-China/articleshow/5092820.cms

44. http://www.voanews.com/english/archive/2009-09/2009-09-14.

45. http://www.dalailama.com/news.456.htm.

46. http://online.wsj.com/article/.

47. http://www.nytimes.com/2008/07/04/world/americas/04iht-prexy.1.14235707.html.

48. http://www.democraticunderground.com/.

49. For the original English text, see http://www.whitehouse.gov/blog/2009/11/16/full-video-and-photos-presidents-town-hall-shanghai. For the Chinese translation, see http://www.news.cn/world/obama/.

50. For the English version, see http://www.whitehouse.gov/the-press-office/us-china-joint-statement. For the Chinese text, see http://news.xinhuanet.com/world/2009-11/17/content_12475620.htm.

51. http://content.usatoday.com/communities/theoval/post/2009/11/.

52. For the text of the interview, see http://www.reuters.com/.

53. He studied Chinese at college and allegedly taught Chinese for three or four years. He obtained a B.A. in government and Asian studies from Dartmouth College in 1983 and an M.A. in international economics and East Asian studies from Johns Hopkins University in 1985. See "Lois Romano Interviews Treasury Secretary Timothy Geithner" (May 22, 2009), *The Washington Post*, May 25, 2009, http://www.washingtonpost.com/wp-dyn/content/article/2009/05/25/AR2009052501246_5.html?sid=ST2009052502536.

54. "Finance Committee Questions for the Record," United States Senate Committee on Finance, Hearing on Confirmation of Mr. Timothy F. Geithner to be Secretary of the U.S. Department of Treasury, January 21, 2009, pp. 81, 94.

55. Jackie Calmes, "Geithner Hints at Harder Line on China Trade," *The New York Times*, January 22, 2009. http://www.nytimes.com/2009/01/23/.

56. Graeme Wearden, "Obama team accuses China of manipulating its currency," *Guardian.co.uk*, January 23, 2009, http://www.guardian.co.uk/business/2009/jan/23/china-us-dollar-yuan.

57. Paul Maidment, "China, New U.S. Administration Make Yuan First Row," *Forbes*, January 23, 2009, http://www.forbes.com/2009/01/23/china-currency-row-markets-economy-cx_pm_0123yuan.html.

58. "China denies that it manipulates its currency-AFP," *Reuters*, January 23, 2009, http://www.reuters.com/article/usDollarRpt/idUSN2335706820090123.

59. "China dismisses US currency accusation," *China Daily*, January 24, 2009, http://www.chinadaily.com.cn/china/2009-01/24/content_7428018.htm.

60. Jackie Calmes, "Geithner Prepares to Meet With Chinese Leaders," *The New York Times*, May 27, 2009. http://www.nytimes.com/2009/05/28/.

61. "Statement by Treasury Secretary Timothy Geithner on Release of Semi-Annual Report to Congress on International Economic and Exchange Rate Policies," April 15, 2009, http://www.ustreas.gov/press/releases/tg90.htm.

62. "Statement by Treasury Secretary Timothy Geithner on Release of Semi-Annual Report to Congress on International Economic and Exchange Rate Policies," April 15, 2009, http://www.ustreas.gov/press/releases/tg90.htm.

63. "Update 3-U.S. again declines to brand China FX manipulator," *Reuters*, April 15, 2009, http://www.reuters.com/article/usDollarRpt/idUSN1551870920090415.

64. Zhou Xiaochuan, "Guanyu Gaige Guoji Huobi Tixi de Sikao" ("Some thoughts on reforming the international monetary system") March 24, 2009, http://news.xinhuanet.com/fortune/2009-03/24/content_11060507.htm.

65. "Geithner says 'quite open' to China's SDR proposal," *Reuters*, March 25, 2009, http://www.reuters.com/article/businessNews/idUSTRE52O43O20090325.

66. Ambrose Evans-Pritchard, "A world currency moves nearer after Tim Geithner's slip," *Telegraph.co.uk*, March 27, 2009, http://www.telegraph.co.uk/finance/economics/5051075/A-world-currency-moves-nearer-after-Tim-Geithners-slip.html.

67. "Zhou Xiaochuan breaths fire into US Treasury markets with bold proposal: SDRs and the fall of the Dollar as global reserve," *China Awakes*, March 26, 2009, http://chinawakes.blogspot.com/2009/03/zhou-xiaochuan-breaths-fire-into-us.html.

68. Office of International Affairs, U.S. Department of the Treasury, "Report to Congress on International Economic and Exchange Rate Policies," October 15, 2009, p. 2. http://www.treasury.gov/offices/international-affairs/economic-exchange-rates/pdf/FX%20Report%20FINAL%20October%2015%202009.pdf.

69. Office of International Affairs, U.S. Department of the Treasury, "Report to Congress on International Economic and Exchange Rate Policies," October 15, 2009, p. 13. http://www.treasury.gov/offices/international-affairs/economic-exchange-rates/pdf/FX%20Report%20FINAL%20October%2015%202009.pdf.

70. U.S. Department of Treasury (http://treas.gov/tic/mfh.txt).

71. http://finance.ifeng.com/roll/20091110/1447917.shtml.

72. http://cn.reuters.com/article/companyNewsEng/idCNN0512983120091105.

73. http://finance.ifeng.com/roll/20091110/1447917.shtml.

74. http://www.chinataiwan.org/english/specialreports/sr/Celebrating/3/4/200908/

75. http://www.census.gov/foreign-trade/balance/index.html.

76. Vaudine England, "Who's right in South China Sea spat?" *BBC*, March 13, 2009, http://news.bbc.co.uk/2/hi/asia-pacific/7941425.stm.

77. "United Nations Convention on the Law of the Sea" December 10, 1982, http://www.un.org/Depts/los/convention_agreements/texts/unclos/unclos_e.pdf.

78. Ibid.

79. "中华人民共和国专属经济区和大陆架法," June 26, 1998, http://www.law-lib.com/law/law_view.asp?id=384.

80. Vaudine England, "Who's right in South China Sea spat?" *BBC*, March 13, 2009, http://news.bbc.co.uk/2/hi/asia-pacific/7941425.stm.

81. "USNS Impeccable (T-AGOS-23)," http://en.wikipedia.org/wiki/USNS_Impeccable (T-AGOS-23).

82. Hans M. Kristensen, "US-Chinese Anti-Submarine Cat and Mouse Game in South China Sea," *FAS Strategic Security Blog*, March 10, 2009, http://www.fas.org/blog/ssp/2009/03/incident.php.

83. Frank Ching, "China shelves dispute over right of passage," *The Japan Times*, March 27, 2009, http://search.japantimes.co.jp/print/eo20090327fc.html.

84. For a Chinese text, see http://chn.chinamil.com.cn/xwpdxw/2009-10/29/content _4070563.htm.

85. Ibid.

86. Ibid.

87. For the English version, see http://www.whitehouse.gov/the-press-office/us-china-joint-statement. For the Chinese text, see http://news.xinhuanet.com/world/2009-11/17/content_12475620.htm.

88. Joseph J. Schatz, "Duet with the Dragon: What's next in U.S.-China Relationship?" *CQ Today Online News*, June 20, 2009, http://www.cqpolitics.com/wmspage.cfm?docID=news-000003149630&cpage=1.

PART 4

Contemporary Issues
in China-U.S. Relations

Chapter 13

Managing the Cross-Taiwan Strait Military Conflicts in a New Era of Political Reconciliation

You Ji

The regime change in Taipei in May 2008 has exerted major impact on the cross-Strait relations. With the resumption of high level official contacts and exchange of good-will between top leaders the overall tension has eased substantially. However, in the military area force deployment, posture and readiness of the two sides have not yet been adjusted to fit in the changed political environment cross the Taiwan Strait. On the mainland side, the numbers of missiles have remained steady, although no further increase has been recorded.[1] The People's Liberation Army's budget is rising steeply and its preparation for war accelerates steadily. Taipei likewise continues to identify the mainland as a military threat and calls for Washington to sell more advanced weapons, e.g., F-16 C/D, as a symbol of US defense commitment to defending Taiwan.[2] There should not be any surprise to this seemingly discrepancy between deepening political rapprochement and lingering military face-off. After all hostility of the Taiwanese toward Beijing remains strong.[3] Mistrust toward Beijing runs deep under whichever government in Taipei, the Nationalist Party (KMT) or the Democratic Progressive Party (DDP). And Beijing is as vigilant as at any time about the prospects of the pro-independence forces returning to power in the future. The KMT's poor performance in the local election in December 2009 further alarmed Beijing. Military deterrence is therefore still regarded as the last line of defense against Taiwan's movement toward *de jure* independence.

On the other hand, leaders in Beijing and Taipei have introduced changes in their basic approach toward the function of military in managing Taiwan conflict. They start to see that peace does not have to be maintained through threat of war, despite the existent state of war between them.[4] Hu Jintao's call for building military security trust and Ma Ying-jeou's revision of Taiwan's defense strategy—from Chen Shuibian's defensive office (境外决战) to his defensive defense (专守防御), conveyed an idea that their search of peace can be institutionalized as a better instrument of security making than the efforts to seek military superiority against each other. This spirit of peace has been captured by U.S. President Barack Obama, who put forward a new concept of promoting healthy military balance across the Taiwan Strait as a way of crisis prevention.[5] Indeed war avoidance has been a lasting and largest common denominator in the tripartite relations between Beijing, Washington and Taipei in the last thirty years. Based on analysis of the sea changes in the Taiwan Strait since May 2009, this paper will evaluate Obama's concept of healthy balance and argues that it actually addresses the fundamental political causes of tension across the Taiwan Strait. Given the rapid rise of Chinese economic and military power and overburdened US global commitment, a parity-based military balance is too dynamic to be maintained. Therefore, Washington has to explore a new approach to deal with the inevitable change in the balance gradually titling in favor of Beijing. The word *healthy* is really about employing a comprehensive mechanism of stability building in the region. While military deterrence is clearly crucial, it would no longer be employed as the only and dominant means to deter emergence of any crisis situations. This certainly serves the best interests of both Beijing and Taipei, each being the relatively weaker military in the tripartite relations with America.

INTERPRETING THE MEANING OF HEALTHY MILITARY BALANCE

Obama's new approach to conflict management is more sensible than the previous administrations' propensity to rely emphatically on military power for achieving political and diplomatic objectives.[6] The latter orientation has proved both costly and ineffective, as far as the Taiwan conflict is concerned. For instance, Washington's dispatch of two aircraft carrier groups to the Taiwan Strait in 1996 not only flared up the tension there but also served as a catalyst for the PLA Navy to strengthen its sea power that has facilitated a naval build up in the region.[7] It is true that the United States has the unparalleled defense capabilities with its military budget exceeding half of the world total. Yet this dose not prevent prominent American security specialists from questioning whether the US has been guaranteed with a satisfactory level of safety because of its military superiority.[8] This is probably the biggest irony in the relations between power and security in human history.

Obama has seen the problem in a dialectical manner and addressed it with a new policy guidance for the employment of force when exerting US global leadership.[9] His search of a healthy balance is to respond to security challenges not solely from heightened military intimidation, as shown by his handling of North Korea's nuclear test.[10] War option is made the last resort to deal with conflicts. Together with his advocacy of exercising "smart power" in diplomacy, a better beginning of US foreign affairs has been set. Now the question is whether Obama's new leadership style can be sustained in the midst of numerous security threats that historically induce the superior powers to consider use of military pressure as a convenient solution to a crisis. Aggressive realism normally finds its way more easily to the decision process of major powers than other IR schools of thought.[11]

The concept of healthy military balance was raised at a time when China's military transformation has made substantial headways. Obama's early mastery of diplomacy is reflected by his choice not to advocate a "security dilemma" response to a dynamic process of military rebalancing across the Taiwan Strait. It may have become part of US hedging strategy for managing inevitable military superiority of the PLA vis-à-vis the Taiwanese military. Here the key word *healthy* is really about a cost-effective, flexible and comprehensive way to meet the challenge. Clearly the core of the concept is politics, not the order of battle. Military capabilities in balance or otherwise do not cause war, politics does. In the Taiwan Strait this politics is embedded in a tripartite consensus between Washington, Beijing and Taipei that war has to be averted. Such a consensus has paved the way for a strategic framework, namely the One-China principle, to be established since the late 1970s. For the time being this principle is practically more of a tacit agreement by Beijing, Washington and Taipei on crisis avoidance than one of sovereignty and geography.[12] What has prevented war from occurring is not the issue of military balance but the three-way commitment to this framework, although differently defined by the parties involved. The reason of heightened cross-Strait tension in the eight-year DDP administration between 2000 and 2008 was largely due to the relinquishment of this framework by one party. Had *de jure* independence become irreversible, it would have been impossible to expect inaction of the PLA, even if it is militarily inferior to combined military strength of the other two parties. Political stake is simply too high for Beijing, as it is related to the very issue of CCP legitimacy to rule the country.[13] Indeed, when political equilibrium is upset, military balancing becomes a zero-sum game.

Further to prove the point, there has never been any military balance across the Taiwan Strait. Taiwan's military alone has never deterred the mainland in the past. It is US commitment to defending Taiwan that has prevented Beijing from taking any decisive actions against the island.[14] At the same time, although the mainland has clearly surpassed Taiwan in force capabilities today, the balance sheet is not complete without counting superior US power in the equation. Short of crisis it is logical to compare the mainland and the island with the existing order of battle that aggressively favors the PLA. Yet in times of war US involvement has to be factored in and this may significantly shift the balance against the PLA. At that time even though the US would not dispatch defense personnel to the Strait, it would provide crucial C4IRS information and other assistance to the Taiwanese military that would substantially increase the difficulties of PLA operations and cause more PLA casualties.[15] The fact of the PLA as a weaker power vis-à-vis the US will not change for a long time to come. One-to-one calculation (the mainland vis-à-vis Taiwan) does not make complete sense in a tripartite relationship.

Politics is thus the main driver in defining the nature of the interaction among the three parties. The centre of cross-Strait tension has been the seesaw battle between reunification and independence. The current tripartite agreement on maintaining the status quo has temporarily reduced the Strait tension, although far from removing the cause of it. Under the circumstances, military balance does matter but it services the political will of the leaders in the three capitals. When the political sense of crisis prevention is absent, military in balance or not does not sway the political leaders over crucial matters. Newly disclosed official document revealed that Mao Zedong indeed had a plan to capture Jingmen in 1958, despite the overwhelming combined military superiority of the US and Taiwan.[16] In office Lee Denghui and Chen Shuibian continued to challenge the mainland's vital interests all the while the Strait military balance strongly tilted in favor of the PLA. Apparently political leaders do not set their key agenda according to mathematical comparison of military strength. Available military capabilities are only one of the factors to weigh against their strategic calculus.

In addition military balance is a dynamic process in which change in comprehensive national power sets the long term trend of balancing. It is a simple and basic understanding that no matter how hard Taiwan tries to keep power parity in the Strait, it would be in vain, being over a dozen times inferior in terms of total GDP and military budget, to name only two relevant factors. In one or two decades this inferiority will become overwhelming, as Taiwan's military modernization remains somewhat stagnant, while the PLA's transformation enters the fast track of development.[17] Even the absolute military superiority of the US vis-à-vis China will gradually be reduced to one in relative terms, making it progressively harder for Washington to contemplate military involvement in a Taiwan war. The human, economic and military cost will one day become unbearable when the PLA achieves creditable MAD (mutually assured destruction) capabilities in two decades. By 2030 the PLA will operate over a dozen nuclear submarines. Among them are six strategic nuclear submarines that can launch an estimated number of 72 *Jiuliang* intercontinental nuclear missiles. With each missile carrying three warheads, a total of 216 war heads can reach most of North America. China's deterrence level vis-à-vis the US will reach a new height, although it is still inferior in overall military power. As the stake elevates, the likelihood of direct Sino-U.S. military confrontation will shrink. Obama's thesis of healthy balance takes a long-term view of changing power parity in the tripartite relationship. It is certainly a more sensible response to changing dynamics of balancing.

First, Washington's preference for stabilizing the status quo has been in agreement with Beijing's mid-term agenda of opposing *de jure* independence and resonated with the main thrust of Taipei's current mainland policy of *Three No-ism* (no independence, no reunification and no provocation of conflict). The lost strategic framework has been restored. This is conducive to the reconstruction of a healthy military balance based on a common ground of *de-warization* (去战争化) in the Strait. Without this political foundation a war is a constant possibility even if the balance is in sharp favor of any of the parties. And if this common ground is upheld, Beijing would acquiesce the fact that

China is divided, even when it takes substantial superiority vis-à-vis Taipei. Therefore, politics is the linkage (☐) and military balance is subordinate (☐).

Secondly, if healthy military balance indeed aims at war prevention, it would guide the three parties to make joint efforts of security building in the Strait: through peace dialogue, political trust measures, economic integration and codified military behavior. Now all these have been jointly pursued by Beijing and Taipei after the regime change in Taiwan. In this regard their search of parity of military power is less pronounced than their pursuit of a peace commitment. If the current momentum of tension reduction across the Strait continues, this peace commitment would be institutionalized in due time.[18]

Thirdly, balance of power is always relative. Efforts to maintain this balance connote an imperative to engage in an open-ended arms race that benefits no party, especially the weakest. The thesis of healthy military balance promotes a smart balancing process to hedge against the worst results of a balance broken up, which is a kind of inevitable between Beijing and Taipei in the short run (the mainland's clear superiority against Taiwan) and between Beijing and Washington in the long run (America's reduced superiority against China). In Asia the U.S. will maintain military dominance against any rising hostile powers. Today it has steadily transferred significant capabilities from the Atlantic to the Pacific Ocean through a vigorous force redeployment program. Strategic nuclear submarines, strategic bombers and an additional carrier battle group are now deployed in the West Pacific with a clear aim to hedge against Chinese military growth. On the other hand, the U.S. would not rely exclusively on adding military capabilities to balance rising powers in the region. As America's economic power will continue to decline relative to that of China, an action-reaction spiral of arms build-up will not be regarded as conducive to US strategic interests. In the Taiwan Strait this would hurt the party mostly in need to be protected—Taiwan. Under the circumstances, America would address the issue of emerging imbalance with more means than one: soliciting positive security cooperation with China; disciplining Taiwan's excessive leaning either toward independence or reunification; enhancing alliance arrangement with regional powers against a Taiwan crisis and so on.

In summary under the assumptions mentioned above, Washington, Beijing and Taipei have their common stake in seeking mutually beneficial arrangement to address the issue of military balance across the Taiwan Strait. The way to realize it is through politics, not simply through adding more weapons systems.

WASHINGTON COMING TO ITS SENSES

As far as Chinese strategists are concerned, the twenty-first century will remain a U.S. century in terms of military power, even when China's rise in military power will be sustained far into the future.[19] In the meantime, the China challenge to the U.S. is not that the PRC would challenge U.S. global leadership with accumulated power but its ability to weaken America's absolute military dominance in the Far East. When the PLA becomes progressively more capable of inflicting heavy damage to US troops within the second islands chain in the West Pacific, Pentagon would not be confident that it would launch a Kosovo type of air and missile strike against China if it gets involved in a Taiwan war. This is especially true when China acquires reliable MAD (mutually assured destruction) capabilities vis-à-vis the US in about two decades, as mentioned earlier. For instance, China understands well that the U.S. has a time-honored policy of not having an all-out war with another nuclear power that has reliable second strike capability. The relevance of the thesis of healthy military balance can be seen by the PLA's Major General Peng Guangqian's argument that even the U.S. could destroy China a hundred times with its superior nuclear power, China could claim victory if the PLA could destroy America once.[20] As the capability gap between America and China is being narrowed, Washington's ability to shape regional order and define the status quo in the Taiwan Strait will relatively decline. Obma's *healthy balance* may indicate Washington's recognition of this power shifting. His new Asia policy, as explained by Deputy Secretary of State Steinberg's vocabulary of *strategic reassurance*, reflects Washington's new thinking on security-making in the region: relying on allies to maintain regional stability and solicit Chinese support to manage regional security challenge.[21]

Healthy balance and *strategic reassurance* are supplementary to each other in informing Obama's strategy to consolidate US leadership in world and Strait affairs. It reflects a dialectical balancing choice: America's superior military strength presents it with the primary leverage to extract Beijing's cooperation, but any excessive use of it would back both in a corner and backlash against US strategic interests. The concept of creating a healthy balance vis-à-vis China guides Washington to rank its hierarchical order of strategic interests properly. Concretely, this raises a question of why the US gets into a major war with another nuclear power when Washington and Beijing share political objective of maintaining the status quo in the Strait. After all Taiwan is not US core national interest in its global pursuits. Chinese strategists argue strongly that talking about a Sino-US war over Taiwan is to put a cart before the horse because Beijing does not have any plan to occupy Taiwan by force. The only source of war is Taiwan's move toward *de jure* independence.[22] Yet this may well be contained when China and the US converge on a joint management agenda against Taiwan's *de jure* independence attempts. Therefore, a Taiwan war is basically a fake topic.[23]

Related to this is a question on the Taiwan Relations Act (TRA) promulgated in 1979 to convince Beijing that the US had the capability and intent to frustrate its unprovoked attack against Taiwan. Now the unpleasant truth to the US seems to be that the TRA may have to be invoked more likely because Beijing is forced to respond Taiwan's declared independence. Then a few more questions can be asked: whether the TRA is meant to protect Taiwan from a unprovoked PLA attack or protect Taiwan's *de jure* independence that is not in Washington's strategic interests. And if the latter is the case, the question is whether Washington has opened the window for the TRA to be manipulated because it is almost a consensus in the U.S. that the possibility of Beijing launching an unprovoked attack on Taiwan remains extremely low.[24]

Along this line of argument, as pointed out by Ted Galen Carpenter, the Taiwan problem highlights the danger inherent in Washington's habit of making ill-advised security commitments to small, vulnerable client states that are not crucial to America's own security and well being. In the case of Taiwan, such an obligation could lead to armed confrontation between the two nuclear powers.[25] Promoting healthy military balance through a two-pronged strategy of security cooperation and smart force balancing can address the inadequacies of traditional US reliance on hard military balancing. Although Washington has been ambiguous about whether it would get involved in a Taiwan war (assist Taiwan's defense), it has all along been unambiguous about preventing a war in the Taiwan Strait. Given the common view that a Taiwan war is most likely triggered by actions of *de jure* independence than those of forced reunification, taking political measures against the former would help the US resolve the dilemma of having to get in an unwanted war ("damned if you do, and damned if you don't"). This is the key to understanding the meaning of smart balancing.

CHINA'S STAKE AND NEW INITIATIVES

Obama's advocacy of healthy military balance across the Taiwan Strait will broaden the space for Sino-U.S. cooperation for stabilizing the status quo in the Strait. Interestingly China's US specialists have largely overlooked this thesis. Taiwan has been a key issue breeding security concerns and mistrust between Washington and Beijing. Each side has been militarily alert for a confrontation. China's decision to accelerate preparation for military struggle in 1999 particularly factored in US intervention against the PLA's action against Taipei's declared independence.[26] In the last decade or so the PLA has been developing asymmetry warfare measures against superior US naval power in the West Pacific, in a form of accumulating relatively stronger capabilities in a limited period of time, in a limited geographic space and over limited campaign objectives. Politically, this anti-independence war is a war Beijing has to fight, with or without any military superiority. Under the situation where the enemy is more powerful, the PLA will have to design smart methods of engagement that would both avoid uncontrollable escalation and fulfill the basic political requirment/objective, such as answering the public pressure at home. This means the PLA will not launch massive amphibious operations to capture Taiwan for the purpose of reunification but aim at forcing the authorities in Taiwan to back down from *de jure* independence.[27]

This politics-led and reaction-based military plan is in agreement with Obama's concept of healthy balance across the Taiwan Strait: the PLA's force build-up in China's coastal flank, including missile deployment, is projected for maintaining the status quo in Taipei rather than undermining the strategic interests of America. In fact China does not seek to challenge US absolute military dominance in the region, as proclaimed by a senior PLA officer in the Strategic Missile Force.[28] Its overall arms inferiority vis-à-vis the U.S. will not change for a long time to come. Yet in protecting its vital national interests, especially in the case of an anti-independence war, it has to have effective capabilities to reduce that absolute superiority to relative superiority, as mentioned earlier. Given the huge capability gap between the two militaries, there is still a long way for the PLA to go before it feels less deterred by US military when protecting China's territorial integrity. This mindset probably reveals an important aspect of China's defense policy, that is, in line with a non-confrontational diplomacy vis-à-vis America, the PLA's overall posture toward the US is defensive oriented. If the essence of healthy balance is to place political measures of crisis prevention above impulse of force employment, it certainly well serves the PLA's interests.

During the eight years of the DDP in power in Taipei between 2000 and 2008, Beijing adopted a two-pronged strategy against *de jure* independence: promoting economic integration and people-to-people exchange, and war preparation. Although the latter was much in the background and was considered as the last resort against a worst case scenario, it had progressively gained centrality toward the end of Chen Shuibian regime that obviously accelerated the pace of *de jure* independence. Yet Beijing realized the high cost of using heavy-handed means against Taiwan independence. The military budget had to increase persistently at a time domestic development requires urgent inputs. Threat of force also contributes Taiwan's negative feelings against the mainlanders. If conditions permit, Beijing would like to see diplomacy as the best mechanism of crisis management in the Taiwan Strait. To this end China initiated cooperation with Washington against the DDP's initiatives of *de jure* independence, such as its UN referendum in 2007/08.[29] This approach turned out to be most cost-effective, allowing Beijing not to use overtly hash language against Taipei that may be played into the hands of Chen Shuibian. In broad terms Sino-U.S. cooperation against *de jure* independence is priced on Beijing's pledge not to challenge US global leadership and exclude US from regional affairs. And in doing so Beijing has to help Washington in dealing with other regional security challenges, such as the nuclear standoff in the Korean Peninsula. Yet considering the importance of the Taiwan issue to the Chinese government, this is a relatively small price to pay.

Sino-U.S. cooperation on maintaining the status quo in the Taiwan Strait has been made easier by Ma Yinjeou's election victory in March 2008. As far as the bottom line of Beijing's Taiwan policy is concerned, which is set around anti-*de jure* independence, Beijing has achieved a decisive victory overnight and almost without a fight. Ma's *Three-Noism* (no reunification, no independence and no armed conflict) matches Beijing's priority of war aversion in the Strait. The regime change in Taipei created a pre-condition for Beijing to concentrate on domestic development. If Ma has a second term in office, Beijing will win eight more years for its strategic period of opportunity. This is crucial for Beijing to acquire true material power that facilitates China's rise. By the end of this precious period of peace, the PLA's transformation will be greatly consolidated in a fast track of development.[30]

Strategically, Hu and Ma have jointly created opportunity for the cross-Strait relations to be deprived of the trigger of war. When Hu made the suggestion to Taiwan to end the state of hostility across the Taiwan Strait in the 17th Party Congress in 2007, his idea was not considered as feasible. Now Ma's administration has reciprocated Hu by putting forward similar ideas. With tension gradually eased in the Strait a trend of *de-warization* between Beijing and Taipei is in the making with profound impact on Sino-U.S. relations. As Taiwan is the only likely spot for the two nuclear powers to fight a war against each other, peace in the Taiwan Strait would help China and America free themselves from an immediate cause of armed confrontation. In turn if the cross-Strait relations are *de-warized*, this would contribute to de-militarization of Sino-US relations. Then Beijing and Washington will have much larger space for security cooperation in regional and global affairs.

More strategically, demilitarized Sino-U.S. relations will serve as a good platform for Obama's idea of healthy military balance to be practiced. Declared political commitment to reducing tension would lessen China's worry about being the inferior party in the equation of military power. And lack of a substantial reason to go to war with China would also address Washington's concern of China's rise in military capabilities. The hedging strategy would oblige Pentagon to keep a good level of general military superiority over the PLA. However, the US effort to maintain force readiness would be short of specific battlefield application against the Chinese. Although there are other sources of bilateral conflicts that are of a military nature, these clash of interests outside the Taiwan Strait may not be as rigid as that related to the Taiwan situation. In a way a healthy military balance paves the way for the three parties to project their long term relations in a manner of reconciliation. This is now happening between the mainlanders and the Taiwanese.

HEALTHY CROSS-STRAIT MILITARY INTERACTION

Cross-Strait military balance has forever gone beyond the stage of relative parity. The PLA's armament superiority over the Nationalist Army has been transformed from a quantitative nature to a qualitative nature. This superiority will become overwhelming in a not too distant future. However, this does not mean worsening security situation in the Strait, especially when an anti-independence party is in power in Taipei. While healthy military balance based on political reconciliation cannot be literally achieved any time soon, non-hostile military interaction can, driven by the emerging bilateral consensus on *de-warization*.[31] Hu has uplifted Beijing's initiative of promoting status quo-based stability in the Strait since Taiwan's regime change in May 2008. The difference before that point of time and now is that Hu's political line of peace development has been transformed from being a pragmatic means of tension reduction to being an end in itself. Despite all the reluctance and domestic constraints, Ma has embraced Beijing's proposal to construct a political foundation for a peace accord across the Strait.[32] As the current momentum of all round cross-Strait exchange continues, the peace consensus of Hu Jintao and Ma Yingjeou would have a chance of being translated into phased, positive military interaction. The PLA participation in the conference *60 Years of Cross-Strait Relations* in Taipei in November 2009 heralded further personnel contacts between the two militaries, and even at more senior levels.[33] Over time the mutual fear of war and the willingness to avoid it could be institutionalized to create mutually abiding rules of the game governing security interaction between the two sides. In the last year or so specific measures have been agreed upon to facilitate construction of mutual trust. The following can be the proof of the progress made in security cooperation in the Taiwan Strait. On the part of the mainland, since 1996 the PLA has occasionally crossed the median line of the Taiwan Strait as an expression of Chinese ownership of the Taiwan island. Indirectly the act has served to challenge the pro-independence authorities in Taipei. Since May 2008, the PLA aircraft and warships have followed the self-imposed restriction not to cross the line. This mainland's concrete gesture of tension reduction has been reciprocated by the Taiwanese military that has taken similar measures. For instance, Taipei's defense authority decided to change the theme of the annual "Zhongxin Military Exercise" in 2009 from countering the PLA's amphibious attack to "responding sudden domestic events."[34]

The gradual accumulation of political trust would be preliminary conditions for setting up a stage for future military contacts, as proposed by leaders in Beijing and Taipei.[35] Today the two militaries are exploring ways to conduct military confidence building measures, something long thought as unattainable.[36] It is happening at a pace beyond our initial imagination. Now a roadmap is being drawn at the operational levels: semi-official and even official contacts at the working levels have become routine, although both sides deliberately keep silent about these activities. According to the spokesman of the Taiwan Affairs Office in Beijing, the contact can be started from retired senior military officers entrusted by decision-making circles, followed by think-tank strategists with access to top leaders and then by active serving researchers from military institutions. This would lead to official negotiation on the ending of the state of war across the Taiwan Strait.[37] In the various workshops in Beijing and Taipei calls for establishment of summit communication channels are frequently mentioned by scholars from both sides, supported by officials responsible for the Strait affairs and military personnel.[38]

To bring about an end to the state of hostility does not need to be based on absolute military balance; it is the result of political reassurance, the core of healthy military balance. Ironically, reconciliation can be reached relatively more easily when military balance is shifting in China's favor because the cause of war lies more likely in *de jure* independence, not in reunification. Manageable PLA superiority can be seen as effective deterrence against the war in the Strait. The cross-Strait interaction has moved in this direction since May 2008. In the meantime other positive measures have been put in place to consolidate the trend of detent, such as deepening economic integration, enhanced human contacts and formal agreements in managing administrative matters concerning cross-Strait affairs.

THE PROSPECTS

Ma's new leadership presents both challenges and opportunities to Beijing. The list of challenges is long: Ma's self-claimed new Taiwanese identity; the issue of international space; anti-CCP mentality; pro-US stance and the emphasis on being president of the all people (taking care of the concerns of the DPP at the expenses of the mainland's interests). However, benefits to Beijing of Ma as Taiwan's leader far exceed challenges. The most valuable one is the removal of immediate war planning in Beijing's top military command in the next four or eight years. For the second time in PLA history since the reforms China has broken away from a sub-war state of affairs (临战状态). As a result the leadership can really concentrate on domestic priorities. And the PLA can implement force transformation in a more coordinated way, as it does not need to add emergent capabilities for a worst scenario in the Strait, capabilities that may become obsolete very soon. As such Ma's challenge is challenge from new opportunities, not opportunities from crisis (危机).

Under the circumstances, it can be expected that Beijing will make further concessions to Taiwan. Politically, trimming missile deployment or providing Taiwan with reasonable international space will be the major items for bilateral negotiations in the years to come.[39] In the short run these concessions would be structured into assisting the KMT to win the next presidential election in 2012. In the long run Beijing seems to be willing to gamble on Ma's inherent Chineseness that may help produce disguised and future policies conducive to eventual reunification. The gambles are concretely reflected by Beijing's shelving of reunification from its current work agenda; dropping "one country, two systems" from its official vocabulary vis-à-vis Taiwan; acquiescing the ROC as the symbol of the status quo; and becoming economically more generous as a way of "depending on Taiwan people" and helping the GMD to win the next election.

Ma's termination of an officially sponsored creeping *de jure* independence movement provides new options for Beijing. Despite all the rhetoric against reunification, Ma's de-de-Sinification (去一去中国化) is a major contribution to the course of eventual reunification. And the framework of the three-Nos does service Beijing's immediate purpose of regime consolidation, e.g., in the lead-up to the next round of leadership succession. Therefore, whatever concessions Beijing has made in adopting a softy policy toward Taipei's new leadership can be said as a true bargain.

On the other hand, behind the Oliver branch is Hu's stick that is made harder with China's rising economic and military power. Despite all signs of reconciliation, two things will not change in Beijing's overall Taiwan policy. First, the military pressure against independence will not be eased. General Ma Xiaotian announced this to the international audience in the Singapore Shangri-la security dialogue on 30 May 2008.[40] On the contrary deterrence will be more pronounced. The difference is that war preparation is more based on general capability enhancement and caters for the PLA's long term transformation rather than focusing on quickly acquiring specific weaponry to preempt an emergency scenario, most likely in the Taiwan Strait. Secondly, Beijing will carefully guard against any attempts by the other side to enlarge international diplomatic space, although Taipei's call for cease-fire on diplomatic recognition is seriously considered on a case-by-case basis. On the whole Beijing's Taiwan policy will be more fine-tuned to individual issues, a departure from a propensity to exercise blanket opposition.

Therefore the seesaw battle will continue. However, this is no longer a struggle dominated by military calculus, a development in line of Obama's concept of healthy military balance across the Taiwan Strait. If the reconciliation is sustained, gradually the conditions for an in interim agreement on the three-Nos may become ripe. From there the foundation for a peace agreement may be constructed. If all goes well, a question naturally arises: will over time a confederate structure emerge as the ultimate solution to the Taiwan impasse? Certainly in the meantime there may arise crisis situations that may sabotage the current cross-Strait détente. The KMT defeat in the local election in December 2009 and its loss of over a million votes as compared with the election in 2008 magnified the possibility of the DDP returning to power, something Beijing has never lost sight of. This is why the three parties in the Taiwan conflict, Beijing, Washington and Taipei, should seize the current positive moment to consolidate the gains in the cross-Strait relations.

NOTES

1. Richard C. Bush, "Cross-Strait Relations Improve; China Still Deploys Missiles," *China Times,* June 27, 2009.
2. For instance, Ma Ying-jeou has repeatedly identified the mainland as Taiwan's only threat and expressed resolve to build strong military capabilities for self defense. His speech to the conference to mark 30th anniversary of the Taiwan Relations Act, organized by the Brookings Institution and the National Chengchi University, Taipei, May 2009.
3. According to a news poll of 1738 high school and university students in July 2009, 83 percent of them identified China as the most unfriendly country, although 79 percent of them ranked China as most important to Taiwan economically, second only to the U.S. "China tops list of unfriendly countries despite improved relations," *China Post*, July 15, 2009.
4. This has been expressed by Hu Jintao's 6-point policy announcement on December 31, 2008. For the first time a Chinese leader suggested to the Taiwanese leader to initiate direct military contacts for the sake of avoiding unwanted clashes (the 6th point of Hu's speech).
5. On this concept, see a roundtable discussion by Robert Sutter and others, "Defining a Healthy Balance across the Taiwan Strait," *Asia Policy*, no. 8, July 2009, pp. 3-40.
6. On this propensity, see Amitav Acharya, "The Bush Doctrine and Asian Regional Order: the Perils and Pitfalls of Preemption," *Asian Perspective*, vol. 27, no. 4, 2003; Monten, J. "The Roots of the Bush Doctrine," *International Security*, vol. 29, no.4, 2005.
7. The event stimulated the Chinese naval commanders to target the carrier groups as the object of attack in a Taiwan war and move to acquire new capabilities in an unusually

fast manner. See You Ji, "China's Naval Strategy and Transformation," in Lawrence S. Prabhakar, Joshua Ho & Sam Bateman, *(*eds.*) The Evolving Maritime Balance of Power in The Asia-Pacific*, Singapore, World Scientific Publisher, 2006, pp. 71-94.

8. Christopher A. Preble, *The Power Problem: How American Military Dominance Makes Us Less Safe, Less Prosperous, and Less Free* (Ithaca, NY: Cornell University Press, 2009).

9. This was best illustrated by the concept of smart diplomacy advanced in Hillary Clinton's testimony to the Congress on her confirmation as Secretary of the State, January 14, 2009.

10. Assistant Secretary of U.S. State Department Kurt Campbell announced in Seoul on 19 July 2009 that despite the DPRK's second nuclear test the US would continue to use diplomacy, such as the Six-Party Talks, to resolve the nuclear standoff, although it would also implement sanctions against Pyongyang as approved by the UN. *Huuanqiushibao*, 20 July 2009. In other words military option is regarded as non-option.

11. John Mearsheimer, *The Tragedy of Great Power Politics* (New York: Norton 2001). Jeffrey Taliaferro, "Security Seeking under Anarchy: Defensive Realism Revisited." *International Security* 25, no. 3, Winter 2000/01.

12. You Ji, "The Anti-Secession Law and the Risk of War in the Taiwan Strait," *Contemporary Security Policy*, vol. 27, no. 2, August 2006.

13. Michael Swine, "Tough Love for Taiwan," *Foreign Affairs,* Vol. 83, no. 2, 2004.

14. Robert Ross, "Navigating the Taiwan Strait," *International Security*, Vol. 27, No. 2, 2002, p. 82.

15. Martin Lasater, *U.S. Interests in the New Taiwan* (Boulder: Westview, 1993).

16. Sun Qimin, *Zhongsu guanxi shimo*, (History of Sino-Soviet Relations) (Shanghai: Shanghai People's Publishing House, 2002), p. 341.

17. Richard Bush, *Untying the Knot: Making Peace in the Taiwan Strait* (Washington, D.C.: Brookings Institution Press, 2005).

18. The four meetings between Chen Yunlin and Vincent Jiang were designed to institutionalize official contact at high levels as part of foundation building for the purpose of institutionalizing the peace initiatives. These have been followed by other trust building measures, such as signing of MOU for financial interaction and a comprehensive economic cooperation framework.

19. Fu Huijun & Yue Shengjun, *Guofangzhengce* (National defense policy) (Beijing: The PLA National Defense University Press, 2006), p. 47.

20. "PLA Generals' View on Sino-U.S. Relations," *Phoenix TV*, June 29, 2004.

21. At a speech on China-US relations delivered at the Center for American Security in Washington on Sept 24, US Deputy Secretary of State James Steinberg proposed the new approach under which China and the US cooperate in managing the effects of China's rise as well as in grappling with a wide range of issues of global significance. The Chinese analysts see it as the successor of the Bush "responsible stakeholder" policy framework coined by former US deputy secretary of state Robert Zoellick. Fu Mengzi, "Reassurance is a two-way street," *China Daily*, 12 November 2009.

22. James Thomson, "US Interests and the Fate of Alliances," *Survival*, vol. 45, no. 4, 2003-2004, p. 214.

23. My interviews with Beijing's experts on US and Taiwan affairs in Beijing in June 2009.

24. *Washington Observer*, no. 12, April 4, 2007; and Michael Swine, "Tough Love for Taiwan," *Foreign Affairs*, vol. 83, no. 2, 2004.

25. Ted Galen Carpenter, *Smart Power: Toward a Prudent Foreign Policy for America*, Cato Institution, July 13, 2007.

26. General Qian Guoliang (commander of the Shenyang Area of Military Command), "Quanmian luoshi 'silinbu jianshe gangyao', gaobiaozhun zhuahao silingbu jiguan jianshe" (Comprehensively implement the guideline of headquarters construction, and do a good job in headquarters construction), *Journal of the PLA National Defence University,* no. 6, 2000, p. 4.

27. More on this point see You Ji, "Revolution in Military Thinking," in Bo Huldt and Masako Ikegami (eds.), *China Rising,* the Swedish National Defence College and the Finnish Defence University, 2008, pp. 335-364.

28. "Getting closer to the Second Artillery Force," *Phoenix TV,* April 12, 2009.

29. The US went an additional length to criticize Chen's referendum efforts. Thoms Christensen, assistant Deputy Secretary of State, said categorically that "bad act is a bad act, even though it is done under a good cover." Such words are very unusual from a senior US official, especially in the Republican Administration.

30. You Ji, "获得地区事务发展方向的主导权: 大国崛起的理论与实践," (Acquire direction leadership over regional affairs: the theory and practice of China's rise), in Yun-han Chu and Jia Qingguo 朱云汉和贾庆国 (主编) (eds), 丛国际关系理论看中国崛起 (China's rise evaluated through theory of international relations) (Taipei: 台北:五南出版社 Wunan Publishing House, 2007), pp. 95-115.

31. Lai Shin-yuan, chair of Taiwan's Mainland Affairs Council, characterized this development with the words "unprecedented change with profound and far reaching implications" in the 38th annual Taiwan-US conference on Contemporary China on 15 July 2009, Washington.

32. According to Taiwan's former ambassador Chen Xifan who is also a foreign affairs advisor for Ma, after the conclusion of a comprehensive trade agreement, the next major work for Ma would be the negotiation of a peace accord., *Taipei Times,* 11 April 2009.

33. Two well known PLA strategists, Liet. General Li Jijun, former director general of the general office of the CMC and vice president of PLA Academy of Military Science and Major General Pan Zhenqian, former director of the Institute of Strategic Studies at the PLA National Defence University, made plenary speeches at the conference. Li proposed concrete cooperative measures as a way to promote CBMs, such as joint protection of China's Nansha (Spratlys) Islands and joint operations for maritime rescure.

34. *China Times,* 26 March 2009.

35. Wang Yi, director of Taiwan Affairs Office of the State Council, briefed Steinberg, deputy secretary of the US State Department in Washington DC on 25 June 2009, *Xinhua News Agency,* 26 June 2009.

36. For an analysis of this discussion, see Bonnie Glaser & Brad Glosserman, *Promoting Confidence Building across the Taiwan Strait,* Center for Strategic and International Studies and the Pacific Forum, 2009.

37. *Huanqiuwang,* March 19, 2009.

38. For instance, speakers expressed this hope at the Conference *Winning the Minds and Hearts of the Taiwan People,* Beijing University, 14-17 September 2008.

39. Zhu Wenzhong, China's ambassador to Washington, made a speech to researchers from US think tanks in Washington D.C. on 10 November 2008 that it was possible for China to reduce missile deployment across the Taiwan Strait if the situation continued to change for the better. Voice of America, 11 November 2008. Without a prior central consent such remarks would not have been uttered.

40. *Strait Times,* 1 June 2008.

Chapter 14

The New Triangle of Power: China, the United States, and the European Union

Jing Men and Youri Devuyst

INTRODUCTION

Since the end of the WWII, the structure of international relations has changed dramatically. In the Cold War era, the competition between the United States and the Soviet Union dominated international relations and involved many other countries in the competition between the camps. After the People's Republic of China (PRC) was founded, Beijing leaned towards Moscow and joined the socialist camp led by this "old brother". It distanced itself from the Soviet expansionist policy in the 1960s and 1970s and since the 1980s it attempted to develop an independent foreign policy. Although far less powerful or capable than either the Soviet Union or the United States, China enjoyed the following position that "when added to whichever superpower, would decide the outcome of an overall global confrontation between Washington and Moscow."[1] By playing between the two superpowers, China was able to maintain its own interests. The triangle relations dissolved when the Soviet Union ceased to exist.

As early as the 1980s, Chinese leader Deng Xiaoping had already stated that "No matter how many poles there will be, three poles, four poles, or even five poles, . . . for the so-called multi-polarity, China should be counted as one of them."[2] China's influence grew in parallel with its rapidly developing economy. In order to realize the strategic goal of constructing a multipolar world in the post-Cold War era, China has established partnerships with all the major powers in the world. Among them, the United States is the most important one. The relationship between the U.S. and China has a direct impact on China's rise. The ability of U.S. to empower others is derived from its hegemonic position in the global system.[3] Yet, due to the changes in international politics and economics in the 21st century, it is getting more and more difficult for Washington to maintain its hegemonic position.

In the international political and economic relations, apart from the five permanent members of the UN Security Council, the G7 group representing industrialized countries, or in recent years the G8 and G20, have become fashionable terms. On top of that, the U.S. took the initiative to introduce a new combination of power—the G2, which consists of the U.S. and China. In the summer of 2008, C. Fred Bergsten—the Director of the Peterson Institute for International Economics in Washington, D.C., former assistant for international economic affairs to Henry Kissinger's National Security Council and Assistant Secretary of the Carter Administration's Treasury for International Affairs—stated that the U.S. and China should provide joint leadership to the global economic system. For the strategy to work, Bergsten argued that "the United States would have to give true priority to China as its main partner in managing the world economy, to some extent displacing Europe."[4] The concept gained credibility when Zbigniew Brzezinski, at a speech in Beijing in January 2009, also promoted the G2 as a comprehensive U.S.-China partnership based on geo-strategic cooperation, and thus going beyond economics.[5] In Obama's state visit to China in November 2009, he also emphasised the importance of cooperation between the U.S. and China in international affairs. He expressed to the Chinese that the two sides should build a new, strategic partnership.[6]

Interestingly, the U.S.'s enthusiasm for the G2 was not reciprocated in China. Underlying the incompatibility between China's foreign policy principles and the notion of a G2, Chinese Premier Wen made clear on several occasions that China is not prepared to forge this G2 with the United States. At the EU-China summit meeting in May 2009, Wen pledged to his European counterparts that "China adheres to an independent foreign policy . . . and is willing to develop friendly cooperative relationships with all countries, and will never seek hegemony." He further added that "Groups of two countries can't solve global problems. Multipolarism and multilateralism are the general trends and common aspirations of the people."[7] At his meeting with Obama in November 2009, Wen repeated again that China would not align with any country or country blocs. As a developing country with a huge population, China still has a long way to go before it becomes modernized.[8]

China's rejection to the G2 concept is due to the fact that it goes against the core principles of Beijing's independent foreign policy. Equally importantly, China needs to take into consideration the feelings and reactions of its other partners, in particular, the EU. As a European think tank pointed out, "The specter of the G2—a China-U.S. condominium—is haunting European governments as much as the specter of revolution haunted its courts in the days of Karl Marx's Communist Manifesto."[9]

China's relations with the EU have become noticeably more important in the twenty-first century. From the establishment of a comprehensive partnership in 1998 to a strategic partnership in 2003, Brussels and Beijing have significantly increased their cooperation. As Mr. Prodi said at the third China-EU summit in Beijing in 2000, "We stand on the threshold of a new era in the relations between Europe and China."[10] The partnership indicates that the EU has recognized China's growing economic and political impact in the world, and that China has brought the EU's status in its international relations to the same level as the other major actors such as United States, Russia and Japan.

For China, partnership with the U.S. is certainly important, however, the partial emphasis on cooperation solely with the U.S. will not solve many of the world's problems. The EU, composed of 27 member states in Europe, is an indispensably influential actor in many important fields of international cooperation. Among the five permanent members of the Security Council of the UN, two seats belong to EU member states. In the composition of the G7, four countries are EU member states. In the G20 framework, the EU, as a supranational organization, has secured membership. With the Lisbon Treaty entering into force, the President and the Foreign Minister of the EU have just been respectively selected. In the past decades, European integration has witnessed huge achievements both in the economic and political domains. The Europeans are getting more ambitious in international affairs. Therefore, it is not exaggerating to say that "the interaction of the United States, China, and the EU will be a defining feature of the international system in the years to come."[11]

Among the three, China is a late comer in the international political system. This chapter will study the relations of the three by first examining China's fall and rise, in order to point out that China is more so a rule follower than a rule maker. The second part will focus on the historical evolution of China-U.S. relations to examine the nature of the relationship. The third part will be structured in the same manner, except that it will focus on China-EU relations. The fourth part will study the most recent developments between China and the other two. It is noticeable that China's rise has obliged the U.S. and the EU to adjust their respective China policies, and consequently, their relationships with China are gradually moving towards more equal and constructive relationships.

CHINA AS A "NEW" COMER

China used to be a world-class power which had accounted for about one-third of the world's GDP before the Opium War (1839-1842). More than a hundred years later, China accounted only for 1 percent of the world's GDP in 1978. Imperial China had maintained a hierarchical system in East Asia, where it was situated at the top for many centuries. European imperialism directly led to the collapse of the Chinese world order and dragged China into the Western world system which transformed it from an empire to "a state among states."[12] China's defeat in the two opium wars ushered a new type of Sino-Western relations. As a means, war helped the Europeans "to cast the world in the European image."[13] China fell from the centre of its civilization to a periphery sovereign state dominated by Western values and rules. The experience suffered during this period was summarized by Chinese Foreign Minister Qiao Guanhua at the UN General Assembly in 1971, "The Chinese People have experienced untold sufferings under imperialist oppression. For one century and more, imperialism repeatedly launched wars of aggression against China and forced her to sign many unequal treaties. They divided China into their spheres of influence, plundered China's resources and exploited the Chinese people."[14]

With hindsight, the clash between the Chinese world system and the international system was a historical process in which the Western powers completed the annexation of the entire Chinese world order and initiated the transformation of Imperial China. With Europe's subjection of China in the international system, a newly-formed universal system was emerging under European dominance. China's entry "into the emerging universal international society was a historical experience and was conditioned on the approval of the European states as original members of that society."[15]

After the PRC was founded in 1949, the Cold War took shape. Ideological differences between China and Western countries contributed to Beijing's isolation in the international community. Due to Sino-U.S. confrontation in the Korean Peninsula in the early 1950s, the U.S. actively opposed Beijing's membership to the UN. From 1951 to 1960, any efforts to discuss the seating of the PRC in the United Nations were blocked by the U.S.-led countries, due to China's intervention in the Korean War. In 1961, when the UN General Assembly's Sixteenth Session was held, facing with the problems of diminishing majority and declining dominance at the United Nations, the U.S. engineered a resolution stating that for the PRC's representation to be restored, it required a two-thirds majority due to the importance of the issue.[16] Kissinger's secret visit to China in July 1971 had an immediate impact upon China's entry to the UN. While no longer actively campaigning to ban China from UN membership, Washington argued that Beijing should gain a seat in the Security Council and Taiwan should be permitted to retain a seat in the General Assembly.[17] The Chinese leadership refused the "Two China" solution, and stated that

> It is crystal clear that Taiwan and the Penghu Islands are an integral part of China's territory and the question of "international resolution" does not exist at all. The Chinese people will never permit the U.S. government to play with the plots of "two Chinas" or "one China, one Taiwan." When and how the Chinese liberate Taiwan is entirely China's internal affair, and no foreign country has any right to interfere.[18]

The PRC was eventually accepted as China's sole legitimate representative at the UN's Twenty-sixth General Assembly on Oct. 25 of 1971.

China's entry to the UN involved a process of mutual legitimation.[19] For the UN in general, the recognition of China's legitimacy in the society of states symbolized the end of the strange anomaly, legitimized the status of the United Nations as a truly worldwide organization, and fulfilled "the imperative need for the United Nations to achieve universality of membership."[20] For the Security Council in particular, the inclusion of the PRC as one of the five permanent members entitled it to be "more representative of the political and geographical realities of the existing international system and reflected more accurately the changing contours of the international strategic landscape."[21] In this way, China was able to exert its influence in international affairs from the inside of the international community. As American President Nixon said, China's political weight no longer rested outside the international framework.[22] For Beijing, UN membership brought to an end its isolation in the world, legitimized the existence of the communist government, and marked the beginning of a process of "China's engagement with the international political and economic systems and with the other member states of the international community within the existing framework of international society."[23]

UN membership allowed China to access other important international organizations. In April 1980, China entered the International Monetary Fund. One month later, China was admitted as a member of the World Bank Group including the International Bank for Reconstruction and Development (IBRD) and the International Development Association (IDA). China obtained a permanent observer status in the General Agreement on Tariff and Trade (GATT) and was affiliated to the Multifibre Arrangement (MFA) in 1984. China applied for the GATT membership in 1986, and engaged in negotiations, mainly with the United States, for the following 13 years. During the years of negotiations, China had attempted to reach a deal with all the members of the GATT and become a founding member of World Trade Organization (WTO) when it was created in 1995. However, some major differences on the conditions of China's accession served as barriers and postponed the finalization of the agreement between China and the WTO members.[24] Only after a bilateral agreement concerning China's WTO membership was reached with the U.S. in 1999, could China finally join the WTO in 2001 as its 143rd member.

During the thirty years from 1971 to 2001, China had become a member of all the important international organizations. From UN membership to WTO membership, access to these political and economic regimes served as a learning process for China to first act as a new comer and a follower to the rules and regulations, and then to act inside these regimes to maintain its national interests and exert its influence worldwide.

For several decades after the foundation of the PRC, due to the hostility between the U.S. and the PRC, most of the Western countries did not recognize Beijing until the 1970s. The United States was directly involved in the reconstruction of Europe with the Marshall Plan, at the end of the WWII, and offered security guarantee to its Atlantic allies by establishing the North Atlantic Treaty Organization (NATO). The dominant influence of the U.S. in Western Europe had a direct influence on the latter's external relations. When France, led by Charles De Gaulle, established diplomatic relations with Beijing, Chancellor Ludwig Erhard of West Germany also intended to do so. However, he had to give up the idea due to the pressure from Washington. He was obliged to assure the U.S. that his country would not recognize the PRC.[25] As Nixon admitted later, the hostile Sino-U.S. bilateral relationship "had global ramifications that went far beyond our bilateral relationship."[26] In the wake of the rapprochement between Washington and China in the early 1970s, the European Community established diplomatic relations with Beijing in 1975. Official relations between Beijing and Washington only came into existence in 1979, after the PRC had been founded for three decades.

The development of bilateral cooperation between Beijing and Washington as well as between Beijing and Brussels only started in the late 1970s, which coincided with China's decision to implement reforms and the open door policy at the Third Plenary Session of the Eleventh Central Party Committee in December 1978. China's reform and open door policy aimed at increasing state power and achieving prosperity. To realize such goals, China needed capital and technology from Western countries. China reached its first trade agreement with the European Community in 1978. An updated agreement—the 1985 Trade and Economic Cooperation Agreement, came into existence in 1985—to reflect the rapidly increasing economic and trade relations. Even up until now, this agreement still serves as the legal basis for EU-China bilateral cooperation. China was granted, by the Carter Administration, the most-favored-nation trading status in 1980.[27] The extension of this grant was based on Washington's performance evaluation of the Chinese government, and only became permanent in 2000 after China reached its WTO accession agreement with the United States.

SINO-U.S. RELATIONS

When Communist China was founded in 1949, the difference in ideology pre-empted the possibility for China to be accepted by the U.S.-led capitalist camp. As a challenge to American values, communism was intolerable and unacceptable. To the United States, a China that was not ruled by Chiang Kai-shek "was a monster controlled by an implacably hostile communist foe."[28] Manipulated by the United States, the UN General Assembly passed a resolution on Feb. 1, 1951, condemning China as an aggressor.[29] In this way, the PRC was made into an international outlaw. As Yongjin Zhang pointed out,

> Only by dismissing the government in Beijing as the legitimate government of China could the United States reject the PRC's claim to China's seat in the UN and the Security Council. Only by denying the PRC its legitimacy as an international actor could the United States justify its policy of ostracizing the PRC from the international society.[30]

The four fundamentals of the U.S.'s China policy, including non-recognition of the PRC, total support of Taiwan, opposition to seating Beijing at the United Nations, and the American trade embargo against the PRC, which served as guidance in U.S.-China relations, underwent little change during the rest of the 1950s and the 1960s.

U.S.-China diplomatic relations were established due to the fact that they both needed each other strategically to counter the Soviet Union's aggressive expansion. Beijing played a triangle game with both Washington and Moscow in the 1980s. The Reagan Administration regarded China as a junior partner in the context of world politics: China simply served as a military-political counterweight to the Soviet Union in America's global strategy.[31] The Chinese were unhappy at the American "card-playing" behavior. Deng Xiaoping once said, "China is fundamentally independent: even if (Sino-U.S.) relations deteriorated to what they were before 1972, China would not perish. The Chinese people will never bow down and never beg or importune for help. . . . If the United States wants to force China to act according to American wishes, China will never agree."[32]

Many Americans regard China as the main challenger to the U.S.'s superpower status.[33] Their competition for influence on both regional and global affairs foretells a relationship built on disagreements and competition. China gives priority to its relationship with the United States, because the latter, as the only true global power in international relations, can exert great influence either to "facilitate or hinder the attainment of vital Chinese foreign policy objectives."[34] Due to the gap between the two countries, both in capability and influence in the world, China is placed in an inferior position in the relationship.

In May 1999, the Chinese Embassy in Yugoslavia was bombed by the U.S. during a NATO air-raid operation in the war-torn country. The incident reminded the Chinese of their nineteenth century humiliation and triggered demonstrations and protests against the U.S. government all over China. Although the U.S. government denied bombing the Chinese Embassy on purpose and apologized for it, many suspected that it was done deliberately. The former Chinese Ambassador to Yugoslavia published a book in 2006 which recounted the incident. In his view, the bombing was a strategic test for China: it aimed at setting up barriers for China's development and testing the Chinese leadership's decision-making capacity in a crisis situation.[35]

When George W. Bush came to power at the turn of the century, China was regarded as a strategic rival. Bilateral relations were frayed following the collision between an American spy plane and a Chinese fighter jet in the South China Sea in April 2001. To make the relationship worse, President Bush authorized the sale of high-tech weapons to Taiwan, insisted on the applicability of National Missile Defense (NMD) system, and attempted to enlist Taiwan into the program. Due to the terrorist attack on the U.S. in September 2001, Washington no longer considered China as an enemy. In an article published in the American journal *Newsweek*, China is regarded as the biggest winner out of the war against terrorism.[36]

Barack Obama and Joseph Biden recognized the importance of a constructive U.S.-China relationship during the election campaign. They explicitly declared that they would "not demonize China."[37] Obama's "carefully crafted" outline for the future of U.S.-China relations was a sign of the rapidly changing geo-economic reality.[38] During the Bush Administration, the main idea had been to welcome China as a "responsible stakeholder" in the international system.[39] As Brantly Womack remarked, this terminology implied status difference rather than mutual respect.[40]

The geo-economic sea changes that took place in 2008 made that such a patronizing attitude untenable during the Obama Administration. In September 2008, China overtook Japan as Washington's largest creditor, holding 10 percent of all U.S. public debt. With nearly US$1 trillion in American treasuries and other government securities, China had—by early 2009—developed the world's largest pool of foreign currency reserves.[41] During the Bush Administration, Washington had strongly encouraged Beijing to buy U.S. treasury bonds to offset the increasing public deficit. This, in turn, allowed China to continue selling its products to indebted America. In other words, China furnished the United States with massive capital infusions that were keeping the American financial system afloat while its factories were producing the goods that were bought by the American general public.[42] Niall Ferguson described this "symbiotic and mutually intoxicating" relationship as the birth of a new nation: Chimerica. "For a time it seemed like a marriage made in heaven . . . . The East Chimericans did the saving, the West Chimericans did the spending."[43]

With the 2008-2009 financial and economic crises, the sustainability of the Chimerican system was put into question. The system had to continue in order to prevent a total collapse of the world financial system. That is why the Obama Administration appealed to the Chinese authorities to continue investing in U.S. treasury bonds.[44] In February 2009, during a visit to Beijing, Secretary of State Hillary Clinton explained that in order to rescue the American economy, the Administration was launching a stimulus package that implied an even further increase of debt. Underlining China's interest in the success of America's stimulus package as a way of pursuing its exports to the U.S. market, Clinton concluded as follows: "[B]ecause our economies are so intertwined . . . . It would not be in China's interest if we were unable to get our economy moving again. So, by continuing to support American treasury instruments, the Chinese are recognizing our interconnection. We are truly going to rise or fall together. We are in the same boat. And, thankfully, we are rowing in the same direction, toward landfall."[45]

Chinese experts made clear that "China, with the responsibility of a big country, w[ould] not make trouble for the international financial markets."[46] Owning a huge volume of dollar-denominated bonds, Beijing recognized that hardly any nation stood to lose more from the financial collapse of the U.S. than China. In March 2009, Chinese Prime Minister Wen Jiabao openly signaled Beijing's concern when stating: "We have lent a huge amount of money to the U.S.. Of course we are concerned about the safety of our assets. To be honest, I am definitely a little worried."[47] A couple of days later, Zhou Xiaochuan, the Governor of the People's Bank of China, recommended creating an alternative to the dollar as the world's reserve currency. He proposed an expanded use of the International Monetary Fund (IMF)'s Special Drawing Rights (SDRs)—a basket of currencies made up of the euro, yen, pound and dollar. Furthermore, he called for a change in the valuation method of the SDRs, stating that the basket of currencies forming the basis of SDR valuation should be expanded to include currencies of all major economies. He also pointed out that China should have a greater voice in the IMF decision-making process through an increase in its voting power at the Fund's Executive Board.[48] Zhou's remarks immediately sparked a reply from Washington that it would do whatever necessary to make sure that the dollar remained the world's dominant reserve currency.[49]

The suggestion made by the Governor of the People's Bank of China for a new reserve currency was an indication of China's re-emergence as a great power. Already, towards the end of the Bush years, Zhou had publicly criticized the United States as the country where the world financial crisis emerged due to over-consumption and a high reliance on credit. To turn things around, Zhou lectured the United States on the need to adjust its policies, raise its savings ratio and reduce its trade and fiscal deficits.[50] The tone of Beijing's comments was interpreted as reflecting an underlying shift in power. Professor Eswar Prasad, previously Head of the China Division at the IMF, formulated it as such: "One result of the crisis is that the U.S. no longer holds the high ground to lecture China on financial or macroeconomic policies. This may actually help turn their relationship into a more equal partnership."[51] At the same time, press reports illustrated the loss of credibility of the American banking executives who—only days before the collapse of the American financial system—had spoken paternalistically of their Chinese counterparts.[52]

SINO-EU RELATIONS

The initial development of Sino-EC/EU relations was rather slow. Although the PRC was founded in 1949, and the European Community came into existence in the 1950s, the official relations between the two were not established until 1975. It took more than twenty years for the two sides to come together, not only because of the international political influence of the Cold War, but also due to the distinct political standpoints held by the Chinese and the Europeans. During the Cold War era, China and the Western European countries belonged to two different ideological camps—China joined the socialist camp led by the Soviet Union whereas the Western European countries stood for the capitalist camp led by the United States. Different political positions and ideological beliefs created animosity between the two sides. China regarded the Western Europeans as the "contemptible lackeys of the United States."[53] In the mid-1970s, encouraged by the Sino-U.S. rapprochement and the mutual recognition between China and most of the Western European countries,[54] the European Community established diplomatic relations with the PRC.

Despite the breakthrough of diplomatic relations between Beijing and Brussels, there was lack of progress in bilateral cooperation during the twenty years thereafter. Both the international and domestic factors exerted their impacts on the relations. In words of David Shambaugh, the Brussels-Beijing relationship is to a large degree derivative from their respective relations with Moscow and Washington.[55] The competition between the superpowers checked the cooperation between Beijing and Brussels. There was no independent motive for the development of the relationship from either of the two sides. As mentioned earlier, before the end of the Cold War, Brussels and Beijing only reached two relatively important agreements: the trade agreement in 1978 and the agreement on trade and economic cooperation in 1985.

In the transitional period from the Cold War to the post-Cold War era, Sino-EU relations faced challenges. The suppression to the students' demonstration on Tiananmen Square on June 4, 1989 by the Chinese government triggered sanctions by the West, with the United States taking the lead. The European Community replicated by sanctioning against China. The relationship between the European Community and the PRC was gradually normalized one year later. Despite different opinions inside the Community, the attraction of the Chinese market, and the benefit brought by economic cooperation with China reminded the Community of China's strategic importance and this convinced the Community to relax the sanctions.

By the time the European Union completed its single market program in 1992, its leadership sought to further stimulate the European economy by enhancing economic cooperation and trade relations with the other parts of the world. Attracted by the dynamic economic development in Asia, the European Commission developed the "Towards a New Asia Strategy" policy paper in 1994. Located at the centre of the EU's Asia strategy, China was given substantial attention. In its first China policy paper "A long term policy for China-Europe relations," published in 1995, the European Commission stated:

> The rise of China is unmatched amongst national experiences since the Second World War. Japan has made its mark as an economic power, the Soviet Union survived essentially as a military power. China is increasingly strong in both the military-political and the economic spheres. China is in the midst of sustained and dramatic economic and social change at home. Abroad, China is becoming part of the world security and economic system at a time of greater economic interdependence and when global problems, from protection of the environment to nuclear non-proliferation, require coordinated commitment from governments worldwide.[56]

This policy paper indicated that the EU had noticed China's rise and considered its relations with China as part of a long-term policy. China's reform and open door policy noticeably promoted its domestic development and external relations. How China would transform itself in the reform process and what kind of role China would play in international affairs would have a direct impact on international peace and cooperation. Close engagement with China became an important EU policy.

From 1995 to 2003, EU-China relations embarked on a fast-tracked development. Bilateral relations were upgraded in many respects. Bilateral trade exceeded US$120 billion in 2003, two times more than that of 1995. In the same year, China overtook Switzerland to become the EU's second largest trading partner behind the United States.[57] About twenty sectoral dialogues and agreements were reached between the two sides, based on which a large number of cooperative projects that were undertaken to enhance exchange, and to support China's transition towards a more open and plural society. The "Country Strategy Paper" and the "National Indicative Programs" were passed by the EU to implement those cooperative projects. The first such document between the

EU and China was published in 2002, with 250 million euros allocated by the European Commission to cover programs running from 2002 to 2006.[58]

Together with the intensified EU-China economic and social cooperation, political relations were also developed rapidly during this period. Political dialogue on sensitive regional and international affairs was established in 1994. Since then, foreign ministers, political directors and experts from both sides are closely involved in the regular and constructive political dialogue. This working mechanism helps to maintain an effective and important channel of direct communication between the two sides. From 1998 onwards, a summit meeting system was created between the EU and China. With all these developments, bilateral relations were noticeably institutionalized, widened, and deepened.

Enhanced cooperation in economic, political and other fields encouraged the two sides to upgrade their bilateral relations. The European Commission, for the first time, used the word "partnership" in its 1998 China policy paper. Five years later, the European Commission recognized that this partnership was reaching maturity. At the summit meeting of that year, the two sides started to talk about promoting a strategic partnership by further deepening and expanding EU-China relations.

The development of a strategic partnership brought the two into a "honeymoon period" between 2003 and 2004. Exchanges of visits by top leaders on both sides became more frequent. For example, EU officials paid 206 visits to China in 2004, an average of four visits per week.[59] The Chinese Premier, Wen Jiabao, was the first foreign leader to pay an official visit to the EU after its historically important eastward enlargement in May 2004. The volume of bilateral trade kept with the momentum of China's rapid economic growth. Bilateral cooperation has been both deepened and widened. Sectoral dialogues have been further increased, with the High Level of Economic and Trade Dialogue (HED) created between the two in 2008.

In its 2003 China policy paper, the European Commission pointed out that the EU and China shared "responsibilities in promoting global governance." The EU and China should work together "to safeguard and promote sustainable development, peace and stability."[60] The strategic cooperation with China, to maintain global order was also highlighted in the European Security Strategy, which recognized that the United States is the pre-eminent world power. But "no single country is able to tackle today's complex problems on its own."[61] Europe should be a pillar in the new world, and it should consolidate relationships with the other great partners, including China.

At the international level, there are lots of issues that the EU and China need to cooperate on in order to maintain international peace and security. After 9/11, the fight against terrorism and weapons of mass destruction became more important to both the EU and China. Apart from the EU Security Strategy issued in December 2003, the Council of the European Union also issued a separate paper on the "EU Strategy against Proliferation of Weapons of Mass Destruction" to highlight the key challenges faced by the EU and the importance of having a multilateral response to these challenges in cooperation with other partners.[62] In the same month, in Beijing, China issued its first white paper on non-proliferation,[63] in which China pointed out that the "fundamental purpose of non-proliferation is to safeguard and promote international and regional peace and security" and "a universal participation of the international community is essential for progress in non-proliferation."[64] One year later, in December 2004, at the 7th EU-China summit meeting, the two sides issued a joint declaration on non-proliferation and arms control in which they pledged to "work together within their strategic partnership" and "to strengthen the international non-proliferation system."[65] The close coordination between the EU and China in their positions on non-proliferation indicated that both regard each other as an important partner in terms of international cooperation on peace and security. It also indicated that there existed a shared understanding between the two sides on these issues of mutual concern.

Economic and trade relations intensified between the EU and China. This represents the founding stone of the maturing partnership. By far, the EU is China's largest trading partner and its most important supplier of technology. China is the EU's second largest trading partner, the biggest source of manufactured imports, and its fastest growing export market. Together with the impressive trade growth, the EU's trade deficit has been rising rapidly. The EU is increasingly complaining about the rising deficit in its trade with China. In its most recent China policy paper, the EU regards China as "the single most important challenge for EU trade policy."[66] Starting from the mid-1990s, the EU's trade deficit with China has been increasing rapidly. In 2008, the EU's deficit rose to 169 billion euros.[67]

In September 2006, at the 9th EU-China summit meeting, the two agreed to start negotiations on a Partnership and Cooperation Agreement (PCA). From the EU's viewpoint, the PCA should cover all the dimensions of bilateral relations, serving as a comprehensive legal document to guide bilateral relations. In the negotiations, the EU expects that the new document will be an upgrade of the original 1985 Trade and Economic Cooperation Agreement. In the meantime, a wide range of issues will be covered in the document to define EU-China relations in the twenty-first century. But the Chinese Ministry of Commerce wishes to separate the negotiation of a new trade and economic cooperation agreement from that of the PCA. Due to the differences in some key issues including, for example, whether China should be granted Market Economy Status, the negotiations are moving very slowly.

CHINA, THE U.S., AND THE EU IN THE TWENTY-FIRST CENTURY

Due to the fact that China is a late comer, the relationship is not equal between the U.S. and China, as well as that between the EU and China. As mentioned earlier, the current international system is the continuation of the system established by the Europeans in the nineteen century. Both the U.S. and major European countries are the founders of many international regimes. The difference between themselves and China is that they are the rule makers whereas China is the rule follower. Furthermore, the PRC's relatively short history of independence and economic development put it at a disadvantageous position in its relation with the U.S. and the EU. China, in most of the cases, acts as a learner and inferior partner.

Such situation has started to change in recent years. Due to China's rising power, both the U.S. and the EU have become more accommodating towards China. Obama's approach to China strongly reflected the new global realities. At the very start of the administration, some observers expected that a hard-line approach was in the making. This impression was in large measure caused by the written answer to a question asked during Timothy Geithner's confirmation hearing as U.S. Secretary of the Treasury. In his reply, the Secretary-designate accused China of "manipulating" its currency and pledged "aggressive" diplomatic action to counteract this practice.[68] Geithner's statement did not come as a total surprise since Obama's election program had promised that "Barack Obama and Joe Biden w[ould] use all diplomatic means at their disposal to achieve change in China's manipulation of the value of its currency, a practice that contributes to massive global imbalances and provides Chinese companies with an unfair competitive advantage."[69] Following Geithner's confirmation, however, the Administration quickly adapted to the new geo-economic reality and Geithner's written comments were blamed on the mistaken language usage of a low-level staff member. When traveling to Beijing at the end of May 2009, the Treasury Secretary did his utmost to underline the pragmatic approach that would guide his mission.[70] Geithner's focus was then to applaud Chinese leaders for keeping up massive stimulus spending, urging them to increase domestic consumption and reassuring them on the seriousness of America's economic policies. Recognizing that "China is already too important to the global economy not to have a full seat at the international table," Geithner pointed out that the U.S.-China economic and political engagement "should be conducted with mutual respect for the traditions, values, and interests of China and the United States."[71] Geithner's soft and conciliatory tone signaled a shift in relations between the United States and China. It seemed to indicate that the "Obama administration appear[ed] determined to make China a more equal partner."[72]

Likewise, Secretary of State Clinton and Speaker of the House of Representatives Nancy Pelosi's political missions to Beijing were examples of the pragmatic attempts to obtain Chinese cooperation in world affairs. While they both had a reputation of harshly criticizing Beijing's human rights record, China's new international stature forced Clinton and Pelosi to focus on broader areas of cooperation.[73] Putting the emphasis on the need for common action on the global economy, clean energy and climate change, and security issues such as North Korea, Clinton explicitly stated that the differences of opinion with China over human rights, Tibet and Taiwan should not be allowed to interfere with attempts to reach consensus on broader issues of global importance.[74] According to Pelosi, the climate crisis demonstrated that "our fates are tied together" and that U.S.-China cooperation had become an indispensable feature of twenty-first-century diplomacy.[75] These highly publicized remarks were seen as a confirmation of the Obama Administration's emphasis on engagement with Beijing.

To give a more structural character to U.S.-China cooperation, President Obama and President Hu Jintao decided, on 1 April 2009, to establish the "U.S.-China Strategic and Economic Dialogue." The Dialogue's "Strategic Track" covers a broad range of political, security and global issues whereas the "Economic Track" covers a broad range of financial and economic issues with the purpose of building a positive, cooperative, and comprehensive U.S.-China relationship for the twenty-first century. In addition, the two sides agreed on the importance of raising the level and frequency of the U.S.-China military-to-military dialogue. The dialogue had been disrupted for half a year following the Bush administration's announcement in October 2008 of arms sales to Taiwan.[76] The May 2009 North Korea crisis only confirmed the importance of this renewed military dialogue.

Obama's policy toward China is a testimony of the profound geo-economic and geo-political changes that have taken place since the 2008 financial crisis. China's economic and political power resulted in the substantially changed tone of American diplomacy when dealing with Beijing. With their fate tied more visibly than before, the need for effective U.S.-China cooperation to master the world's crucial economic, environmental and security challenges, seems to have gradually transformed their relationship. President Obama's recent visit to China was criticized by American conservatives, who stated that he acted too softly and that the Chinese held firm against most of the American demands. In response, White House officials argued that "Mr. Obama's foreign policy is rooted in recasting the United States as a thoughtful listener to friends and rivals alike." In the meantime, they also pointed out that "it would be counter-productive" if "Mr. Obama to confront Beijing with loud chest-beating."[77]

A much more visible sign of profound geo-economic and geo-political change is the leading role attributed to the G20 in steering the world out of the world economic crisis. With the participation of such countries as China, India, Brazil and Saudi Arabia, the G20 indicate the shift in power away from the Western-dominated G7. The prominence given to the G20 is seen as a recognition that the world has changed and, in particular, that the old industrial West no longer has sufficient economic and financial resources to individually resolve the crisis.[78] According to Timothy Garton Ash, China's leadership at the April 2009 G20 Summit in London marked the day on which, through the catalysis of a global economic crisis, Beijing definitely emerged as a twenty-first-century world power.[79]

The U.S. has always been the top priority for Chinese foreign policy since the PRC was founded, whereas the EU has only developed itself into a key partner for China in the 21st century. Similar to the Americans, the Europeans in one way or another held a patronizing attitude towards Chinese. In all of the EU's China policy papers, it is noticeable that words such as "support," "help" are often used to express the EU's possession of experience which may assist China's participation in the international community and transform it into an open society based on human rights and democracy. In contrast, it is interesting to note that in the only EU policy paper produced by the Chinese government in 2003, the words "equal" and "equality" appeared 9 times and the word "mutual" appeared 25 times.[80] This demonstrates that China requests an equal relationship with the EU and stresses that bilateral relations are mutually interdependent.

As a matter of fact, the Europeans have gradually realized that without cooperation from China, it will be difficult to reach agreements on many important issues such as climate change, disarmament and nonproliferation and sustainable economic development. In the first HED dialogue between the EU and China in 2008, the fact that the European Commission President Barosso went to China with 9 other Commissioners highlighted the degree to which the Commission perceives the importance of its relationship with China.

In the meantime, as a result of the rapid development of national power and its rising influence in international affairs, China gradually becomes more assertive in its foreign policy.[81] China decided to cancel the 2008 summit meeting, due to French President Nicolas Sarkozy's scheduled meeting with the Dalai Lama in Poland. The EU obviously felt disappointment with China's decision. According to John Fox, "China doesn't place much value in Europe any more."[82] The Chinese government regards the Tibetan issue as part of its core national interest. National sovereignty and territorial integrity are the priority of its external relations. The meetings between European leaders and the Dalai Lama, from the Chinese viewpoint, indicated European interference in China's domestic affairs. Chinese Premier Wen, in his speech at the news conference of the May 2009 summit meeting, stressed that the EU-China strategic cooperation is based on the principles of mutual respect and mutual non-interference in each other's domestic affairs.[83]

The U.S. has a strong impact on EU-China relations. Different from EU-China relations, EU-U.S. relations are based on common values, a common cultural and historical background, similar political systems and a long tradition of alliance. In comparison to the relatively recent EU-China partnership, the EU-U.S. partnership has been, for more than half a century, a much deeper and more stable partnership. On the other hand, the United States has been the first priority, for several decades, in China's foreign policy. How to maintain a workable relationship with the U.S. in order to maintain a favorable international environment has always been of important concern to the Chinese government. Therefore, how the EU and China deepen their partnership and keep their commitments to their respective relations with the U.S. is not an easy task.

The PRC's legitimation in the international community paved the way for its economic development and its rising influence worldwide. As a consequence of the implementation of reform and the open door policy, the country has undergone tremendous changes and achieved successful developments. Up till now, China has built itself into the world's third largest economy. It has replaced the United States in the past several years to become Japan, South Korea, Taiwan, Brazil, India, and Australia's largest trading partner. Although the Chinese government refused to embrace the concept of the G2, it is interesting to note that in the dialogue between Washington and Beijing, an increasing concern is given to key regional and international issues instead of just bilateral concerns.

Nevertheless, it is necessary to point out the asymmetry that exists between the U.S. and China in terms of influence and capability. There is no doubt that the United States remains the most important player in the international system. In order to facilitate its national and strategic interests, the U.S. has noticeably strengthened cooperation with China in the twenty-first century. As Mr. Talbott pointed out, "The transformation of U.S.-China relations is one of the most complex and consequential developments of the twentieth century, and it has major implications for the twenty-first."[84]

The future of Sino-U.S. relations is without doubt uncertain. Stated by David Lampton, "the process of economic and information globalization have landed America and China increasingly near one another in the same global bed, but our respective national institutions, interests, leadership and popular perceptions, and the very characters of our two peoples, ensure that our nations have substantially different dreams."[85] This is also applicable to Sino-EU relations. However, as China is the largest beneficiary of the economic and political order established by the U.S. and the EU, China will not challenge the international system at the sacrifice of its own interests. China's power and influence will further grow after the financial crisis, but will not match the power of the other two in many aspects. What is certain is that the three will further strengthen cooperation for their own and the world's interests.

NOTES

1. Yongjin Zhang, *China in International Society Since 1949: Alienation and Beyond* (Houndmills, Basingstoke, Hampshire and London: Macmillan Press Ltd., 1998), p. 67.
2. Deng Xiaoping, *Selected Works of Deng Xiaoping [Deng xiaoping wenxuan],* (Beijing: Rebmin Chubanshe, 1993), Vol. 3, p. 353.
3. Rosemary Foot, *The Practice of Power: U.S. Relations with China since 1949* (Oxford: Oxford University Press, 1997), p. 16.
4. C. Fred Bergsten, "A Partnership of Equals. How Washington Should Respond to China's Economic Challenge," *Foreign Affairs*, Vol. 87, No. 4 (2008), p. 67. For an earlier use of the G2 concept by Bergsten, see his "A New Foreign Economic Policy for the United States," in C. Fred Bergsten (ed.), *The United States and the World Economy. Foreign Economic Policy for the Next Decade* (Washington, D.C.: Peterson Institute for International Economics, 2005), p. 54.
5. Zbigniew Brzezinski, "The Group of Two that could change the world," *Financial Times*, 13 January 2009.
6. "President Obama seeks strategic relationship with China," BBC News, 16 November 2009, http:// www.bbc.co.uk/worldservice/news/2009/11/091116_usa_china_dm.shtml.
7. "Chinese premier rejects allegation of China, U.S. monopolizing world affairs in future," *Xinhuanet.com*, 20 May 2009.
8. "Wen: China Disagrees to So-called G2," *China Daily*, 18 November 2009, http://www.chinadaily.com.cn/ china/2009-11/18/content_8998039.htm.

9. François Godement, "Obama in Asia - G2 of China and the U.S. haunts Europe," *Global Arab Network*, 17 November 2009, http://www.english.globalarabnetwork.com/200911173633/World-Politics/obama-in-asia-g2-of-china-and-the-us-haunts-europe.html.

10 . "EU-China Summit Beijing 23 October 2000," http://www.ecd.org.cn/pr/press2000/2001023e.htm.

11. David Shambaugh, "The New Strategic Triangle: U.S. and European Reactions to China's Rise," *The Washington Quarterly*, Vol. 28, No. 3 (2005), p. 7.

12. Yongjin Zhang, "System, Empire and State in Chinese International Relations," *Review of International Studies*, Vol. 27, No. 5 (2001), p. 58.

13. Yongjin Zhang, *China in International Society since 1949: Alienation and Beyond*, p. 9.

14. Quoted in *Beijing Review*, No. 46, Nov. 19, 1971, p. 6.

15. Yongjin Zhang, *China in International Society Since 1949: Alienation and Beyond*, p. 11.

16. Ibid, p, 25.

17. Michael Schaller, *The United States and China in the Twentieth Century* (New York, Oxford: Oxford University Press, 1979), p. 173.

18. "Opposing a 'Two Chinas' Solution," *Renmin Ribao (People's Daily)*, May 4, 1971, quoted in Alan Lawrance, *China's Foreign Relations since 1949* (New York: Routledge, 1975), p. 214.

19. Yongjin Zhang, *China in International Society Since 1949: Alienation and Beyond*, pp. 73-76.

20. Lincoln Bloomfield, "China, the United States and the United Nations," *International Organization*, Vol. XX, No. 4 (1966), p. 654.

21. Yongjin Zhang, *China in International Society since 1949: Alienation and Beyond*, p. 76.

22. Richard Nixon, *U.S. Foreign Policy for the 1970s: A New Strategy for Peace* (Washington, DC: U.S. Government Printing Office, 1970), p. 2.

23. Yongjin Zhang, *China in International Society since 1949: Alienation and Beyond*, p. 72.

24. See Xiang Cheng, Hung Yee Ching, *Handbook on China's WTO Accession and Its Impacts* (Singapore: World Scientific Publishing Co. Ltd., 2003).

25. David Shambaugh, "China and Europe: Developing from Derivative Relationship to Independent Relationship," in Song Xinning and Zhang Xiaojin (eds.), *Zouxiang ershiyi shiji de Zhongguo yu Ouzhou (China and Europe Towards the Twenty-first Century)* (Hong Kong: Social Science Publishing House, 1997), p. 43.

26. Richard Nixon, *U.S. Foreign Policy for the 1970s: Shaping a Durable Peace* (London: United States Information Service, 1972), p. 16.

27. Q. S. Tan, "The politics of U.S. most-favored-nation treatment to China: The cases of 1979 and 1990," *East Asia*, Vol. 9, No. 1 (1990), pp. 41-59.

28. Michael Schaller, *The United States and China in the Twentieth Century* (New York, Oxford: Oxford University Press, 1979), p. 125.

29. King C. Chen, *China and the Three Worlds: A Foreign Policy Reade* (Armonk, NY: M.E. Sharpe, 1979), p. 10.

30. Yongjin Zhang, *China in International Society Since 1949: Alienation and Beyond*, p. 22.

31. Roy Medvedev (translated by Harold Shukman), *China and the Superpowers* (Oxford: Basil Blackwell, 1986), p. 141.

32. *Ming-bao (Daily Information)*, Hong Kong: August 25, 1981, quoted in Roy Medvedev (translated by Harold Shukman), *China and the Superpowers*, p. 136.

33. See for example, Richard Bernstein and Ross Munro, *The Coming Conflict with China* (New York: Knopf, 1997).

34. Steven L. Levine, "Sino-American Relations: Practicing Damage Control," in Samuel S. Kim (ed.), *China and the World: Chinese Foreign Policy Faces the New Millennium Boulder* (Colorado: Westview Press, 1998), p. 91.

35. Pan Zhanlin, "Zhanghuo zhong de waijiaoguan: wo shiguan beizha zhimi" [My Encounter with War: Why Our Embassy was Bombed], 29 September 2006, http://news.xinhuanet.com/book/2006-09/29/content_5152207.htm.

36. Fareed Zakaria, "The Big Story Everyone Missed," *Newsweek*, December 30, 2002, http://www.newsweek. com/id/66987.

37. Barack Obama and Joe Biden, "Protecting U.S. Interests and Advancing American Values in Our Relationship with China," 2009, p. 1, http://www.barackobama.com.

38. Brantly Womack, "Washington Tea Parties: Managing Problems and Imagining Solutions in U.S. China Policy," in Daniel Gros, Brantly Womack and Alexei D. Voskressenski, *The Rise of China: Policies of the EU, Russia and the U.S.* (Brussels: European Security Forum Working Paper No. 30, February 2008), p. 8.

39. The key statement in this context was that of Robert B. Zoellick, Deputy Secretary of State, "Whither China: From Membership to Responsibility?," Remarks to National Committee on U.S.-China Relations, September 21, 2005. See also Thomas J. Christensen, Deputy Assistant Secretary of State for East Asian and Pacific Affairs, "China's Role in the World: Is China a Responsible Stakeholder?," Remarks Before the U.S.-China Economic and Security Review Commission, Washington, D.C., August 3, 2006.

40. Womack, "Washington Tea Parties," p. 9.

41. Geoff Dyer, China's dollar dilemma," *Financial Times*, 23 February 2009, p. 5.

42. Mark Landler, "2 economic giants addicted to credit," *International Herald Tribune*, 1 December 2008, pp. 27-28.

43. Niall Ferguson cited by Fareed Zakaria, "A Path Out of the Woods," *Newsweek*, 1 December 2008, p. 23.

44. Ariana Eunjung Cha and Annys Shin, "Geithner Tells China Its Holdings Are Safe," *Washington Post*, 2 June 2009.

45. Hillary Rodham Clinton, "Interview With Yang Lan of Dragon TV," Beijing, China, 22 February 2009.

46. Hu Angang, Director of the Center for China Studies at Tsinghua University, cited by Jim Yardley and Keith Bradsher, "An 'economic miracle' in peril," *International Herald Tribune*, 23 October 2008, 12.

47. Michael Wines, Keith Bradsher and Mark Landler, "China's Leader Says He Is 'Worried' Over U.S. Treasuries," *New York Times*, 14 March 2009.

48. Zhou Xiaochuan, "Reform the International Monetary System," People's Bank of China, Beijing, 23 March 2009.

49. Pedro Nicolaci da Costa and Steven C. Johnson (Reuters), "Geithner says dollar to be reserve currency for long time," *Washington Post*, 25 March 2009.

50. Geoff Dyer, "China officials take turns to lecture Paulson," *Financial Times*, 5 December 2008, p. 3.

51. Quoted in Dyer, "China officials take turns to lecture Paulson," p. 3.

52. Peter S. Goodman, "U.S. banks fail as a role model for China," *International Herald Tribune*, 18 May 2009, p. 1.

53. Donald W. Klein, "Japan and Europe in Chinese Foreign Relations," in Samuel S. Kim (ed.), *China and the World: Chinese Foreign Relations in the Post-Cold War Era* (Boulder, Colorado: Westview Press, 1994), 3rd edition, p. 113.

54. Since the Sino-U.S. relations improved in the early 1970s, many Western European countries established their diplomatic relations with Beijing in a short period. Among them, Italy recognized the PRC in 1970; Belgium and Austria in 1971; UK, Western Germany, Luxemburg, and the Netherlands in 1972. Much earlier than these countries, France, against the opposition of the United States, established official relations with China in 1964. West Germany wanted to follow suit, however, due to the great pressure from Washington, it had to give the attempt up. The historical development showed that the United States played an important role both in hampering and promoting the bilateral relations between China and the Western European countries.

55. David Shambaugh, "China and Europe," *Current History*, Vol. 103, No. 674 (September 2004), p. 245.

56. Communication of the Commission, "A Long-term Policy for China-Europe Relations," COM (1995) 279 final, Brussels, 5 July 1995, http://www.europa.eu.int/ comm./external_relations/china/ com95_279en.pdf.
57. "Sino-EU trade relations trending up," *China Daily*, October 23, 2003, http://www.chinadaily.com.cn/en/doc/ 2003-10/23/content_274686.htm.
58. See "China: country strategy paper 2002-2006," http://ec.europa.eu/externalrelations/ china/csp/index2002.htm.
59. Benita Ferrero Waldner, "The EU, China and the quest for a multilateral world," 4 July 2005, http:// www.delchn.cec.eu.int/en/eu_and_china/30th/sp05_414.htm.
60. Commission policy paper, "A Maturing Partnership - Shared Interests and Challenges in EU-China Relations," COM(2003) 533 final, Brussels, 10 September 2003, http://europa.eu.int/comm/external_relations/china/com _03_533/com_533_en.pdf.
61. European Council, "A Secure Europe in a Better World – European Security Strategy," Brussels, 12 December 2003, p. 1, http://www.consilium.europa.eu/uedocs/ cmsUpload/ 78367.pdf.
62. See the "EU Strategy against Proliferation of Weapons of Mass Destruction," http://www.trade.ec.europa.eu/ doclib/docs/2004/august/tradoc_118532.en03.pdf.
63. Information Office of the State Council of the PRC, "China's Non-proliferation Policy and Measures," December 2003, http://www.china.org.cn/e-white/20031202/index.htm.
64. Ibid.
65. "Joint Declaration of the People's Republic of China and the European Union on Non-proliferation and Arms Control," Ministry of Foreign Affairs of the PRC, 9 December 2009, http://www.fmprc.gov.cn/eng/wjdt/2649/ t173749.htm.
66. Commission Working Document accompanying COM (2006) 631 final: Closer Partners, Growing Res-ponsibilities, "A Policy Paper on EU-China Trade and Investment: Competition and Partnership," COM (2006) 632 final, Brussels, 24 October 2006, p. 3, http://trade.ec.europa.eu/doclib/docs/2006/october/tradoc_130791.pdf.
67. Press Release of the EU, "EU-China Trade in Facts and Figures," 4 September 2009, http://europa.eu/rapid/pressReleasesAction.do?reference=MEMO/09/375&format=HTM L&aged=0&language=EN.
68. Alan Beattie and Geoff Dyer, "U.S. says China 'manipulating' renminbi," *Financial Times*, 22 January 2009.
69. Barack Obama and Joe Biden, "Protecting U.S. Interests and Advancing American Values in Our Relationship with China," p. 1.
70. Anthony Faiola, "Geithner to Pursue Practical Goals, Tone in Trip to China," *Washington Post*, 29 May 2009.
71. Timothy F. Geithner, "The United States and China, Cooperating for Recovery and Growth," Speech at Peking University, Beijing, China, 1 June 2009, pp. 5-6.
72. David Barboza, "Geithner Softens Tone in Approach to Beijing," *New York Times*, 2 June 2009.
73. Ariana Eunjung Cha and Glenn Kessler, "Pelosi Mum on Rights Before Trip To China. Speaker, as Clinton Has, Plays Down Topic; Focus Will Be Climate Talks," *Washington Post*, 24 May 2009.
74. Geoff Dyer, Christian Oliver and Demetri Sevastopulo, "Clinton in pragmatic mood for China visit," *Financial Times*, 21-22 February 2009, p. 3.
75. Nancy Pelosi, "Remarks at Tsinghua University," Beijing, China, 28 May 2009, p. 3.
76. "The President meets with Chinese Foreign Minister Yang Jiechi," The White House, Washington, D.C., 12 March 2009.
77. Helene Cooper, "China Holds Firm on Major Issues in Obama's Visit," *The New York Times,* 17 November 2009, http://www.nytimes.com/2009/11/18/world/asia/18 prexy.html?r=1&th&emc=th.
78. James Traub, "Shaking Up the Boardroom at World Government Inc.," *New York Times*, 4 January 2009.

79. Timothy Garton Ash, "China arrives as a world power today—and we should welcome it," *Guardian*, 2 April 2009.

80. Chinese Government, "China's EU Policy Paper," 13 October 2003, http://www.fmprc .gov.cn/eng/topics/ ceupp/t27708.htm.

81. Jing Men, "EU-China Relations Need More Mutual Understanding," *EU-China Observer*, Issue 1 (2009), p. 7.

82. Quoted in Chris Buckley, "Dumped summit exposes China-Europe disenchantment," 1 December 2008, http://www.reuters.com/article/reutersEdge/idUSTRE4B013820081201.

83. Xinhuanet, "Chinese Premier Attends 11th China-EU Summit," 21 May 2009, http://news.xinhuanet.com/ english/2009-05/21/content_11409921.htm.

84. Strobe Talbott, "Forward," in Robert L. Suettinger *Beyond Tiananmen: The Politics of U.S.-China Relations 1989-2000* (Washington, D.C.: Brookings Institution Press, 2004), p. ix.

85. David M. Lampton, *Same Bed, Different Dreams: Managing U.S.-China Relations 1989-2000* (Berkeley and Los Angeles: University of California Press, 2001), p. 11.

Chapter 15

The Change and Continuity in the U.S. China Policy after the Cold War

De-Yuan Kao[*]

INTRODUCTION

The People's Republic of China (PRC) and the U.S. signed the *Joint Communiqué on the Establishment of Diplomatic Relations* on December 16, 1978, a windy day in Beijing. This communiqué not only signified the mutual diplomatic recognition of both countries, it also opened a new page in the history of the complex Sino-U.S. relationship. The Cold War ended ten years after this communiqué. A hostile Soviet Union no longer exists. China has become an important player in regional and world affairs. The U.S. now has to work closely with China in resolving many important international issues, such as denuclearizing the North Korea, deterring terrorism, reviving the global economy, reducing global warming, and so on.[1]

When a new host of the White House is elected, his[2] China policy is always one of the major focal points that people closely examine. Although some argue that there has been no dramatic change in the U.S.-China policy, others point out that many incidents happened during the Bush Senior, Clinton, and Bush Junior administrations which somewhat affected their policies toward China. For example, President Bush Senior did not clearly adopt a tough policy toward China when he assumed the presidency. However, the Tiananmen Square massacre in 1989 forced him to impose economic sanctions on China. President Clinton adopted a tougher attitude toward China in the early days of his presidency, but later his administration adopted the policy of engagement and enlargement in order to benefit the U.S. economy. Likewise, President Bush Junior referred to China as a strategic competitor when he took up his office. However, he had to treat China as one of American's major partners on anti-terrorism activities after the 9/11 terrorist attacks in 2001. Facing the highly changeful situations and various challenges, the U.S. needs to respond with different policies and strategies. The U.S. China policy has also needed to chart a path consistent to and keep up with the times.

When we talk about the U.S. policy toward China, it is true that some parts of the policy change over time, while others remain stable under either Republican or Democrat governments. Most discussions on the topic of foreign policy focus on what factors or theories lead to policy changes,[3] but they neglect considering that those unstable factors might be interchangeable with other fixed factors. Although we have seen great improvement in the relationship between the U.S. and China, disputes over issues relating interests such as economics, security, and Taiwan continue to flare up from time to time. These three issues could be regarded as the most important issues that Washington has to consider when making its policy toward Beijing.[4] The question is from amongst this cycle of flare-ups and cooling-off periods, whether or not we can ascertain which of those malleable and unchangeable aspects of the U.S. China policy are. What are the respective logical principles, if any, behind any changes and any aspects of the policy or relationship which tend to exhibit continuity? This chapter focuses on the U.S.-China relationship after the Cold War with discussion of three U.S. presidents (George H. W. Bush, Bill Clinton, and George W. Bush) over the past two decades. Their policy emphases with respect to three major issues of national interests involving the economy, security, and Taiwan will be reviewed concisely reviewed.

After the 1978 opening reforms in its economy, China's economic power had risen rapidly. For the United States, China is now the second largest trading partner next to Canada. Trade has been a hotly debated issue within the U.S., especially with regard to the massive trade deficit with China. How complexities of the trade relationship affect U.S. policy toward China is worthy of much further analysis.

On the issue of security, we have seen many debates about the China threat, as well as what policies the U.S. government should adopt to respond to this "threat." The official Chinese defense budget has increased at a double-digit pace annually since 1989 (except 2003).[5] With the possibility to parlay its increasing economic power into stronger military power, China has been seen as the country that could potentially compete with the U.S., not only in East Asia, but also in the global arena. Scholars have debated whether conflict between the U.S. and China is inevitable.[6] However, the threats that Washington faces come not only from Beijing, but also more urgently from terrorist attacks, environmental deterioration, and regional disorder which are the issues needed to be dealt with on a more urgent basis. However, it is important to recognize that most of these issues likely cannot be resolved without China's cooperation.

The last topic that this chapter will discuss is the Taiwan issue, which has always been the flashpoint between the interests of the U.S. and China. How the U.S. deals with the Taiwan issue is important to its relationship with China. Does Washington ever change its position on Taipei in order to cope with Beijing? If so, when, how, and why?

This chapter will offer a preliminary discussion on these issues according to the following structure. The first section introduces the main idea of this chapter. The two sections following thereafter briefly explain the three presidents' China policy in terms of U.S. interests in the economic, security, and Taiwan issues. It will also highlight the changeable and unchangeable elements in the U.S. China policy. The fourth section discusses some implications of President Obama's

China policy, as well as the importance of these two sets of variable and invariant China policy elements. The last section provides the conclusion.

THE CHANGEABLE ELEMENTS IN THE U.S. CHINA POLICY

The relationship with the People's Republic of China has become one of those most important issues that any U.S. president cannot afford to handle carelessly. Since the establishment of official diplomatic relationship and the recognition of the PRC as the sole legitimate government of China in 1979, the U.S. has consistently adopted a serious attitude toward this bilateral relationship. Any slight commotion can upset the delicate balance of national interests and make Washington and Beijing deeply worried and anxious. David M. Lampton, one of the most prestigious experts on the Sino-U.S. relationship, points out that both countries have been wrestling over their competing interests in the economic, security, and Taiwan issues over the past three decades.[7] From Bush Senior, Clinton, to Bush Junior, the U.S. has had several disputes with China over these issues, and the relationship could not be regarded as a perfectly smooth one. Although this chapter will only discuss these disputes briefly, it is obvious that any country's foreign policy cannot be completely fixed and unresponsive to changing environment and strategic considerations or interests. On the contrary, any country will necessarily adjust its policies in order to accommodate different circumstances or to respond to various critical precipitating events. In the evolution of the U.S. China policy, the three main issues noted above come to our attention.

Economy Could Prevail over Human Rights Issue

Since beginning its economic reform in 1978, through rapid growth in bilateral trade and commerce, China had become the United States' tenth largest trading partner in 1989, the fourth largest in 1999, and the second largest in 2009.[8] According to official data, total imports from China to the U.S. increased over 28 times if we compare the numbers from 1989 with those for 2008, producing a huge trade deficit of 268 billion in 2008.[9]

Readers might wonder if the Tiananmen Square protest had any ill effects on the U.S.-China trade relationship since it was the major incident during Bush Senior's presidency. Interestingly, the answer is in the negative. Although President Bush Senior immediately decided to impose economic sanctions on China after the bloody suppression, not even one single sanction was enacted by the Congress as law before February 1990. Just one month after the massacre, President Bush Senior lifted several sanctions' measures. At that time, the only weapon that the Congress could use to respond to President Bush Senior's "friendliness" toward China was the review of China's most-favored-nation (MFN) status. However, Bush Senior himself was not opposed to extending China's MFN status. Although this decision helped keep the amount of trade increasing between both countries, criticism of China's human rights record in the Congress and in the American society did not quiet down. Bush Senior's deeper connection with China did not give him a better chance to solve the crisis. On the contrary, granting a higher priority to the economy without paying as much attention to the poor human rights performance in China became one of the strongest criticisms from the Clinton camp during the 1992 presidential campaign.[10]

Clinton attacked President Bush Senior's China policy harshly during the campaign. He accused the president of being indifferent to democracy.[11] With great emphasis on domestic economic affairs and the determination to promote a better human rights situation abroad, Clinton, as expected, won the presidential election. However, policies do change. Although he held sharp attitudes towards Bush Senior's weak China policy, Clinton's position changed soon after the election ended. In November 1992, Clinton told the press that China should not be isolated as this was relevant to U.S. interests.[12] His way to engage China and maintain the U.S. interests at the same time was to link China's human rights performance with the extension of its MFN status.[13] By so doing, President Clinton might be able to show the American people that he still kept good on his words.

But even this policy did not last long. Facing great pressure from business circles and the Congress, President Clinton and his advisors decided to de-link the two issues in 1994. Instead, the U.S. government adopted an engagement policy toward China, hoping that the human rights condition in China could turn for the better if there were more interactions with the U.S.[14] The major tactical tool that Washington could use to demand Beijing to comply with international human rights standards has since been powerless.[15] The same scenario happened in late 1999 when the Clinton administration finalized the negotiations with the Chinese government for China's entry to the World Trade Organization (WTO). The U.S. Congress tried to push the government to use the WTO issue for further pressure on China's human rights performance. President Clinton realized that he could not ignore the strong opposition voice; hence, he did not sign the agreement with the Chinese Premier Zhu Rongji in April 1999. However, through numerous later rounds of bargaining, the U.S. and China reached agreement about market openness in November 1999, disregarding the dissatisfaction in the U.S. society.[16]

Clinton is not the only U.S. president who sharply changed his China policy. The Republican presidential candidate Bush Junior harshly criticized Clinton's China policy during the campaign. He further argued that the U.S. should adopt a tough realism to deal with China.[17] China was no longer a "constructive strategic partner" in Bush Junior's point of view; on the contrary, he regarded China as a "strategic competitor" and it was not wise to accommodate China simply for economic interests as this could sacrifice the U.S. security interests.[18]

Bush Junior himself did not completely eliminate the possibility to cooperate with China. During the presidential campaign, he emphasized that free trade and China's entry into the WTO were also part of his policy.[19] An announcement in June 2001 made by Robert Zoellick, the U.S. Trade

Representative, indicated that the U.S. would help China to finalize the procedure to enter the WTO. This statement signified and reaffirmed the importance of economic issues in the Sino-U.S. relationship.[20] After China formally joined the WTO in the end of 2001, the bilateral trade between China and the U.S. grew rapidly. The total U.S. exports to China increased over 29 billion dollars by the end of 2002, and this number went up to 62 billion dollars by the end of 2003.[21] China has become the U.S. second largest trading partner, next to Canada, and the gap between these two is narrowing.[22] As some progress in the bilateral economic relationship came into view, the Bush Junior administration also realized that direct engagement had its positive effects Although there are still some trade disputes between the U.S. and China, Henry Paulson Jr., Secretary of the Department of Treasury, mentioned that "engagement (with China) has helped us (the U.S.) manage the current financial market crisis . . . and China's growth is an opportunity for U.S. companies and consumers."[23] The Secretary of the Department of Commerce Carlos Gutierrez further clearly made this point that "as China's economy has developed, so has our trading relationship . . . maintaining openness in the U.S.-China economic relationship is not easy, but it's necessary . . . a prosperous China is in America's interests."[24] China has become one of America's most important trading partners,[25] and its weight in U.S. foreign policy cannot be ignored.

Engaging China Could Be Good for U.S. Security

The making of foreign policy involves not only concerns for domestic needs, security factors also matter in the decision-making process.[26] On the one hand, since the end of the Cold War, the global environment has become more complicated. Conflicts over cultures, resources, borders, and power occur in an endless stream.[27] The U.S. is the sole superpower now, but it cannot solve these conflicts alone, especially when several external factors simultaneously threaten or impair its national security. On the other hand, security issues could have a negative impact on the economy's development which, in turn, hurts the government's authority. Therefore, from Bush Senior, Clinton, to Bush Junior, we have seen that the leaders have tried to engage China as an important partner, and hope that persistent economic interactions could decrease the possibility of a future conflict against each other. For these reasons, the economic relationship has become a major pillar in the Sino-U.S. relationship, and all the U.S. government clearly understands this development. However, security concerns do not disappear from the considered calculations of America's China policy as the potential threats do not only come from China.

China's brutal suppression of the demonstration at the Tiananmen Square in 1989 showed the world once again just how a communist regime could be merciless to its people. As discussed earlier in this chapter, although the Bush Senior administration imposed economic sanctions on China, the sanctions were soon diluted.[28] Although the pressure from business circles was huge, another possible factor for this policy change could be the first Gulf War against Iraq in

1990. In order to gain China's support in the United Nations, it was helpful to offer some inducement for China to cooperate. Another friction between both countries during Bush Senior's presidency was China's arms sales to Pakistan and the Middle East.[29] President Bush Senior imposed sanctions on China when Chinese companies sold missile components to Pakistan in June 1991, but the sanctions were again soon lifted.[30] The main object in Bush Senior's mind had been the North Korea issue. As one of the rogue states,[31] North Korea was just a particular thorn in the America's side. In order to encourage Beijing to help persuade Pyongyang to participate in the proposal of denuclearization in the Korean Peninsula, and allow the International Atomic Energy Agency (IAEA) personnel to carry out their inspection mission in its nuclear bases, minor issues could be set aside temporarily.

This cooperation in security issues has two major implications. On the one hand, being more flexible in the policy toward China could increase the bilateral economic interests that pleased domestic business circles. On the other hand, the U.S. hoped China could make an effort on the North Korea issue. In short, President Bush Senior applied engagement policy toward China for the sake of economic and security issues, and he did reach some positive results.

However, the North Korea issue was still there after Clinton assumed office. Pyongyang's withdrawal from the *Nuclear Nonproliferation Treaty* (*NPT*) in 1993 weakened Washington's authority in East Asia. In order to break the deadlock, Beijing stepped in and helped Washington and Pyongyang sign the *Agreed Framework*. In other words, the crisis further promoted the cooperation between the U.S. and China in security issues. It is true that China's role in the 1994 *Agreed Framework* was not the most important one, yet, without its influence on Pyongyang, President Clinton would have faced more difficulty in reaching agreement with the North Korea.[32]

Another security issue attracting attention from Washington and Beijing was the Taiwan Strait Crisis in the 1995-1996. Many articles and books have detailed analyses and discussions of this event.[33] Although conflicts between the U.S. and China might have been triggered at any moment during this crisis, both countries realized that the lack of military-to-military direct dialogue channels could make the uncertainty more dangerous that could lead to unthinkable results.[34] Therefore, how to increase bilateral interactions and build mutual trust became an important mission for both sides. Unfortunately, the Belgrade embassy bombing incident in 1999 interrupted the process, and the official military hotline was not established until 2008.

The terrorist attacks in 2001 shocked the whole of America. The urgent demand for international cooperation against terrorism became the first task in the Bush Junior administration. China also expressed its willingness to work with the U.S. both economically and militarily. On the days following after the attacks, Chinese President Jiang Zemin agreed to support the anti-terrorism campaign and to strengthen the dialogue with the U.S. government.[35] Since then, Bush Junior modified his previous judgment regarding China's role. In the *2002 National Security Strategy of the United States of America*, the Bush Junior administration clearly pointed out that "China is an important part of our strategy to promote a stable, peaceful, and prosperous Asia-Pacific region." Moreover, the U.S. "welcomes the emergence of a strong, peaceful, and prosperous China."[36] Beijing was no longer seen as a strategic competitor but as a constructive partner.[37]

In addition to the anti-terrorist cooperation, China also helped the U.S. to hold the Six-Party Talks with the North Korea. Although there was no clear sign that North Korea would utterly abandon its nuclear program, this initiative did reach some positive results. In the latest national security strategy report, the White House reconfirmed that China is an important actor in the world stage, and expressed that U.S. government hopes to see China become a responsible stakeholder.[38] In March 2008, the U.S. and China finally agreed to sign an agreement on the establishment of a military hotline between the two countries' defense chiefs.[39] This mechanism not only led to a closer relationship between China and the U.S., it also meant that there will be less chance of misjudgment and more opportunity for smoother dialogues.

In short, Washington has realized that engagement is beneficial in its relationship with Beijing. Engagement will lead to mutual understanding, and increase the cooperation across different agendas, while decreasing the chances of possible conflicts and disputes, thereby enhancing the U.S. security.

Taiwan Card Might Become Less Useful

Among issues that involve the Sino-U.S. relationship, Taiwan has been one of the most sensitive ones. Since Washington established official diplomatic relationship with Beijing in 1979, its relationship with Taipei has been closely monitored by the Chinese government. Any further contact between Washington and Taipei might make a ripple on the seemingly peaceful pond of the Sino-U.S. relationship. Over the past two decades, Bush Senior, Clinton, and Bush Junior did have some positive contacts with Taiwan, and China complained about these movements from time to time.

After the People's Republic of China replaced the Republic of China (ROC) as the Chinese member of the United Nations in 1971, the ROC has lost its membership in many international organizations. Although it was one of the earliest signatories of the General Agreement on Tariffs and Trade (GATT) since 1948, the ROC was forced to withdraw from this organization in 1971. The Nationalist government in Taiwan sought to participate in the GATT since 1988, and submitted an application to the GATT for new membership in 1990. The Chinese Premier Li Peng soon made representations to the GATT, but the Bush Senior administration promised to grant its support for the ROC's membership.[40] One year later, during the presidential campaign in 1992, President Bush Senior announced that the U.S. decided to sell 150 F-16 aircraft to Taiwan.[41] China was again upset about this decision and regarded it as "a very serious incident."[42] However, if there had been no Tiananmen Square incident in 1989, and if President Bush Senior had the possibility to win the election, there would not have been the F-16 sale.[43] During Bush Senior's presidency, Taiwan could be a handy card to play when the U.S. needed to admonish China from engaging in further behavior that violated human rights. In addition, Washington's speaking in support of Taipei's participation in international organizations could also force Beijing to open China's market sooner.

Nonetheless, the winning presidential candidate Clinton did not restrain the contact between the U.S. and Taiwan. A former U.S. president even argued that Taiwan's market was larger than mainland China.[44] The close relationship kept developing until the 1995-1996 Taiwan Strait Crisis occurred. On the one hand, the U.S. government did not want to infuriate China further after granting a visa to Lee Teng-hui, the Taiwan leader in 1995. On the other hand, the Clinton administration had to take some measures to prevent a conflict in the Taiwan Strait. Finally, President Clinton sent two carrier battle groups to international waters near Taiwan in 1996. At the same time, in order to reassure Beijing about Washington's policy toward China, President Clinton gave China his Three No's promise in writing in 1995, and reaffirmed this policy during his 1998 visit to Shanghai.[45] The Belgrade embassy bombing incident in May 1999 roused another wave of dissatisfaction in China, and Lee Teng-hui's "special state-to-state relationship" statement[46] in July 1999 further worsened the triangular relations. The Clinton administration soon distanced itself from Lee's statement and asked China to act with restraint.[47] With a more powerful China that had more confidence in itself and a more provocative Taiwan whose leader was more inclined to go to extremes, it seemed that the U.S. government had gradually lost its checking power over Beijing and Taipei as they could easily take provocative actions without notifying the U.S. in advance.

Obviously, the Clinton administration's China policy became one of the critical issues that Bush Junior attacked during the presidential campaign. Compared with Clinton's engagement policy, Bush Junior saw China as a competitor and hoped to check China's power more efficiently. For this reason, Taiwan became a bargaining chip that the U.S. government could use. For example, Bush Junior decided to sell Taiwan a range of weapon and said he would do "whatever it took" to help Taiwan defend itself.[48] The President of Taiwan, Chen Shui-bian, soon proposed his interpretation of the China-Taiwan relationship as "one country on each side (of the Taiwan Strait)."[49] Taiwan would have gained more support from the U.S. if the leaders did not adopt such brinkmanship.[50] To some extent, Chen's statement backfired, and the U.S. also restated its one China policy, both publicly and privately.[51]

In addition, with the terrorist attacks, Washington reversed its policy toward Beijing. In just eight months, China had become America's constructive partner, no longer a strategic competitor. The financial crisis pushed the U.S. even closer to China.[52] As Washington needed Beijing's assistance in several international issues, Taiwan's status could even be disregarded.[53] Thus, it could be seen that the Bush Junior administration did not play the Taiwan card deftly, and could not accomplish the mission of "regularizing relations with both Taiwan and China at the same time" either.[54]

The U.S., although still the most powerful country in the world, has become weaker to some extent as challenges and crises come one after another. Issues such as North Korea denuclearization, terrorist attacks and financial crises could not be solved by the U.S. alone, and China, with its growing influence, has proven to be able to offer necessary assistance on these issues. From this point of view, it seems that Washington has become more reliant on Beijing after the end of the Cold War, not vice versa. In other words, with internal and external crises, the U.S. has seemed to gradually loss its bargaining chips in the economic and Taiwan issues while China has gained more.

THE IMPERVIOUS ELEMENTS IN THE U.S. CHINA POLICY

It is true that Washington's China policy has experienced pendulum swings over the last two decades, with some modifications as the circumstances changed.[55] However, regarding the foundational issues of human rights, national security, and Taiwan, Washington has its consistent position, and these elements could not be changed easily.

The Human Rights Issue Is Still Important

President Jimmy Carter established the official diplomatic relationship with the PRC in 1979. Carter might be the U.S. president who openly supported the idea of human rights the most.[56] The U.S. Department of State has submitted the review report on the human rights conditions in other countries annually to the U.S. Congress since 1977. China, as one of the countries that have a consistently bad record for human rights performance, has been criticized by U.S. legislators every year.

During the Cold War, the U.S. needed China's assistance in counterbalancing the Soviet Union, and the contact between both countries has become even closer since the 1990s. As discussed above, the bilateral trade relationship did not really suffer because of China's human rights violations. The U.S. government and Congress argued over China's MFN status every year until President Clinton managed to delink the human rights and trade issues in 1994, even though China had not made as much progress on human rights issues as he had hoped. However, Clinton himself pointed out that after the separation of these two issues, Washington would have more serious dialogues with Beijing.[57] One reason for the Clinton administration to make the decision to engage China more broadly was to hope that the U.S. could find another approach to improve China's human rights performance.[58] However, there has been no obvious improvement in the annual human rights practices report submitted by the Department of State. China is still regarded as a "not free" country according to the Freedom House.[59]

Although there is no substantial checking power from the human rights report, the U.S. government has often used this review to persuade the Chinese government for further openness and reform. Furthermore, the U.S. president also tries to mention or even condemn China's poor human rights record on different occasions.[60] These criticisms, whether in written form or in rhetoric, signify that as long as China has no obvious and notable improvement in its human rights performance, the U.S. government, whether it's a Republican or a Democrat one, will keep using the human rights card to press China for progress in according the natural dignity owed the Chinese peoples.

National Security Is Emphasized Repeatedly

The U.S. has occupied the status of a sole superpower in the world for the past decades since no country has the capability to challenge its power. It is true that the U.S. won several wars under the Bush Senior, Clinton, and Bush Junior administrations, and the superiority of the U.S. military force has shown the world that the U.S. has the power to fight against its enemy in the name of counterterrorism or humanitarianism. However, the U.S. arbitrary decision to wage wars makes Beijing worry about the possibility of coming conflict between the U.S. and China.

Therefore, after the U.S. victory in the first Gulf War, and the mobilization of its forces in the 1995-1996 Taiwan Strait crisis, the Chinese government decided to develop and modernize its military forces. With continuous double-digit growth rate in its military spending since the mid 1990s, a rising China has emerged. Awareness of the so-called China threat has spread over the U.S. and the world. For this reason, whether China could challenge the U.S. status in international society has been hotly debated.[61] Of course, even if Beijing is a threat, it will not be the only threat that Washington must face. The U.S. leaders have repeatedly mentioned the importance of national security.[62] If it is the moral factor that makes the U.S. to push China for better human rights performance, it may be practical reality that forces the U.S. to balance China.

Taiwan Policy Remains Stable

According to official statements, the U.S. policy toward Taiwan has remained stable. The three communiqués (the *Shanghai Communiqué* of 1972, the *Joint Communiqué* of 1979, the *817 Communiqué* of 1982) and the *Taiwan Relations Act* of 1979 are the major documents that explain or regulate the U.S. policy and relationship toward China and Taiwan. However, as the economic and security policies, there is no preset and unalterable Taiwan policy that the U.S. government must follow. In fact, those documents represent basic guidelines for the U.S. leaders to make decisions. This explains why it is that even as Taiwan leaders reject U.S. pressure, they still have confidence that Washington would feel it their impervious duty to come to their help if ever there is a crisis.[63]

As discussed in the previous section, of course, with different strategic considerations, the actual policy choices could be different, as long as the core elements in the documents are not vitiated. Thus, we see that President Bush Senior could sell F-16 fighters to Taiwan, President Clinton could publicly talk about his Three No's policy, and President Bush Junior could boldly assured the Taiwanese of strong U.S. support. That is the flexible function of the Taiwan card. After the terrorist attacks and the financial crisis, the U.S. has been seeking international cooperation, especially from China. With fewer bargaining chips in economic and security terms, the U.S. leadership must rethink the importance of the Taiwan trump card.[64]

Ultimately, as the only superpower in the world, the U.S. must take a broader view when making China policy. However, the discussion of the permeable and impervious elements throughout the Bush Senior, Clinton, and Bush Junior administrations shows that in order to promote U.S. interests, economic interests in particular, human rights, national security, or aspects of the Taiwan issue could be disregarded. After all, ordinary people pay more attention to the numbers of their bank accounts, and they happen to be the electorate of the U.S. leader. Therefore, if the presidential candidate wants to be elected, it is rational that he or she focuses on the bottom line economic issues. This inference seems plausible, but in fact, the U.S. government still holds to its steadied position on the unchangeable elements. The adherence to these elements also presents itself in the current Obama administration.

WHAT NOW? AND SO WHAT?

The above sections have discussed the changeable and unchangeable elements in the past three U.S. administrations' policy toward China. One liberal argument regarding foreign policy goals, especially for the United States, is that one of the goals is to spread liberal ideology, such as democracy, human rights, free trade, and so on.[65] The United States has been a liberal democracy since its beginning, and liberal ideologies do matter, to some extent, in formulating U.S. foreign policy. We have learnt that economic, security, and Taiwan issues construct the core of U.S. China policy in the past two decades. However, what are their positions in the current Obama administration's China policy? In addition, we must ask which set of elements is more important, the changeable or the unchangeable elements?

Current Situation

In fact, in order to resolve the current slate of global and domestic problems, the U.S. needs further international cooperation, and China has a key role in this cooperation. Before he was elected as the U.S. president, Mr. Obama clearly argued that the U.S. would have more "high-level dialogues" with the Chinese government in economic, security, and global issues.[66] The Taiwan issue is of course one of those important global issues. In the previous chapter, Dr. Bo Zhiyue has proposed a detailed analysis of the continuity and change in President Obama's China Policy. Therefore, this section will only briefly discuss the current situation regarding the above three issues after President Obama's visit to China in November 2009.

First, in terms of the economy, China has held almost $800 billion in U.S. treasury bonds as of the end of September 2009 and replaced Japan's position as the U.S. biggest foreign creditor.[67] Therefore, if China were going to sell its holdings, the dollar would likely precipitously depreciate immediately. With the severe global recession originating from Wall Street, President Obama naturally also hopes that cooperation from both sides could revive the economy, and bring back the domestic prosperity. The U.S., facing severe internal recession and the global slump, has to rely on China's assistance to manage the current global setback. Therefore, on the one hand, the U.S. government should also encourage China to follow global financial and economic practices to make sure that the Chinese government truly observes the relevant norms and rules. On the other hand, Washington will need to seek other countries' cooperation to reinvigorate the global economy.

China's GDP was $1 trillion in 2000, only one tenth of the U.S. GDP. However, the ratio changed dramatically in 2008 when China's GDP reached $4 trillion; it is close to one fourth of the U.S. GDP in that year. An economically strong China has attracted many European countries, who want to work with China to construct a new international financial regime. This attraction grants China a larger say in global economic affairs. To overly rely on China without looking for other approaches to solve the crisis is just like a two-edged sword. It might hurt U.S. national interests if this policy backfires.

Secondly, in the case of security issues, the Obama administration needs China's help not only to mediate the nuclear crisis largely caused by North Korea in the Northeast Asia, but in other regions, such as South Asia, and Africa, China can also provide positive contributions to maintain stability. The Six-Party Talks has been suspended since April 2009. President Obama has decided to work with the Chinese government to resolve the Korean Peninsula.[68] In addition, it is also important for the U.S. to have China's assistance in counterterrorism in all of South Asia, especially in Afghanistan.[69]

As regards the Iran issue, China has not agreed to the U.S. suggestion for imposing tougher sanctions on Iran. Chinese President Hu Jintao said "it is only normal that our two sides may disagree on some issues."[70] Yet, in the *U.S.-China Joint Statement* that the U.S. and China signed after the leaders' summit, China expressed its willingness to share responsibility with the U.S. to address regional and global security challenges, not only including denuclearization of the Korean Peninsula, the nuclear issue in Iran, but also disarmament, nuclear proliferation, and the relations between India and Pakistan.[71] It is clear that the Chinese government now has more confidence in keeping up its own position, and any tough gestures would surely strengthen the authority of its leadership. What is worth more attention, however, is by granting so much emphasis and responsibility with China, the U.S. might sooner or later lose its influence on the global stage.

Thirdly, with regard to the Taiwan issue, it is clearly that President Obama will follow his predecessors' policy.[72] The U.S. shall abide its One China policy, the three *Joint Communiqués*, and the *Taiwan Relations Act*. Although there is no mention of the *TRA* in the *Joint Statement*, President Obama did refer to the *TRA* in the press conference after his talk with the Chinese President Hu Jintao. He is the second U.S. president to talk about the *Taiwan Relations Act* in Beijing and in the Chinese leader's presence.[73] President Obama's visit to China again reflects this continuity of position, policy and practice. If it is unavoidable that Washington needs Beijing's assistance in regard to the economy and security, how the Obama administration will play its Taiwan card is worth our serious attention.

Which Set of Elements Is More Important?

Policies can also change because different leaders have distinct thoughts and considerations. Although it is logical to differentiate the changeable and unchangeable elements in the foreign policy making process, it is also true that change and continuity are in fact two sides of same coin, and they can be interchangeable when necessary. We should not too harshly divide these two sets of elements in the U.S. China policy.

For example, President Clinton delinked the human rights issue from the annual extension of China's most-favored-nation status in 1994. President Obama did not touch the human rights issue during his first visit to China in order not to hurt the Chinese leaders' feelings in order to gain more support of economic and security issues. Yet, the U.S. Department of State criticizes China's human rights performance every year in its human rights report. That is to say, although some elements have lower priority at times, that does not mean they will be ignored or left aside. Sooner or later, these issues will arise under a somewhat different guise.

As discussed in the previous sections, trade issues have become the most important focus in the U.S.-China relationship for the time being. In order to cope with the changing circumstances, the U.S. is now diverting its focal points. Other issues have to wait until the economy revives. Policies are seemingly not designed as transparently as before, but are being made in a mythical black box. As president, Obama receives a lot of information, regarding both domestic and international concerns. By consulting the information at hands, leaders want to make the decisions that comport with securing their best national interests. Hence, there might be no definite answer to the questions regarding whether the changeable elements are more important than the seemingly immutable elements or not. The only way to tell which element is more important is to see what its current rank in the leader's priority list of priorities.

CONCLUSION

Thirty years have passed since the U.S. and the PRC established their official diplomatic relationship. This evolution shows the world that as long as both parties can dialogue from the premise of mutual respect, a peaceful coexistence, in spite of basic difference in position and competing interests, is not impossible. This bilateral approach to reconciliation also tells us that confrontation is not the best policy to solve bilateral differences; on the contrary, to understand your counterpart's needs and thoughts is the key to reach mutualism. If Washington and Beijing want to maintain their amiable relationship, both countries should not go backtrack.

From 1989 to 2008, although disturbances and disputes happened occasionally, we have seen a lot of progress in the U.S.-China relationship. Since Mr. Obama came into power in 2008, there has not been much fluctuation in his China policy. Three factors might be able to explain this phenomenon. First, many of the administration members have experience in Asian affairs, and their opinions are mostly practical and objective. Since these senior officials in those important Departments and agencies know how to deal with China, and they are well acquainted with U.S. national interests as well, President Obama does not have to re-design or implement a new set of China positions, policies or practices.

Secondly, to maintain the continuity and steadiness of the U.S. China policy is a guiding principle for the Obama administration. President Obama clearly pointed out this principle before he won the presidential election.[74] He will rigorously follow a policy of engaging China so as to produce more benefits for both sides. Lastly, the U.S. economy is now in a somewhat dire situation. The financial storm has swept across the U.S., so it is President Obama's first priority to concentrate on economic recovery. For these reasons, therefore, to maintain China policy on its existing tracks is the most convenient approach for the Obama administration to handle issues related to China and avoid any drastic dislocation caused by derailment.

It is clear that a healthy Sino-U.S. relationship is good for international society; yet, one important trend generalized from the above discussion remains noteworthy. That is, that if the U.S. would like to keep trading with China and hoping China will contribute to global affairs, sooner or later, Washington will gradually lose its checking power over Beijing. In fact, with more bargaining chips in hand, whether China will be willing to cooperate with the U.S. will be debatable. Although China has not caught up with the U.S. in military capability at present, it is possible that Beijing will use its advantage to make the current balance (if there is a balance) in the relationship with Washington a more favorable one, with the fulcrum swinging toward itself in the future.[75]

China has become one of the most important actors that the U.S. could not ignore after the Cold War. People still pay close attention to the development of the bilateral relationship between the U.S. and China. A rising China could be a constructive strategic partner in the Clinton administration, the strategic competitor before the terrorist attacks in the Bush Junior administration, a responsible stakeholder in Bush Junior's second term. Yet, these conceptual changes could be adjusted from time to time as long as the relationship is going in what is perceived to be a positive direction. Although some differences do exist between the two countries, and some scholars regard China as the threat to the existing balance of power, dispelling mutual divergence, and strengthening the bilateral relationship is more important. If no surprising incidents occur, then some core elements in the U.S. China policy will hardly change no matter who is the host in the White House. Confucius once said "at thirty, I could stand firm and act on proprieties." The official diplomatic relationship between the People's Republic of China and the U.S. has now matured to thirty years, and both countries have learned a lot from their past. If the U.S. and China are willing to tolerate its counterpart's economic and political ambitions, with moderating foreign policies and smooth communication channels, a win-win relationship for both countries should not be unexpected.

NOTES

* De-Yuan Kao is a Ph.D. Candidate in the Department of Political Science at Boston University, Boston, MA, U.S.A. He can be reached at <dykao@bu.edu.. The author would like to thank all the comments received at the Association of Chinese Political Studies (ACPS) annual conference (2009).

1. Thomas Freedman has argued that China and the U.S. are inseparable. See Thomas L. Freedman, *The World is Flat: A Brief History of the Twenty-First Century* (New York: Farrar, Straus and Giroux, 2005).
2. I use male appellation here because no female presidential candidates have been elected as the U.S. President since its establishment.
3. For example, Steve Smith, Amelia Hadfield, and Tim Dunne, eds., *Foreign Policy: Theories, Actors, Cases* (New York: Oxford University Press, 2008); Robert S. Ross, eds., *After the Cold War: Domestic Factors and U.S.-China Relations* (Armonk, New York: M.E. Sharpe, 1998); and Raymon H. Meyers, Michel C. Oksenberg, and David Shambaugh, eds., *Making China Policy: Lessons from the Bush and Clinton Administrations* (New York: Rowman and Littlefield, 2001).
4. Kerry Dumbaugh, *China-U.S. Relations: Current Issues and Implication for U.S. Policy*, CRS Report, R40457, April 2, 2009. http://italy.usembassy.gov/pdf/other/R40457.pdf. Last retrived on November 20, 2009.
5. The military increased 9.6 percent in 2003. See Willy Wo-Lap Lam, "Budget Surprise for China's Army," CNN (March 6, 2003). http://www.cnn.com/2003/WORLD/asiapcf/east/03/05/china.forces/index.html. Last retrieved on August 15, 2009. More detailed analysis of China's military power, see Robert M. Gates, *Annual Report on the Military Power of the People's Republic of China* (Washington, D.C.: Department of Defense, March 25, 2009).
6. Zbigniew Brzezinski and John J. Mearsheimer, "Clash of the Titans," *Foreign Policy*, Iss. 146 (Jan/Feb 2005), pp. 46-50. More theoretical debates see Aaron Friedberg, "The Future of U.S.-China Relations: Is Conflict Inevitable?" *International Security*, Vol. 30, No. 2 (Fall 2005), pp. 7-45.
7. See David M. Lampton, *Same Bed Different Dreams: Managing U.S.-China Relations, 1989-2000* (Berkeley, California: University of California Press, 2001).
8. See Warren John Tenney, "U.S. Response to the Tiananmen and Kwangju Incidents: American Relations with China and Korea," *East Asia*, Vol. 11, No. 4 (December 1992), pp. 58-76; "Top Trading Partners—Surplus, Deficit, and Total Trade," in U.S. Census

Bureau. Online statistics at http://www.census.gov/foreign-trade/top/index.html#2009. Last retrieved on November 23, 2009.

9. These numbers only reflect the trade in goods. See "Trade in Goods (Import, Export, and Trade Balance) with China," in U.S. Census Bureau. Online statistics at http://www.census.gov/foreign-trade/balance/c5700.html#top.   Last   retrieved   on November 23, 2009.

10. James Mann, *About Face: A history of America's Curious Relationship with China, From Nixon to Clinton* (New York: Vintage Books, 2000), pp. 229-232, 260-262. Also see Peter Baker, "Bush, Clinton and China," *The Washington Post*, April 8, 2008. http://voices.washingtonpost.com/44/2008/04/08/bush_clinton_and_china.html.   Last retrieved on Nov. 23, 2009.

11. Edward Walsh, "Clinton Indicts Bush's World Leadership," *The Washington Post*, October 2, 1992, p. A12.

12. Thomas L. Friedman, "The Transition: The President-Elect; Clinton Says Bush Made China Gains," *The New York Times*, November 20, 1992, p. A1. http://www.nytimes.com/1992/11/20/us/the-transition-the-president-elect-clinton-says-bush-made-china-gains.html. Last retrieved on November 23, 2009.

13. David M. Lampton, "China Policy in Clinton's First Year," in James R. Lilley and Wendell Willkie II, eds., *Beyond MFN: Trade with China and American Interests* (Washington, D.C.: AEI Press, 1994), pp. 16-20.

14. Vladimir N. Pregelj, "92094: Most-Favored-Nation Status of the People's Republic of China," *CRS Issue Brief*, December 6, 1996. http://www.fas.org/man/crs/92-094.htm. Last retrieved on November 10, 2009

15. Many U.S. Congressmen were not satisfied with the decision to decouple the human rights performance and MFN status. They argued that the segmentation in 1994 only made the situation worse in China. See "Country reports on human Rights Practices for 1994: Hearings before the Subcommittee on International Operations and Human Rights of the Committee on International Relations," House of Representatives, One Hundred Fourth Congress, first session, February 2 and 15, 1995. http://www.archive.org/stream/countryreportson00unit/countryreportson00unit_djvu.txt. Last retrieved on Oct. 12, 2009.

16. See James H. Nolt, "China in the WTO: The Debate," *Foreign Policy in Focus*, Vol. 4, No, 38 (December 1999), pp. 1-4. Regarding the political and economic entanglement, please see Keiji Nakatsuji, "Essence of Trade Negotiation: A Study of China's Entry for WTO," *The Ritsumeikan Journal of International Studies*, Vol. 14, No. 1 (June 2001), pp. 15-33.

17. George W. Bush, *A Charge to Keep* (New York: William Morrow and Company, 1999), p. 239.

18. Condoleeza Rice, "Promoting the National Interests," *Foreign Affairs*, Vol. 79, No. 1 (January-February, 2000), pp. 47-60. The negative result of Clinton's engagement policy is also discussed academically. See John J. Mearsheimer, *The Tragedy of Great Power Politics* (New York: W. W. Norton & Company, 2001), p. 4.

19. Bush Junior made this statement to win over the support from the agricultural and financial sectors in the U.S..

20. Bill Savadove, "U.S. China Reach Consensus on WTO, Eye Geneva," *Reuters*, June 9th, 2001. http://www.nettrash.com/users/socialjustice/chinarchv.html. Last retrieved on October 18, 2009.

21. See "Trade in Goods (Import, Export, and Trade Balance) with China," in U.S. Census Bureau. Online statistics at http://www.census.gov/foreign-trade/balance/c5700.html#top Last retrieved on November 23, 2009.

22. See "Top Trading Partners- Total Trade, Exports & Imports," in U.S. Census Bureau. Online statistics at http://www.census.gov/foreign-trade/statistics/highlights/top/index. html#2009. Last retrieved on November 23, 2009.

23. Henry M. Paulson, Jr., *Preview Upcoming Strategic Economic Dialogue Meeting in Beijing*, Treasury Secretary's Speech on U.S.-China Economic Relations, December 2, 2008.   http://www.america.gov/st/texttrans-english/2008/December/2008120217272 1eaifas0.8715326.html. Last Retrieved on November 12, 2009.

24. Carlos M. Gutierrez, speech delivered at the 2007 George Bush China-U.S. Relations Conference. Washington, D.C., October 23, 2007. http://www.commerce.gov/ NewsRoom/SecretarySpeeches/PROD01_004381. Last retrieved on November 22, 2009.

25. Jill Dougherty, "U.S., China Agreed on Economic Strategies," *CNN*, June 29, 2009. http://edition.cnn.com/2009/POLITICS/07/28/china.stimulus/index.html. Last retrieved on November 11, 2009.

26. Ryan K. Beasley, Juliet Kaarbo, Jeffery S. Lantis, and Michael T. Snarr, eds., *Foreign Policy in Comparative Perspectives: Domestic and International Influences on State Behavior* (Washington, D.C.: CQ Press, 2002).

27. See Samuel P. Huntington, *The Clash of Civilizations and the Remaking of World Order* (New York: Simon & Shuster, 1996).

28. For example, President Bush Senior sent Brent Scowcroft and Lawrence Eagleburger to Beijing in July. The U.S. also permitted the sale of four Boeing 757 commercial aircraft to China about the same time. See Harry Harding, *A Fragile Relationship: The United States and China since 1972* (Washington, D.C.: The Brookings Institution Press, 1992), pp. 229-229.

29. Harding, *A Fragile Relationship*, pp. 331-333.

30. "The sanctions were supposed to last for at least two years, but it was lifted less than a year." In Gary Milhollin, "Testimony before the House Committee on International Relations and National Security," June 17, 1998. Also see Robert Suey and Shirley A. Kan, "Chinese Missile and Nuclear Proliferation: Issues for Congress," *CRS Issue Brief*, IB92056, February 2, 1995.

31. A general model of "rogue states" became popular in the national security discourse from 1990. See Michael Klare, *Rogue States and Nuclear Outlaws: America's Search for a New Foreign Policy* (New York: Hill and Wang, 1995).

32. Ji-Yong Lee has a thorough investigation on the role of Korean factor in Sino-U.S. relations in Chapter 4 in this book.

33. See for example, Robert L. Suettinger, *Beyond Tiananmen: The Politics of U.S.-China Relations, 1989-2000* (Washington, D.C.: The Brookings Institute Press, 2003), pp. 200-263; chapters in Suisheng Zhao, ed., *Across the Taiwan Strait: Mainland China, Taiwan, and the 1995-1996 Crisis* (New York: Routledge, 1999); Allen S. Whiting, "China's Use of Force, 1950-1996 and Taiwan," *International Security*, Vol. 26, No. 2 (Fall 2001), pp. 120-123; and Andrew Scobell, "Show of Force: Chinese Soldiers, Statesmen, and the 1995-1996 Taiwan Strait Crisis," *Political Science Quarterly*, Vol. 115. No. 2 (Summer 2000), pp. 227-246.

34. Admiral Joseph Prueher mentioned this point in China. He was wishing that he could call the Chinese Navy directly during the crisis. See Shirely A. Kan, *U.S. China Military Contacts: Issues for Congress*, CRS Report, RL32496, August 6, 2009. http://www.fas.org/sgp/crs/natsec/RL32496.pdf. Last retrieved on November 11, 2009.

35. See "News letter of 2001," No. 1107, September 2001, Embassy of the People's Republic of China in the United States. http://www.china-embassy.org/eng/ sgxx/sggg/sstx/2001/t35029.htm. Last retrieved on November 11, 2009.

36. The White House, *National Security Strategy of the United States of America*, September 2002, p. 30.

37. *Ibid..* But there are still other concerns about the bilateral cooperation. See Shirely A. Kan, *U.S.-China Counter-Terrorism Cooperation: Issues for U.S. Policy*, CRS Report, RS21995, May 12, 2005.

38. The White House, *National Security Strategy of the United States of America*, March 2006, p. 46.

39. Cao Li, "Sino-U.S. Deal on Military Hotline Inked," *China Daily*, March 1, 2008. http://www.chinadaily.com.cn/china/2008-03/01/content_6498577.htm. Last retrieved on October 15, 2009.

40. "Bush to Support ROC GATT Bid; President Promises to Push Taiwan Accession," July 23, 1991. http://taiwanjournal.nat.gov.tw/site/tj/ct.asp?xItem=12421&CtNode =122. Last retrieved on November 26, 2009. Also see Harding, *A Fragile Relationship*, p. 349.

41. Mann, *About Face*, pp. 266-269. After the U.S. and China signed the *817 Communiqué* in 1982, the U.S. decreased its arms sale to Taiwan gradually. The total amount in 1990 was about 660 million dollars. See Jaw-Ling Joanne Chang, ed., *China-U.S. Relations: 1985-1987* (Taipei: Institute of American Culture, Academia Sinica, 1989), p. 3.

42. Mann, *About Face*, pp. 280-271. Regards the more detailed analysis of the U.S. arms sale to Taiwan, please see Shirley A. Kan, *Taiwan: Major U.S. Arms Sale Since 1990*, CRS Report, RL30957, August 20, 2009.

43. This decision was not really meant to strengthen Taiwan's military force. President Bush Senior made the decision in order to attract more votes in Texas. Mann, *About Face*, pp. 266-268.

44. Richard Nixon, *Beyond Peace* (New York: Simon & Schuster Inc., 1993), pp. 133-134.

45. Mann, *About Face*, pp. 330, 366.

46. Richard C. Bush, *Untying the Knot: Making Peace in the Taiwan Strait* (Washington, D.C.: The Brookings Institution Press, 2005), pp. 218-219.

47. Bonnie Glaser, "Beginning to Thaw," *Comparative Connections*, Vol. 1, No. 2 (October 1999), pp. 15-16.

48. David E. Sanger, "U.S. Would Defend Taiwan, Bush Says," *The New York Times*, April 26, 2001, p. A1.

49. Bonnie Glaser, "China's Taiwan Policy in the Wake of 'One Country on Each Side'." *American Foreign Policy Interests*, Vol. 24, No. 6 (December 2002), pp. 515-524.

50. The more detailed analysis of the relationship between Washington and Taipei, please see Kerry Dumbaugh, *Taiwan-U.S. Relations: New Strains and Changes*, CRS Report, RL33684, October 10, 2006. http://www.au.af.mil/au/awc/awcgate/crs/rl33684.pdf. Last retrieved on May 12, 2009.

51. Ibid.

52. Wang Zhuoqiong, "Crisis 'Can Bring China, U.S. Closer'," *China Daily*, March 5, 2009. http://www.chinadaily.com.cn/china/2009-03/05/content_7538000.htm. Last retrieved on October 20, 2009.

53. Ted Galen Carpenter, "Wild Card: A Democratic Taiwan," *China Security*, Vol. 4, No. 1 (Winter 2008), p. 52.

54. Joseph A. Bosco, "Bush Deftly Plays the Taipei-Beijing Card," *Los Angeles Times*, March 25, 2002, p. B9.

55. And President Clinton was attacked harshly for his vacillation. See Lawrence T. DiRita, "Read My Flips: Clinton's Foreign Policy Reversals in His Own Words," Heritage Foundation, June 20, 1994. http://www.heritage.org/Research/Europe/ FYl18.cfm. Last retrieved on November 29, 2009.

56. Jimmy Carter, *Keeping Faith: Memoir of A President* (New York: Bantam Books, 1982).

57. See Press Briefing by National Security Advisor Tony Lake, Assistant Secretary of State for Human Rights John Shattuck, Assistant Secretary of State for Asian and Pacific Affairs Winston Lord and Assistant to the President for Economic Policy Bob Rubin, May 26, 1994. http://www.presidency.ucsb.edu/ws/index.php?pid=59758. Last retrieved on September 20, 2009.

58. David M. Lampton, "America's China Policy in the Age of the Finance Minister: Clinton Ends Linkage," *China Quarterly*, No. 139 (September 1994), pp. 597-621.

59. Freedom House, *Freedom in the World: 2009 Edition* (Washington, D.C.: Freedom House, 2009). http://www.freedomhouse.org/template.cfm?page=22&country=7586&year=2009. Last retrieved on November 20, 2009.

60. See for example, Jane Macarthney, "President Bush Condemns China Human Rights Record on Eve of Olympics," *The Times*, August 8, 2008. http://www.timesonline.co.uk/tol/news/world/asia/article4476593.ece. Last retrieved on November 20, 2009; Steven Lee Myers, "Bush to Urge China to Improve Human Rights," *The New York Times*, August 6, 2008. http://www.nytimes.com/2008/08/06/sports/olympics/07prexy.html. Last retrieved on November 20, 2009; "Clinton Urged to Tackle China on Human Rights," *The Birmingham Post*, June 23, 1998. http://findarticles. com/p/news-articles/birmingham-post-england-the/mi_7996/is_1998_June_23/clinton-urged-tackle-china-human/ai_n35897078/. Last retrieved on November 20, 2009; and Susan F. Rasky, "Bush Nudges China on Anniversary of Crackdown," *The New York Times*, June 5, 1990, p. A9.

61. See for example Aaron Friedberg, "The Future of U.S.-China Relations: Is Conflict Inevitable?" *International Security*, Vol. 30, No. 2 (Fall 2005), pp. 7-45.

62. See the emphasis on national security in the *National Military Strategy of the United States* in the past years.

63. Carpenter, "Wild Card: A Democratic Taiwan," pp. 42-60.

64. However, since Ma Ying-jeou took his office in 2008, the relationship between Taiwan and China has become closer. The triangular relations among these three parties have shown the asymmetric development, which, in turn, might decrease the U.S. influence on Taiwan, and make the Taiwan card less useful.

65. Stanley Hoffmann, "The Clash of Ideas: The Crisis of Liberal Internationalism," *Foreign Policy*, Iss. 98 (Spring 1995), pp. 159-177.

66. Barak Obama, "US-China Relations under an Obama Administration." *Time*, September 15, 2008. http://china.blogs.time.com/2008/09/15/obama_and_mccain_on_china/. Last retrieved on November 11, 2009.

67. Li Na, "China Increases US Treasury Bonds Holdings," *Global Times* (November 18, 2009). http://business.globaltimes.cn/china-economy/2009-11/486178.html. Last retrieved on November 20, 2009.

68. "Hu, Obama Agree on Resolving Korean Peninsula, Iran Nuclear Issues through Dialogue," *People's Daily,* November 17, 2009. http://english.people.com.cn/90001/90776/90883/6815578.html. Last retrieved on November 20, 2009.

69. Peter Ford, "Obama Bids China Farewell with Great Wall Tour, Modest Expectations," *The Christian Science Monitor*, November 18, 2009. http://www.csmonitor.com /2009/1118/p06s04-woap.html. Last retrieved on November 20, 2009.

70. Helene Cooper, "China Holds Firm on Major Issues in Obama's Visit," *The New York Times*, November 18, 2009, p. A1. http://www.nytimes.com/2009/11/18/world/asia/18prexy.html?scp=9&sq=obama%20china%20iran&st=cse. Last retrieved on November 20, 2009.

71. See *U.S.-China Joint Statement*, The White House, November 17, 2009. http://www.whitehouse.gov/the-press-office/us-china-joint-statement. Last retrieved on November 20. 2009.

72. President Obama said: "there was no need to change Washington's one-China policy." Stephen Collinson, "Obama Hails China, Taiwan Ties, Talks on 'Rights,'" *AFP*, November 16, 2009. http://news.yahoo.com/s/afp/20091116/wl_afp/chinausdiplomacy _20091116065107. Last retrieved on November 22, 2009.

73. The first one is President Bush Junior. He mentioned the *Taiwan Relations Act* in Beijing in 2002 after the summit with then-Chinese President Jiang Zemin.

74. Yuan Peng, "Obama's China Policy," *Beijing Review*, January 18, 2008. http://www.bjreview.com.cn/report/txt/2009-01/18/content_175419.htm. Last retrieved on November 20, 2009.

75. Thomas J. Christensen, "Posing Problems without Catching Up: China's Rise and Challenges for U.S. Security Policy," *International Security*, Vol. 25, No. 4 (Spring 2001), pp. 5-40.

Index

stability/order, as harmonious values, 187(table)
State Environmental Protection Administration (SEPA), 222
Steinberg, James, 286
Stevens, Ted, 108
Straits Exchange Foundation (SEF), 123
Strategic and Economic Dialogues (S&ED), 11, 85, 89, 91, 93, 95n37, 125, 127
strategic goals/policies: of China (PRC), 9–10, 65–68; of U.S., 6, 58–60
strategic reassurance, in Sino-U.S.-Taiwan relations, 286–87
Super Girl Contest, 248–49
Sutter, Robert G., 99
Swaine, Michael D., 202, 218

Taiwan: Democratic Progressive Party (DPP), 11, 115, 130–31, 283, 288, 292; Five-nos, 146; Hu Jintao'six points, 122–23; provocative moves, 146; and rapprochement negotiations, 28–29; and Sino-U.S. relations, 11, 44–49, 122–24, 169–70; Three-no's principle, 146, 284, 288, 291–92, 322, 325; U.S. arms sales to, 154(table), 258
Taiwan Relations Act (TRA), 154–55, 327
Taiwan Strait missile test incident, 144
TaiwanRelations Act (TRA), 186
taoguan yanghui concept, 178
teenagers, and popular media, 248–49
terrorism: and global strategic environment, 118–19, 123–24; September 11 (9/11) attacks on U.S., 11, 118, 121, 123, 130, 141, 253–54, 263, 305, 315; Sino-U.S. relationships, 130–31, 139, 144, 326
Thailand, 61, 64
Thayer, Bradley, 37
Thompson, William, 42
Tiananmen Incident, 144; and fragmentation of intellectual elite, 241; Pelosi's criticism of, 260; and U.S.-China relations, 3, 59, 100
Tibet, 260
tourism, 105–107

trade: China-E.U., 303–6; China's diversity, 122; China-U.S., 4, 102–5, 142 (table), 170–72, 255 (fig.); and complex interdependence, 115–16, 125, 327; correlation with normalization, 125–28, 161–64; cross-strait, 147 (table); decline of in political stagnation, 164–69; Pan-Beibu project, 64; and politics, 161, 164–67; unfair trade policies, 126; U.S. protectionism, 267–68; U.S.deficit problem, 126
trade protectionism, to be avoided, 121
trade unions (U.S.), and China's rise, 5
treaties, 197
Treaty of Good-Neighborliness and Friendly Cooperation, 62
Tucker, Nancy Bernkopf, 44

Uighkur terrorists, 130
U.K.-U.S, trade, 255 (fig.)
Union of Soviet Socialist Republics (USSR). *See* Soviet Union (USSR)
United Airlines (UA), 107
United Nations Convention on the Law of the Sea (UNCLOS), 269
United Nations General Assembly, Bush/China meetings, 273(table)
United Nations general assembly, China's entry into, 298
United States: ambitions of, under Kennedy, 179; arms sales to Taiwan, 154 (table), 258; and balance of power, 285–87; China policy, 253, 300; East Asian strategy and Chinese perceptions, 57–60, 65–69, 88–90; financial crisis and decline of influence, 127–28, 295; holdings of treasury securities, 125, 257 (fig.), 302; market populism, 244; military supremacy of, 46; on North Korean nuclear development, 85–86; rapprochement and secret negotiatins, 30–31; role of in East Asia, 44–46, 84–93; three-phase relationship with China, 2–8
unity, in Confucian philosophy, 185
University of Hawaii at Manoa, Center for Chinese Studies, 31
urban youth culture. *See* teenagers
U.S. Congress: China Caucus, 108; House Select Committee on Energy

Breinigsville, PA USA
22 July 2010
242208BV00005B/1/P